OUTFOXED

Alexandra Kitty

Introduction by Robert Greenwald

disinformation®

© 2005 Alexandra Kitty & Robert Greenwald
Published by The Disinformation Company Ltd.
163 Third Avenue, Suite 108
New York, NY 10003
Tel.: +1.212.691.1605
www.disinfo.com

Library of Congress Control Number: 2004114765
ISBN 1-932857-11-7
Printed in USA

Design by raisedBarb Graphics
www.raisedbarb.com

10 9 8 7 6 5 4 3 2 1

Editor: Jason Louv

Distributed in the USA and Canada by:
Consortium Book Sales and Distribution
1045 Westgate Drive, Suite 90
St Paul, MN 55114
Toll Free: +1.800.283.3572
Local: +1.651.221.9035
Fax: +1.651.221.0124
www.cbsd.com

Distributed in the United Kingdom and Eire by:
Turnaround Publisher Services Ltd.
Unit 3, Olympia Trading Estate
Coburg Road
London, N22 6TZ
Tel.: +44.(0)20.8829.3000
Fax: +44.(0)20.8881.5088
www.turnaround-uk.com

Attention colleges and universities, unions and other organizations: Quantity discounts are available on bulk purchases of this book for educational training purposes, fund-raising, or gift giving. Special books, booklets, or book excerpts can also be created to fit your specific needs. For information contact Marketing Department of The Disinformation Company Ltd.

Contents

"Fox News? You're Crazy!"

Introduction by Robert Greenwald

When I told a few people, in whispered tones, that I was thinking about pursuing Fox News[1] as the subject of my next documentary, the responses included both cheers and condolences. There were also a few patronizing pats on the head (as though I had completely and totally lost my mind), and of course one or two epithets that can't be printed in a book intended for family consumption. Nobody was neutral—virtually everyone felt strongly and intensely about this "so-called news network" and the importance of focusing an objective, critical lens on it.

What was most shocking to me was how little had been written or produced in the way of a critique of Fox News. All my media contacts—writers, producers, editors, reporters—seemed to accept without question that Fox News was biased; that Fox was obviously parroting the Republican party line; that in fact there was a clear connection between the RNC and Fox News; but very little was being written about it. Fox was not being held to any standard; there was no accountability; there was no sense of outrage—at least not in the public media.

As I probed further, talking to some good friends, colleagues and others in the media for whom I have enormous respect, it became pretty clear that Rupert Murdoch, Roger Ailes and John Moody had cleverly set up a seemingly "no-lose" situation for themselves; that is, if other news organizations talked about or wrote about the bias of Fox News it would seem as though they were simply attacking a competitor, and their motives and conclusions would thus be suspect. But by ignoring Fox, the rest of the media was in effect allowing a real tarnishing of our free and Democratic society, because an organization that was partisan was pretending not to be, and not being called on it. Thus I was inspired to set the record straight, and there followed seven months of incredibly hard work, seven days a week, to produce the film *Outfoxed*.

The support from my amazing partners at MoveOn—Wes Boyd, Noah Winer, Eli Pariser, Peter Schurman and Joan Blades—was instant and unwavering. The only thing they wanted, understandably, was to get the film done before the media became focused on the summer political conventions. They didn't want it to get lost in accusations of political demagoguery—ironic given Fox's partisanship, but nonetheless something that I respected. John Podesta, Raj Goyle and the other terrific folks at the Center for American Progress were equally enthusiastic and understood the importance of the film. John wisely counseled that we tie it into the larger issues of media consolidation, in that Fox News was truly part of the larger problem of having a few folks in the media controlling so much of the message we get.

So I began in early December, 2003—a perverse Christmas, Hanukkah and Kwanzaa present to myself—and was able to enlist some of my extraordinary colleagues and partners who had worked on *Uncovered*, including Jim Gilliam, Kate McArdle, Devin Smith, Chris Gordon and Lisa Smithline. I supplemented them with a team of researchers and editors who would come in at seven in the morning, work until seven or eight at night and be followed by a second team who would arrive and work through the night until the first team was back, in order to make our summer deadline.

---

1 Though the FNC at times refers to itself both as "Fox News" and "FOX News," we have used "Fox News" exclusively in this book for consistency.

MoveOn, through the wonderful work of Noah Winer and his media group, sent word out to their constituents that they were looking for some volunteers to work on a project. The specifics were kept vague, because I was deeply concerned that Fox would undertake legal action to stop the film from going ahead. In short order, I was on a phone call with 9 or 10 people, all women, from around the country, whose only real commonality was their passion for democracy and their conviction that the distortion of news had to stop.

These wonderful women—our "media monitors"—spent hours and hours every week watching Fox News at specific assigned times (Jim Gilliam worked out a master chart), noting the times of certain topics and incidences I was looking for and sending in daily e-mail reports. So, for example, somebody might be watching "Hannity & Colmes" each day; they would then record that at 2:15 p.m. on Tuesday, Hannity made an anti-Kerry statement. The person monitoring Bill O'Reilly might note that on Wednesday at 6 p.m. he mentioned gay marriage, etc. We would use that information to make video copies of those incidences from our master videotape of the Fox News broadcast, which was being recorded 24 hours a day at my production office. These "incident" tapes then went to the editors, who were compiling the record of what Fox News was doing.

Similarly, the terrific folks at FAIR—Peter Hart, Steve Rendall and former head Jeff Cohen joined the effort by giving me guidance, and undertaking the very important and STILL overlooked study that FAIR did of the Brit Hume show, which revealed that Hume's "fair and balanced" guests were 80% Republican, 20% Democrat. At the same time, I reached out to a council of wise men and women whose ideas and viewpoints became helpful voices in the overall creation of the film, and who in some cases became on-camera interview subjects—everyone from Jeff Cohen to David Brock to Chellie Pingree. And then, perhaps most critically, we began the process of finding those former and current employees at Fox News who felt so strongly about the politics of Fox that they were willing to jeopardize their careers and either get me material or speak out publicly. The amazing Kate McArdle, with her wonderful, energetic and chatty phone voice, spent hours talking to and following up on leads that I generated, tracking people down. Slowly but surely, current and ex-"Foxies" (as they came to be known by our team) came forward, and their accounts became the heart and soul of the first-hand reports and stories in the film, that affirmed what everybody with any common sense knew—which was that Fox was not biased by accident. Partisanship was built into the DNA at Fox News, and was legislated at the highest levels.

I had started out thinking that Fox News was simply a conservative network, but what I discovered after months of research was that there were actually many conservative voices that were rarely or never heard on Fox—if they were in disagreement with the Bush administration. There are conservatives whom I disagree with who have positions about some classic conservative issues—budget deficit, careful and prudent foreign policy, protecting the environment—but none of those voices were heard on Fox News. Instead, I began to realize that there was an almost direct connection between Fox News and the Bush administration's policy lines of the day or the week. The fact that Fox had become this absolute mouthpiece for the Republican party and power only increased my passion to finish the film as quickly as possible and to be as objective and scientific as I could be in proving this. I knew I would be attacked if I did not have irrefutable evidence to prove the case.

The editing process was hard, particularly given our time pressure. It was brutally difficult to structure the separate elements (the media experts, the Fox insiders, the Fox News footage, the statistics and studies) into coherent storylines that would hold the interest of a general audience.

I knew I was on to something very strong after I interviewed Jeremy Glick, who told me the story of his brutal on-air attack by Bill O'Reilly. Then when Doug Cheek put Jeremy's interview together with the O'Reilly clips, and I saw it for the first time, I got chills. I was working with Chris Gordon and the "shut-up" sequence, and we started seeing the number of "shut-ups" that O'Reilly used. Chris, in his very creative fashion, did the quick cutting that has now become famous. I was practically leaping up and down, knowing it was a sequence that captured on film forever one of the most overt and obvious of O'Reilly's overstatements.

From there, it was a rush to the finish. Thank goodness for the technology that allowed the editors to work around the clock, which allowed me to see sequences posted at all hours of the day and night on secure FTP sites, and allowed different versions of the film to be cut, re-cut and cut again and again. Jane Abramowitz probably did 20 versions of the Clara Frenk section before we were happy with it.

Then, finally, we were finished. We had managed to keep the production a secret, and Fox hadn't stopped us. Every step of the way the film had moved forward because of the amazing pro bono legal work of Larry Lessig, a visionary in the realm of intellectual property rights. He and his associates at Stanford Law School and the law firm of Fenwick & West gave hundreds of hours of their time, going over versions of the film and making sure I stayed within my fair use rights. I learned more about fair use and copyright than I ever dreamed possible, and along the way became convinced that we should make all our interviews available for anyone else to use, to make their own film, after we had finished. This was accomplished with the help of a wonderful nonprofit organization, Creative Commons (www.creativecommons.org).

The plans for the launching of the film via alternative DVD distribution went ahead. Center for American Progress organized the premiere in New York; David Fenton and Trevor Fitzgibbon worked their magic in organizing a press conference and alerting the media; and a coalition of grass roots groups promoted the film on DVD via their e-mail lists and websites. These included MoveOn, the *Nation*, AlterNet, Buzz Flash, Media Matters, American Progress, Center for Digital Democracy, Center for Public Integrity, Common Cause, Citizens for Media Literacy, Consumer Federation of America, Consumers Union, Fairness & Accuracy in Reporting, Free Press, Media Access Project, Media Channel and Youth Media Council. The DVD was marketed and distributed to retail by the Disinformation Company and Ryko Distribution, and they managed to place it in stores around the country on July 13th, just two days after a lengthy *New York Times Magazine* article about *Outfoxed* started the whole media bandwagon rolling. Pretty much every video outlet you can think of stocked the DVD, with the very notable exception of Wal-Mart, who claimed it was not appropriate for their customers.

We had an amazing burst of interest and attention that I had never expected, because the very thing that had prevented people from writing about Fox News had now been overcome. Here was a legiti-

mate reason to write about Fox News—a film about Fox News. It did not put other organizations or journalists or editors in a position of attacking the competition, but instead allowed them to write about the film and its accusations, allowing for many discussions on talk radio, television and in print. And write and talk they did, despite Fox's threat that "Any news organization that thinks this story is legitimate is opening itself to having its copyrighted material taken out of context for partisan reasons."

Within a short period of time there were literally hundreds and thousands of articles, not just around the country but worldwide, about the film. Cinema Libre stepped in to release it in movie theaters. The Disinformation Company did a brilliant marketing campaign for the stores and we were number one on Amazon.com for an extended period of time. We had distribution offers from all over the world, and I literally spent weeks on the phone doing press interviews and trying to explain Fox News to reporters from Jordan to Japan. Not surprisingly, several papers owned by Murdoch in Australia refused to run ads for the film when it opened in local theaters. Regardless, Outfoxed became a phenomenon (or, as one friend said, "The liberals' *Rocky Horror Picture Show*"). People would go and laugh and talk back to the screen and have a good time.

And finally, Jim Gilliam e-mailed me one day toward the end of the summer with the announcement that if you "Googled" Rupert Murdoch, the first reference was *Outfoxed*.

My work was done (for the moment) but the film was and is only the beginning of a long term battle to create a media that serves democracy—a media that is not controlled by a few companies—to build alternative media and to hold the primary media accountable, as we do in this book and in the film. There is still much to do in the struggle ahead, and I hope you will join us and the many terrific groups doing this work. Please go to www.outfoxed.org to sign on to the campaign.

Thanks,

Robert Greenwald

OUTFOXED

Part One:
Consolidating the NEWS

Chapter 1

Monopolistic Tendencies

"There should be no limit to diversity."

Rupert Murdoch

Without free speech there can be no accurate news: people generally do not want to air dirty little secrets about their dangerous, immoral, corrupt or vile practices, and if they have the power to censor any unflattering dirt that can hurt their reputation, bragging rights or careers, they will do it. Why face scorn, punishment or accountability when a sunny press release touting your latest pseudo-achievement works more in your favor? Human nature craves secrecy and self-preservation, but society's preservation depends on transparency and the freedom to expose and express.

Personal or collective inconvenience can put a damper on a person's aura, yet those self-serving reasons aren't enough to justify the blacking out of information. If a government obstructs the press from investigating an army's atrocities or a politician's illegal and corrupt dealings, then news is reduced to propaganda, carny tactics, lies, delusions and advertising—all of which may be perfectly useful to those who are scamming the public, but are useless to those who are being fleeced.

People need unfiltered and accurate information to navigate through and make the right decisions in their lives. Without knowing the real story, the public is lulled into believing that everything is all right with their world, even as all the subtle, muted signs are desperately screaming that a cataclysm is fast approaching. Lies hurt both individuals and society in the longrun; that's precisely why journalists are supposed to tell their audience exactly what's happening around them. Anything less can do irreparable harm to both journalistic credibility and the audience's quality of life.

For a profession that prides itself on being objective, truthful, accurate, unbiased, fair and balanced, journalism is shamelessly careless and vague with its terms and definitions. Exactly what does objectivity mean? What is defined as a credible source? Precisely how many facts are supposed to be included in any news report? Who can be considered a qualified reporter?

The answer to all these questions is simple: it depends on who you ask and at what time of the day you ask them. Though journalism is supposed to rely on hard facts, it is often muddled with qualifiers, speculations, vague terms and waffling. Objectivity means being fair and balanced for *some* journalists, but not for others. Some believe in objectivity; others renounce it, but both may have vastly differently ideas of what it means.

The realm of journalistic ethics is also a quagmire of ifs, buts and maybes. Is it ever all right to interview close colleagues? What are the rules of disclosure? When is it ethical to interview parents of murdered children? Is it moral to name an alleged rape victim? Should obituaries dredge up past sins? Should ethics and morals even be a consideration?

In other words, the purveyors of precise data have never had the discipline to work within well-defined and precise boundaries.

The American model of journalism has been both one of the most liberating and most confining paradigms for the profession. This model is based on the honor system and the fundamental belief that a free market, lax regulation, freedom of expression and a strong commitment to objectivity will all inevitably lead to reporters producing reliable and credible information. Both journalists and their employers will work together in harmony: the first group free to disseminate information, the second free to make as much profit as they can and regular citizens free to use their products without suspicion. Just leave reporters and news owners on their own to do their jobs, and they will be compelled to report the Truth.

But neither how that truth will be uncovered and presented, nor whether journalists and media owners will have clashing interests, has ever been adequately addressed by the American model of reporting. In fact, the economic realities of the news business never come into play in the theory of how journalists are supposed to do their jobs. Economics is economics and journalism is journalism, and the two schools are kept separate. The focus on the editorial side of the business was key to the American model. The paradigm was supposed to give journalists the freedom to report the news as it happens—the way it happens. Truth and transparency were the reporter's main worries, not the profit margins, branding fancies or the consolidation aspirations of their employers. What the news consumer ultimately read in the paper or saw on the newscast was the unvarnished truth. Journalism focused on the reporters, producers and editors who were uncovering and processing the news, not the ones who owned the news.

Except that reporters and editors aren't the ones who have the ultimate say in how they deliver information; they are hired by others to deliver the information. Audiences almost never point an accusatory finger at media conglomerates when a journalist goes astray; they blame the reporter, his editors and perhaps the individual outlet itself. Few news consumers cast a wary eye on the people who issue the reporter's paycheck—they write abusive e-mails to journalists, not to the Chairman of the Board. Theorists never envisioned a media landscape where only a handful of companies controlled the flow and slant of stories. Somehow, in all of the various debates as to how journalists should do their jobs, no one remembered to think about the biggest constraint and obstacle reporters contend with: their own employers.

> At the new media conglomerates, the biggest constraint and obstacle that reporters had to contend with was their own employers.

Journalism theories have a tendency to assume a reporter's biggest oppressor is the government—whether the oppression takes the form of censorship, denied access to classified information, stifling laws or the promiscuous misuse of slander and libel suits. But governments are not the only ones who have the power of oppression, censorship and intimidation. A corporation that pulls in billions and employs thousands of people has comparative powers to a government: it can not only discredit, banish and exile the heretics, but it can also propagandize, sanitize, demonize, bureaucratize and do just about any other -ize it feels is warranted.

But in a country of many mini-nations, oppression doesn't have to necessarily come from the media conglomerate: it can be attacked by another corporate state that feels threatened. Sometimes the oppression comes from industries and corporations who will pull advertising from a media outlet for informing readers and viewers about a company's dangerous or unethical conduct. Other times the oppression comes from the public relations department of a company that bombards reporters with press releases and VNRs, but denies access to crucial interviews and documents. Still other forms of oppression come from confidentiality agreements that ensure that the weak and the fearful take the company's disturbing secrets to their graves.

Not all companies fudge their books, expose their workers to appalling conditions or dump toxic sludge into the environment, but with many audiences offended by bad news, reporters are often attacked by the very people that would benefit most from their warnings. Focus groups will frown on long stories. Keeping advertisers happy means keeping audiences happy. News is supposed to be important and useful information that helps citizens know who to trust and who to avoid. But with the number of internal and external factors hovering over journalists, sometimes that mandate is difficult to execute.

And if those obstacles weren't enough of a headache, reporters have to concern themselves with how they look and how they package their information. Depressing and offensive news items are taboo, longer stories are shunned in favor of snarky sound bites and a television reporter with bad teeth can lead to a plunging audience share and an exodus of advertisers. More and more, image is king; so long as things *appear* safe or at least solvable, then everyone is happy. Pictures of limbless soldiers are banished in favor of prettier pictures of scantily-clad starlets. That hard bodies take precedence over hard news is a fact in the newsroom, but they don't always teach this to the new recruits at J-school.

 **When public service is a private business,** flash will inevitably be intermixed with fact. Editorial content takes a back seat to profitability, yet that corporate mindset is nothing new. Lord Thomson of Fleet once quipped that owning a television station is like having a license to print money. Though the theory is that news is a vital tool used to enlighten a mass audience, those who own media properties seem to see their product as a commodity such as crude oil or pork rinds.

The core beliefs that drive journalists are obviously not the same ones that drive their employers. Journalists still concern themselves with the news; owners concern themselves with their empires. Expanding and maintaining empires to stay competitive is key to survival. That can mean that the line between news companies and other media companies is virtually nonexistent: companies who own news outlets also own entertainment ones. It doesn't matter what type of bricks are used for building the fortress: it's only the size that counts. Journalists no longer make the bulk of a media outlet's work force: the paycheck they receive comes from the same account that pays reality show contestants.

Most newspaper publishing companies used to have flagship papers that were considered crown jewels: these days papers are traded back and forth between companies looking to stock up on profitable vehicles. News outlets get gobbled up to build communications kingdoms: Viacom owns CBS, UPN, Comedy Central, Paramount Pictures and King World Television; Time Warner owns *Time*, *People*, CNN, HBO and America Online; and Gannet owns *USA Today*, *Army Times*, a score of community papers and twenty local television stations. No American network is without a conglomerate overseeing the expense sheets: Disney owns ABC and General Motors owns NBC. Big may not always be beautiful, but it is a way of journalistic life.

If the press is supposed to be immune to the maneuvers and shenanigans of parent companies, many have been bitterly disappointed in that regard. For many news outlets, the ones who control the purse strings also control the quality of the editorial product. Every media baron wants to be the one with the biggest kingdom. The drive to expand leads to battles for mere survival. In the world of business, there is no room for a tie. The quality of the news product isn't even tertiary: what counts is the bottom line, and the influence a behemoth media machine can bring its rulers.

For some news outlets, being a little fish in a big pond means that the pressure to succeed economically, rather than editorially, drives the news product to new lows. It doesn't matter if the circulation department wildly overstates the number of newspapers sold; it doesn't matter if a journalist fabricates stories whole cloth or disseminates whoppers without an ounce of trained skepticism. What matters is printing more Lord Thomson currency, not the quality and thoughtfulness of stories. Whether improving the journalistic product itself while ignoring the branding and paid consultancy urges would result in a real increase in circulation isn't considered; after all, one tactically careless exposé and the outlet's biggest sponsor may just decide to advertise in another newspaper.

OUTFOXED

The lecture halls at J-schools have professors who still teach reporting, ethics and the importance of objectivity, but they don't focus on what their students will have to face once they find employment in their chosen profession—editors or publishers who will exclusively talk about scoops and angles, branding, leveraging, synergy, focus groups, attracting key demographics and psychographics, and partnerships with advertisers. How any of that relates to improving the quality of the news is anyone's guess. What counts is improving profit: beefing up a news product won't necessarily make a significant impact on a company's earnings.

The solution to improving the bottom line seemed simple enough: keep buying and getting bigger until you are the biggest and most influential empire on the block. Consolidation looked promising, but there was just one hitch: if you weren't devouring fast enough, there was a very good chance someone else would eat you instead. For others, getting bigger was easy, even if there were borders, competitors and government rules to contend with. The ones who knew who played the best were the ones who could insert their own rules into the game.

The King of the Giants

News Corporation happens to be one of those players that seems to have an uncanny knack for growing exponentially: it's one of the world's largest media companies, owned by Rupert Murdoch, a man who began his empire in Australia before he expanded it to include properties in Britain, China and the United States. Murdoch has seen his kingdom flourish, despite the fact that government regulation would have normally stopped his expansion dead in its tracks.

News Corp's Murdoch has many talents, yet for someone who owns as many journalism products as he does, producing quality news isn't one of them. Most of his holdings are hopelessly schlocky, simplistic and vapid, yet he has managed to capture an audience around the world.

King Rupert: The world is watching.

Murdoch's News Corp is a global media outfit: its outlets reach billions, meaning that more people than not are being exposed to a Murdoch product at any given moment. Murdoch owns newspapers (the *Times of London*, the *Sun*, the *Australian* and the *New York Post*), magazines (the *Weekly Standard*, *TV Guide*), television stations (WTTG, KTTV, WNYW), television networks (FX, FNC), book publishers (HarperCollins) and even a movie studio (20th Century Fox). In 2004, Fox News began to offer programming for radio. With *Forbes* magazine pegging his personal worth at almost seven billion dollars, Murdoch is truly a multimedia king.

Yet the Kingdom of Murdochian Media is revered for its sensationalist and/or right-wing leanings. Just look at News Corp's print holdings: the *New York Post* has a nasty track record for publishing hoaxes and erroneous information (the paper once gloriously declared on its front page that

Democratic Presidential candidate John Kerry chose Dick Gephardt as his running mate when Kerry in fact chose John Edwards). The paper serves its job as a quick fix for daily gossip; Liz Smith, Cindy Adams and *Page Six* are as salacious and gratuitous as the British tabloid the *Sun*'s "Bizarre" section (also a Murdoch-owned publication). On the other hand, the *Weekly Standard* is the right's trusty voice, dutifully preaching to the converted.

Murdoch's broadcast holdings haven't fared much better in the editorial content department, either, particularly News Corp's all-news vehicle Fox News Channel. The title promises news, but what kind of news isn't specified. It doesn't take long for a viewer to pick up the nuances of the kinds of stories that this all-news channel specializes in—a thirty-second investment in watching the July 15, 2004 edition of Fox News' biggest hit, the "O'Reilly Factor," tells the viewer everything he needs to know about where the network's priorities lay—in sounding more like the *National Enquirer* than *Newsweek*:

 O'REILLY: Tonight, Whoopi Goldberg loses a million bucks. She's canned as a spokesperson for Slim-Fast. We'll tell you what happened.

Will Martha Stewart go to jail? The smart money says yes. Tomorrow is her day of destiny.

Judge says the Kobe Bryant tapes are admissible and there's a lot of sex talk on them.

Also, what is the truth about J.F.K., Jr. five years after his tragic death?

As for objectivity, the FNC has its own ideas on the subject—and none are in agreement with the status quo. Why settle for detachment when a crowd loves a good taunt? Why worry about keeping emotions in check when unleashing them attracts bigger crowds? The September 29, 2004 edition of the "Factor" showed that newsmen can let off a little steam on the job:

O'REILLY: "Factor" follow-up segment tonight. How the Bush-Kerry race is playing in Europe. This survey by the Program on International Policy Attitudes, an independent group, shows the following. In France people favor Kerry over Bush sixty-four to five. No wonder we're boycotting those people.

Has nothing to do with Bush, but come on. Germany, seventy-four to ten. In Italy fifty-eight–fourteen. In the Netherlands, sixty-three–six. Remember, drugs are legal there.

As is watching porn stars strut their stuff in the U.S., except that the Fox News Channel allows viewers to see a rarity: their favorite porno star with her clothes *on*. But just as perky bosoms are a staple in Murdoch's British tabloid the *Sun*, the FNC parades flesh in the news, but at least they are clever enough to mix the hooters in with round table discussions. Monica Crowley had the privilege of having a serious discussion about politics with busty porn actress Mary Carey in the August 27, 2004 edition of "Hannity and Colmes":

CROWLEY: All right, so tell us what your beef is here with the U.S. military.

CAREY: Well, basically, right now, the military—you know, our tax dollars are being used to give soldiers plastic surgery when they come out, you know, especially

women. They're offering it kind of as a way to get extra soldiers in, to recruit new officers. I don't think that's right, considering we've already spent $135 billion on the war on Iraq. I think there's a lot better things our tax dollars could go towards, other than giving plastic surgery. It sends a bad message.

CROWLEY: Also, and I'm sort of with you on this, Mary, you know. Your slogan, "bullets, not boobs," makes sense to me. I want the military to get their essentials, and breast implants is not exactly an essential here.

FNC anchor Brit Hume wasn't so lucky: he only got to interview National Security Advisor Condoleezza Rice without so much as her showing an ounce of her cleavage. But at least he gets to play her publicist when she's on his program. The June 27, 2004 edition of "Special Report With Brit Hume" showed that a real journalist can make loaded comments to guests who are in positions of authority:

HUME: Tell me, if you can—obviously you got a favorable reaction from the European nations there, who will of course be the main element in NATO at this summit—what is it you expect that NATO will now be prepared to do to support our mission in Iraq?

RICE: We have been getting a very favorable reaction from European nations, all saying that, with the U.N. Security Council resolution, it's time for everybody to pull together and support this new Iraqi government, as it tries to build a stable and secure Iraq.

Though FNC reporters and executives alike have repeatedly denied the network works as an image broker for the Republican Party, their actions sing a different tune. It was difficult to justify the "fair and balanced" argument when Fox News personality Rita Cosby interviewed Defense Secretary Donald Rumsfeld on October 2, 2004:

COSBY: Let's set the record straight. Is there any effort to reinstate the draft?

RUMSFELD: Oh, my goodness no. I have seen a couple of people on Capitol Hill, Democrats in the House and Democrats in the Senate have introduced legislation. I don't believe there's any Republican support for it up there. And I am dead set against it. There is no need for a draft in the United States of America. We have no problem, none, in attracting and retaining the people we need. And my view is that anyone who is talking about the draft, very likely, in this context may very well be making mischief. I just can't imagine reinstituting the draft.

COSBY: Mischief for a political reason?

RUMSFELD: I have no idea.

COSBY: Do you question the timing? Maybe it's being put out there pre-election as a scare tactic?

RUMSFELD: Oh, I'm not supposed to get into politics.

COSBY: What do you think, though?

RUMSFELD: I think I'm not supposed to get into politics, Rita.

A political figure who refuses to discuss politics was both impudent and outrageous, but Cosby never challenged her guest on his arrogant declaration. She just asked a series of loaded questions, all favorable to her evasive guest. His critics were mischief-makers, and employing scare tactics to frighten the masses. The guest could innocently rebuff the question, while she did all the talking for him. When a reporter becomes a mouthpiece for a government official, her product is anything *but* real journalism, fair and balanced.

Of all the regions of the Murdochian Kingdom, only one property is a real success and a threat to the journalism product, simply because it has captured the imagination of its audience. King Rupert relies on General Roger Ailes to rally his troops; Colonel John Moody issues the daily orders to the troops; Captains Sean Hannity, Alan Colmes, Carl Cameron and Neil Cavuto competently fight for the cause, but they are not in charge of individual strategy; that exclusive privilege is reserved for Murdoch's best soldier, Major Bill O'Reilly, whose specialty is luring and trapping unsuspecting and overconfident enemies into his own personal torture chamber, the No Spin Zone. Fear and promises alike are used to control the troops, and all the soldiers work together to expand King Rupert's influence and empire. The troops comply with the General's odious orders, all in the false hope that they will one day be elevated to enjoying the same perks and rewards as the Major. But the King's plans are made all the more unstoppable for one reason: his enemies don't have armies, and he does.

This is a story about a man who controls the flow of information to billions of people; about his company that controls an arsenal of information weapons that can shape public opinion; about one prime property that has shattered all the rules of a profession that has until recently dutifully followed a model that was one with the soul of its country's core beliefs; about his foot soldiers, who unquestioningly follow the man's strict orders while wrapping themselves in the very flag they are desecrating.

Welcome to the Fox News Channel. We hope you enjoy the guided tour.

Chapter 2

Shrinkage

"There is a general trend, a downward trend in journalism that Fox has taken a hand in . . . it has created an atmosphere in newsrooms around the country that makes news a commodity, that cheapens our trade and [is] creating a less informed, more vapid public."

A Former Fox Employee

Some barons are better at holding the reins of massive media power than others. Conrad Black's Hollinger empire was always a controversial outfit, both during its rise and its predictable fall. In his drive to be king of all he surveyed, Lord Black took enormous and unpopular risks that made his stockholders and employees openly seethe with anger, but the worst they could do was mock him behind his back with the puerile moniker "Lord Tubby." Their collective disdain proved ineffective: their stocks weren't performing up to snuff and reporters were finding themselves pink slipped, but Black lived the life of a jet setter with a bottomless pit of cash as he devoured more and more newspaper holdings.

The way Hollinger conducted business was also cutthroat: Black (with his number-two-in-command David Radler) was known mostly for squeezing his media assets by reducing newsrooms to skeletal staffs and cutting costs to the bone. It seemed Black's empire would forever expand, though his company was much smaller than those of some other rivals, such as Rupert Murdoch. Throughout his reign, Hollinger shareholders continued to be displeased with their returns, Black's lavish lifestyle and the company's debt. Black merely rattled off numerous bloated diatribes while he thumbed his pudgy nose at his increasingly vexed critics. Nor did vocal opposition stop him from continually buying and selling more newspaper properties. Both employees and investors alike weren't informed about important company decisions. There were even rumblings that Black used shell companies, and bought and sold properties from and to himself. Despite the rumors of various irregularities, Black's hold on Hollinger was firm.

However, nothing lasts forever: Black's unrepentantly pompous and vainglorious wife Barbara Amiel helped blow down her husband's castle of cards with her infamous August 2002 *Vogue* magazine interview where she so snootily and smugly put her Manolo-clad foot in her big mouth by announcing to the common plebs that "I have an extravagance that knows no bounds" (though this obnoxious statement came at the tail end of a longer comment—that she was outrageously spendthrift because someone's mother once put down her modest attire when she was a teenager—her comments were still a chilling justification and revelry for her living-beyond-her-means excesses).

With that infamous interview and other Black-instigated irritations piling up and taunting Black's detractors, the already peeved shareholders snapped and revolted; Black's empire started to crumble and slip away from him; a special committee report accused Black and Radler of "self-righteous and aggressive looting" and dubbed their management style "corporate kleptocracy." Suddenly, Amiel learned that it was her stupidity that knew no bounds, though her extravagance soon discovered them. Life is hard.

The priorities of Hollinger brass were questionable: editorial quality was pushed aside so that Black could throw a lavish $43,000 Hollinger-funded birthday party for his wife—one complete with Beluga caviar and lobster in order to be able to hobnob with the likes of Oscar de la Renta and Charlie Rose. As one reporter who wrote a book about Black noted at the time, "When I did all that research years ago I definitely concluded that his first priority was to pay himself."

To do that, Black was accused of having an "overwhelming record of abuse" according to the special report. This bastardized model of "smash and grab" capitalistic enterprise let readers know exactly where Black and Radler's priorities lay: not with putting out a quality product, but with lining their own pockets at the expense of readers, employees and shareholders. As the special committee report noted:

> **To fully gauge the level of Black and Radler's disregard for shareholder** interests, one must step back from individual transactions and note the myriad of schemes, fiduciary abuses and fraudulent acts that were used to transfer essentially the entire earnings output of Hollinger over a seven-year period to the controlling shareholders.

In those seven years, Black and his cohorts were accused of siphoning 95% of the company's net income, translating to roughly $400 million dollars of play money to buy expensive homes to show off in a *Vanity Fair* spread (being fully confident the magazine's scribe wouldn't probe further to ask where the money to obtain such prime real estate came from).

With such a large, unwieldy company buying and selling papers at a frenetic pace, who could see that those at the top would be accused of engaging in the corrupt and self-serving rape of an industry that prides itself on exposing those very same practices?

The disintegration of Hollinger also leads to a laundry list of disturbing and unanswered questions for media critics and other non-shareholders alike:

◆ Why didn't journalists and editors—who had worked there day-in and day-out for decades—spot what was going on with their fearless leader?

◆ How aware were they of their own surroundings and their employer? If they did know that the king's gold crown was in fact made of tin foil, why did they keep silent?

◆ Can these same journalists and editors rebuild trust with their readers?

◆ Can news consumers trust that other large media conglomerates aren't playing the same complex games with readers, shareholders and employees?

Why didn't journalists and editors spot what was happening at Conrad Black's Hollinger Empire?

◆ Can a media conglomerate get so big that those at the top can plunder, cheat, prevaricate, manipulate and intimidate without detection? Who will hold them accountable?

◆ How do editors and reporters respond to edicts issued from their pretentious and vaunting lords whose reality consists of liberally stealing, lying and bullying while maintaining a faux aura of refined and overpriced sophistication?

◆ What kind of accurate and unfiltered picture could these news producers ever present to their audience?

No wonder a twenty-six-year-old Black said in 1969 that journalists were "ignorant, lazy, opinionated, intellectually dishonest and inadequately supervised"—how could he possibly have any respect for those who were sleepwalking on the job and letting someone like him operate undetected and unchallenged *for years*? Of course journalists were not being adequately supervised, their employers were too busy smashing and grabbing to pay attention to the editorial product. Unfortunately, media consolidation restricts a reporter's freedom and ability to operate—if he burns his bridges at one outlet, he will be de facto blacklisted in any of the conglomerate's other holdings.

Those investigative reporters who *were* rock-turners Black dismissed as "swarming, grunting jackals"—an insincere way of saying that he didn't like journalists who were skeptical of press release propaganda and insisted on thinking for themselves. If a media baron has contempt for the muckrakers and the analyzers, news consumers cannot possibly expect to get the whole ugly truth from their news sources—reporters will be barred from doing their jobs properly. The more outlets a belligerent news baron owns, the greater number of journalists will lose their freedom to report on events as they see fit.

Size Does Matter

Even if other media outlets are on the level and do care about editorial quality, they too can find themselves in a precarious situation if they face a prolonged economic stagnation or even a sudden catastrophe: if one of these goliaths begins to collapse on its own weight (as News Corp almost did in 1991), what happens to individual media properties? Do they get divvied up among the few remaining giants, or will some inevitably be forced to shut down? What happens to communities who relied on those fallen outlets for their information?

No one in the upper echelons of news media companies seems to care much about the people they are supposed to serve: executives are trained to look at the bottom line—if profits aren't meeting expectations, staff is cut, financial resources are slashed and cheaper wire copy is used to replace old-fashioned rock-turning. The final product becomes a pale imitation of its ancestors—even the actual size of newspapers has shrunk and the number of minutes of a typical newscast has decreased. Opinion pieces and soft news stories are cheap filler used to replace investigative stories.

It isn't just the number of real news stories that has dwindled. Fewer owners are controlling more and more outlets; with fewer regionally based owners controlling the information flow, the emphasis on hometown news has also diminished. As Mark Cooper, Director of Research at the Consumer Federation of America noted, "You have twenty-four hour cable stations that give you an immense amount of national news and international news, but they don't deal with local issues at all."

The number of players owning media properties has also shrunk over the years: Viacom, Disney, Time Warner, Clear Channel, News Corp and General Electric all own broadcast news properties; Gannett, Condé Nast, Hearst, Times Mirror, Liberty and CNHI all own print properties. The companies that own the metro and national papers have control over the local properties, too. Not to mention that every one of these media companies also has substantial Internet holdings. On the other hand, independent news media outlets have slowly disappeared from the American media landscape, making it harder for independent voices to be heard. As former network television writer and independent producer Len Hill said, "We now find that in the [amalgamation] of power within these five media titans, there is anything but transparent and competitive dealmaking."

Yet some larger media companies also find themselves less than invincible. Conrad Black's mini-empire may have imploded, but the Hollinger media kingdom was no different from the previous kingdoms before it: to stay competitive, it needed more properties, even if the outfit wasn't equipped to run them properly. Why settle for one vehicle that makes you comfortably wealthy when you can own ten that will give ten times the riches?

Unfortunately, what makes a media titan wealthy won't necessarily make him care about the quality of his product. Properties are no longer vital organs of a community; they become bargaining chips in a familiar game of corporate chess. Former flagship papers and stations are discarded if a more profitable holding suddenly becomes available. The difference between Black and Murdoch is that Murdoch is a shrewder performer who knows how to play the game: Black always seemed to bully,

bluff and bluster his way out of jams with his shareholders, board and employees.

As companies merge and devour their smaller rivals, some larger companies become autocratic. Others are more concerned with their mandates with shareholders than with their mandates to their audience: operations are streamlined, which is just a psychopathic way of saying a large number of workers are going to lose their jobs, while the ones who escaped the slaughter are going to have to do twice the work at the same or lesser pay. Since hard news and investigative stories can't be done properly without sufficient funding, cutbacks inevitably mean less hard-hitting stories. As Jeff Chester, Executive Director for the Center for Digital Democracy said, "the media industry, the big media companies in the United States, have a vision for the future; they know where the media system is going and they're using their political clout to shake the policies in Washington to ensure that they end up on top. The problem with the public, and with progressives in particular, is that we're always fighting the battles of the past." He added that in the mainstream, "media lobby is fighting tomorrow's battles today, right now."

When News is a Commodity

Media companies act no different than any others, in that they like to "brand" themselves (i.e., make their product distinct and widely recognized for its unique set of traits). Branding may seem more like "dating," "coasting," "stagnating" and "playing it safe at the expense of creative growth, risk and innovation," but branding is all the rage with their peers in other industries; so it must be right. However, since news is a commodity like soft drinks, running shoes, Barbie dolls or feminine hygiene products, rival outlets want to set themselves apart.

Media conglomerates also like the concept of branding for another reason, according to Jeff Chester:

> The danger here is that in the absence of positive change we will unleash the most powerful, commercial media system ever witnessed on the planet. It will be interactive, it will be personalized, the content will be integrated with the advertising. And it will be irresistible in many ways to many people, particularly young people, because they'll know what you're watching, they'll know what you're buying. The reason these big media companies have opposed privacy policies on the Internet is because they want to be able to do that kind of micro-targeting for this one-to-one video system that's at the heart of their plans. I call this the *brand-washing* of America.

The news industry sells a product to consumers—information and an individual company's survival is not dependent on the amount or quality of information it disseminates, but on how much revenue it can generate. Public good is not a consideration. If that's the case, then outlets should be allowed to stand and fall based on market considerations and not on public need for information. As Robert McChesney opined:

> The great myth of our media system is that it's a natural free market system, that as long as the government sort of stays out of the way and does nothing, a free press

Conglomerates make a good profit—it's just not necessarily very good journalism.

will sprout up with entrepreneurs competing to give us the best product at the lowest possible price. Nothing could be more incorrect about our media system [which] is the direct result of government policies and subsidies that create it. Rupert Murdoch's empire, for example, is built on getting for free massive gifts of monopoly rights to TV channels. He doesn't pay a penny for it in the government. Those are government created and enforced monopoly privileges to TV channels. I mean it's corporate welfare pure and simple; his whole system is built on it[...] Across the board Rupert Murdoch['s News Corporation], like all media companies, depends on government largesse, policies, monopoly privileges and subsidies to do their business.

Think globally, act locally has been taken to mean something new entirely. While the ultimate goal for these titans is to become a worldwide powerhouse, the way to reach that goal is by buying more and more smaller community outlets, removing the local content of individual properties, draining resources from them, then pumping smaller outlets with content produced from bigger outlets or from headquarters.

But this method has negative repercussions according to Peter Hart, media activism director at the progressive watchdog group FAIR: "What you see is a collision of values. You have commercial values, these are commercial enterprises, and you have journalistic values, too. Too often, commercial values win out over [those] values that should exist in journalism: independent, aggressive investigation." Hart added that large conglomerates, "make a good profit out of it; it's just not necessarily very good journalism."

Producing individual local stories for smaller outlets is more expensive in the long run for larger media operations; it is far cheaper to produce stories from a single source, then distribute them to the smaller properties. As writer and media critic Eric Alterman noted, "it reduces the number of ideas for the market place—instead of a hundred ideas, there's only six. And so a lot of good ideas are not there anymore… Americans believe in choices; [as] consumers, our choices are being reduced by consolidation." As Walter Cronkite observed about the nature of the shrinking media landscape:

> Media consolidation could mean control of all means of communication in a given community. The possibility is there for owners to control a television station, a radio station, the newspaper; in a smaller community that might be all the sources of information, and it's therefore possible for an owner to dictate how the news shall be presented and interfere with a free flow of information that the public needs to intelligently exercise its franchise in a democracy.

If a company is willing to skimp on the total number of stories it produces, then it shouldn't be surprising that the more expensive investigative stories will be rejected in lieu of cheap and easy news. Celebrity gossip and sensational murders are easier to churn out than an in-depth series on

government corruption. Modern day "celebrity" reporting is not even similar to arts reporting: in many cases, stories about the content and impact of films, plays, art, literature and music are resoundly ignored in order to devote time and space to the dysfunctional private lives of people who aren't even professional entertainers, such as failed contestants on serialized game shows. In many cases, news has been reduced to feeding into the insatiable media beast with junk food because nutritious fodder is too expensive. As former broadcasting journalist and writer Av Westin noted, "At the local level particularly, beginning in the eighties when the Reagan administration deregulated the control of buying and selling television stations, many stations which had previously been locally owned by people who were residents in their communities, many of those stations were bought by what I call distant owners." He added, "Those distant owners whose headquarters were not in the town where the station was, but New York or Chicago or wherever they're located, became much more concerned with the bottom line than they were with the editorial content."

Westin also bluntly described the two-step mindset of corporate media: "One, you cut the size of your staff and [two...] you do anything you have to do to get ratings." However, many people aren't fully aware of the problems with the shrinking media landscape until it hits home and their local news suddenly disappears. As former Maine Senator and current President and CEO of Common Cause Chellie Pingree lamented:

> I come from a community in the state of Maine that's mostly fishing towns, small coastal communities, and for many years we were served by one radio station that everybody listened to, WRKD AM and FM. Almost all of the fishermen in the morning would turn it on, to find out what the weather was going to be; we'd listen to local basketball games; all the political candidates would always debate there; it was just where you tuned in for local news.

> A few years ago, they were bought out by Clear Channel Radio, and that was my first introduction to what the issue around media was, and I didn't even understand then what the big implications of it were.

What happened next may have been business as usual for the conglomerate, but it was certainly a surprise to the small community, who were ignorant of the nature of the media industry:

> The fascinating thing was Clear Channel, of course, moved [the station] to an aluminum building ten miles outside of town; there was no longer a local announcer. It used to be when you walked down the street in Rockland, Maine, you'd walk by, you'd see Don Shields, who was the announcer, and he'd say, "Oh, there goes the kindergarten kid getting out of school," or he'd say, "Another politician is going to get another coffee." I mean it was local radio. Every time I debated an opponent, everybody would tune in, in their cars, or their home radio, and they would hear what we were feeling differently about. And when Clear Channel bought [the station], that was the end. You couldn't even count on somebody looking out the window and telling you if it was a good day or a bad day, or if the fog was coming in. It wasn't the station the fishermen could tune into anymore.

Clear Channel's resistance to the notion that the free flow of information is central to the Democratic system did not deter many Rockland citizens, who decided that local news from a local source was important enough to fight for:

> [...] People got so angry, [that] there was a local group that got organized and attempted to get a low power FM radio license. They said, "We need to have somewhere to tune in so that when people want to know what's going on in this town, they can find out the local news..." They had a hard fought battle: Clear Channel opposed them, but [the group] actually won and now there is a little radio station operated out of a garage in that town, all volunteers; anybody can play the music they want, but at five every day, [people] tune in to the dialogue of what's going on in that community.

Residents of Rockland weren't the only ones ignored by big media. A consolidated press can also mean that an entire group of citizens lose their collective voice. Malkia Cyril, the founder of the activist group Youth Media Council, studied news coverage on KTVU, a Fox affiliate station in San Francisco, and discovered some unsettling problems with the channel:

> We studied three months of Fox News coverage in the Bay Area, and what they had to say about young people... One thing that we found was that white adults speak on behalf of people of color nine times out of ten. So prosecutors, police and politicians tend to be the primary spokespeople in coverage of youth of color. We found that problematic not only in that young people don't get to speak for themselves, but because they're portrayed so often as criminals; they're not even perceived as deserving to speak for themselves... There were more stories about pets and animals than there were about youth poverty.

Cyril said that, "if you're covering young people, you're primarily covering young people of color, and you're primarily covering them in crime stories and other kinds of stories like that. So when you look at that coverage, separate from the business coverage, separate from its transportation coverage... [the coverage] fails miserably." She quipped that "either the kids are dead, going to jail or they have a dog."

As a result of the study, Cyril's group held an editorial meeting with KTVU and convinced the station to host an annual youth journalist roundtable. Cyril noted "they said it was the first time in probably ten or fifteen years that a constituency group locally had ever come in to demand anything from them. They just get to do whatever they want."

If reporters such as Jayson Blair, Jack Kelley and Stephen Glass can fabricate stories without they and their employers being criminally charged for fraud or negligence, citizens should not expect media owners to be held responsible for the consequences of their governing style. But still, people expect "the government" will take care of any problem that arises from media concentration.

The government may not want to interfere for many reasons, and some of those reasons may be self-

serving, as Greg Kimmelman, Senior Director for Public Policy with Consumer's Union (publishers of *Consumer Reports*) explained:

> **The media is special because every politician knows they want to look good on television.** They want to be on television a lot. They want the newspaper to write a good editorial and they want them to write them often. They want to be in the positive news, not in the negative news. So they are so fearful of media companies, journalists, that they have to be a little more responsive, they think, to their policy desires.

As media companies become larger, they become more powerful: politicians need the news media to get their messages across, to sell their legislation to the public and to persuade their constituents to vote for them once again come election day. By letting the invisible hand regulate the press, many politicians fear that the same phantom hand will slap or crush them if they try to make unpopular changes. Those who know how to work the press have no reason to interfere. They already know how to get their message across; it's less work to handle a few large news outlets than to handle a myriad of smaller ones.

If some politicians fear the wrath of the invisible hand, then more journalists ought to, as well. For instance, when Ted Koppel decided to devote one episode of "Nightline" to reading the names of the U.S. soldiers who fell in Iraq in 2003, Sinclair Broadcasting, which owned several ABC affiliates, wanted to censor the controversial program from its airwaves, including WLOS, a local ABC affiliate in North Carolina (in a stroke of pure cheeky genius, it was a local Fox affiliate who ran the broadcast). Wally Brown, the Executive Director of the Mountaineering Information Network, decided to take action by challenging WLOS' license renewal, stating: "We saw this as a tremendous opportunity to really galvanize citizens in this community, raise public awareness about what's going on with the ownership of WLOS and bring some pressure on Sinclair to let our local journalists do their jobs and stop slanting the commentary here in our community."

Brown also said that "one of the things we hope to do in this community is to make common cause with the media workers at WLOS. They are being victimized just as much as viewers in this community are being victimized by the heavy hand of Sinclair out of Baltimore. So we want the journalists at WLOS to know that we're on their side. We want them to be free to practice the art and craft of journalism."

News companies refusing to air the news? Reporters as corporate hostages? Citizens as liberators of the press who have to fight media conglomerates to air easily accessible information? Is this what journalism has come to—being pitied and having to be rescued by concerned citizens? How did journalists lose their clout and their power? Free market implies little or no government interference in the way businesses are run; it does not mean that professionals are free to ply their trade without interference from others. Reporters who still wish to be employed as reporters have to toe the company line.

Journalists who work for big media companies know that they are only a small part of their employer's empire. The "Big Three" networks may have impressive news divisions, but they still deal mostly with producing fictional programming—in other words, networks are literally *broadcasters*. They cater to a broad audience and they offer a broad variety of genres; news and current events being only one part of the content they produce. Resources are shared—the focus will always be on the next promising actor on a popular television program, and journalists will always be second-tier players, at best.

If network television reporters are limited, then we should expect that TV reporters from "all-news" channels will have more freedom to do their jobs properly. After all, they are the sole talent driving their networks. Unfortunately, some cable news reporters may have even fewer freedoms than their network counterparts, although it wasn't supposed to be that way.

The Rise and Fall of CNN

The Fox News Channel may be in first place, but it wasn't the first to be there. It was media tycoon Ted Turner who offered Americans something momentous that no other television network had before him: the choice to watch a newscast whenever they wanted. There were the national early morning news shows running from 6 a.m. to 9 a.m.; local news popped up again at noon and at 6 p.m.; national news came on again at 6:30, and the last call came at 11 p.m.

Turner changed the rules by offering cable subscribers a twenty-four hour news channel; now insomniacs could get informed on their time and news junkie shut-ins could finally have their peace. The idea of a cable news network (conveniently called CNN) was novel, but the results were promising, even if headquarters were in Atlanta and not in New York or Washington, the two competing centers of the universe.

CNN didn't come into its own as a nationally respected brand name until the 1991 Gulf War. It was a war that saw three CNN reporters—Peter Arnett, Bernard Shaw and John Holliman—reporting in darkness on the first night of U.S.-led bombing of Iraq. They were the only ones who managed to communicate to the public that night, and their reports made for riveting news: the "Boys of Baghdad" were a beloved hit and CNN became the go-to place for the news junkie. Larry King lived up to his last name, and shows such as "Crossfire" and "Burden of Proof" were fairly well known. People watched CNN for any soap opera-like super-story that messily unfolded in front of rolling cameras. CNN's formula of instant analysis and blanket coverage of big stories worked.

By 1996, Turner sold his sterling empire to Time Warner, which effectively became Time Warner-Turner. CNN was to play a major role in this brand new media fiefdom—that is, until AOL officially merged with Time Warner-Turner in January 2001 and rechristened their new media mammoth AOL Time Warner. Though he stayed as Vice Chairman (only to quit in early 2003, though he remains a shareholder), Turner, known as "The Mouth of the South," found himself shut out of the limelight and the action.

As did a lot of Republicans who griped that CNN had to stand for "Clinton News Network." They were sick of the man who left his calling card on some intern's blue dress and the high profile pundits who seemed, in their eyes, to embody the "liberal" point of view. Ted Turner did support leftist

causes. Where were the conservative commentators? Where were right-winged subjects and topics covered in a rightist way? Why didn't CNN present a conservative skewed version of reality? Who validated the thoughts and beliefs of those on the far right?

But even those viewers who were not conservative began to shuffle in their seats. People became tired of the same old predictable format, the CNN cable spin offs (CNNSI for example) and the sudsy stories. The "synergy" between CNN and Time Warner's print publications were yawners, and CNN's various attempts at regaining audiences were flops (such as hiring Connie Chung and Jamie Kellner, a former television entertainment executive who had no news background). Nothing new or fresh was being offered; it was just the same limited number of tricks and stories being repeated and stretched thin.

Ratings reflected this viewer fatigue; somewhere along the way, CNN lost its innovative spark and rested on its past glory. Even the once-buzzworthy Larry King has taken a decided back seat to current cable news ratings champ Bill O'Reilly and even Sean Hannity and Alan Colmes.

Once upon a time, CNN was the news channel Americans watched for their information. Now, the era of CNN seems to be waning in favor of a brash upstart called the Fox News Network.

The Rise and Rise of Fox News

Rupert Murdoch was a busy man in 1996: his company News Corp was running, among other things, newspapers, magazines, a movie studio, a book publisher and a major U.S. television network. Yet all those properties would not be enough to satisfy him. The most fascinating and troubling of his outlets appeared later that year: a little cable news network called the Fox News Channel. Even though it captures, on average, less than two million viewers in the U.S., it has still managed to take on the once powerful CNN and bring the cable newser to its knees.

At first, Fox News didn't catch on with viewers overnight. People were happily tuning to CNN, trying to catch the latest news on the O.J. Simpson trial and the death of Princess Diana. What the United States *didn't* need was another all-news station: there were already plenty of other channels that carried news some or all of the time. Audiences seemed generally comfortable with the already-proven CNN.

Eventually, though, the audience's tastes would shift: Fox looked slick and quite different than the standard and dry offerings from the other networks. Fox was different: it didn't just offer news, it offered attitude. So how did attitude pave the way for Fox News?

The Fox News story begins with the Fox television network. In the 1980s, News Corp began buying independent stations and creating a fourth network to rival ABC, CBS and NBC. The Fox Network's early entertainment shows were predictably bad ("Good Grief," a funeral home comedy starring Howie Mandel); others were good, but short-lived ("Get a Life!"); while others found an audience (such as "Melrose Place," "Married... With Children" and the still running "The Simpsons" and "America's Most Wanted").

When other media outlets talked about the Fox network, they mostly discussed its push-the-limits-of-good-taste fictional shows or noxious "reality" programs, such as the notorious "Who Wants to Marry a Multi-Millionaire?" The terms artistic, intellectual, innovative or critically acclaimed just aren't in Fox's dictionary; they don't need them to snag a sizable audience.

It was Fox's entertainment programming that caught everyone's attention. No one really took much notice of the news division on a national or even local scale, mostly because Fox News wasn't News Corp's strong point, on either level. Many of the local Fox affiliates did not score high ratings with their evening newscasts. How on earth did the Fox News Channel ever get off the ground in the land of brides-for-purchase and steamy Aaron Spelling dramas?

Before They Were the FNC: Fox's WTTG Experiment

Before the 1996 launch of FNC, two events stand out as those that helped pave the way. The first occurred when Rupert Murdoch scooped up WTTG-TV from Metromedia in 1985. WTTG was a non-Big Three affiliated station in Washington, DC. Though it did not have the backing from ABC, NBC or CBS, its news broadcasts still drew in large audiences; in fact, WTTG had the country's highest-rated evening newscast. Those strong ratings, coupled with airing its newscast at 10 p.m., helped ensure that the station was a profitable one. WTTG wasn't the first American television station bought by Murdoch, but it was a crucial one in the FNC nexus.

The second occurred in 1986, when Fox launched the show "A Current Affair," giving American audiences a taste of the syndicated tabloid "news" program. "Affair" was a Fox-produced number, and brass tapped Maury Povich, a WTTG on-air personality, to host the show. "Affair" stories were centered around sleazy characters, sex, crime, over-the-top scandal and other emotionally manipulative "shame on them" pieces. The production values reeked, and the show obsessed over the news of the cheese.

But back to WTTG.

What WTTG excelled at was its sensible approach to news and current affairs, and its profitability seemed to insulate it from corporate meddling. As Frank O'Donnell, a former WTTG producer recalled about WTTG's pre-Murdoch days:

> [WTTG] had a very different approach to the news during the time I was there. Rather than trying to do a lot of sensational cop and robbers, mattress-fire type news, we actually did serious national news and actually got high ratings for it in DC because the audience here wanted to know what was really happening with the government, with the White House, with the Congress, with the federal bureaucracy. That was our formula for success, until the Murdoch influence began to creep in and take charge of the newscast.

O'Donnell maintains that Murdoch did not interfere with the editorial product for the first three years of his ownership. But that was before it was time for America to elect a new President.

Vice President George Bush was battling former Massachusetts governor Michael Dukakis for the country's top job. O'Donnell recalled the moment when WTTG entered a new, troubling phase:

We first saw the influence of Murdoch in the middle of 1988, during our coverage of the Republican convention, where we received an order from one Murdoch "apparatchik," if you will, that we should cut away from our newscast and start carrying a fawning tribute to Ronald Reagan that was airing at the Republican convention. We were stunned because up until that point we were allowed to do legitimate news, and suddenly we were ordered, from the top, to carry propaganda—Republican right-wing propaganda. It's the sort of thing I think carried on into the Murdoch empire, into the Fox News Channel to this day.

The factually-devoid tribute ran on WTTG uninterrupted for fifteen to twenty minutes; however, O'Donnell said how executives treated WTTG staff when their edict was handed down, "There was no explanation, there was no context; it was obviously a partisan-political decision to promote a guy who had been President at a time when you had a very contested election."

The mandated airing of the sugary kissy-fest was a sign that worse things were to come to those who both prided their abilities for finding hard news and those who cherished their autonomy. It would be a slow evolution from hard news to slanted sensationalism; especially after several new employees were brought in (some who had little reporting or television experience). However, O'Donnell and other WTTG employees were in denial that their enclave would be affected:

Those of us who had seen it, had seen it happen in Australia, we had seen it happen with the *New York Post*. We thought that eventually it might happen to us. And it was kind of like being in an office and seeing people come down with the flu around you. We knew the flu eventually might reach us, but we were hoping if we took enough vitamins that we'd never catch the flu, and so when it finally happened, we were stunned because we thought maybe we had warded off the flu for a number of years.

The flu came in the form of a series of decrees that seemed to be based on something other than editorial considerations. The changes to WTTG were both patronizing and repugnant, according to O'Donnell:

We started getting orders on a regular basis to run excerpts of "A Current Affair," on our newscast. This is something we would have never done in the old days... We knew it was bad news and so we never touched the stuff until we started getting daily orders to carry stuff from [the show.]

Whether it was WTTG's previous dry approach to news reporting or its lack of overt partisan reporting that turned off Fox executives in the first place isn't clear. David Burnett, a former journalist with WTTG recalled those same edicts that came down from head office:

Murdoch wanted to kind of spice it up a little bit. There were things he wanted to introduce in the news, but even though that's what he wanted, most people were a little resistant to that.

How Fox executives wanted to change WTTG's news product was by skewing its point of view, as Burnett recalled:

> They wanted to bring in a more conservative newscast. They wanted to, I think, use us as a sort of experiment, to see how a conservative approach to the news might work... But I do believe what happened in 1993 served as essentially the genesis for what ultimately became Fox News Channel, which ultimately supplanted CNN as the number one cable newscast.

The exact mechanisms of this ideological shift became painfully clear to staffers by 1993. Joe Robinowitz, WTTG's newly appointed news director was gearing up to get the station in line with management's desires. Burnett described Robinowitz as someone who was "not really savvy about television news at all," and that Burnett "didn't really respect his intellect—none of us did." WTTG staff stumbled upon his August 31, 1993 memo (entitled "Pending openings at WTTG") to Fox News chairman Les Hinton on their computer that was filed under a previous news story. The memo stated in part:

Metromedia WTTG Washington, D.C., 1985.

> [I]t is going to be a pleasure in coming months to replace WTTG news staff who are inept, politically correct, shallow and/or unsuitable for the jobs we have here in our newsroom. Since I'm very much a newcomer to this market, I am relying on the expertise of the following individuals to help me in this regard.

The "experts" Robinowitz planned to consult were Tony Snow, Herb Berkowitz (from the Heritage Foundation), Brent Bozell (of the conservative "watchdog" group Media Research Center), and Reed Irvine (of the other conservative "watchdog" group Accuracy in Media)—all far right-wing ideologues. Though Robinowitz was dismissed from WTTG (though he went on to work for News Corps' *New York Post*) when news of the memo was leaked to the *Washington Post* (some referred to the episode as Fox's "memogate"), it was a signal that change was in the air.

But employees at the time did not blame Robinowitz for the chilling memo. One employee at the time said, "This verifies there is a conservative agenda being funneled from top Fox management down to this station." Even now, Burnett agrees with that assessment: "If you looked at the [memo], he was responding to directives from Los Angeles. It was not his making. He was responding to what he was being told to do."

The head office orders were something entirely new for the local affiliates, who were used to making independent decisions about editorial content and voice, as Diana Winthrop, a former producer at WTTG, sees it: "Murdoch did not have any commitment to—like a number of stations or networks do—the local community. What he was there for is he wanted to be number one, that was his goal."

Within eight years, WTTG went from reflecting the voice of the community to reflecting the party line and "attitude" of someone who did not have any interest or knowledge of the region. The influence of Murdoch led to WTTG giving then-U.S. Supreme Court nominee Clarence Thomas positive coverage (despite allegations of sexual harassment), while Ted Kennedy received negative coverage, as per L.A. office orders. For instance, WTTG staffers were ordered to run a supposedly long, uncut "Current Affair" story about Kennedy's fateful car accident at Chappaquiddick—never mind that the scandal happened thirty years earlier. Though the story had no news value, WTTG was forced to run it.

Increasingly, reporters were criticized over what stories they wanted to cover. Winthrop said there were numerous management complaints "that there was too much being done on AIDS." She added that "anything about gays, AIDS, race, affirmative action" was also repeatedly criticized; however, pseudo-stories that conveniently tied in with various Fox products were perfectly acceptable. One story about the Fox movie studio also made it on air, as O'Donnell recalled:

> We were also ordered at one point to try to make up a sensational news story about something that had sounded like somebody was trying to sell a movie idea to Fox. It involved a couple of Fox reporters coming to DC on what they called some sensational scoop, where the Ku Klux Klan had allegedly abducted dozens of African-Americans from the streets, taking them out to a farm somewhere, tortured them and then killed them—and then buried them on some farm. One of the reporters described it to us as "maybe bigger than *Mississippi Burning*." And this was the attitude they were taking. Later we actually had to air this thing, even though the reporters themselves were very skeptical; they told us that it was true. Later the FBI investigated it and said there was absolutely nothing to it. We learned later that the whole idea originated with a guy trying to sell a movie idea to Fox.

Dubious filler crept in, despite the newsroom's efforts to resist the shift from usefulness to sensationalism. Winthrop also noticed the shift at the Fox affiliate:

It was different. You felt that there was a clear cultural mission on the part of Rupert Murdoch. And the news director at the time, and the subsequent news directors, apparently tried to impose those kinds of views on me.

There were other signs that professionalism wasn't the main item on the agenda at the Foxified affiliate. One of the parachuted news producers referred to African-Americans as "those people." Alexander Kippen, a former reporter for Fox's Washington bureau, recalled another equally dubious incident regarding one news director:

> [The news director] was hilarious in a lot of ways, but he would say on occasion the most extraordinarily offensive things. I remember at a news meeting once, [the director] was sitting there and all of a sudden he says, "now, what about all these wetbacks taking all the jobs? Why don't we do a story on them?" And I sort of looked up around the room and looked at everybody else to see if I'd heard what I thought I heard. And I see these

bugged eyes and sure enough, he said it... I said, "You know, I don't think you should really use those terms like 'wetback'; it's offensive; it's a slur, you're going to get in a lot of trouble if you talk that way." And he just looked back at me with a big smile and just said, "[...D]on't let the political correctness squad get to you, that's my rule." He waved me off and that was pretty much that.

Not surprisingly, there was some resentment and antagonism from seasoned reporters towards the new kids on the block. The changes that came from head office meddling made for an unpleasant atmosphere. Fox management may have made numerous missteps (bad production values, opinion clumsily inserted into otherwise solid editorial product where the difference would be glaring), but they at least learned from their mistakes.

It must have dawned on someone in the upper echelons at Fox that biased opinion mixed in with real stories would only draw attention toward the shameless attempts at slanting news coverage for personal gain. Then there was the problem that old guard journalists were only human, and no previously independent individual is going to relinquish autonomy without resistance and hostility. Brass must have also realized that mediocre news plus mediocre production values equals a snickering and fleeting audience. Finally, no one can make a conservative news channel fly without someone who has both political and television experience.

The solution was simple: one, reduce the amount of news being covered and increase the amount of opinion-spewing; two, start hiring from scratch, only recruiting those reporters and producers who either share your ideology or are too desperate for a media job to challenge management; three, concentrate on and improve the "look" of the network; and four, find someone to run the network who has both Republican party and TV cred.

 In other words, start your own all-news station from scratch. And so the Era of the Fox began.

The Birth of the Fox News Channel

The year 1996 was a busy and eventful time for many Americans. A sexually-charged Democrat who could get Republicans to fly into a childish rage just by existing was still President; having your own personal website devoted to your favorite extreme sport or has-been starlet was still considered to be chic; people were perfectly cool about being defined by the television shows they watched or by the coffee they drank and twenty-somethings could get away with impressing other people by peppering their conversations with obscure pop culture references. Everything was about vanity projects, indulging your ego and one-upmanship leisure. People were in a shallow mood—and why not? The economy seemed white hot with the dot-com boom going on, and on the surface, profits continued to soar upwards by defying old economy rules.

Yet not everyone wanted or could gain access to this me-centered economic bliss. Not everyone was an Instant Internet Millionaire; not everyone could brag about vacationing in Whistler or Bora Bora; not everyone could afford a Moschino outfit. Not everyone could indulge in their fantasies.

But Rupert Murdoch could, with the help of the disenfranchised—and Roger Ailes.

In 1996, the new cable newser was launched with little fanfare or general respect. In a few short years, Fox News became the highest rated cable news channel, surpassing former reigning champ CNN— this despite the fact that CNN was available in twenty-three million more homes than Fox. In the 2000s, more television viewers seem to have suffered from CNN fatigue and have tuned into the vixen network instead. With shrinking audiences and fewer media conglomerates, Fox has managed to thrive in this constricted environment.

Fox News didn't start as a profitable venture. In fact, in its infancy the FNC was losing about seventy-five million dollars a year according to estimates, and the most it could hope to do, according to conventional logic, was beat out MSNBC. One *USA Today* article began the premature FNC deathwatch in 1997 when it noted: "Some analysts wonder whether Murdoch will continue to have the stomach for such losses after his recent flurry of expensive deals to buy such marquee properties as the Los Angeles Dodgers and the Family Channel. The question is, how long does Fox have to improve?" So much for analysts.

The staff at WTTG started getting orders to run excerpts of "A Current Affair" and other non-news material on the newscast.

When Murdoch first announced the creation of Fox News, he was overshadowed by other media titans, such as Disney (with ABC) and NBC (with Microsoft), who had declared their designs to launch CNN-like networks. No one in the industry took Murdoch's foray into televised news seriously. As one newspaper account noted in January 1996, "Murdoch's venture would appear to be in the weakest position, as Fox does not have a strong news division..." Another scribe agreed: "Though Mr. Murdoch said the service will draw on the news operations of his Fox Television network in the U.S., in reality the Fox stations have only rudimentary news-gathering capabilities that are vastly inferior to those of NBC and ABC."

But with other profitable ventures, Murdoch could afford to take the hits common with all untested entities. Fox News wasn't like the other news channels or network newscasts. Once viewers got adjusted to the strange mix of more abrasive style and sweet come-ons, they were hooked. With that buzz came confidence: Fox News began psyching out its rival CNN with glorious results. Five years after it first launched, Fox was regularly beating the tar out of CNN. By 2004, it looked like even MSNBC would push CNN aside and leave it alone in the ratings cellar. However, it was Fox that threw the crippling punches at CNN; while the original cable newser would falter and hesitate, Fox had a comfortable lead and was in no danger of losing out to its demoralized competition. With fewer news resources than any of its rivals, the FNC still managed to become the news destination of choice for cable watchers.

Fox News' success doesn't just lie in its product, but also in the way News Corp has been allowed to side-step important rules. As independent producer Len Hill noted, "Without federal regulation [Rupert Murdoch and News Corporation] never would have had enough independent stations to create the fourth network, and yet no sooner was the Fox network on the air than Fox began arguing [to] the FCC that there was enough competition. They tried to shut the door behind them. It is particularly ironic that Fox, born of regulation, would now become the leading cheerleader for deregulation."

Mark Crispin Miller, who teaches Media Studies at New York University, noted that "What corporate concentration of ownership has done has been to basically blow away the ideal of good journalism."

As long as the ever-expanding titans are allowed to make and break the rules, viewers should expect nothing less.

Chapter 3

Survival of the Fittest

"It is sometimes hard to hear yourself think over the noise of grinding axes as our competitors cloak their pleas for protection and special privilege in the language of public interest."

Rupert Murdoch

W hen it launched, on October 7, 1996, Fox News was seen by most to be destined to be the perennially tatty and guffaw-inducing underdog. Newspaper articles of the day made references to Fox's lack of deep journalistic credentials, its small offices with used and timeworn furnishings and its lack of competitive financial resources. As one journalist snidely put it: "After all the years, all the talk, all the flubs and miscues, this company is on the verge of launching a real, live, honest-to-goodness network news division. Who would've thought?"

Unfortunately for CNN, the new kid with the seemingly rich chiseler of a dad had bigger goals for himself: in early 2000, Fox was beating MSNBC for total viewers; by the end of the year, it was regularly beating CNN in the prime-time category. By January 2001, Bill O'Reilly overtook Larry King in the ratings for the first time; by October 2002, "Hannity and Colmes," the direct competitor, also managed to topple King. The year 2002 also marked the first time that Fox overtook CNN in both daytime and prime-time ratings. In 2004, during the Republican Convention in New York City, the vixen network was the choice of over 5.2 million viewers, beating the Big Three networks in total viewers (CNN barely garnered a million and a half viewers, lagging behind MSNBC). The year 2004 also marked two other milestones for Fox News: first, the ratings for CNN, CNN Headline News, MSNBC and CNBC combined still lagged behind Murdoch's baby; second, the first of three Presidential debates between George W. Bush and John Kerry saw the cable newser's audience peak at over nine million viewers. CNN was clearly behind Fox News in the race for viewers, and the venerable newser was looking to get back in top form.

The (arguably) biggest problem for CNN was its lack of competition during its formative years: competition was not something CNN could understand. For years, CNN was the only child, and had grown up never fully knowing what real direct competition was or how dangerous a vindictive rival could be. The game plans never truly took into account what CNN would have to do if a contender was suddenly vying for the top spot on Nielsen's hit parade.

Fox, on the other hand, was created with the full knowledge that it had a rival it would eventually have to overtake. This meant that Fox's mandate was always to conquer; CNN's mandate never included such a survivalist proviso. As Peter Hart, media activism director for FAIR (a progressive media watchdog group), noted: "It's warfare, a sort of campaign-style war against other media outlets, so when Fox went on the air, the idea was to bash CNN."

While Fox was busy adopting and refining its role as bashing predator, CNN was busy running scared. After slashing hundreds of jobs and revamping its lineup starting in 2001, CNN brass had hinged their hopes on well-maintained, middle-aged, second-wave female television news personalities such as Connie Chung and Paula Zahn, with mixed and middling results. The old guard were ushered out post haste, and Time Warner brass had even hired Jamie Kellner, whose success mainly lay in fictional entertainment programming at the WB netlet. Kellner could do "Buffy"; he could bring ratings and some respect to a fledgling network. From an entertainment standpoint, Kellner had all the right credentials. The question was whether he could help CNN get back some of its former glory.

Things didn't look too promising for CNN: for one, Kellner's news experience was nil. AOL Time Warner (now known as just plain Time Warner) was hoping to inject a little glam into the newscasts, but how would Kellner direct the editorial content of the country's first all-news network, particularly when he was saddled with other responsibilities as well?

Kellner's idea of journalistic reinvention was hiring new faces to produce and present the same repackaged format. One of those fresh new faces included former "NYPD Blue" actress Andrea Thompson, who was hired to tell viewers all the words she saw on the teleprompter. The move outraged journalists and did nothing to boost sagging ratings. By March 2003, Kellner was out and headed back to his old alma mater.

By then it became clear that CNN had lost its punch and prowess and, more importantly, it still had no clear plan of attack: most at CNN continued to behave as if it were still the only all-news choice around. As *Vanity Fair* contributing editor and author James Wolcott explained: "When CNN started out Ted Turner had a much more global view of what the media was, what cable news could be. That has really shrunk over the years. Now, maybe there was no way to maintain it, but there was this dream that cable news would be the thing that would really bring us the global village." He added, "I don't even know if CNN's been moved so much to the right as if it's simply been neutered. It doesn't seem to stand for anything anymore; it doesn't even stand up for itself... CNN might as well just be albino." CNN is hopelessly lost: it still hasn't gotten over the shock that it isn't special anymore.

Somehow, the once virile cable newser faced a mid-life crisis and the results were ugly, indeed: botched plastic surgeries, desperate, unhip makeovers and failed dalliances with faded beauties. Fox News, on the other hand, continued to climb in the ratings while openly snickering at its once-powerful rival. CNN didn't seem as assured anymore; it reeked of the desperation of trying to compete with a younger model. CNN never clued in that its competition was uttering sweet nothings to keep its audience aroused. The gangly little kid in geeky clothes grew up to be an alpha male ready to prove his manhood.

And this new stud on the block was a vibrant showman who swaggered and sounded confident: with its snarky, embittered and flagrantly partisan attitude, Fox News became everything CNN could never be: overtly opinionated, flirty to its favorites and crass to any group or person it disliked. Fox News could allow its reporters and anchors to bully and insult their prey with reckless abandon. Murdoch's underlings were given free reign to have uncontrolled outbursts while calling anyone they didn't like a boob and a pinhead. While CNN journalists held on to their dry style and their long arc-serialized news stories, the Fox News kids could roll around in the mud like pigs, hurling both muck and insults at passersby. What CNN couldn't grasp was that TV viewers were no longer content with mere up-to-the-second gossipers; now the talking heads had to act like sneering brutes at a freak show.

The divergence of strategies continues to show in the final products; Fox sets the agenda in terms of how other news outlets cover the news and what will be the top water cooler talk in the country, while CNN merely tries to retain its relevance, with disappointing results. Because Fox News has taken the cool, decisive lead in the news race, its methods have become imitated. As Wolcott observed, "One of the things I've seen happen, particularly under Bush, is that the media is even more America-centric than before. The foreign bureaus have been cut back; they send reporters off to cover wars but not much else. You could see the contrast if you watch CNN International and compare it to CNN Domestic Service. The CNN Domestic Service is pitched to a slightly lower maturity level, but all of these networks act as if America is the center of the world..." Patriotism has little to do with it; it's cheaper to have a local focus than a global one.

Let's Do the Time Warp Again

The change in fortunes can be boiled down to one simple fact: CNN is fighting not to lose while Fox is fighting to win. It is this difference in mindsets that can explain why Fox is capturing the news consumer's imagination. Those who work at Fox fancy themselves as fearless innovators who do journalism different than the fuddy-duddies over at CNN.

Though Fox fans and CNN critics alike maintain that CNN is old school and passé in its appearance and delivery, while rival Fox is innovative, fresh and new in theirs, such a superficial and self-serving assessment couldn't be further from the truth. Despite the funky graphics, snide remarks and female anchors' over-processed hair extensions, the Fox News Channel has absolutely no hip, cutting edge format, formula or strategy going for it. The Fox formula is an old, trusty one that has been used by past media titans with resounding success. The FNC mindset and method of conducting business is older than even your oldest living relative.

The days before the Penny Press (pre-1830) era were openly partisan, not because newspapers truly believed in the ideological tripe they peddled, or merely because they were trying to boost circulation, but because many owners, publishers, editors and reporters were auditioning for lucrative patronage positions from the reigning government of the day.

The self-appointed right-wing chroniclers of the Truth were as openly and shamelessly looking to the government for a handout as their rivals were. Why inconvenience yourself toiling for paltry journalist's wages when you can move up in the world in style with the same sugar daddy you're supposed to be chronicling? Since there were no regulatory laws or self-regulating governing bodies overseeing the news media, there was no need for editors and reporters to worry about whether what many of them were doing was wrong and unethical. Besides, elites read the papers more than regular citizens, and it was the decision-makers and the players who kept up with larger events. Currying favor with the ruling government of the day was just the price of doing business.

Partisan reporting ruled newspapers for a long time. It was only when media owners finally realized that politically neutral stories can grab a larger audience that their paradigm began to shift. That, coupled with the beginning of the Penny Press era, when news products finally became accessible— or at least trendy—to the working classes, brought a change to how the news was reported. As time progressed, these outside influences (economics and populism) were internalized in the news product, and the net result was called objectivity. This commercially practical approach to reporting the news has been the driving force in journalism and still influences journalists to this day.

However, Fox News has openly turned its nose at this method of doing journalism. While those at News Corp's crown jewel may pride themselves on finding a new way of reporting, they have in fact taken a time machine to the nineteenth century. By dusting off the old media play book, the FNC has managed to beat their rivals not with new methods, but with tried and tested old ones.

Graduating With Honors From the Partisan School of Journalism

Fox News has overtaken its most powerful rival to set the tone for how news is presented and interpreted. CNN may have been the trailblazer, but Fox has become the agenda-setter. In the last ten years, television news has taken a right turn; Fox News has simply led the way. The network is an elite playground for the Republican in-crowd: here you will find the likes of Newt Gingrich and Ann Coulter freely getting access to the swings and seesaws, while their progressive counterparts are left sitting on the benches. Fox News has given a platform to the likes of Bill O'Reilly and Sean Hannity, making it fashionable to abuse Democrats and bully them on the playground.

But its conservative leanings aren't the only traits that make the cable newser an old school follower: from its glorification of certain powerful politicians to its revelry in executing its numerous personal and professional vendettas, the network has closely followed the partisan bible to gain a devoted following and crush the competition.

Not that anyone at Fox News would admit it: they claim to be a populist product, yet much of how

their operations are run indicates otherwise. While Fox News does have the Penny Press sensibilities that appeal to the have-nots, its machinery all points to an elitist setup. Murdoch's channel has taken the most commercial aspects of both the populist and partisan models and created a network that both regular folks can enjoy and their rulers can benefit from. In that regard, the network is a partisan one: it is the most powerful Republican faction and the network that reaps the most rewards.

The Fox News Channel is a hybrid of both populist and partisan methods. Instead of relying on journalistic objectivity, Fox brass have decided to follow the formula of old school newspapers during the pre-Penny Press era. News was secondary to its delivery and the motives behind disseminating information to the public; so how does Fox adhere to old school journalistic values? It does so by following the seven golden rules of ideological reporting:

Fox News became everything CNN was not.

1. Be openly partisan. Ideological or political beliefs are based in opinion, personal convenience and values more than mere fact. Partisan-slanted information can be inaccurate, but also manipulative: each story has a purpose and is a means toward an end. Positive and negative stories alike are meant to persuade the audience in order to support the media outlet's point of view.

Before the era of journalistic objectivity, newspapers mostly served the upper classes and depended on the financial support and patronage of political parties, and not advertising, to keep them going. The Penny Press era saw for the most part the end to that act of journalistic lordosis by giving newspapers the option of appealing to common citizens and accepting advertising from a variety of different businesses, but the editorial product still tended to appease the upper echelons of power.

Today, that sort of shameless support of corporate and governmental elites has found a new home at Fox News. Sean Hannity openly slobbers over Republican ideologues who come to hawk their various wares, particularly books, on his program, while Neil Cavuto saves his truckled saliva for corporate kahunas. Speaking of guests, more Republican pundits and guests are showcased than are Democrats, and the token Democrats who are allowed to enter the Fox's den are less known and far weaker than their Republican counterparts. Not only does Fox not give equal time to all parties in any given issues, but it seems to stack the odds of winning the public's hearts and minds clearly against one side.

Fox News must have hedged their bets to one side for a reason. During the impeachment hearings of former President Bill Clinton, the FNC was relentless in its negative coverage of the beleaguered leader—why? One reason may be practical, rather than ideological in nature: since Bill Clinton was well into his second and final term in office, it could be argued that there was no benefit for Fox News to cover him in a neutral manner: what would be in it for them to show mercy to a lame duck President? What could he possibly do for them after forced to leave office?

The messages minions receive from the Fox's den also point to partisan methods. Murdoch's crew receive daily memos from higher ups, instructing them how Fox News coverage on certain events will be presented. These dictates are significant: how can the non-news gatherers make a determination on how a story should be covered without all of the facts? Shouldn't journalists gather information first before they come to a conclusion, rather than the other way around? As former CBS News anchor and journalistic legend Walter Cronkite observed, "I've never heard of any other network nor any other legitimate news organization doing that—newspaper or broadcast. That is, that comes down from on high, of course, as the edict for coverage. There have been newspapers in the past that certainly did that. There were the days of the newspaper, in the newspaper world where newspapers were open advocates of one set of circumstances or another, politically being the most obvious. But that day has pretty well passed. Really, Rupert Murdoch is about the only practitioner in the United States, anyway, who conducts his news organizations in that fashion."

Because Fox News has been loud and confident in their methods, it leads to the impression that their vehemence equals correctness. Since other news outlets aren't as strident, they seem less correct and more wishy-washy by comparison. Suddenly, being partisan never looked so righteous. As Robert McChesney noted:

> A number of media that have come to see themselves as explicitly conservative, self-described conservative often times, even implicitly conservative and their justification is "we're conservative and we're allowed to be conservative and one-sided because the rest of the media is liberal and one-sided against us, so we're just balancing them. The historical evidence doesn't back that up at all and what we have instead basically is a mainstream journalism, NBC, CBS, CNN, the mainstream print media which is rigidly centrist, which tries to be fair to each side of the range of elite debate and is scared to death of being accused of being liberal; the last thing mainstream journalists want to be accused of is being ideological.

The schism between Fox News and the rest of mainstream journalism in America has had another consequence: it has given the new kid on the block the right to change the rules of television journalism. McChesney noted that Fox News acts like "rabid pit bulls that say 'we don't have to play by those conventions; we're just here to advance our interests, pure and simple.' And so they get to set the tone." Since the tone at Fox News is "we're always right and our competitors are always wrong," the direction of the debate becomes troubling for any news organization not owned by News Corps.

Even those who worked for the Network have essentially admitted that Fox is a skewed news channel: when Canada rebuffed Fox's advances to allow the channel to air in that country, a scorned Bill O'Reilly complained that his northern neighbors didn't allow Fox "to balance" out the coverage given by one left-leaning news network—a de facto admission that Fox News is not a complete or balanced news channel in and of itself. Those words could not have come from someone who honestly believed he was working for a "fair and balanced" news channel.

As Dave Korb, a former freelance news writer who worked for Fox News noted, "Fair and balanced, or in newsroom jargon, F and B, was the code, without a doubt. To the audience it was meant to

convey the idea that they could turn to Fox for news that would balance the events, or the issue against whatever progressive spin might have been..." On the other hand, "to the staff it was meant to convey, in code which everyone understood, it was kind of 'wink, wink, nod, nod,'" Korb adds, "it was Fox's to give it a 'fair and balanced' spin, which meant to give it a conservative spin or, if you will, a Republican spin, or an administration spin. They were very clear about that." Peter Hart noted that, "You look at Fox News Channel and it's no wonder that [Rupert Murdoch] has so many friends in conservative politics; he gives them exactly what they want." As will be discussed in Chapter Seven, Fox is not necessarily a conservative news network, but a George W. Bush Republican one.

2. Be overtly arrogant and pompous. Would anyone expect any self-respecting professional news producer to tell a guest he invited on his program to "shut up"? Would a serious newsman such as Edward R. Murrow or Walter Cronkite ever have called someone a "boob" while reporting the news? What serious journalist would have the gall to demand respect without actually earning the honor to which he believes he is innately entitled?

For partisan news outlets to work, they cannot concede that any ideology outside their own can possibly be right on any issue: if they open the door to outside beliefs, some readers may just like those fresh ideas enough to drop the publication for other ones. The partisan press of yore could more easily throw slurs and insults to their rivals and targets; once the United States began to more confidently form, evolve and refine itself, those same methods suddenly seemed too crude to be accurate. People began to trust news outlets that didn't resort to those degrading tactics.

Fox News has revived the practice of strategic name-calling as a legitimate form of reportage, but shrill temper tantrums are nothing new: newspapers of the partisan age used to stoop to the same puerile antics in order to degrade the competition and to elevate their own stature in the public arena. But since modern day audiences have not encountered editorial snapping before, the tactic seems fresh and fun. Bill O'Reilly doesn't need to attend anger management classes, since his serially explosive schtick keeps packing in loyal viewers. Sean Hannity doesn't need to come to terms with the possibility that he may have a narcissistic personality disorder, since his fans love him just the way he is. The Fox News kids get to swagger and rudely cut off guests who want to pop their balloons with a dose of reality. When guests with one expertise are dressed-down by hosts for not having another expertise, such as when O'Reilly dismissed media critic Steve Rendall for not also having military expertise, the situation can only be described as bewildering and pompous.

3. Rely on style over substance. During its infancy, Fox News was not the most attractive-looking news channel around, but within a few short years, the network has in many cases surpassed its rivals in the aesthetics department. Fox News has eye-catching graphics that announce that it is a patriotic outfit that keeps its finger on breaking and important news, but when "Fox News Alerts" are used to report on the latest celebrity press releases, the value of the images flashed on the screen becomes questionable.

Yet the distinctive style is undeniable. The Fox News kids dress better than anchors on other networks. The production values seem edgier and sleeker. While the actual news content leaves much to be desired, there is no doubt that next to Fox News, CNN and MSNBC look dowdy and slow. However,

The seven golden rules of ideological reporting

1	Be openly partisan.
2	Be overtly arrogant and pompous.
3	Rely on style over substance.
4	Focus on sensationalism, crime and reactionary opinions.
5	Openly support war and the reigning government of the day.
6	Appeal to the disgruntled, disillusioned and neutered male.
7	If a critic voices a complaint, go for his jugular.

it is cheaper to create impressive visuals than create impressive investigative stories. If content isn't important to the outlet, then the focus has to be on presentation; why would people be attracted to your product if it were both sparse and homely? Fox News creates a world for those who appreciate aesthetics more than content.

4. Focus on sensationalism, crime and reactionary opinions. A news outlet is supposed to report on issues and events that affect the audience's lives: politics, environment, education, career, family, crime, environment, business, labor, law and health are all areas that impact everyday lives, but many of these topics are underrepresented on Fox. Conversely, the more lurid murder and rape trials, porn, war, rap music and the positive deeds of CEOs seem to get more coverage on Fox News than other stories, such as women's issues or palliative care. As former broadcast reporter, producer and writer Av Westin noted, "cable operations... are desperate to find anything to fill their airtime and so they frequently will report ad nauseum, with no new detail, a scandal, an 'O.J.' case, Laci Peterson. All of that is designed of course to get the ratings and they can see it. They do track ratings now minute by minute on programs and they can tell what subjects are bringing them ratings and which ones are not. And clearly prurience and tabloidization [are] very effective in bringing up the ratings."

Political pundits and other opinion spewers also get a lot of face time on Fox rather than those who have first hand knowledge of an event or issue, but manipulating emotions is vital for a partisan news outlet: since biased thinking is illogical, the outlet can't appeal to intellect or reason since the glaring lies and faults will be quickly uncovered. In order to conceal the shoddy reporting, emotions have to be used as misdirection and distraction; that way the news consumer will be too busy feeling enraged or frightened to notice that they are being fed suspect information.

There are other reasons for choosing sensational stories over dry ones: many people prefer an emotional story over facts and logic. Finally, using emotional manipulation leads to behavioral control. As Wolcott observed about Fox News' post 9/11 news coverage, "There was a real orgy of fear-mongering after 9/11 and one of the things that they do to keep the anxiety level high is... have an anchorman interviewing somebody about one doomsday scenario, but the crawl at the bottom of the screen is giving you details about another one; so you're getting two or three at once." He adds, "In the Age of Terror, terrorism has become the all-purpose fear weapon because now everything is converted to terrorism, even what we used to recognize as legitimate or illegitimate forces of resistance are now simply called terrorists."

A fearful audience is a devoted audience: how else will they know where danger lurks, who can be trusted, and how to save themselves? Striking fear into the audience is essential, according to Wolcott, because "if you have a constant sense of unease then you're going to look to the government to protect you. You're going to look to strong government because the people can't do it."

If a large enough audience does respond to the emotional manipulations, the media outlet, in turn, can exploit those individuals in future ad campaigns. For example, Bill O'Reilly regularly reads his viewers' letters on air, complete with his commentary. Foxnews.com has its own "Fox fan section." It is a form of free advertising and bragging rights that also helps cultivate a closer relationship to the news consumer. When viewers have an emotional investment with a news channel, they may become a more loyal audience.

5. Openly support war and the reigning government of the day. Few ongoing news stories can be as riveting and mesmerizing as war stories, particularly if the home team is one of the combatants. When it is "our" men and women who go over to a foreign country to battle, people back home are worried for their safety, root for their soldiers and despise the enemy. War stories guarantee decent and stable ratings for as long as the war is fought. News outlets have a lot to gain by running with these types of stories; they're unpredictable, frightening, yet if the home team wins the war, there is a great emotional payoff for the audience.

But war coverage can also lead to a dilemma: the war may be prolonged, ugly and may not go as well as viewers hope. Images of shredded soldiers and body bags are unwelcome since no one wants to root for a losing team or face the prospect that their own flesh and blood is physically and strategically inferior to another group. In order not to offend their audiences, news outlets will gloss over the grittier and bloodier parts of the battles.

The Fox News Channel promotion of the Iraq war was notable for several reasons: glamorized war shots were used in their promos, the U.S. seemed as if it had not lost a single casualty, antiwar activists were portrayed as dangerous and unpatriotic and Fox News emphasized stories that only showed the positive benefits of the war. Wolcott believed that "Fox, even more than other networks, depends upon war fever to keep going, and when the war fever dissipates, you can see them sort of floating around; they're sort of waiting for the next war to get galvanized."

Fox News didn't merely cover the war in Iraq; they shamelessly supported it. Cheerleading masquerading as coverage reeks of partisan reporting, but viewers didn't care whether hosts such as Hannity and O'Reilly openly ridiculed and demonized anyone who questioned whether Iraq actually had weapons of mass destruction, whether they had the capability to launch these alleged weapons toward the United States, or whether sending young men and women to be traumatized, disfigured, tortured and killed was really worth it. What would happen if soldiers were busy fighting in Iraq, and a real threat came on U.S. soil? The cable newser never entertained any of those tough questions.

And that Fox News never considered that there might be another side to the war was chilling, not because the network took sides, but because it showed shoddy and careless reporting. Do they not ever have a Plan B if things do not work according to plan? Are they so naïve and intellectually stunted that they can't entertain the fact that every story has at least two sides? As Robert McChesney, a professor at the University of Illinois and cofounder of Free Press, noted about Fox News, "what's considered legitimate political news is basically being stenography to people in power." McChesney adds that "by 'we report; you decide,' it basically means we report what people in power say and we're not going to tell you whether it's true or not, that's up to you to figure out. Basically, it's an aggregation of the responsibility of journalism wrapped in being professional journalism."

6. Appeal to the disgruntled, disillusioned and neutered male.
A young man's fantasies don't just involve babes in bikinis, but also achieving monster success. What could be more exciting to a young turk than becoming a star athlete turned A-list actor and rock singer who is envied for his great looks, obscene wealth, creative genius and sexual prowess?

But life for the dreaming adolescent male often doesn't turn out to be so unlimited. The girl he married was the neighborhood floozie who tricked him into marriage by way of an "accidental" pregnancy, the menial job he has is grueling and unglamorous, the boss is a bullying slave driver, the crippling bills flood his modest mortgaged home located in a bad part of town and deep down he knows his fading talents are taunting him at every waking moment. He will never be the handsome and athletic young turk he once was. His glory days spit in his face every morning he looks in the mirror. To some, it's a fate worse than prison. At least the inmate knows it was a judge and jury who convicted and confined him. The inmate has some identifiable outsider to blame for his predicament. It's the American Dream turned into a Nightmare.

And yet there are people all around him succeeding and surpassing him: vapid movie starlets who bag multimillion dollar paydays and gangster rappers who glorify crime can afford Cristal and Gucci. The people he went to school with are doing well in life, too, particularly the ones who seemed to be lost causes. The children of immigrants he went to school with now own their own businesses. The nerds who were thrown into the school swimming pool became multimillionaires. The girls who were called dogs became beautiful and successful careerists. Everyone who looked like they'd have it worse ends up having it better than he does. He is angry at his lot in life, but who's to blame?

Whoever it is, it can't be him.

It has to be the foreigners who are taking jobs away from him or the gay couples who seem to have more disposable income than he ever will. It's the rappers that are corrupting his children; the criminals who have turned his neighborhood into a war zone and the leftist women who have taken all the fun out of a little sexist humor at the work place. His failures can't be because he didn't keep focused on his goals, relied too much on his natural talents, gave up too easily or allowed himself to be fooled by sweet nothings and old tricks.

The problem is that he may have fallen for those old tricks, but he keeps falling for them, anyway. Instead of it being a nubile girl promising a no-strings-attached good time, it is a bunch of talking heads surreptitiously holding his hand, assuring him he's not to blame for his world and his country falling apart.

If Fox excels at any one specialty, it is digging up a motley crew of outsiders who can, on cue, point a finger of blame at someone who does not belong in Fox News' demographic. The exploitation of their viewers' anxieties and weaknesses has helped the network gain a following and loyalty. As former WTTG-TV reporter Alexander Kippen noted about the pre-FNC days of News Corps affiliates:

> *The exploitation of Fox's viewers' anxieties and weaknesses has helped the network gain a loyal following.*

> In those days [during Kippen's tenure as correspondent for the Fox Network] they were really experimenting with different ways to develop a distinctive profile and I guess what started out when I was there as news for maybe the young and hip, evolved into attitude for the middle age and the angry... I think perhaps it was the beginning of a discovery at Fox that maybe there was this unserved need for conservatives, for middle age white suburbanites who felt unserved by the news business at that time, and it was an unfilled niche and if they could fill it, if they could serve that need they could make a lot of money. And that seems to have come to pass.

Fox News has beautifully and masterfully exploited a psychological weakness with its vulnerable audience: don't blame your real and perceived failures on your unrealistic goals, your jealous streak, your poor critical thinking or planning skills, your aversion to working around obstacles and your self-imposed boundaries; blame your failures on someone else. Wolcott noted that:

> [Fox] "always stoke anger. They love the idea of anger. If you go back and think about [the] Iraq [war], it wasn't just [former Iraqi leader Saddam] Hussein that they kept talking about; it was the French and the Germans, anyone who was not with us. If you go back and look at what they were saying about the French and the Germans on Fox News leading up to the war because they would not participate. All the talk, Neil Cavuto, Bill O'Reilly, talking about boycotts...

Because Fox News blends elitism with populism, the channel can serve both elites and validate its audience. As Mark Crispin Miller noted:

Murdoch plays a very dangerous role. It's interesting that he would defend his bluntly commercial enterprises in Britain especially by attacking the BBC as elitist, and thereby clothing himself in the rags of populism... So his lowbrow programming was something for the little guy, the common man, anti-elitist and therefore a breath of Democratic fresh air.

7. If a critic voices a complaint, go for his jugular. Why listen to reason when your own self-affirming delusions work so much better for your sense of self and self-esteem? Who wants to hear that his grandiose life theories are too impractical, unrealistic, expensive, ridiculous, dangerous, psychopathic or just plain stupid for a real-world application? Why be inconvenienced by reality when fantasy is just so much cooler?

Nasty comments to critics were an important part of the FNC. Bill O'Reilly was never fired for yelling "shut up" to guests who did not share his point of view. Fox is not a forum for public debate; it is a forum for anchors and hosts to hurl a variety of ignoble insults and put-downs to those who simply do not agree with their beliefs.

People at Fox News don't have a sense of humor. When CNN's former resident conservative Tucker Carlson was asked on-air for his home phone number (he had defended telemarketing on his program) in 2003, he instead gave the number for the FNC's Washington bureau. After getting flooded with calls, Fox News retaliated by posting Carlson's unlisted number on their website and refused to take it down until he apologized. Even though the Carlsons were deluged with a torrent of obscene phone calls from sexually frustrated Fox News watchers who obviously could only get their jollies in this impotent fashion, the network still claimed to have taken the high road: an FNC spokesuit sniffed, "CNN threw the first punch here. Correcting this mistake was good journalism." Judging by their past and current news stories, it seems as though the FNC may not be entirely aware of what good journalism actually resembles.

But the Carlson incident is merely one in an endless stream of Fox's overzealous attacks on critics, rivals and irritants. The same underlying vindictiveness drives Fox News to not just disagree with their rivals, critics or ideological opposites, but to shred their reputation and dignity to shreds. Public debate has to be stifled in a partisan outlet, or else viewers may begin to trust other outlets for their information and abandon ship and elites to retaliate or shut out the outlet for not supporting their patron.

Public debate only works when both parties have carefully thought out and researched their positions and truly have a genuine respect for their fellow man. Debating is futile for those who just belch their hardened opinions without well-researched facts: after all, debating might just reveal the debater's blaring flaws and profound lack of knowledge. People who don't want to debate don't want others to know how limited, desperate or opportunistic they are.

Besides, there is a coolness to rudeness: people admire those who can retort with a snappy put down. But rudeness in the media is nothing new: newspapers in the pre-Penny Press era were filled with various insults directed at those who did not toe the party line. In those cases, and in Fox's, while the

vitriol may be amusing, what it has to do with reporting the news isn't clear: if your mandate is to report the facts, why are you wasting time sticking your tongue out at your enemies?

Fox News has simply resurrected a well-worn formula of journalistic survival and updated it for a modern audience. While there are some elements of populism, the shift toward partisanship is clearly present. Media barons such as William Randolph Hearst mastered the hybrid method of populist and partisan reporting; the Fox News Channel is merely following the same cutthroat strategy with better results.

> *But the Fox News Channel would be nothing without its two main architects:*
> *Rupert Murdoch and Roger Ailes.*

Part Two

Darwin's Darlings

Chapter 4

Murdoch

"I am not a monopolist as some claim. I have given people choice."

Rupert Murdoch

Lots of men make money, and while some take decades to build up their fortunes; others seem to have a knack for racking up wealth naturally. Some of the wealthy are uncanny strategists who have a gift for exploiting the zeitgeist or ortgeist to increase their bottom lines and influence; others simply grow richer without bothering themselves with power or games. But being rich and powerful isn't as special as it used to be: what's paltry millions compared to someone else's billions? Even news media titans have a hierarchy: some are rich, some rich and powerful and some are rich, powerful, influential and ubiquitous. Rupert Murdoch falls into the last category.

News Corp's Rupert Murdoch is a self-appointed entrepreneurial populist who proves that the "you scratch my back and I'll scratch yours" method works wonders for one's bank account. Though he has repeatedly denied being a monopolist over the years, he was also quoted as saying "Monopoly is a terrible thing, 'til you have it." Perhaps he isn't quite a monopolist yet, but he is an undisputed oligarch: in a shrinking field of media titans, his empire has expanded globally over the years.

Murdoch was once referred to as the world's "unofficial Minister of Information" for a good reason:

his media empire's tentacles are firmly rooted in Australia, the United Kingdom, China and the United States. In fifty years, he has seen his reach expand: in 1954, when his father passed away, a young Rupert Murdoch took over his father's newspaper business in Australia. Two years later, he acquired his first magazine, and two years after that he acquired his first television station. He acquired a book publishing company in 1981 and his first cable network in 1983. He now owns one movie studio, nine satellite television networks, forty television stations, 100 cable channels and 175 newspapers that reach a worldwide audience of 4.7 billion people. As of this writing, Murdoch has expressed his intention to launch a Fox Financial News and Fox Entertainment Network as well.

Murdoch has an indisputable reputation for making money, but what he does not have is a reputation for being the vanguard for quality journalism—or quality programming or quality editorial product in general. He is the avatar of nicely packaged disposable schlock that soothes the troubled souls of the vulgar classes. He's got his hands in all sorts of gossipy ventures: the "Bizarre" and "Page Six" brand names of crotch-gazing belong to his newspapers. Britain's *Sun* is a newspaper stacked with stacked naked girlies with cutlines such as "Leah, aged twenty-two, from Hastings." Leah from Hastings would simply fall under the *Sun*'s radar if she were a fully clothed medical researcher who discovered the cure for AIDS or ALS.

Murdoch is a man who has claimed he has given people choice. At least the man doesn't lie; just look at all he has done for the United Kingdom. He has given the British the choice to read their newspapers with one hand while simultaneously learning about the not-so-fresh details of Britney Spears' well-worn bikini and deep, piercing insights about monikerly-doomed living silicon storage unit Abi Titmuss (how would England ever get informed without Victoria Newton?) As Mark Crispin Miller observed, "Murdoch was kind of a byword for journalistic sleaze, for tabloidism at its worst; so the mainstream press likes to speak in fearful tones of the danger of Rupert Murdoch taking over a newspaper and dumbing it down, putting in a lot of cheesecake photography, beefing up the sensationalism."

Murdoch's peddling in salacious scuzz in his news products makes him something of a tin foil titan and a glorified garage sale peddler: he gets people to buy junk they don't really need and then feel good about their purchase. Instead of making his wealth providing useful products, services or information, he lines his coffers by having naïve girls exposing their nipples in newspapers or having journalists spend time and resources interviewing the disgruntled former mistresses of the rich and famous.

There are people who may want fluffy, primal distractions, but they also don't want to be caught dead buying those kinds of openly nosy and smutty rags at the supermarket check-out counter: they'll only buy or watch them if they have a patina of respectability. It is these people that Murdoch gives exactly what they want: News Corps balances their various news vehicles with jingoism, sensationalism, smut, gripes, fear-mongering and a small dash of real information to justify the label "news." But even here, the news will take one side of an issue over another. The *Weekly Standard* is not going to have articles that will upset their conservative audiences or that will run counter to their political views.

In other words, Murdoch came by his success in two ways: either by stuffing cotton in his audience's ears or by allowing them to freely roll around in the sewer. Murdoch simply acquires the rights to charge admission to the sewer-rolling and sells the cotton. He is an entertainer, propagandist, pornographer, gossiper, spoiler, mudslinger and cheerleader all rolled up tightly in one dignified-looking package.

The rise of the American empire is largely based on the notion of utility and creativity: either make something useful or something innovative. The automobile, electricity, airplane, computer and light bulb are inventions that propelled the United States to the dominant position it enjoys today. Its movie, music and entertainment industries take care of the artistic or leisurely side of human nature.

Murdoch has blurred the line between news and entertainment.

Somewhere along the way, utility and creativity were joined together to create something entirely different. Computers weren't just glorified typewriters, but game consoles, matchmakers, oracles, bankers and message carriers, too. On the surface, it is in this hybrid realm where Murdoch seems to have the advantage. He has blurred the line between news and entertainment: nude girls resting their breasts beside hard news, gossip sandwiched between political and business coverage, mouthy pundits snapping and discussing the latest breaking military news. Murdoch, it seems, has an eye for combining the two greatest American strengths to create cheery utility. His news is like an SUV: it's big, shiny, great to drive and gets you where you want to go.

But News Corp products aren't known or respected for their informational or investigative value: the company is not one that produces quality information and analysis, but one that banks on using carny tricks. Murdoch's news properties only look useful and entertaining on the outside: inside, they simply push a single point of view. Murdoch has been credited with (or accused of) blurring the lines of information and entertainment, but whether his news properties are entertaining at all is questionable: how entertaining is it for a middle-aged man to tell a young guest who has lost his father to "shut up"? How entertaining is it for a grown man to accuse those who have a different political point of view of being on the same level as terrorists? Murdoch's news vehicles may offer a lot of things, but data or thrills won't be on the top of the list.

The Murdochian Candidate

Murdoch's attitude toward the journalism profession isn't one of respect or reverence. As David Brock noted, "[Murdoch] doesn't believe in objectivity, he has a contempt for journalism." In that regard, he is no different than other media barons—such as Conrad Black, who has sneered at the line of work his employees toil in. Media owners don't like the media, making their journalists' jobs all the more difficult.

Murdoch's main interest isn't improving the quality of his product, but expanding it. Acquisition of more properties is the name of the game and Murdoch has a rare ability to skirt around rules to get his own way with government. According to John Dunbar, Murdoch is "a very smart man and he is not someone who is going to big foot anybody. He's very persistent, that seems to be the one word that comes out the most. He's looking down the road; he's looking for the long haul, and he's going to continue to... gently, gently persuade regulators to go his way."

The News Corporation honcho has an insatiable appetite for buying more properties. As he told one interviewer: "I would never say that our company is complete. If an asset comes along that is a good fit at the right price, we would always look at it and make an assessment—we've always been opportunistic." It's never big enough, and there is no such thing as limits.

A man who shuns limits in his professional life is likely to shun limits in other areas, too. Murdoch has a reputation for vindictive behavior: when the *New York Daily News'* Pete Hamill wrote a 1977 column that directly criticized Murdoch, the News Corp titan did not take kindly to the slight. Murdoch went for his opponent's most vulnerable spot and attacked.

At the time, Hamill was dating Jacqueline Kennedy Onassis and Murdoch—who obviously has an impeccable memory—had an underling find one of Hamill's earlier columns that was particularly critical of the former First Lady. That embarrassing column was reprinted in most of its entirety in the rival *New York Post*. One slap obviously deserved another.

Rivals aren't the only ones who need to fear the wrath of Rupert. Andrew Neil, a former editor of the *Sunday Times* told *George* magazine in 1999, "[...] you must never forget the duty of a courtier. It is fatal to make the mistake of taking him for granted. 'I wonder how the king is today?' is the question you must ask yourself every day you spend at Rupert's court. Otherwise you'll be finished. Just like that."

Even politicians have to be careful not to step on Murdoch's feet. As media critic Eric Alterman noted about Murdoch's influence over lawmakers, "There was nothing in it for the politicians to resist Rupert Murdoch; he could make their lives very difficult. He has a daily newspaper that he treats as an attack dog, so what did they need the headache for?"

No one wants a Murdochian headache and giving in is wiser than playing chicken with a man who can shape your image to an audience of billions. He is aware of his power and knows how to use it. As Miller explained, "Rupert Murdoch is not some marginal predator with especially low standards. Today [he] is in charge of a vast transcontinental corporation that has countless interests all over the world and is involved with governments all over the world for that very reason." Robert McChesney added that Murdoch is "more effective and more brazen about linking up the politics and the economics than the other media bosses are." Murdoch is a savvy negotiator and is willing to swap his media power for something he can use. But the merging of both corporations and the government, according to McChesney, is a trait of a classical fascist regime. Murdoch may not espouse fascism, but it could be argued that his business style precariously flirts with the darker side of conservatism when left unchecked and unchallenged.

Playing the Game of Murdocholy

Rupert Murdoch aligns himself with conservative ideology and ideals: for example, he once said of the aftermath of the Iraq War that "I think it's been misrepresented... all the kids are back at school, 10% more than when Saddam Hussein was there." As Diana Winthrop, a former news producer for WTTG in Washington, observed during her time at the station:

> It was clear during those years that Murdoch, who had absolutely adored Ronald Reagan, and had a lot of admiration for the group of Republicans that controlled Congress... He really adored Reagan more than anything, and I think it's because their background was quite similar [...and Murdoch] admired that Reagan wasn't a liberal establishment guy who had gone to Harvard [...] This was a man that he really thought walked on water.

He may have admired Reagan, but Murdoch prefers any politician who is best described as pliable: he has parted the red tape sea in order to expand his already mammoth empire. As Peter Hart, Media Activism Director for FAIR explained, "I think he's more brazenly gone in and had things altered specifically for his own benefit... You pour money into politics, you make friends with politicians and you get favors in return. Murdoch has always been good in understanding the intersection between politics and the media, and he understands making friends in politics means getting things in return."

But Murdoch is not a stubborn fool: when he cannot get his way with buying or bullying, he will back down. Discouraging Murdoch is not an impossible task, and the Chinese government learned that in 1994 when they openly expressed their anger at Murdoch's satellite offerings, particularly the BBC, which had the audacity to air documentaries that pointed out the various ways the government walked all over the basic human rights of their citizens. As Cohen explained:

> [Murdoch] once, years ago, made this comment about how satellite technology was going to open up authoritarian societies because information-hungry residents of closed societies would have access to new information that their repressive government wouldn't allow them to have.

Cohen added that instead of belaboring the point or challenging his hosts, Murdoch took another approach to the problem:

 The BBC can often cover human rights well, and was covering human rights in China, and the authorities in China complained to Murdoch, and what did he do, for the people he had once crowed about—the information-closed societies? He simply took BBC off the air.

As former News Corp newspaper journalist Bruce Page bluntly put it, Murdoch was the Chinese government's "favorite Westerner because he never gives them any trouble. He rushed in there looking like he'd give them trouble, but they tamed him very fast." Page remarked that Murdoch "started off in China talking very revolutionary talk. But, as [at] many times in his life, he has changed

direction quite abruptly at no very great pressure... He has made his way by being subservient to powers greater than himself; so changing him is not a big problem—there's not a hell of a lot there to change."

The all-powerful News Corp head is flexible in other areas of his life, too. Despite his strong affiliations to the Republican party, above all else, Murdoch is a pragmatist. In 1985, when he wanted to own certain media properties in the states, but was prohibited because he was a foreigner, he simply jumped the queue and became an American citizen. Whatever it takes to be the kid with the most toys, Murdoch will do it.

Don't let that flexibility confuse you into thinking Murdoch's a pushover. As Jeff Cohen noted: "Rupert Murdoch is a real example of a guy who knows how to pull political strings, in country after country across the globe, to shape political power in those countries in a way that allows him to build his economic power. He's done it from Australia to England to the U.S.; he'll endorse people for office, and when they get in, they'll allow him to have more media power, and if he decides they're not helping him enough, he'll switch parties, [and] endorse someone else..."

As to the rewards Murdoch reaps from his various corporate expeditions, Cohen adds:

> It's something William Randolph Hearst from the 1930s would be astounded [at]—I mean, there have always been media moguls, but they operated within one country. Murdoch was the first that went transnational, and he showed this agility for working political levers in country after country to allow himself to amass media power. The more media power he has, the more the politicians are afraid of him and it becomes easy for him to exert more political power...

The art of the deal is an exact science, and Murdoch is both an artist and a scientist who can read his marks, regardless of their cultural differences to him. As Robert McChesney noted, "What Rupert Murdoch does is in country after country where he operates, China, Australia, Great Britain, the United States, he goes in to the government in power and is basically willing to trade on his media power, for his coverage to get the best possible deals, more monopoly licenses, a license to get bigger and bigger, to get more commercial success." In that respect, Murdoch has succeeded beyond anyone's wildest imagination.

Freedom of Choice—News Corp Style

Because Murdoch's corporate combat methods involve oiling squeaky back room doors, his networking skills have helped him cultivate important relationships. Miller noted Murdoch's "wide range of properties has given [him] a special amount of clout with various governments, with world leaders. He's an extremely pragmatic man, although very, very right-wing; so he will back whatever horse he thinks will win. Murdoch, for example, worked very closely with [former British Prime Minister] Margaret Thatcher to break the Printer's Union in Britain." As David Goodfriend, Executive Vice President and general council of Air America noted, "Influence is almost subliminal. The influence that Rupert Murdoch has when he walks a member of Congress through the local TV station."

Young Rupert Murdoch

1954	First Newspaper
1956	First Magazine
1958	First Television Station
1960	First Record Label
1981	First Publishing House
1983	First Cable Channel

His bravura and persistence have also helped him get around those pesky ownership rules, too, as Miller noted: "Murdoch owns newspapers and TV stations in the same cities; this is a violation of FCC regulations... but the FCC issued a waiver in Murdoch's case, as the FCC often has done for him." As Gene Kimmelman noted, Murdoch "owned newspapers; he wanted to own more newspapers, he wanted to own more broadcast outlets, he wanted to own [a] satellite in this country. He had to get licenses. He had to get waivers of rules in some instances, all of this overseen by the Federal Communications Commission. So he has had his army of experts and lawyers, lobbyists at the Federal Communications Commission, like many other companies, day in and day out, for years. He's visited himself many, many times, and he plays the political process to get the changes in rules, changes in laws he needs to consummate a merger, to buy more properties, to get around limitations on foreign ownership." In other words, Murdoch plays by the partisan press rule book. He may claim to be a populist, but his courtship of powerful government elites firmly places him with the media ownership of the pre-Penny Press era.

Murdoch's cozy relationship with useful politicians has come in handy in other areas of his empire as well. When Fox News launched in the mid-1990s, its biggest problem was securing nationwide broadcast distribution. Fox News needed cable service providers to pump the FNC into the homes of subscribers, but one company in particular proved to be stubborn in its resistance. Time Warner, which owned CNN, also happened to be the cable service provider that didn't want to carry a rival network. Exercising the power to keep contenders at bay, Time Warner shut out its competitor. News Corp wasn't going to take the shut out lying down. The spat would find its way into the courts and New York City Hall, where the city's get-tough mayor would be recruited into the battle of the network titans.

There was also a third, smaller contender caught in the crossfire of the two mud wrestling corporate giants, as Mark Green recalled:

> My office read in the paper that [former New York City Mayor Rudy] Giuliani was proposing to give over one of the public access channels. Time Warner was a franchisee

Old Rupert Murdoch

175	Newspapers	
9	Satellite Television Stations	
100	Cable Channels	
40	Book Imprints	
40	Television Stations	
1	Movie Studio	

over to Murdoch's Fox News, and we thought it was an odd selection because a public access channel is supposed to be for community news, governmental news. It's supposed to be for public education and governmental purposes. It's called a PEG channel for those three words, and the argument that Fox News was a public channel was odd because if you ask who's the biggest capitalist in the world, who is the least public access person in the world, the answer would probably be Rupert Murdoch.

The solution wasn't viable to Green, who recalled the reaction upon hearing about the FNC's special treatment:

> When we saw that the mayor was trying to coerce Time Warner into giving over one of its very few public access channels to a private entity called Fox News, I contacted Time Warner, heard out their concern and their arguments, and I, the public official, joined with Time Warner to try to stop and enjoin Mayor Giuliani from forcing Time Warner to carry something which is obviously not public, governmental or educational, but was commercial.

The taxpayer pays for PEG channels; not to mention that a commercial network taking over those airwaves would be a violation of the Cable Act. Green joined in Time Warner's lawsuit to stop the takeover and the judge issued an injunction against Fox. Green noted that the maneuver was "consistent with the way Murdoch often operates, which is trying to get waivers around normal rules because of political favors." Time Warner eventually had to carry the rival network, and the rest is history. Murdoch got his way and gave people a choice between CNN and the FNC.

Even the FCC has not put its foot down to Murdoch's multiple requests for special treatment. As John Dunbar, director of the Telecommunications Project at the Center for Public Integrity, wryly noted, "the FCC is more interested in ensuring a free flow of commerce in the industry than it is in looking out for the public interest." Dunbar also noted how Murdoch has bypassed those annoying plebeian rules to build his American media empire:

Back in the mid-nineties, he bought ten very large television stations; [they were] owned by a Criss Craft Industries at the time. It was a highly controversial sale and it was a huge deal. There were three separate ownership issues that were all created in the public interest that would be violated if that sale was allowed to go through. Virtually the entire transaction took place, and the deal was done before Murdoch and News Corp ever came before the FCC to ask for permission because they were banking on the fact that the FCC was going to grant a waiver, and [their] waivers are just notorious. This is a particularly obnoxious instance of the public's interest being virtually ignored because there's this presumption that the FCC is going to do what the industry wants it to do.

In July 2001, News Corp was ordered to sell a New Jersey television station within two years after buying ten new stations from another media company, but News Corp never sold the asset since brass assumed the FCC would simply rewrite ownership rules that would allow the company to keep all of its toys. The Commission did rewrite the rules, but the free pass was nixed by a federal appeals court in 2004, and what the FCC will do to remedy the situation remains to be seen as of this writing. The mindset of News Corp has always been the same: rules are for commoners.

Murdoch has given people a choice all over the world: in China, citizens have a choice between watching state-run television and Murdoch-run television that conforms to state-run dictates. As Bruce Page noted, "the main outcome [is] television assets in China are very, very carefully monitored by Murdoch and the Chinese to make sure that they never, ever say anything that might bother the government, like refer to AIDS or SARS or anything of that sort. They concentrate on pretty brain dead entertainment that won't cause any hassles. My feeling is that Murdoch would like to do that everywhere."

For giving people the choice between real news and the poseur variety, Murdoch has been duly rewarded. For those who refuse to believe that their opinions cannot be anything but fact, Murdoch has created a world that conforms to those beliefs. If one were skittering on paranoid ideations, a person could convince himself that the shrewd, opportunistic and endgame-obsessed Murdoch's ultimate goal was to divide the American people in order to conquer them. The country's left-right schism has widened and become more perilous to divergent views over the years. Why not take advantage of the rifts to profit from them? The bickering sides will be too busy fighting to notice that they were being exploited by rabble-rouser outsiders, who quietly grow rich as the battling sides grow bitter. Why would an outsider care about a foreign country's unity and health?

The above musings may be an overstatement, but the FNC only adds fuel to the ideological fire.

Murdoch is not an ideologue: he is a capitalistic pragmatist who caters to a devout and sizable market that clamors for redemption. According to Bruce Page, "Murdoch is the classic authoritarian type where there is no real core. Murdoch will change at any time according to what the circumstances dictate. There isn't any fixed set of beliefs or any strong personality at work there."

With his brilliant corporate maneuvers, one would assume that Murdoch's empire is and always

has been on solid financial footing; however, he has had his share of close scrapes with securing his scratch: in the early 1990s, he nearly lost it all when one bank almost refused to roll over one of his $10 million debts. He's vastly overpaid for some of his holdings, such as *TV Guide* and the broadcast rights for the NFL. The extent of red ink he can withstand is also curious: the *New York Post* loses money. Murdoch has poured hundreds of millions into the Fox News Channel. He has mastered the perception of invincibility and profitable risk-taking, and for his believers, to whom he has given a choice, that is good enough.

> Who is Rupert Murdoch? He has changed religions, beliefs, wives and even citizenships in order to get what he wants.

Murdoch the Changing Man

So, who is Rupert Murdoch? He described himself once as being "selfish" when he gave the reason for the end of his first marriage to his wife Anna. By other accounts he is described as calculating, power-hungry, vengeful and opportunistic. It is the last quality that makes him troubling to his enemies and critics, but not in the way many people think. Sure, an opportunist may take advantage of an opponent's weak spot, but it also means he will quickly drop his old methods in favor of something that will work better. And when someone changes his signature, pinning him down or defining him becomes that much harder.

Despite the size of his global media empire and his penchant for retribution, Murdoch isn't a larger than life persona who can be easily described or spoofed. Though he has remained steadfast in his admiration of former President Ronald Reagan, Murdoch has changed religions, beliefs, wives and even citizenships in order to get what he wants in both his personal and professional endeavors. If that's the case, Murdoch becomes a chameleon: he is someone who has changed the most definable and fundamental aspects of his life. Without a definable and standout personality, in many ways Murdoch can safely blend into the background and quietly go about his business without drawing attention to himself, as the more flamboyant and mouthy Conrad Black did in his heyday. Rupert Murdoch is not an easily identifiable target: he talks in annoying, banal phrases that only seem frightening when his words are squared with his company's size and influence. His comments about his European holdings—"We are a relatively small part of an ever-widening rainbow of outlets for the dissemination of diverse views"—seem harmless until one realizes that his global outlets have a reach of almost 80% of the planet. Rupert Murdoch always underplays the extent of his influence.

Murdoch's ability to fade into the background makes him dangerous to his opponents and harder to detect: he's not an easy-to-identify rogue who can become an object of mockery, scorn and derision. He's not a distinctive-looking man; he is a faceless titan who has a cabal of colorful characters who have a bigger profile than their leader. Murdoch's low-key approach is a stroke of pure brilliance: instead of critics all focusing their energies on the source of their grief, they instead criticize Murdoch's various employees; thus diluting their potency. Even if detractors manage to unseat a few of Murdoch's underlings; these magpies *du jour* are easily replaced with a younger crop of underlings who are willing to push the envelope even farther than their predecessors have. As usual, the kingpin is safe from harm; there are countless other pawns and soldiers willing to do Murdoch's bidding for the chance at fame, power and fortune.

Rupert Murdoch is an ironic figure: he has one of the largest media empires in the world and yet still refers to his small, less global rivals as the media elite. Murdoch was quoted as saying (presumably with a straight face) that "the traditional media in this country is in tune with the elite, not the people... That is why we're not liked by the traditional media. That's not us." This knee-slapper of a comment is vintage Murdoch: the wealthiest and most influential media mogul the world has ever known continues to insist that he is a humble underdog and populist.

The Fox News Network is an ideological reflection of its master. The conservative cable newser may bend over backwards to present itself as common people reporting for other common people, but its true mandate is to make a ruling regime's whims and dictates seem palatable to those it was meant to exploit. His empire made Margaret Thatcher's regime seem brilliant to Brits and the Deng Xiaoping regime seem humane to the Chinese, and the Fox News Network makes the Bush regime seem functional and competent to the Americans. He is the official propagandist to the Machiavellians, in charge of spin that is made to look as if it were produced by your friendly neighborhood commoner.

And all the while, Murdoch can sit back, reap the benefits of his empire and smile.

Chapter 5
Ailes

"I feel terrible now that I trashed him. I wish I hadn't. There's no dispute, really. I disagree with what he wrote, and he agrees with what he wrote. We have since moved on."

Roger Ailes
(After claiming the *Washington Post*'s Bob Woodward was not as wealthy as novelist Tom Clancy because "while he and Clancy both make stuff up, Clancy does his research first")

E very king needs a loyal, clever and faithful servant who will cater to the needs, whims and orders of his master without too much fuss or lip. Every leader needs a second-in-command to do the dirty work, while giving his master most of the glory. In other words, every Elahrairah needs a Rabscuttle.

If any one person in the news business can be described as a Rabscuttle, it is Roger Ailes. Clever, agile, swift and a survivalist who can still—despite his advanced age and regal professional background—stomach taking orders and guff from another person. Ailes is a media mogul's dream second-in-command: someone who relishes his power as he relinquishes it. If all media titans could be as lucky as Rupert Murdoch, they would not be seeing their ratings crumble in a pathetic free fall.

Devastating and precise proficiency describes the Ailes method of television news combat, though on the surface his credentials would seem to paint him as some sort of dilettante-savant. Ailes went from being the son of a factory foreman to becoming a twenty-five-year-old executive producer of the "Mike Douglas Show" to working on improving the image of former President Richard Nixon. He was "discovered" when Nixon came on as a guest on the program and Nixon became Ailes' first Svengali. He was a media advisor to both Presidents Ronald Reagan and George Bush, Sr. The man got around.

His media credentials are also equally praiseworthy: he was the executive producer of Rush Limbaugh's television show and from 1993 to 1995, before his move to Fox, he was President of CNBC,

59

resulting in impressive ratings growth and the creation of Chris Matthews' "Hardball" program. In his early career he produced Off-Broadway plays; he studied theater in college. Understanding the science and art of showmanship would be his foundation; all his other talents would be built on that flair for flash and giving people what they want.

He can also command respect from his colleagues, a difficult feat in a profession known for deep

Roger Ailes
Fox News CEO & Chairman

Roger Ailes: Manservant general.

rivalry and cutthroat maneuvers. One television trade magazine glowingly described Ailes as "unconventional" and as known for "kicking tail." It also described Fox as being an extension of Ailes: "combative, blustering, straightforward, conservative and thoroughly middle American." Ailes' best PR flak could not possibly think up any better copy.

Aside from the illustrious television background and the good press he can finagle for himself, Ailes has deep roots in Republican politics. He also has experience in consultancy, entertainment, news and network management. He has unified his vast knowledge, making his sharp, conciliated mind a formidable force to his intellectually and philosophically weaker rivals, and proving that E.O. Wilson, who famously discussed the unification of all knowledge in his bestselling book *Consilience*, was right all along. Though Roger Ailes shines as a leader, he is also proficient in making other people look smart while he stands quietly in their shadows—and he is also used to taking orders and stomach-turning sass from forceful Republican ideologues.

In other words, Roger Ailes was born to run the Fox News Channel.

A leader who can follow has a rare quality, and Ailes seems to have it in spades. He is a star who never gets top billing and a bright light who always lives in someone else's shadow. Though it was Ailes who helped boost CNBC's ratings when he was its President, he didn't get the deserved promotion as President of NBC News or of MSNBC, but found himself to be redundant when NBC planned to merge CNBC with MSNBC; he then quit. There was no "thank you" from the mainstream press for Ailes; only a swift kick in the rear. Though he can masterfully manipulate public opinion, Ailes seems to be exploited by those who have a bigger marquee value. Ailes is at his best when he willingly submits to someone who is from a higher social and economic caste than he.

Not that this unrepentant Republican groupie hasn't gone into business for himself (he was chairman of Ailes Communications), but even then, the business was all about consultancy. He was busy; always choreographing the clueless and power-hungry chieftain wannabes; showing them how to mask their weaknesses from the public in order to get into or maintain their power.

If NBC brass were too dense and shortsighted to see the power of an unleashed Ailes, at least the opportunistic Rupert Murdoch had the shrewdness to procure a valuable pawn when he saw it. It was Ailes who was at the fateful press conference when Murdoch launched the Fox News Channel. The Fox News CEO warned his future rivals that Fox News would herald a new era in journalism.

The move alone should have put CNN on full alert.

If any one news outlet needed Ailes, it was Fox. With the exception of WTTG, the network had little respect from the journalism community. Though Murdoch owned news media properties overseas, those who were imported to the United States to help shape the U.S. news division did not have the required finesse to satisfy the visually picky and jaded American audience. It was not until Roger Ailes whipped the Fox News division into shape that it got any respect from colleagues or viewers—not respect for its editorial content, but for its ability to pass itself off as a news channel without having to produce the goods.

But that describes Ailes' *modus operandi*: cleaning up other people's messes, then keeping the house in top form, all the while making his masters richer than he makes himself. The FNC would not be the powerhouse it is today without him. Ailes rallies the troops while keeping them in check, he attacks the enemies and then he sits down and devises the strategies for the next battle. Ailes is the manservant general: he can win his chosen battles in the name of his master. He is a complex man who defies simple explanations; yet he can easily crunch complex concepts into simple and simplistic units. He has made both Republican Presidents and news accessible to the general public.

When Rogers Ailes gets mad, he can spew vitriol like nobody's business: he has told jokes at the expense of the Clintons and both Paula Zahn and Bob Woodward have felt the stinging lash of his crude, punitive tongue. He looks—and on an intellectual level behaves—very much like a portly and elderly Han Hoogerbrugge[2] clown: impudent, self-indulgent, oblivious to the casualties falling around him and strictly focused on his own goals and ambitions. He isn't a sore loser, but a sore winner: he has no difficulty trash-talking his rivals, such as those at CNN, as well as any left-leaning icon who has the nerve to open his mouth.

Ailes has a notoriously thin skin, as Peter Hart observed: "I think... he's very passionate and probably can get angry. We know over the years there have been incidents behind the scenes at Ailes' various places of employment where people have learned not to cross him." Ailes' "you're either with us or against us" mentality echoes George W. Bush's sentiments to the global community after the 9/11 attacks. In Ailes' world, there are only two choices: agreeing with him or being wrong.

Ailes has uncomfortably straddled the objectivity fence. He mused that the notion of objectivity was "crazy," since journalists "Have friends. They have an education. They've gone to school where some professor spun their brain out. They've got history. They've got parents. They have a view based on experience. And they bring all that to journalism." Ailes was simply politely saying that he sees journalists as hapless drones incapable of breaking away from the influence of others. Worse, if it's a battle of the will between reporters and everyone else, it seems the journalist has a weaker will than his parents, friends and teachers. In this regard, General Jeeves has a grim view of the moral and intellectual fortitude of his underlings.

2 Hoogerbrugge is a flash artist from the Netherlands who uses impudent clowns in his online artwork. Ailes just looks like one.

The Ailesian Philosophy

Despite his tendency to give in to his primal vendettas, Ailes has an acute business-savvy. He has a feel for which foot soldiers can deliver him victories: he recruited Bill O'Reilly to anchor the flagship show for the FNC startup. He knows how to motivate the troops: employees received a quasi-inspirational how-to-cover-the-news book with Ailes' mug right on the cover. And he knows how to chip away at his rivals' self-esteem: with his pointed jabs at CNN, the once cool kid of cable news is suddenly facing an ugly mid-life crisis.

Who is Roger Ailes? He is rumored to have a notoriously thin skin. He isn't a sore loser, but a sore winner.

But an army's limited rations must be used wisely, and Ailes can make less go further. Perhaps FNC's newsrooms didn't look all that spiffy in the beginning, but then the wallpapering of a boiler room isn't as important as the strength and unity that both the enemy and the citizens back home see. Ailes' troops may be paid less than those of his rival armies but, then again, a hungry soldier will be a grateful soldier for any extra scraps and opportunities for advancement his leaders give him. It also makes those scruffier fighters envious of their more pampered opponents and ready to pounce and destroy them. Hunger and the drive to quickly work up the ranks are both powerful motivators, and Ailes uses them well.

Ailes understands carny tactics, emotional triggers to galvanize an audience and playing with the minds of opponents. He was media advisor to two Presidents and helped make their elections a cakewalk. He's transferred those skills to managing cable news, and a triumphant Ailes has broken the spirits of the pampered pussycats over at CNN, instilled panic and then walked all over their well-tended faces. He can cannily pick his pawns to win his battles; he is a strategist who understands his enemies better than they understand themselves. Cable news has followed his lead and shifted their shows to the right instead of attempting to counter-program their lineups with innovative shows with a variety of viewpoints. When the pioneer tries to imitate his younger competitor, the pioneer has lost face and the war. What Ailes can do is win his battles by breaking his rivals.

What he can't seem to do is carry out his business with a moral compass. Former employees fear his retribution if they speak against him. Current employees know better than to question him. One former Fox News employee noted that there was no formal code of ethics at the cable newser. Rivals are not there just to be bested; they have to be crushed, taunted and humiliated in the most vile way imaginable. Fox's taunting billboards have an underlying psychological sickness to them; the malicious and gleeful sky-high messages are meant to haunt their rivals in their sleep. There is something decidedly venomous and grotesque about comparing an employee to an animal carcass (as he did with Paula Zahn), but Ailes does it with relish. His competitors try to take the public high road and not return the taunts, but their lack of passion only makes them seem afraid of the Fox.

At times, Ailes is a modern day Ignatius J. Reilly; a bellowing monarchist leading his crusaders for

OUTFOXED

Moorish Dignity who uses his tools to pass remarks on the cast of liberal characters, from gays to feminists. At times, you half expect him to charge at CNN, blustering to know which degenerate produced this abortion and that those liberal doxies ought to be impaled upon the member of a particularly large stallion. But Ailes is content to let King Rupert make the official decrees, while Ailes himself is in charge of maintaining Fox's theology and geometry—in the end, everything will be all right with the world.

As writer David Brock noted:

> Some of the themes of Fox... of appealing to the base in the Republican party on the issues of religion, race and sex, which are kind of the organizing, in my view, principles of the Republican base. And this is what Fox tends to be preoccupied with, in terms of a lot of its subject matters. This is the same thing that Roger Ailes was doing when he was doing ads for Richard Nixon; it was the same thing he was doing when he was doing ads for the first President Bush. It's a culture war approach and very pugnacious.

David Brock
President/CEO of Media Matters for America

David Brock: Conservatives bought my brain!

With Ailes' illustrious connections to the Republican party, it should not be surprising that the network employs both faded former Republican politicians and disseminates a partisan point of view. Traditional Republican hot issues—such as the problems associated with crime, foreigners and the discontent—get more play than the problems associated with governments, armies and corporations. That each segment of the FNC has the feel of a Republican campaign ad should not be surprising, given Ailes' background and passion.

The Rules of Disengagement

Every leader of consequence is at the top of his game because he knows how to draw up the rules that he knows he can use to his advantage. Leaders don't look for unnecessary challenges; they merely look to win. If the rules are those that rivals can't follow, then so much the better. If rivals are so stupid as to try to follow some enemy's un-winnable rules, better still. While other rival news networks have decided to follow the rules decreed by Roger Ailes, he can smile in satisfaction, knowing that his intellectually and morally weaker competitors have decided to follow his lead. Because they follow his rules and do not create new rules by which they can win, Ailes is assured a lengthy stint at the top of the television news world. They make it too easy for him to win, but that's their problem, not his.

Ailes' rules of engagement may be straightforward and even curiously predictable, but it hasn't stopped his combat system from being effective or reliable at making his competitors tremble in their boots. He understands the shallow nature of his business—where the knee-jerk answer to sagging news ratings is to hire a few more news bunnies whose scripted and vapid happy talk is sandwiched between a bizarre and cornball hybrid of jazzy and electronic music, rather than pouring resources into finding important and offensive hard news that will gain attention, outrage and snap their fellow flabby citizens out of their perpetual slumber. Ailes must know this; otherwise he would spend more time beefing up the content of Fox's factually sparse newscasts rather than thinking of novel and feral ways of putting down the now-impotent CNN. With the potent combination of Rupert Murdoch and Roger Ailes, none of their soft and ill-prepared competitors stood a chance. Both men understand that their audiences are looking for more than news read by well-groomed and cordial anchors: they are searching for a message and reassurance.

Fox News does more than report the news with snazzy graphics, while patting their jittery audiences on their backs: it uses theatrics to scare them and warn them that outsiders are gunning for them. But concentrating on the image and the message takes away from the amount of editorial content a news outlet can show; besides, reality can't always conform to a network's worldview, meaning that some news will be ignored in favor of news that does.

If the presentation and opinion are more important than the mandate to inform viewers, at least the network should be skilled at making their opinion seem as if it were real news. In the areas of show, molding data to fit the message, and passing opinion as information, Ailes has had plenty of practice, as David Brock observed:

> **Ailes went to work for Nixon in his 1968 Presidential campaign,** and there were a series of events called "Man in the Arena," which were efforts to portray Nixon as a warm and accessible person. And these were paid events, these were paid political ads, but they were structured to kind of look more like news events, and that was one of the innovations Ailes had at the time. They were kind of town hall meetings, but it was all staged. The questions were staged in advance; so this is the kind of thing Ailes does well.

Ailes' set of rules for running cable news are different than those of his competitors: pump ideological filler in to the watered-down product; dress it up to look appealing to the eye and the mind, then attack your rivals for allegedly doing the same thing that you are. Ailes may fight dirty, but this is an ideological and economic war he is fighting at the behest of his employer. As long as Ailes is in charge of whipping his FNC troops into shape and priming them into attack mode, his competitors are cooked.

OUTFOXED

Part Three
The World According to Fox

Chapter 6

The Foxification of Reality

"...Most of Iraq is doing extremely well."

Rupert Murdoch

"We report, you decide."

Fox News Motto

N ews is supposed to present an accurate and truthful picture of reality. Watching a newscast is supposed to give the viewer the lowdown on what really transpired, who were the good guys and who were the bad. The trouble is that our wishes and beliefs continually cloud our assessment of what's really out there. The same biases that distort our vision also distort the vision of journalists. No one is truly safe from subjective biases, but an honest reporter takes extra effort to address his or her own personal prejudices before filing a story. Gathering and presenting news can be a difficult process for the diligent journalist.

This task is made harder by a myriad of other factors that are beyond the control of the reporter: time and budget constraints, dishonest or cagey news sources who have mastered the art of spin, viewers who get easily offended by life's brutal nature, advertisers who wish to sweep unflattering news under the rug and the limitations and biases of reporters. No matter how careful a reporter may try to be, the reality he presents to the public gets distorted through the media filter. In the end, what the viewer or reader gets is a picture which is either better or worse than what's really out there. Wars get sanitized, petty criminals become demonized and the economy either seems to be preternaturally bullish or on the edge of Armageddon, depending on which outside influence has the bigger pull with the reporter—the Wall Street analyst or the homeless activist.

However, most of these constraints have to do with problems rooted in almost everyone's daily reality: news outlets do not have a bottomless pit of resources available (i.e., time or money) to present the most accurate view of the world they can. Still, if the reporter is competent and enterprising, he can come close to reporting a reasonable facsimile of the Truth. The journalist's mandate is to find enough news and relevant hard facts to clue in his audience about what's happening around them.

What separates Fox from its predecessors is that Fox doesn't conform to the traditional view of reality: if it did, it would not generate the buzz and ratings it currently holds. Why go to the fairly newish Fox News if you already get the same perspective and presentation from CNN, MSNBC or the other three mainstream networks? Fox doesn't break different stories or provide more details than its competitors. It doesn't offer more facts or different facts. Fox News can't boast about having superior investigative journalists who dig up superior scoops. If that's the case, then what is it that Fox brings to viewers that its rivals do not? What's the pull?

What Fox News does offer its viewers is something entirely different: not a staid world full of hard data, but one full of attitude and opinion. When Democratic Presidential hopeful John Kerry effectively bested President George W. Bush in the first of three 2004 Presidential debates, the FNC general spin did not concede that perhaps a Democrat could best a Republican on any account. On the October 1, 2004 edition of "Hannity and Colmes," Sean Hannity and guest William Bennett made the debate sound as if the results favored Bush more than Kerry:

HANNITY: All right. Just give me your general thoughts first, and then I've got some specific questions to ask you.

BENNETT: I think that Kerry won the debate and Bush won the argument. I know Kerry did a very good performance, the best I've seen him engage in. And he was on offense and you know my rule; you're on offense or you're on defense. He was on offense the whole night, kind of relentlessly on offense.

He was well briefed. He was well prepared and he went on attack. He sounded good; he looked pretty good. And he made it seem as if he was winning the points. The problem is there's a short run and there's a long run. He created some issues for himself which I think are going to be very harmful.

HANNITY: Yes, I do as well.

Hannity also opined that "it was Bush who was more likable, Bush who was more believable." Never mind that it was Bush who was smirking more, and Bush who had a harder time controlling his temper. A fair and balanced newsman would acknowledge that the President did stumble for more than he scored, a troubling scenario given that he had had practice with Presidential debates four years before. Nor was the show's guest particularly helpful or insightful: instead of discussing

the content of each candidate's speech, and squaring it off with what was true, logical or possible, Bennett was the usual GOP cheerleader. Fan boy devotion can be blinding and devoid of actual information.

While other TV news outlets have flirted with making punditry and opinion a prominent part of the news for years, Fox News has made opinion the backbone of its product: news merely supports opinion, not the other way around. The FNC offers its viewers better-tasting cookies than its more tight-assed rivals: from validation to guidance to entertainment, the FNC excels at offering irrelevant fillers as news. It sacrifices hard facts for opinion, though the watering-down effect doesn't bother Fox News viewers one jot.

Who Put the Opinion in My News?

Instant tele-analysis is hardly a Fox News Channel invention: in the 1970 book *The Adversaries*, author William Rivers recounted a 1957 CBS interview with then-Soviet leader Nikita Khrushchev and its surprising aftermath: Jack Gould, the legendary *New York Times* television scribe blasted the network in his column for not critically analyzing the Communist leader's statements and positions. CBS listened to Gould, and the rest is history.

Television journalists enthusiastically embraced the idea of commentary and analysis: instead of just presenting dry information, commentators and anchors could offer their insights into the day's events and newsmakers. Analysis became an increasingly popular staple in television news: adding perspective and some personal commentary gave television news insight. For those non-journalists who were blessed with the ability to succinctly or reliably dispense a *bon mot* on cue, they too could get in on the commentary action. The fact that many of these commentators weren't journalists seemed hardly troubling; these were the experts whose outside expertise could add a breath of fresh air. Military specialists, lawyers, doctors and former politicians could all be counted on to weigh in on current events from their own expertise. Facts still mattered, but they could be enlivened with perspective. Analysis was never meant to be the main course; it was a diversion and an enjoyable break from a long stream of mundane information.

As time progressed, meaningful analysis and logical conclusions were replaced with their more troubling and less practical cousin, opinion: if misused, opinions didn't have to be based on expertise, knowledge or experience. Opinion didn't have to be thoughtful, impartial, practical or relevant. All opinion needed was attitude and lively delivery, but still contain enough factual information to be credible.

Some of these pundits were better at forming a quick opinion than at analysis, but they still could use facts as the basis of their opinion. Some could interpret facts in a pointed and amusing way. For the Andy Rooneys of the news world, analysis meant getting known for attitude rather than reportage. For the John Stossels, it meant a greater freedom to cultivate a marketable persona. In either case, reporters and other pundits still had to base their opinions on some hard data (though many times the data was sparse). For the most part, audiences could still easily disagree with the reporter's or outside commentator's opinion, since viewers were presented with enough news in other segments and programs to make an informed opinion. It was just that the actual news time got watered down.

Fox News took modern day tele-analysis one step further: why not simply replace all those boring facts with the more glamorous opinion? Or, if facts are used, they are secondary to snarky or upbeat assessments; data was used to bolster someone's worldview. Programs were filled with a smattering of information and commentary flecked throughout the day. With the final obstacle out of the way, Fox News managed to do something that no other TV news outfit before it could: offer a new version of reality.

However, opinion can never truly mimic actuality: since nature has no obligation or desire to conform to our wishful thinking, life is a lot crueler and more unfair than most of us would care to admit. Finding happiness is a difficult proposition when you're fighting personal bankruptcy, family discord and colon cancer. Prozac is a popular medication for a reason. Reality is a hard concept to deal with, and so we oversimplify the world around us based on our own limited knowledge and emotional and psychological weaknesses. Since opinion requires no outside information or adherence to how things really are, it won't be able to represent reality; what it can do is sound like a more palatable version of what's really out there.

What Fox specializes in is slacker news. Journalists at Fox don't break their backs covering information in the same way their colleagues at rival outlets do; what Fox offers is strong, galvanizing opinion that doesn't quite jive with what's truly out there. On Fox News, crime is more prevalent than what national numbers suggest, yet wars seem to be much simpler and more sterilized than what history has repeatedly shown us. There is a specific worldview that Fox can disseminate and promote without worrying about alienating their audiences. It's a prefab world their audiences clamor for.

The formula has worked so well that the FNC has, in less than ten years, climbed out of the ratings cellar and into top spot, threatening and occasionally besting even network news ratings. Other TV news outfits have made crude, embarrassing attempts at replicating the FNC style of monster success, but no one seems to be able to outfox Fox. The reason why the FNC can present information in a different and attention-grabbing way is that does something differently than its older competitors.

Fox News does not report on reality like any other news outfit; for Fox, some versions of reality are more salient and appealing than others. Battered women bring yawns, as do polluted waters where the cancer rate for people living nearby is several times higher than the national average; however, naughty nutjob foreigners and salaciously-motivated murderers are exciting and worth attention on Fox. A surprising number of Fox News stories follow the "Us Versus Them" formula: who is trying to corrupt or destroy the good American citizen?

There is also something harsh and bitter with that Manichean view of the world: terrorists, killers, pornographers, perverts and Democrats alike are all running loose on the street, making America a scarier and more dangerous place to live in. Children get exploited every second of every day, antiwar

activists are worse than foreign terrorists and feminists are simply just whack and out of sync with the rest of the country.

The Fox News Channel reports about the world with an odd mix of reassurance and outrage.

The motto may be "we report; you decide," but who decides on what Fox is going to report? When Fox's website was redesigned in 2004 to be more advertiser-friendly, the cable newser made it clear that it wasn't looking out for the best interests of their viewers, but their own. The Fox News Channel is not journalism, a reenactment of journalism or even a reasonable facsimile of journalism. Most journalistic outfits do not resort to an over-saturation of flag-waving graphics and empty mottos to tell a story. Hard sells aren't usually used for high-quality products.

Jon Du Pre
Former Fox News Anchor-West Coast Bureau

Jon Du Pre was told to "foxify" his newscast.

It seems that even those who work at Fox know a thing or two about the hard sell. Fox doesn't just call itself a newsroom, but "America's newsroom"—as opposed to what? Uganda's newsroom? "Real journalism, fair and balanced"—why say it this way? Is it because viewers wouldn't know it was actual journalism just by watching it? Does Fox brass assume that the confusion lies in the defective nature of their product or with the intellectual deficiency of their viewers?

The FNC school of journalism has become so distinct and successful that other networks refer to copycat attempts as "foxifiying" the news. As former Fox News reporter Jon Du Pre noted:

> In short order, the bosses, the news directors, the general manager and the executive producers were instructing us to "foxify" our newscast. We wanted it to be punchier; we wanted it to be faster paced; we wanted it to be more conversational; we wanted it to be pithier; [and] we wanted it to have more of an edge than the standard sort of traditional newscast delivery. So it was a style question more than anything when it came to working in a local affiliate. "We want you to 'foxify' your newscast," simply meant "we want you to take most of the verbs out if you can, and read the news in a faster pace with more energy, with more urgency or at least seem that you have more urgency with as few verbs as you can in a sort of headline fashion."

Blurring the lines between news, propaganda, advertising and opinion is all in a day's work at the FNC. While those at the Fox News Channel conduct themselves in a somber journalistic style, their words all hint that the newser has a vastly different agenda. As Peter Hart observed:

> "Special Report" is anchored by Brit Hume Monday through Friday and we are to believe that Brit Hume is the anchor of a news outlet—he doesn't bring strong politics to it; he just happens to anchor the newscast like Peter Jennings. On Sundays, Brit Hume turns into a rather caustic, right-wing pundit on "Fox News Sunday," sometimes the most conservative on their panel. You can hear him say all kinds of things on Sunday

that make you wonder, "well, Monday through Friday, does he set these things aside and do something else?"

A Foxified newsworld can have anchors that double as pundits. It can have porn stars jiggling while discussing politics. It can even have journalists with multiple master's degrees discussing the contents of an amateur porn film while screeching childish put-downs to guests. FNC brass can deny it all they want: their world just doesn't turn the same way as everyone else's.

What You'll Find in the Fox's Den

Watching Fox News is very much like looking at Salvador Dali's "The Discovery of Christopher Columbus": what you see in the first viewing versus what you see when you take longer, more deliberate glances are two different things. On the surface, the masterwork is pretty to look at, busy and overwhelming for the eye, and seems to represent all that Americans are most proud of—America, religion, patriotism and compliance, but if you look more closely at the painting, all the painting really does is indulge in the deification of the morally questionable muse and the glorification of the egomaniac creator himself. Replace the angel's face with George W. Bush and Dali's visage with that of Rupert Murdoch and you could just as well be watching Fox News.

Just as Dali's painting can be both pretty and grotesque, so is Fox News. The FNC may be pleasing to the eye, but its bitter and simplistic messages ooze with decrepit hatred and frustration. A Fox News reality almost seems like a breath of fresh air: the network's take on events and people is markedly different from the reality presented by its rivals. If that's the case, then how does Fox present reality?

The short answer is that the FNC presents the world with blinders. The network seems to behave like the slacker who skips all the hard work such as research and writing for a school assignment, but will try to gloss over those deficiencies by adding lots of bright colorful pictures and putting his shoddy piece of work in a snazzy looking plastic folder. He may even include flattery, including a few zingers and blatantly writing filler that supports his teacher's beliefs. His report may be easy on the eyes, but the content is appalling. The FNC's American flag graphics seem to be more memorable than the news that precedes it.

When there is content in its news stories, it focuses on a few types of issues; stories and slant must conform to the network's point of view. As David Brock noted, "a lot of Fox's content is organized around religion, racial matters and sexual matters, particularly the highest-rated show, 'The O'Reilly Factor.'" Affirmative action, homosexuality and child molestation may be common content, but the slant those stories take will also be a specific one, according to Brock: "they set up, say, the [North American] Man-Boy Love Association to stand-in for liberalism."

As Miller noted:

> Murdoch is always going for the lowest common denominator. This is true whether what we're talking about is entertainment properties or his news division. What we're talking about is a kind of visceral, nasty, largely hateful propaganda machine that deals

in a sort of pornography. The shouting heads on Fox TV... give viewers what they call "red meat." This is a kind of porn. It is to civil discourse what pornography is to art... It represents a move toward the lowest common denominator and tacit suggestion—sometimes not so tacit—that this stooping, deliberate low-browism is Democratic; the assumption being that the American people *en masse* are lowbrows and apes who want to be enraged and infuriated and mobilized all the time.

The FNC's method of maintaining ideological continuity is issuing frequent memos that set the tone of the show for that day. John Moody, Senior Vice President, News Editorial, has been responsible for firing off these FNC missives that shape the message the network disseminates. As Av Westin noted, "The message of the day is a very political device. We know that the Reagan administration, the Clinton administration and now the Bush [administration] have raised to a very high level of sophistication, the manipulation of news and information to essentially promote their particular agenda." That is reasonable politics; what's now happened is that that political game has shifted into the news side." So, according to Fox News, what issues are important and who can be trusted?

> Fast-moving graphics called "teases" subtly tell viewers that no mental exertion is required.

Eye Candy

Though content and slant help shape the Fox News world, so does style. After all, the Fox News logo, with the two searchlights, emphasizes the network's entertainment roots, not its journalistic mandate. The studios look sleek, and clothes also play a role in cultivating a hipper-than-thou image. Some of the female talent wear skirts that are shorter than their sound bites and (as was the case with Brooke Alexander), the cameras seem more focused on the bust line than the headlines. As Fox News spokesman Rob Zimmerman told one reporter, on-air Fox talent had to be told by consultants how to dress to "keep things hip," and that they had to "try not to have that boring, conservative look shared by other network news anchors." In other words, what separates Fox News from other news outlets is that Fox brass have undeniably confused voguing with reporting.

Yet a news outfit cannot rely on blonde highlights alone to grab eyeballs; graphics are fast-moving and striking, not only appealing to the ADHD generation but also evoking strong patriotic themes. American flags are repeatedly flung in viewers' faces. Even certain logos have a certain Presidential seal quality to them. As Peter Hart observed, "the idea, I think, is to make sure people never pull their eyes away. Graphics are always moving in the background. They've sort of pioneered the use of the American flag as an icon of your news broadcast." So much so, in fact, that one would expect the FNC's official website to be www.foxnews.gov.

Yet that waving flag doesn't look like it's being embraced by steady, cool winds: the speed of the images make their flags look as if they're being beaten and shaken by angry overactive hands. The light speed of the moving images is too reminiscent of the disjointed images of the movie *Head* to

The Fox Formula

1	Elbow Grease Logic: People get what they deserve
2	Body Counts and Conspiracy Theories: More blood = higher ratings
3	War Games: Our side is always winning
4	Getting Caught With Your Pants Down: Famous people having sex sells
5	Sex/Crimes: Offensive sex sells
6	Steroid Economy: Our side is always winning

claim any real reverence for mom and apple pie. There is no respect for the red, white and blue: even the very symbol of the U.S. is being forced to shake it a little faster for the nice folks at home.

Besides gyrating flags, the FNC relies on other visuals to draw in their audience. As an FNC memo from senior producer Jerry Burke simply requested: "need good, visual tease." In another April 28, 2003 memo, Burke lectured to underlings:

> Teases are the most important part of your show, especially now that the war is over... Please give them full attention. Keep tease copy short&sweet, use a catchy title, use sexy b-roll... AND GET THE TEASE WRITTEN IN TIME, SO IT CAN BE COPY-EDITED. Do not ever go to break without a good tease.

In other words, facts and analysis take a back seat to a good tease. As one former Fox employee recalled:

> It goes beyond the flying stars and stripes corner of every newscast and the banners that seem to take up like 50% of the space on a TV screen. It's the increasing focus on quick and easy news...

Jeff Cohen believed FNC graphics had more troubling consequences:

> I think the techniques of odd polling and odd graphics of Democrats [sic] and weird banners in the lower third of your screen, these are all pretty sophisticated techniques and they work in collaboration with the most ingenious marketing slogan in history, which is "fair and balanced"—because remember, "fair and balanced" is operating on several levels and it really works [...] For people who are not that sophisticated—they're not well-informed, they don't have a well-formed ideology, and they're coming to this channel every ten minutes that's telling them "fair and balanced"—it's a stroke of genius. It has nothing to do with truth in packaging...

Yet there *is* a certain truth in the packaging. The FNC's viewer-friendly graphics subtly tell viewers what kind of news they can expect to see on the vixen network: punchy stories with flash that can be told quickly. Though mental exertion is not a requirement when watching a Fox News story, it helps to pay attention to what stories are chosen and how they are told. The Fox News world is a very different place than reality: complications are removed, dangers seem closer and more imminent, blame is easily assigned, villains and heroes are separate and distinct and wars can be fought without shedding blood or losing limbs. It may be a world that is both a better and worse place than the one you live in, but its novelty hooks in viewers who can't resist but to take a look at this brave new world.

The Propagandization of Fox Reality

It isn't just the graphics that are rushed: Fox News relies on knee-jerk reactions to their stories. The FNC seems to want viewers to jolt out of their chairs on a regular basis; after all, even the most trivial news gets the "Fox News Alert" treatment. The news doesn't even need to be current, as Hart noted: "Fox News Alert is something that's thrown on your screen whether… it's big news or not. President Bush gives a speech. Two hours later, it's still a Fox News Alert that President Bush gave a speech." Alerts have been used when a potential Vice Presidential running mate declined John Kerry's offer, or when George W. Bush speaks at a fundraiser or wins an award. When Martha Stewart meets with her parole officer, it is given the same treatment as when a dangerous hurricane is touching down on a populous area. Fluffy stories are given equal treatment to important ones.

Despite the punchy and cheeky delivery of information mixed in with lowered standards of "breaking news," the FNC presents a Manichean view of the world and a bunker mentality. Emotional manipulation creeps into the news product, but for that to work, stories that evoke strong feelings are more likely to be broadcast. As James Wolcott observed:

> I think [fear-mongering] is very deliberate because one of the things we know from people who have left Fox News is that they get a memo every day and they're told what to hit, what notes to hit, what stories to hit very hard. It becomes a way of silencing critics.

Because Fox News relies heavily on the "Us Versus Them" paradigm, story structure and texture are extremely limited. This makes their stories easy to understand and follow without any background knowledge or need for concentration. Interestingly enough, the Fox formula is similar to the propaganda formula, making their messages all the more worrisome. In one May 2004 memo, Moody's directive showed he didn't want the line between the good guys and the bad to get blurred:

> Thursday update: the pictures from Abu Greb [sic] prison are disturbing. They have rightly provoked outrage. Today we have a picture—aired on Al Arabiya—of an American hostage being held with a scarf over his eyes, clearly against his will. Who's outraged on his behalf?
>
> It is important that we keep the Abu Graeb [sic] situation in perspective. The story is beginning to live on its own momentum. The facts of the story may develop into the

need to do much more in the days ahead. For the moment, however, the focus appears to be changing to finger pointing within the administration and how it plays out as an issue in the Presidential campaign.

If one of FNC's designated good guys has the slightest chance of incurring bad publicity, the Fox News kids are careful to preserve his image. One March 23, 2004 Moody memo cautioned minions to cover one potentially negative Bush story with care for the sake of the nation:

> The so-called 9/11 commission has already been meeting. In fact, this is its eighth session. The fact that former [President] Clinton and both former and current Bush administration officials are testifying gives it a certain tension, but this is not "What did he know and when did he know it" stuff. Do not turn this into Watergate. Remember the fleeting sense of national unity that emerged from this tragedy. Let's not desecrate that.

The moral of the memos was simple: raw and damaging truth should be sacrificed for the sake of good press and stifling debate. Some details can be played up; others must be hidden or at least downplayed. The problem is that the trivial gets full FNC attention while other more crucial information is swept under the rug. Viewers merely get a Foxified version of the truth—and that truth has to fit the Fox News mold perfectly. Contradictory facts are to be dismissed and shunned, not pondered or debated. FNC's formula relies on the beliefs that we get what we deserve or that wars we wage are, by definition, just. Some of the basic tenets of Fox News' version of reality include the following:

1. Elbow Grease Logic

A Foxified world is a just world: all baddies get their comeuppance, while all the saints get their rewards; thus sympathy is virtually unnecessary since people get what they deserved anyway. In a Foxified world, the downtrodden don't need our empathy; they need a swift kick in the rear. For example, Sean Hannity gave his viewers the standard nagging dad lecture on his April 26, 2002 program:

HANNITY: I got to tell you something, because look, I had to drop out of college twice because I couldn't afford the bill anymore. My first car that I bought was $200, because that's all that I could afford. My second car was $350. So I struggled to pay my rent like a lot of people, and I had to work two jobs to make this happen.

But with unemployment as low as it has been, I don't think you can blame the economy. Do we develop marketable skills? Do we go to school and get an education? Would we rather not get up early in the morning but would rather stay home? Do we choose to do drugs and alcohol?

While Hannity did not go on about how he had to walk twenty miles to school in a blizzard every day, he did reveal a lot about the FNC's underlying view that people who are down are there simply because they refuse to work hard enough to dig themselves out of a hole.

2. Body Counts and Conspiracy Theories

Action movies pack in theaters with the promise of convoluted plots and plenty of movie extras being used as cannon fodder. The higher the body count, the more exciting the film. The FNC seems to like certain types of violence and plays up to certain kinds of carnage. This mindset was best described in one of John Moody's memos from April 22, 2004:

> [L]et's rock n roll with the korean [sic] train explosion. korean websites are speculating freely that it was a mistimed hit on kim [sic]. that gives us the right to quote them, and let guests etc. speculate. it is eerie that it happened just hours after the dear leader finished his business in china and pointedly took the train home.

Carnage linked with a conspiracy is a double ratings whammy, but by the next day, Moody downgraded his assessment of the senseless bloodshed:

> As we worried yesterday, the death toll in the N Korean train wreck looks like it's being drastically revised downward. [T]hat doesn't mean we won't follow the story, to the exten [sic] we can get information from the Hermit Kingdom. The chance that it was an assassination against Kim is slim (i took a poetry class to do this stuff). But it's not impossible.

So long as it's not the blood of fallen U.S. soldiers, the FNC will provide viewers with a steady optical diet of the messy aftermath of tragedy.

3. War Games

The 2003 Iraq War provided the FNC with plenty of fodder to spin according to its core beliefs. As John Nichols noted, "There's simply no question that Fox has made a decision to present the Iraq war as a success and as an ongoing success, and Fox in this sense has actually moved into a fascinating role within media. They are not simply competing, trying to do the best job; they're actually trying to shape the news done by other networks. They're creating a pressure that says we alone are reporting the truth of Iraq; the networks, liberal media, are aggressively trying to undermine our troops, undermine the war by presenting only negative images." Nichols added "the goal there is to fool the American people into believing something which no one in the rest of the world believes; i.e., that the war is going well."

When the official end of the Iraq war turned out to be anything but, the FNC kept presenting a positive view of events; as Peter Hart noted when U.S. casualties seemed to decrease, Fox News reporters would "talk about whether we've turned the corner;" when fighting escalates the coverage is muted. "You're not going to see a long conversation on Fox about the following month when violence spiked up again and if you do, there's always some strange explanation for it." As James Wolcott stated:

> Shortly after 9/11 you began to see all of these think tankers, all of these right-wing neo-cons going on MSNBC, CNN, but mostly Fox, and they were talking about Iraq almost

immediately. Now at that point we hadn't nabbed Bin Laden, and we still haven't, but they were already looking ahead, and at that point I was very perplexed. I [thought], "Why are we talking about Iraq?" I mean, no one's shown a connection... We were all in shock and in grief; they saw an opportunity and they seized it.

War coverage is carefully choreographed; images, graphics and words are blended to create a Nerfworld battlefield where every moment of every American soldier is a symbol of his country's justness. Paul Morantz, an attorney who specializes in cases of cults and brainwashing was troubled with the network's integrated methods: "With Fox during the war, there was sort of a drumbeat I thought within the network, the American flag being portrayed, I thought that the use of journalism was wrong."

Spinning facts to suit a mindset seemed to be one of John Moody's functions at the FNC. In a memo dated March 25, 2004, Moody opined, "As is often the case, the real news in Iraq is being obscured by temporary tragedy." In other words, the rising body count of both Iraqis and Americans was obscuring all the great and wonderful things that were happening in the country.

John Moody's April 2004 memo had this observation:

> Fighting overnight in Najaf didn't go the way the militants there had hoped. Reports say forty-three of them were killed, with no U.S. causalities being reported. This is one of the few times we've gotten a count of enemy dead. Let's use that to make the point [of] what happens when terrorists take on the coalition.

Because the result of the battle was in tune with Fox News' version of reality, it would get prominent play. Moody had this to say in his April 4, 2004 memo regarding his opinion on the fighting in the region:

> MONDAY UPDATE: Into Fallujah: It's called Operation Vigilant Resolve and it began Monday morning (NY time) with the U.S. and Iraqi military surrounding Fallujah. We will cover this hour by hour today, explaining repeatedly why it's happening. It won't be long before some people start to decry the use of "excessive force." We won't be among that group.

Moody also seemed to think American lives were disposable and didn't seem at all troubled by the body count:

> Err on the side of doing too much in Iraq rather than not enough. Do not fall into the easy trap of mourning the loss of U.S. lives and asking why are we there? The U.S. is in Iraq to help a country brutalized for thirty years protect the gains made by Operation Iraqi Freedom and set it on the path to democracy. Some people in Iraq don't want that to happen. That is why American GIs are dying. And what we should remind our viewers.

Another memo also reiterated Moody's cold logic about the price of fighting:

If, as promised, the coalition decides to take Fallujah back by force, it will not be for lack of opportunities for the terrorists holed up there to negotiate. Let's not get lost in breast-beating about the sadness of the loss of life. They had a chance.

Yet whether the bloody toll was justified just wasn't questioned. Critical analysis was shunned: Moody simply assumed there was ample reason to go to war with Iraq. There were claims that former Iraqi leader Saddam Hussein had weapons of mass destruction and that he planned to unleash them on the United States. The evidence was never scrutinized, nor was contradictory information taken into account. The FNC would present viewers with a simple and clean war that was entirely justified. Evidence that whispered otherwise would be drowned out by the premature victory screams bellowed from the bowels of Fox News.

4. Getting Caught With Your Pants Down

Former President Bill Clinton's impeachment hearings over his handling of his fling with White House intern Monica Lewinsky provided the FNC with a motherlode of stories: the network relentlessly condemned the President for his sexcapades, while talking endlessly about the details of the deeds that got him into big trouble in the first place.

But you don't have to work in the Oval Office to have the FNC talk about your sexual shenanigans: even ordinary people who screw up, so to speak, are Fox News fodder. Bill O'Reilly had a serious discussion about what happens to naïve girls who enter wet t-shirt contests on the April 22, 2004 edition of the "O'Reilly Factor":

> **O'REILLY:** Look, I don't think these four girls are going to get any sympathy at all from my audience. They are not. You know, they did it, whether they were drunk or not, that's their own fault, seventeen years old is old enough to know. But the system, you know, you might have to run up a big lawyer tab to defend yourself here, Paul. Are you ready to do that?
>
> **PAUL PREWITT:** Well that is part of the reason why I am coming on your show [to] bring this story out to the press. I want people to learn from it. Photographers need to know, the youth need to know and the parents need to know.
>
> **O'REILLY:** Yes. Everybody needs to know, stay away from this stuff, I mean, this stuff, no good is going to come out of any of this. All right, Paul. We are going to follow the case. We appreciate you taking the time.

On the same program, O'Reilly then talked about the perils of anchorwomen who doff off their clothes in front of a camera:

> **O'REILLY:** And now we have an update for you on that Ohio anchorwoman, TV anchorwoman who went down to Key West, Florida, and took her clothes off in a bar. She is thirty years old. Federal court has ruled that an Internet site may publish the photos of Catherine Bosley, who lost her job over the incident. Joining us now from Cleveland is Ms. Bosley's attorney, Mark Colucci.
>
> **MARK COLUCCI:** Hi, Mr. O'Reilly.

O'REILLY: So I feel bad for your client. I don't know how dumb—this is one of the dumbest things I've ever seen, a Youngstown, Ohio anchorwoman getting naked in Key West. I don't know how that happens at thirty years old, but I feel bad for her because her career, damaged. I don't know whether she can come back. And now the judge says these pictures can go anywhere.

Just in case Bosley wasn't feeling like a heel, O'Reilly would correct her emotional insight:

O'REILLY: All right. But neither did these guys on this website, I am not going to mention the name, I don't want to give them publicity. They didn't have Ms. Bosley's written consent, yet the U.S. Court of Appeals in the Sixth Circuit said they can show it.

COLUCCI: Well, it's not quite over. I mean...

O'REILLY: No, no, no, no, no. But it is over in the sense that you lost this. Those pictures are up there right now. Your client is being embarrassed all over the United States. I don't like this. I think this is bad. But again, it's a cautionary tale to women and men. If you're going to do crazy things in public, you're going to pay a price.

Wherever a woman takes her clothes off when she shouldn't, be assured that the FNC will be there to record her infamy—for purely journalistic reasons, of course.

5. Sex/Crimes

Is the Fox News Channel a real news channel or a tele-tabloid? Tabloids thrive on crimes and sex, preferably crimes with sexual underpinnings. Crime stories drive the FNC, but their attitude toward the seedier side of the human condition tends to be cold: as one April 1, 2004 Moody memo macabrely quipped: "Marjorie Alexander, the girlfriend of Peter Gotti of mob fame, was found dead with a plastic bag fastened around her head. Our own button man, Eric Shawn, tells the tale of the duct tape." Another Moody memo simply noted, "We have good perp walk video of Eric Rudolph which we should use."

His March 31, 2004 memo seemed miffed at a foreign body's opinion:

The... [International] Court of Justice ruling against the U.S. is something that many Americans [sic] might find offensive. We'll take a look at just what this court is, and what gives it the right to tell U.S. courts what to do with death row prisoners.

Besides crime, porn is another Fox News staple—though stories warn about the evils of pornography, the FNC won't hesitate to show lurid images of nymphets and show them often. Here, a Foxified reality dictates that journalists must pretend to be appalled at the pornographers while simultaneously titillating audiences with flashing images of semi-naked women warming up for paid mattress-smashing. One March 25, 1999 "Fox Files" program (since canceled) began with the announcer making the decree: "Hard-core, X-rated, living out sexual fantasies in front of the camera, but there's a dark side." The journalist then began to tease her viewers with a visually stimulating story:

ARTHEL NEVILLE: Porn—many women believe it's their road to money, glory and fame, but for most it's a highway to oblivion.

The segment showed just how far FNC reporters go to get the scoop:

NEVILLE: "Fox Files" went behind the scenes of the making of a porn movie to find out if today's porn stars feel like victims or superstars.

CHRISTI LAKE: The best part for me is the sex, and I enjoy it a lot.

JOHNNIE BLACK: We're providing something for, you know, thousands of people out there to enjoy. I mean, you know, we're promoting freedom of expression.

NEVILLE: But what we saw on the set isn't what you call good old family values.

CHLOE: This industry has been so good to me.

Of course the segment couldn't end without this pseudo-saccharine self-congratulatory statement:

SCOTT: What a heartbreaking story, Arthel. Thanks. Hope you've helped some people.

NEVILLE: I hope so, too.

More marketable sex trade workers have also found themselves receiving free publicity on Fox. While there were other, more important news events of the day, Bill O'Reilly still managed to squeeze in an interview with empowered porn plaything Jenna Jameson, who was grilled by the host on his February 25, 2003 show:

O'REILLY: So there's never been a time, Ms. Jameson, in your whole life, where that's given you pause, that what you do may be harmful to a child? Never one moment?

JAMESON: The only thing that's ever given me a pause about my career is when it comes to me having my own children.

O'REILLY: In what way?

JAMESON: Well, I'm very family-oriented, and I know that it's going to have a major impact on my children, no doubt about it. I've already laid down the law that I am going to quit before I have children. I will certainly never, ever do another adult movie or a magazine...

O'REILLY: Why is that? Why will you quit?

JAMESON: Well, I think it's important to turn a new leaf once it comes to family. It's important for my children to know that that's something that I did in my past.

Despite her vows of putting her future children's welfare ahead of her career, Jameson would still be nubile cannon fodder for the perpetually peeved O'Reilly:

O'REILLY: But if there's nothing wrong with it?

JAMESON: There's nothing wrong with it when it comes to being a single woman.

O'REILLY: Have you ever gotten into psychological trouble doing what you do? Do you go to a therapist, or when you were younger, did you have any problems in that regard?

JAMESON: Absolutely, yes. I've been to a therapist and, you know, I mean, there is absolutely no doubt that this industry is hard. You are having sex with strangers and people—the way people identify with you or look at you on the street, a lot of the time I feel myself having to constantly prove myself, that I am an intelligent woman, that I am an honest, good person. You know, they automatically think, you're a porn star, you're nothing, you know?

If Jameson thought she could use her feminine wiles and play up on the pity card to disarm O'Reilly, her plan may have seemed to have worked at first:

Fox uses the concept of good morals as an excuse to trash those who do not conform to specific norms.

O'REILLY: They think that you're a slut.

JAMESON: Exactly.

O'REILLY: But doesn't it hurt your feelings when people judge you and call you "whore," "slut," things like that?

JAMESON: No, I've never had anybody call me a whore or a slut to my face.

O'REILLY: To your face.

JAMESON: To my face.

But Jameson's gambit was an old one, and she proved that she was no match for the savvy and streetwise O'Reilly, who was ready for her with his blunt and less-than-compassionate reply:

O'REILLY: You know they say it behind your back.

Game, set and match.

Though Jameson complained bitterly and publicly about O'Reilly's hard line of questioning and that he didn't grasp the difference between a prostitute and a porn actor, she herself failed to grasp that there was only one role for her to play on Fox: a sexually deviant villain who must be the target of scorn and derision. A Foxified news program will exploit those who thrive on the fringes in order to prove that the mainstream value system is the only one to live by. Foxification means that the only course of action O'Reilly could possibly take was to wipe the floor with this woman as if she were a dirty rag. Jameson was the cannon fodder, and she willingly jumped right into the cannon.

O'Reilly's choice of words was cunning and subtle, yet a brilliant stroke: he told her that others snicker "behind her back"—a subtle way of invoking insecurity in his guest. Viewers and O'Reilly could themselves snicker at Jameson as they cruelly gossiped about her when she wasn't in earshot. No, Jameson wasn't an object of desire, but an object of ridicule: could she trust anyone? After all, O'Reilly made the cutting remark as if he had good authority. He effectively isolated Jameson from the rest of society with a single comment, though whether she or the viewer could consciously grasp the significance is questionable.

Morals are the excuse used to either rake or pity those who do not conform to those specific Foxified norms. It didn't matter if Jameson was a porn star, hooker or antiwar activist, she was considered to

be un-American scum in the Fox universe, as O'Reilly wryly hinted when he responded to her public gripe on his February 26, 2003 show:

> **O'REILLY:** Time now for the "Most Ridiculous Item of the Day." Our pal, porn star Jenna Jameson, is mad at me for criticizing the Pony sneaker company for hiring her as a pitch woman.

O'Reilly gleefully informed his guests that he heard from the Pony pitchwoman's mouth:

> **O'REILLY:** Jenna e-mailed us today and said, in part, "I hope Bill understands the difference between a porn star and a hooker. I assume he has done some research on the subject because he requested some of my videos after we finished taping my appearance. I imagine he wanted them for professional reasons." Of course I did, Jenna. Having any other motivation would be ridiculous. Enjoy your sneakers.

Jameson may have simply prolonged her time in the dentist's chair with her naïve missive; of course O'Reilly would ask for copies of her work, not out of hypocrisy as her e-mail suggests, but as one more smug jab at a guest who gave O'Reilly a free and easy ride in the No Spin Zone. Jameson simply added a new chapter to the ongoing "Factor" soap opera.

But pornography-related stories pop up on the "Factor"; O'Reilly introduced the exclusive world premiere of a gonzo porn film on December 5, 2002:

> **O'REILLY:** Now for the top story tonight, we've been telling you about the administration at Indiana University apparently covering up a sex scandal there. A California porn outfit arrived on campus, shot a movie in a dormitory at IU featuring Indiana students. Now, we can't show you the hardcore stuff, obviously. All right? This is just a little bit of the tease stuff they have in the movie. Can't show you the hardcore stuff.
>
> And here's—this is a first look at the film. Nobody else has it.

Some news outlets waste their time trying to find incriminating documents of corporate or governmental wrongdoing; Fox News spends time digging for Z-list porn—but they still deliver the goods. But just in case "Factor" viewers weren't sure what sorts of scenes were found in a typical porn movie or why these films were made in the first place; O'Reilly brought them up to speed:

> **O'REILLY:** These are students. These are students that are going to be in this porn movie, doing sex acts. Which, of course, will be sold for profit by the California outfit.

He went on to wag his finger at University honchos:

> **O'REILLY:** Now, the administration at Indiana continues to say it knew nothing about the situation, which is almost impossible to believe, because the porn outfit went on the campus radio station to recruit the students. In addition, some faculty members have been told if they comment to the "Factor," their raises could be in jeopardy.

The "Factor" wasn't the only FNC program to engage in crotch-gazing. The June 3, 1999 edition of the "Fox Files" let viewers know they could spice up their get-togethers in a unique way:

> **JOHN SCOTT:** Here's another new trend from Los Angeles, roving sex parties.

> **CATHERINE CRIER:** But don't let the word party fool you. As Arthel Neville reports, this is really risky business.

> **NEVILLE:** Tom Cruise rocketed to superstardom in the early 80s playing a high school student who charged his friends to have sex with prostitutes in his parents' home. But it's not just a movie anymore. Now these women are making big bucks conducting risky business selling sex in Hollywood homes.

Neville went the extra mile to enlighten her Fox News viewers:

> **NEVILLE:** Men pay at the door for sex and the more sex they want, the more they pay. If partygoers just want to watch, they'll see sexcapades up close and personal. "Fox Files" hidden cameras take you behind closed doors into Hollywood's booming illegal sex industry. For men who want more interactive entertainment, this house party offers lap dances that are anything but private.

Even crusty old Tony Snow got into the act on the January 12, 2003 edition of "Fox News Sunday":

> **SNOW:** Former stripper Barbara Scott wishes to lead Nevada's Democratic Party. Her press release states in part, "I believe my unique political background, experiences and abilities provide me with the qualifications to best solidify and unite the Democratic Party in Nevada," blah, blah, blah, thus proving conclusively that political rhetoric can make even strippers boring.

According to the FNC, Tony, strippers are never boring.

6. Steroid Economy

But porn actresses' bosoms aren't the only things pumped up on the FNC screens: the U.S. economy is also perpetually pumped. Stocks always go up, profits always rise and the standard of living always improves, so long as the Republicans are controlling it. Neil Cavuto kicked off his program on January 5, 2004 with this declaration:

> **CAVUTO:** If the Democratic candidates are trying to score points talking about a stumbling economy, they're wasting their time. So says my next guest, who just so happens to have accurately predicted the good economic numbers we are seeing right now. I'm talking about the commerce secretary of the United States and one of the President's most-trusted advisers, Don Evans.

Here, Fox News is more like a socialist government than a private broadcaster operating in a free and Democratic country: just as state-run news channels only report information that presents the national economy as bright and rosy, here too FNC makes the U.S. economy sound as if it were innately healthy. No matter how sluggish the economy may be at any given time, the FNC makes it sound as if everything is white hot and popping. Even one on-air graphic showed Uncle Sam as a steroid-pumped bodybuilder. On July 31, 2004, "Bulls and Bears" host Brenda Buttner asked her guests about the health of the American stock market:

BUTTNER: As for stocks, it was an up week with the Dow breaking its five-week losing streak, posting a triple digit gain. So is the worst finally over for the stock market?

SCOTT BLEIR: YES! The worst is over and we have started our summertime rally. Expect at least a 100-point NASDAQ rally and a 400-point rally on the Dow in the next four to six weeks.

Everything about the economy is just great. And even if there is a little glitch here and there, every dark cloud has a silver lining, even according to the gloomiest of Fox analysts:

TOBIN SMITH: The worst is NOT over! Stocks need to be cheaper so investors will "own" them and not "rent" them. In the short-term it is better if the market goes down, increasing investors' fear, and making stocks cheap. Once this happens, stocks will head higher.

ROB STEIN: The worst is over, but the best might be over too. I don't expect the market to move too much one way or the other for the rest of the year. However, I'm still bullish on the market for the next twelve to eighteen months.

Even those who tend to straddle on the fence think everything is fine:

GARY B. SMITH: It's a tough call, but we do seem to be bottoming. The NASDAQ is right at support and is oversold, so I think it's time for the "big bounce."

PAT DORSEY: Stocks are cheaper, but are not cheap. We have not seen fear yet. Fear was the big bottoms the market suffered last year and a few years ago. Valuations are improving, as is the economy, but there will be no sustained move higher until after the election, when a lot of big issues are cleared up for Wall Street.

The hot, hot, hot American economy is just bustling, according to Fox, even if the signs of robust growth just aren't there. And if things look just a teensy bit sluggish to the skeptical or the personally affected, it's just because no one else has reported on all the positive signs. Gee whiz, everything is just dandy foo, peachy keen, hunky dory and all that jazz, as Hannity and Cavuto enthusiastically concurred on October 15, 2003:

HANNITY: You know, I think the economy clearly has shifted dramatically. We have projections of nothing but significant economic growth all throughout next year. But I don't think you see a lot of—it's only now we're beginning to get the news.

CAVUTO: Yes. It is good. There's no denying how strong it is.

In a Foxified world, George W. Bush must be continuously credited with pumping up the economy, as guest host Stuart Varney seemed to suggest on August 4, 2004:

VARNEY: The Bush-Cheney campaign says corporate support for the President's reelection has never been stronger. And doesn't my next guest know it. Joining us now is Treasury Secretary John Snow. Mr. Secretary, welcome to the program.

JOHN SNOW: Thank you. And great to be with you.

Varney's guest seemed to wholeheartedly agree with the host's assessment:

> **VARNEY:** I don't suppose you can quantify this for us, can you? I mean, we've got 200 people, execs supporting Mr. Kerry. Is everybody else in the executive suite for Mr. Bush?

> **SNOW:** Well, what I know is, when I travel the country and talk to business leaders, small business, medium-sized, large business, they applaud the President for his leadership on the economy, for the tax cuts, for getting the economy going again, for the jobs and growth bill, for his leadership in torte reform, for his leadership in education, for his leadership in bringing the deficit down. So I think you will see the business community and business leaders support the leadership that the President has brought to the economy.

Neil Cavuto's July 17, 2004 guest seemed to believe that Democrats were all just jealous:

> **CAVUTO:** It could be the only question that really matters this election year. Are you better off now financially than you were four years ago? Tom, that's the $64-thousand dollar question: are we better off than four years ago?

> **TOM ADKINS:** Democrats can lie, but the figures don't. We are absolutely better off. The only thing that hasn't recovered is jobs. The reason we had a recession is because of Alan Greenspan raising rates for no good reason.

If you're not the owner of several villas and expensive vehicles, you're just not doing it right, according to Foxified logic.

Slacker Analysis

Asking hard questions ("Why were you negligent in your job?") is uncomfortable to many, but asking insulting questions ("Are your breasts real?") is much more fun. Insulting questions also tend to be the easy ones: it takes probing and research to find evidence of wrongdoing, while it only takes a mean-streak to come up with demeaning queries. Easy questions lead to easy analysis: you don't need to study the way you do with thoughtful analysis, just say the first thing that pops into your head to shock your guest, then watch him squirm in his seat the same way he would have if you asked a hard question. Since the reactions are identical, why bother with all the extra work?

Analysis that comes from Fox News may be devoid of any real-life value, but it sure sounds tough and on the money. For those who have both anger-management issues coupled with attention deficit problems, Fox News makes perfect sense in their fragmented, upsetting world. Analysis from pissed off commentators has the same amount of forethought as analysis coming from someone who was just cut off in traffic. Easy analysis is readily available from FNC's stable of pundits, such as regular Laura Ingraham who showed America just how brilliant she really was on the December 5, 2003 edition of "Hannity and Colmes" (note the equally clever retort from Ellis Henican):

> **INGRAHAM:** No, Sean and Alan. The difference here is that Howard Dean is playing to a crazy, lunatic, embittered fringe in his own party.

HENICAN: Like George Bush does it with the religious right?

Both pundits made their statements without a single shred of evidence, logic or genuine analysis. But then again, it's awfully hard to think about how to properly interpret facts when you are preoccupied with coming up with cool insults and zingers. Who cares about thoughtfulness, when pundits can insult a person's honor without having to actually prove anything? As Alexander Kippen noted, "It's easy, it's attitude, it's simple and it goes down quickly." He added:

> In contrast, clearly there's very little appetite for complicated, in-depth examination of infuriating and/or bedeviling issues that may never be solved. Television's not interested in that because viewers are not interested in that.

Even if viewers could get a nexus of cutting factual analysis, a Foxified world prohibits it: facts can get in the way of a good story.

The Fox Syndrome

Other rivals have tried to mimic the formula of Fox News' growing success in the hopes of boosting their ratings the same way. As Walter Cronkite remarked, "I think that the rapid success of the Fox News operation, which is, by my note anyway, particularly conservative, it has affected the other news organizations in the sense that, as a competitive member of the broadcast community, if it is successful with this approach to the news, it puts on warning those who are in the old standard more impartial, even accused of being, at times, liberal." Jeff Cohen agreed:

> You see the "Fox effect" throughout television news. I was at MSNBC for a year in 2002 and 2003 and like all channels, what you found at MSNBC was this eagerness for celebrity stories, crime stories, fear stories, matched by an equal and opposite timidity about offending anyone in power, especially conservatives... At MSNBC, I worked as a senior producer on the Phil Donahue prime-time show. What's interesting or what's telling about the corporate media is no one will counter program against Fox News. Because of the corporate ownership of television news, there's no one who will say, "Hey, I'm going to take my multimillion dollar investment and I'm going to help the left-wing social movements like Fox helps the conservative movements."

With cable news' tendency to follow the ratings leader, those news producers who preferred to offer original programming found themselves left out in the cold, but Cohen admitted he was still feeling optimistic that MSNBC would make a small, if significant concession to the more politically progressive news producers:

> At MSNBC I was hoping for at least one hour a day with the most unabashedly liberal host in the history of American television, Phil Donahue. For one hour a day they would counter program and they would see that there are millions of people in America hungering for an alternative to Fox, but at MSNBC, from the beginning they were saying to us, we have to be balanced and for months they were telling Phil, giving

him instructions not to be too confrontational. Don't be too partisan, don't be too angry, you have to be balanced. Now if Roger Ailes at Fox, who had built up his channel being partisan and angry, if he heard the instructions that Phil Donahue was getting at MSNBC, he would have laughed his ass off and indeed Roger Ailes is laughing all the way to the bank.

Jeff Cohen: Outfoxing Fox.

However, Cohen soon discovered that the network wanted a Foxified version of the liberal host:

At the end of our tenure with "Donahue" at MSNBC, balance wasn't enough, and this was the "Fox Effect": they mandated that any time we had—if we had two left-wing guests—we had to have three right-wing guests; if we had one antiwar guest, we had to have two pro-war guests. So that's how we ended the show; we were trying to outfox Fox—you cannot outfox Fox. But MSNBC and the others have tried. Since the corporate ownership of the other channels does not allow anyone to counter program against Fox, in television the inclination is imitation and they imitate Fox.

Donahue made his mark being an unrepentant liberal who proved that success in the personal and professional sphere didn't require reactionary beliefs. A Foxified Donahue would have been an impossible figure, but in the drive for Foxified ratings glory, the network didn't seem to care about the deeper ideological consequences of a watered-down Donahue.

Roger Ailes once quipped to a reporter when Fox News launched, "Maybe the words 'fair' and 'balanced' are more terrifying than we realize." It was a comment that revealed more about the mindset of its author than most people realized. It also revealed the heart of the FNC: a Foxified world is a terrifying one. First, it is unfamiliar territory for most since it is a world that doesn't truly exist. Second, for those who do not fit in this world, what becomes of them? Are they destined to become societal pariahs for the rest of their lives? Must they assimilate to the beliefs of an artificial world to escape persecution? What if the reality you experience runs counter to a Foxified one? How does someone square what he knows to be true with what he is told is true?

It's cheap news that takes cheap shots, and cheap shots are plentiful in the Fox News world. As one Moody memo (dated April 30, 2004) callously quipped, "Should food stamp recipients be allowed to buy junk food with their government-subsidized coupons? The governor of Minnesota thinks not. Steve Brown's on the case of the taxpayer and the twinkie." Moody did not opine whether taxpayers who owned Fox's airwaves should be outraged that they saw no returns from their investment, but the pot reveled in pointing out the kettle's blackness.

But a Foxified world doesn't merely stem from ideology; it also comes from miserliness, as Nichols remarked:

I don't believe [that] they do it for purely ideological reasons. I think it's also [that] those stories are very easy to do, very cheap to report. You can just pick up a little video from Florida, a little video from Massachusetts, from California or wherever and the sort of visceral issues that are in play, issues of morality, issues of safety, are easy to blow up into big stories. That's in a way one of the journalistic crimes of Fox. They don't like to spend money doing serious stories. They like to do cheap, easy stories that will get a gut reaction, an emotional reaction, without going out and spending the money on stuff like figuring out whether crime is up or down...

If it can be done on a shoestring budget, FNC brass seems to be all for it—except that you get what you pay for. The FNC has very few foreign bureaus, and almost no exclusive breaking scoops. Fox News is reactionary in more ways than one: it reacts to news already reported by other news outlets. *Times* columnist Jack Gould's call for analysis has now reached a new disturbing level: instead of reporting news and then adding instant analysis, the FNC is merely reporting opinion, then calling it news. Sure, being cheap and easy will get you an unsavory reputation in your neighborhood, yet the talking heads at Fox News can at least do it with an air of authority. But in the end, what makes Bill O'Reilly any better than Jenna Jameson? Don't both try to satisfy their audiences by appealing to their primal desires, but then justify that by putting an empowerment spin to it?

Chapter 7

The Partisan Press

*"A word about Laci Peterson revelations:
we need to be extra careful that we know from
whom we are getting our information.
There is no doubt that Mark Geragos is a
skillful manipulator. That doesn't mean that
he's wrong or deceitful. But everything he tells
us, or anyone else, will be to benefit his client.
The same is true of prosecutors and Ms. Allred.
We don't need to discount what they say, but we
need to be aware that it comes with attitude."*

One of John Moody's memos to Fox News staff

S hameless political cheerleading by the press isn't a new concept: reporters who have had illustrious (or at least semi-functional) careers in the news world frequently find themselves working for the same politicos they once covered. This type of crossover shouldn't be much of a surprise: reporters know how the news media works, they know how the government is run and, most importantly, they inevitably make the right connections with the same powerful people they interview and report on day after day. It does cross the minds of many reporters that positive coverage of a certain politician or a party can lead to lucrative scoops—or even a lucrative career.

Contrary to popular opinion, most journalists (both full-time and freelance) don't rake in hundreds of thousands of dollars in yearly wages. While a few "star" reporters and columnists do bring home hefty paychecks, many more live on a working class or lower middle class salary. For some journalists, (particularly those in television), their media careers are cut short by corporate "restructuring," wrinkles, a "difficult" reputation, management or ownership changes or negative focus group feedback. Unlike other professions, landing another job in the field can be difficult or impossible, meaning some of the displaced wind up teaching in J-schools or working in public relations. Others go on to work with the same people they were responsible for observing.

There have always been reporters who have crossed the line between observer and participant even while still gainfully employed as a journalist. In August 2004, Monica Armenta, a television news anchor, read a glowing introductory speech for New Mexico Governor Bill Richardson, giving

effusive praise such as "Governor Richardson has done more for New Mexico in two legislative sessions than any previous governor accomplished in decades." In fact, the Governor's own flunkies wrote the rosy remarks for Armenta to read. It was another stunning example of real journalism, fair and balanced.

Not every reporter who benefits from his past connections gets a plum government post: sometimes a nice corporate "thank you" is the reward. In 1998, after ABC newsman David Brinkley retired from the network, he became a pitchman for Archer Daniels Midland—the same company that ran ads on his "This Week" program (ADM was also fined $100 million for price fixing in 1996).

The news world can be a revolving door: reporters work for politicians (some of who have worked as reporters themselves) or become politicians themselves (such as California Senator Bruce McPherson); those who worked for politicians become journalists (Diane Sawyer, George Stephanopoulos and even Fox News honcho Roger Ailes); and former politicians end up working for the news media themselves (such as Fox News' John Kasich and Newt Gingrich). The line between power brokers and their chroniclers has always been blurred and uncomfortable, but most people don't seem to raise serious questions with either their fellow journalists or the public. For a profession that claims to be objective, the spinning door isn't as conducive to objectivity as one might expect.

A Quick History of Journalists and Their Ideas About Objectivity

If there are people today who angrily complain that the media is too politically slanted, it is because they have not read news stories from earlier decades; since they have nothing to compare today's coverage with, they assume that the news media is overly rampant with personal and political biases. Compared with the journalism of yesterday, modern reporting seems quite neutral and even bland in comparison. While the media's "conservative" or "liberal" bent may have done old readers' hearts good, they would have been unhappy to learn that brazen, biased reporting was generally used by owners, editors and reporters alike as a stepping stone to curry favor with elites, not with readers. In a way, news consumers of the past were being used and exploited by many unscrupulous news producers.

Patronage appointments were the hallmark of the pre-Penny Press era: many editors and reporters would openly praise, support, deify and generally propagandize for their targets, hoping that the brazen bootlicking would translate to a better paying career with perks. In many cases, the "good old days" of journalism were nothing more than strategic advertising wrapped in newsprint.

Once some media owners, editors and reporters realized that their calculated boot-licking wasn't a guarantee of better things, the journalism model slowly began to change. Somewhere along the way, a few enterprising wire services discovered that politically neutral stories were more likely to be picked up by both right- and left-winged publications; why appeal to only 50% of the market when you could easily double your profits just by keeping your smart-assed opinions to yourself? Eventually, newspapers also hit upon the same revelation: publications who appealed to both (or more realistically, all) sides of the political spectrum would have a more robust circulation and bottom line than those who courted the fringes. And so, modern-day journalism was born.

Eventually, the savvy marketing ploy was sugarcoated with the usual ethical justifications journalists love to spew: We must be objective! We must be fair! We must be balanced! We must get both sides of the story! We must keep opinion out of editorial! *Liberté! Égalité! Fraternité!* It was the journalistic equivalent of the French Revolution. Eventually, journalists began to see objectivity as dogma: by 1923, the American Society of Newspaper Editors decreed that objective journalism—and only objective journalism—could be considered to be ethical journalism. Any other dissemination paradigm need not apply, thank you.

Put bluntly, journalistic objectivity was a capitalistically enterprising and pragmatic idea that was eventually framed in murky moral posturing. Once the chain of ethics and morality became attached to the concept, the necessary revising or improving upon the notion of objectivity was out of the question. Debate and testing were shut out. At no time was journalistic objectivity measured, quantified, defined or properly tested in the academic J-school halls, nor was it ever framed as a logical or intellectual quantity; thus, it could never properly evolve as an empirical method or gold standard for the profession in the way that other professions could define their own concepts of objectivity.

What, precisely, journalistic objectivity really meant was anyone's guess: maybe it meant being fair and balanced, who really knew? But it sure sounded good, and so reporters and editors alike ran with it for decades and passed on their beliefs to future journalists. As Robert McChesney noted, "Throughout the history of television, there's been this notion in professional journalism of neutrality, sort of standing centrist between the Democrats and the Republicans, between the range of debate and elite opinion."

Interestingly, "objectivity" and "journalistic objectivity" are considered one and the same idea. They are not. Scientific objectivity is an entirely separate concept from what reporters consider to be objectivity. Scientists and researchers grapple with the complexities and nuances of their version of objectivity: control groups, double blind conditions, placebos and the removal of outside influences are the methodology with which academics conduct experiments and see the world around them. There is debate, revision and even disagreement (for example, noted psychologist Robert V. Guthrie's 1976 book was entitled *Even the Rat Was White*). In this sphere, the ideas about what is objective have evolved over time.[3]

Journalists, on the other hand, never bothered to tinker with or test out their definition of objectivity (with chasing leads and rushing to make deadlines, they were apparently too busy to verify the

---

3 Some less illuminated academics have argued that there is no such thing as objective truth; however, saying that everything is relative is an absolute statement, and hence a contradictory and logically impossible situation. Crush these same academics' hands under the wheel of a car and those smart alecks will discover that the objective truth is they will be in serious pain and will need medical attention—but that's another subject.

beliefs that defined their profession). On the whole, reporters have an aversion to both theory and academia. For far too many, intellectual exploration and theories are time-wasters that will bore the news consumer and bog down the reporter. What this means is that the basic ideas about objectivity have never changed, never grown and never been revised. If it worked for reporters in the 1940s, it will work for reporters today. Journalistic objectivity is a static concept.

Though there aren't many, if any, journalism studies backing up the usefulness of objectivity, reporters believed in their definition of neutrality and fairness. Facts were in; opinion and emotion were out. This is how reporters and editors conducted business for decades: don't take sides, cover *both* sides of the story, give *both* sides equal time and be fair and balanced in your politically neutral stories. It seemed to work: people consumed news, and a healthy percentage trusted the media's credibility.

Objectivity Today

The journalistic ideal of objectivity was nearly impossible to adhere to for many reasons: first, objectivity was always ill-defined for the profession; second, personal opinion and feelings creep into a story no matter what, never mind that the artificial idea of a two-sided world left out many ideas and voices in the press. Finally, why bother toiling as an opinionless and useful muckraker when there is a more lucrative career in being a loud and useless opinion-spewer?

Objectivity wasn't a perfect concept, but journalists didn't bother to look for other, *differing* models of objectivity. Some simply gave up on trying to appear objective. Others are still in denial that anything is wrong.

Modern American journalism has suddenly found itself on the verge of a new era: somewhere along the way, a few critically-thinking media owners and reporters discovered that ideologically neutral stories were troublesome. After all, how can anyone be completely neutral? How can you be fair to unequal sides, especially if you see that one side is clearly wrong or at least unpopular with an audience? Why do we assume that there are only two sides to every story? How healthy is it to discard your feelings during a tragic event? In the Internet Age, how can a media outlet expect to retain audiences if they don't add a few pointed zingers in their stories? What if the audience is actively looking for subjectivity?

Journalists are still unofficially mandated to give an accurate and truthful account of the world around them (though they can be sued for libel or slander, they aren't going to end up in the slammer for flagrantly lying or distorting facts)—but because objectivity was created in a capitalistic and not an intellectual or ethical foundation, the concept could never really ring true in the hearts and minds of those in the news media. A gold-digger might try to ease his conscience by convincing himself that he actually married for love, but if his spouse loses her wealth, he is not going to stand by her and help her through her slump. He is going to dump her so he can find another wealthy pigeon to fleece.

From the beginning, objectivity was used to boost circulation and revenue. Since more and more viewers and readers are questioning the very notion of objectivity, many media owners and workers are willing to discard objective reporting if it means gaining audience share. Modern-day biased reporting has nothing to do with being "honest" with an audience or telling them "the way it is"; it is about catering to a segment of the public who wishes for some form of validation. Journalistic ideology has always been virtually nonexistent: it really is all about the Benjamins.

Which brings us to Fox.

Some individual journalists and media owners have realized how lucrative partisan reportage can be. For example, some reporters who cultivate relationships with power brokers will get the juicy pseudo-scoops that will, of course, be flattering to and serve the purposes of their secret source. That cultivation will require that the reporter present the information in a certain way: he must take

Anonymous 1
Former Fox News Employee

Fox News Channel has eliminated traditional journalism altogether.

care that his source is presented in a positive way if he is to get any more information. The filter the reporter will use will be somewhat rosier than if he found the information independently of the source.

Fox News goes several steps beyond the cynically enterprising tightrope act: their reporters and hosts make grand generalizations and declarations about world events without having to toil and dig—never mind that the little scratches of information that are reported are self-serving and one-sided. CNN has over forty foreign bureaus; Fox has less than half of that. Fox News is water-cooler talk with an attitude. What major

scoops, investigative hard news or groundbreaking stories have ever been associated with Fox? Where is their Watergate? Where are their Boys of Baghdad?

For Fox, there is no Watergate or even *a* Boy of Baghdad: what Fox has to offer is attitude, neatly packaged in a news format. It's journalism for people who hate journalism, but still want to seem as if they're informed and in the know. Advertisers peddling infomercials have been mimicking newscasts for years, but the final result always oozes with cheese. Fox News' GOP infomercial has truly broken a barrier: their product looks and sounds like regular news, as Robert McChesney observed:

> [...M]uch more than its partisanship, the real revolutionary breakthrough of Fox has been its eliminative journalism—that's the thing to understand. What Fox News Channel has done is it's stripped out any notion of journalism as we've traditionally understood it from its product. There is no journalism at the Fox News Channel... Journalism should provide a vigorous accounting of people in power and people who want to be in power. Journalism should provide a wide range of informed opinions on the crucial issues that face the people of the day. Journalism should find some way to let the truth rise up so lying is exposed.

McChesney went on to describe Fox News Channel's modus operandi:

> Fox News Channel is sort of at the forefront of going against all three of those [things].
> It does that by eliminating traditional journalism altogether... [such as] investigations
> of people in power, how they operate, real original work, big stories... real coverage.
> Instead what... is much less expensive to do, what Fox specializes in is punditry, basically
> getting marching orders from the Republican National Committee or some political
> operative, then having people pontificate about it, have guests come on to talk about
> it, have pseudo-experts come on and discuss it, but they don't actually break anything
> themselves. They don't actually study anything; they don't go out and actually find the
> truth themselves.

For the Fox News system to work, it needs people who are willing to vouch for FNC's version of truth,
or what McChesney described as "stripping out the journalism" and replacing it with "pundits and
pontificators." Fox's colorful commentators aren't any different from the ones who provide similar
services for football games; Fox pundits may have taken their cue from John Madden or Howard
Cosell rather than Walter Cronkite. Fox has taken disrespectful scowling and brought it to a whole
new level—instead of exposing spin and cheap opinion as one-sided shysterism, mouthing off has
become glorified as a respected method of funky reportage.

Mind you, journalism is still only at the *verge* of a devolution: it hasn't reached the point of no return
yet. While some outlets may have decided to shuck the old model of journalistic objectivity, it is
still too dicey and dangerous to openly admit to the deliberate tilting and slanting of news coverage.
There may be a consumer backlash and a professional stigma attached to admitting that an outlet
will thumb its collective nose at colleagues and will actively replace reportage with propaganda.
The instigators of the new journalistic devolution are pushing the envelope while simultaneously
maintaining that they are adhering to and improving the established norms and rules of the
profession. It's too early in the game for the instigators to show all their cards. The best that they can
do at the moment is to count cards and bluff.

When Rupert Murdoch and Roger Ailes first announced the creation of the Fox News Network
in front of a gaggle of reporters in 1996, they made themselves up as if they were out to save the
American public from the current roster of "elite" media outlets. They promised the dawn of a new
journalistic era, but that they would do it better than their colleagues. They delivered by calling
what writer David Brock dubbed a "cable opinion channel," rather than a cable news channel, and
attempted "to define news as opinion."

As Roger Ailes warned his future rivals at the news conference, "We'd like to be premier journalists.
We'd like to restore objectivity where we find it lacking... We just expect to do fine, balanced
journalism."

It was too risky to freely admit that they were starting up an ideologically biased network, but they
could hint at it while figuratively nudging and winking to their potential audience. As David Brock
reflected:

The very notion of balance, I believe, is troubling. Fox says it's fair and balanced, and by that they mean that there are a number of liberals who appear on various shows throughout the day on Fox. That's correct, one can see liberals on those shows, O'Reilly has several liberals on as guests. Journalism used to be about objectivity, not about balance. The conservatives like balance... Balance means that if you have 99% of scientific consensus on an issue and 1% over here, and this 1% is funded by [a major] industry, in balance you have to quote them both; they both have to be on the show; they both get equal time. So for the viewer or for the reader, it appears as if there's equal weight.

Truth in Advertising?

He added that what Murdoch "really wanted to do was bring us back to the nineteenth century when everything was partisan; it was all polemics and so that's really his view, it's all just a matter of opinion." Those at Fox News seem to like to play it both ways: their incessant tagline insists that what they are presenting is "real journalism—fair and balanced," but their stories skew toward the sensational and their guests lean heavily right. When a host for a news program openly counts the days until his favorite political candidate wins an election, the insistence that Fox is "real journalism" or is in any way "fair and balanced" flies right out the window. It's time to take a look at both the "objective" window-dressing and the actual slanted content.

Trust Us—Really!: We're Fair and Balanced

The phrase "fair and balanced" is a problematic and vague concept. What does "fair" mean? "Fair" to whom? How is "balanced" defined? Just as the profession never precisely defined the term "objectivity," Fox, too, has cleverly refused to precisely define the terms fair and balanced. In that regard, they can claim no more moral high ground than their colleagues and rivals.

But just because the people at Fox News don't have the courtesy to spell out what they mean, it doesn't mean that an outsider can't decipher their methods and intentions. In essence, what Fox uses is a licked finger barometer to determine what they will cover and how they will cover it. To Fox, "fairness" seems to be a code word for lobbing softballs to those who have "traditionally" had a harder time getting fawning coverage in the news media, though rapists and serial killers aren't included in this category. The fact that these "persecuted" individuals may have done something to warrant hard-nosed coverage doesn't seem to be a factor, nor that a real news story shouldn't sound like a fawning press release. But at the FNC, they are fair to certain people, but not to others. "Balance," on the other hand, seems to mean justification for covering certain stories more than others.

In terms of both fairness and balance, Fox News is not an entity that can stand on its own; everything it does is relative to what its rivals are doing. Taken alone, Fox News isn't fair and balanced; it is simply whatever its rivals aren't. Fox News is supposed to be a companion channel: read or watch other sources of news and then compare their information with what you hear on the FNC. It provides an alternate reality, not more in-depth information.

Because the FNC markets itself as an alternative or companion news channel, they take much of the pressure off themselves to have to perform in the same way as their older rivals. They can proclaim to "correct" the ideological faux pas of their competitors, even if they incite anger toward certain people through their coverage. How can a network that claims to be fair and balanced have hosts who insult and belittle people who hold one set of views, but not another? Jeff Cohen believed the motto "amounts almost to consumer fraud" since, as Mark Crispin Miller quipped, "politically, Murdoch's enterprise is little more than a kind of PA system for the extreme right-wing of the Republican party." How can a report that contains very little information be considered to be fair and balanced? Or hosts who believe that people who hold a different political view than theirs are tantamount to terrorists?

Just as girlie magazines have just enough words to convolutedly justify their "magazine" status, Fox News has just enough information to convolutedly justify its "news" status. But Fox News does tend to stay clear of serious issues: there are plenty of stories about celebrities, local and sensational crime, and other soft news. Shows hold serious discussions about Michael Jackson, Britney Spears and Jennifer Lopez's private lives, as if knowing about their problems is actually useful. As Cohen noted: "I would have nothing against a channel that oriented toward right-wing causes and the right-wing agenda as Fox News does; what offends me is that there is no truth in packaging."

At least the packaging is pretty to look at—but that doesn't always hold true with Murdoch's television entities. News Corp's earlier forays into U.S. television were somewhat embarrassing and fifth rate. As Frank O'Donnell recalled about the early days at WTTG:

> It was done very clumsily; there was no attempt to say we need to be balanced in this matter—it was simply an order to run certain pieces of propaganda as if they were news. I think in that era the Murdoch team was really still feeling its way into how it operated. I don't think they were smooth in that era. They knew what they wanted; they wanted to have more of this kind of right-wing propaganda; they wanted it to be sort of packaged in an entertaining fashion when they could, to make it seem more palatable to the viewer. But they didn't really have a smooth transition to it, and that's why these kinds of things came in fits and starts with their newscast.

It took the propagandistic prowess of Ailes to transform Murdoch's entities

from low rent sleazecasts to the more sophisticated *ideologicasts* of FNC today. Not only are the hosts swimming on the right side of the ideological pool, so are the guests. As Peter Hart observed, "look at the interview guests on Brit Hume's show, for instance; there's usually a one-on-one interview that Hume does with a newsmaker. They tend to be conservative politicians, conservative academics, conservative pundits. So you're basically turning the floor over to someone like that for fifteen minutes out of a one hour newscast every night." He adds, "Those are the tactics Fox uses every day to subtly and sometimes not-so-subtly skew its newscast, and I guess the clever thing about Fox is that it has all the other appearances of a normal news outfit... Fox is a little bit more insidious [than a personality such as Rush Limbaugh] in that regard. They discovered a formula that has the look and feel of news when it's more propaganda than news."

The FNC is the United States' first truly successful and mainstream conservative channel that appeals to the party faithful. As David Brock noted, "People seem to be coming to Fox to learn not the news, but what to think about the news. And once you don't have a solid basis of information and you don't have news, that has implications for democracy." He added, "the desire on the part of the conservatives to both have their own media, to have explicitly conservative media and then infiltrate, penetrate and influence the culture of the rest of the media goes back at least to the early 1960s and the sense that conservatives didn't have a major presence in the media." Fox News now showcases some of the most combative conservatives in America today, while keeping their equally matched ideological opposites at bay.

Toeing the Party Line

If Fox News' success is any barometer, then selling news alone isn't enough: the news has to be presented with "attitude," but then again, attitude is the modern day euphemism for bias. The word "bias" sounds ugly and narrow-minded, while the word "attitude" sounds cool and courageous. But attitude is just the same ugly concept dressed up by a shrewd image consultant. Fox News has attitude in spades. It leans to the right on many issues and in general demeanor. Av Westin noted that, "you can observe that there is an attitude on the part of the news personnel on the air in Fox programs. I'm not talking about Bill O'Reilly or any of those programs... I'm talking about those straight news programs where presumably it is 'We report; you decide,' [but] you're getting quite a spin. Just in body language..."

Gene Kimmelman also echoed similar sentiments: "Murdoch's form of journalism... I think is shocking to many people who thought journalism was all about ethics and fairness and true balance in presenting news and information... He's brash. He has the money to buy media outlets, he has a point of view he wants to present and he wants to make money as well. He'll entertain you, he'll put on different points of view periodically, but he clearly has his own political message he wants to get across."

A Partisan Primer

Fox isn't merely political: Fox brass can rightly claim that it isn't a conservative news channel. Traditional conservatives would not approve of running endless stories about a young woman giving blow jobs to a world leader, and many did not approve of the war in Iraq. Yet these conservative voices weren't exactly readily heard on Fox News. Fox is a *partisan* news network, as James Wolcott observed:

It has very little to do with conservatism. For one thing, conservatism isn't conservatism anymore. Conservatism used to have a very different complexion; it used to be about avoiding foreign entanglements, not being militarily aggressive across the

world. There [was] this sense that you should mind your own business unless you were attacked.

Old guard conservatives aren't held in as high of esteem as their smugger counterparts, Wolcott noted:

> This is the debate that's held between the Paleo-conservatives and the Neo-conservatives because the Pat Buchanans are more isolationist-minded and so they see the new conservatism as just a total betrayal of the old conservatism. But what it really is is simply power politics; it's simply power grabbing and that's what we're really seeing in the Bush Era. It's all about power. It's about power in taking over the Senate; it's in power controlling the bureaucracy so that you can control the regulatory process, or take the regulations off. It's not really conservatism; it's just a Republican corporate power at work. That's what they're pushing.

So is Fox a Republican network? Not entirely. Fox News does not seem to echo the sentiments of moderate or less influential Republicans. What Fox News has done is hedge their bets and have decided to be a George W. Bush Republican news network: whatever the Bush administration has decreed to be noble, important and good, the FNC concurs with fervently. Fox is a fanboy haven because it appeals to a zealous and devoted fringe just as cult fans are devoted to a particular character (Spider-Girl), writer (J.K. Rowling), show ("Star Trek") or comedian (Andy Kaufman). It adheres to the "Great Man" school of thought: it does not like to criticize George W. Bush or his disciples. Whether the Reaganphile Murdoch is trying to resurrect Reagan by reinventing Bush or trying to merely curry favor in order to expand his already corpulent empire isn't entirely clear. In any case, Bush should probably be feeling more exploited than flattered.

The partisan way of covering the news is enforced at the FNC: reporters are expected to toe the party line and cover certain events in certain ways. One former Fox News reporter recalled how the cable newser made sure journalists knew what was expected of them:

> The Fox News Channel was just getting started, and I was excited. I thought that this would be a good, good opportunity. It was, you know, very conservative [and] I knew that going in… This [network] was going to be kind of conservative, but their idea was they were going to put on a cable newscast that was "balanced," that was unbiased, and they were going to do these great in-depth news pieces, and we were all going to do great journalism… When we were in New York, they passed out this [little paperback] book to everyone that Roger Ailes wrote. It was kind of a "rah-rah" book about how we're going to approach this new network, and how we're going to approach journalism.

The Ailes manifesto is only one tool FNC honchos use to ensure ideological continuity; the Moody memos are another. For example, to make certain that U.S. soldiers in Iraq were presented in a positive light, Moody wrote in an April 2004 memo to "refer to the U.S. marines we see in the foreground as 'sharpshooters' not snipers, which carries a negative connotation." In another case, FNC executive producer Brian Gaffney lectured in his May 2, 2003 memo: "*Fox News Sunday* hosts Donald Rumsfeld. Let's promote the dickens out of it."

Why was the Secretary of Defense's interview considered such a get? Because of the hype surrounding the surrender of former Iraq Deputy Prime Minister Tariq Aziz; the event was seen as proof of the White House's success against the tyranny of foreign terrorism. So how did Fox News hosts handle this key interview? By lobbing Rumsfeld an easy question on a May 4 broadcast:

> **HUME:** Now people who are saying, Mr. Secretary, in the aftermath of the success in Iraq, military success in Iraq and after Afghanistan, and after the warnings that have been made to Syria, that the stage is being set here for some sort of perpetual conflict in which one government after another will be taken on and maybe—and that the whole "axis of evil" may now be the focus of military undertakings. What about that?

Hume's long-winded question received another long-winded reply from Rumsfeld:

> **RUMSFELD:** Oh, I don't know that that's the way to look at it. It seems to me that the way to look at it is that the United States and the United Kingdom and Australia and sixty-five nations in a coalition made a decision to change the regime in Iraq. The effect of that was a demonstration to the world that an awful lot of countries don't think it's a good idea for countries to have weapons of mass destruction, or to be on the terrorist list, or to have relationships with terrorist networks. And that's—that message is a good message for the world. It isn't a good thing for countries to be on the terrorist list, or to be cooperating with terrorist networks, or to be developing weapons of mass destruction. So, I think that the message that's going out is a solid one. It's a healthy one. It's good for the world. And, we may see some behavior modification.

> **HUME:** What about North Korea?

No brain-cramping follow-up questions from Fox's crown jewel; no tough or probing questions from either Hume or Tony Snow who seemed to opt for the deferential line of questioning. The love-fest not only assured Rumsfeld face time, but praise and soft questions as well. However, this wasn't an off day for either Hume or Snow; those who were in the Bush cabinet—and even the big guy himself—usually don't find themselves in Fox News' hot seat.

Regardless of the motives behind the rah-rah Bush attitude, the Fox News support of the most powerful faction of the GOP is clear and present. Sean Hannity did not count the days until the Republicans retain their majority in the House or Senate; he counted the days until President Bush could again park his heinie in his chair in the Oval Office. With this attitude, Fox News has taken America right back into the days when journalists curried favor with powerful elites. Despite the patriotic and psychedelic graphics, FNC isn't reinventing journalism or offering a new journalistic ideology or paradigm. It isn't a progressive news outlet, but a regressive one. Its mandate seems to be to create news stories that promote George W. Bush as a stoic and productive super-President.

Who could guess that the former party boy turned world leader with the perpetual smirk was a fallible mortal from watching Fox News? The Bush love-fest was more than evident in a March 6, 2003 edition of "Hannity and Colmes":

SEAN HANNITY: [...W]e're joined by Fox News foreign affairs analyst, Mansoor Ijaz, is with us. Mansoor, first of all, your thoughts on the President's press conference tonight. I thought he was superb. What did you think?

MANSOOR IJAZ: I can't disagree with that.

No, Ijaz couldn't disagree with it, unless he wanted to shut the door to future FNC appearances. But no one at Fox is likely to knock a Republican President: every action can be justified and spun into something that sounds heroic or just. Bush's various predicaments and plights are reported with care at the FNC. As John Moody opined in a June 3, 2003 memo to his faithful staffers:

Sean Hannity: Herr Hairdo

> The President is doing something that few of his predecessors dared undertake: putting the U.S. case for mideast peace to an Arab summit. It's a distinctly skeptical crowd that Bush faces. His political courage and tactical cunning are worth noting in our reporting through the day.

A "fair and balanced" newscast would simply report on the event itself without the slanted commentary; whether a news producer thinks that the move is one of "political courage and tactical cunning" is irrelevant. Instead of asking anchors to stick with what is observable, talking heads at Fox are asked to behave like drones: just tell the nice viewers what the President's actions "mean."

But Bush's actions were justified by Moody on more than one occasion, as he did in one of his memos on June 2, 2003:

> Heads of state don't leave G-8 meetings early unless they have good reasons. President Bush has two: he has to get to Egypt, and he doesn't like the French. Let's explain to viewers that despite the tepid handshake, Bush and Chirac are far from reconciled, as are the U.S. and Germany. The early departure from Evian should take the sparkle out of the bottled water spa.

In other words, Fox logic dictates that it is perfectly kosher for a grown man to take his toys and go home when others do not wish to blindly follow his wishes. Just as a wounded child will bitterly and unquestionably defend the actions of his morally ambiguous parents, Fox News defends its daddy, regardless of how convoluted those justifications may sound to the nonbelievers. For a partisan press, facts are secondary; it is interpretation that is key to disseminating information.

Yet how that interpretation is disseminated is also unique at Fox News. With a top-down model of reportage, Jim Moody spins events in his memos to fit a Foxified reality, while hosts and foot soldiers fall obediently into place. What the facts show is irrelevant; as long as the facts can be interpreted in a partisan way. Blurring the line between news and opinion becomes a key ingredient in a partisan news outlet, as Cohen noted:

It's very hard at Fox News to separate news from the commentary because it all blends together. That's what makes it so ridiculous, that slogan *we report; you decide* because there's no TV news channel in history that's ever reported less. It's mostly opinion and punditry, and I think if you pinned them down at Fox News they'd admit it.

One easy way to facilitate a partisan agenda is to report on certain types of stories; in FNC's case, those stories are ones that dovetail nicely with the Bush platforms of crime, terrorism and business. But it also helps a partisan network parade about a group of pundits who can be counted on to passionately reinforce the network's ideological talking points.

Friends of Fox

Filling up the airwaves with a constant stream of information is an extremely difficult task: finding information costs money and requires competent and ambitious news producers to work round the clock to find breaking stories that interest viewers. News is expensive to unearth; opinion is cheap. Finding reliable pundits to distract and entertain the crowd takes less time and resources than fighting the government to open classified files or following a tangled paper trail into a shady company's dealings. Fox News heavily relies on pundits to give their take on the issues of the day.

Guests who get the kid glove treatment at Fox usually fall into two categories: people who make regularly scheduled appearances to chit chat with attitude (and are thus paid for their random thoughts) and those who are newsmakers who actually have a real job and do something more than just observe and pontificate. It is the former category that don't need to give viewers any new information; they just have to give attitude. Pundits are filler and, as Brock noted, "it used to be the job of the journalist to weigh the conflicting claims and make some judgment, and now it's just the conflicting claims."

With pundits, journalists don't have to dig for dirt: aggressive yakkers can take the place of research. Gratified and relieved reporters don't have to worry about the analytical quality of the opinion spewer. As Brock observed, there is "no actual discernment anymore," since these pundits "cancel out the expertise." Fox News viewers don't seem to know the difference or even care.

The Usual Gang of Idiots

The regular pundits, or what Cohen refers to as the "hot air brigade," are the ones who "can fill up an hour with speculation and so-called analysis and it's very cheap..." All TV news outlets rely on punditry, but Fox News' spewers are a *Who's Who* (or even, during more charitable times, a *Who Was Who*) of the most aggressive right-wing pundits the U.S. currently has to offer. Right-wing fan boys can rejoice every time one of their "tell-it-like-it-is," "in-your-face," "world-according-to-me" pseudo-gladitorial mouthpieces throws the proverbial vitriol in the faces of moderates and left-wing opponents.

Despite their high profile, these nag hags aren't usually newsworthy in and of themselves. They haven't been recently indicted, elected or suspected in any terrorist activity; these are people who make their living showcasing the forcefulness of their personalities alone. They give their opinion and analysis on the issues of the day, whether or not they have any direct knowledge or experience in the area. It's punditry, it costs nothing to spew and it's their living.

These pundits are the *creme de la creme* of the right: passionate, surly, articulate and well known. Most have roots in politics; all of them have had other media exposure and have written books. The key here is the books: the pundits write book after book so that the fair and balanced newsmen on Fox can ceaselessly plug them on their programs. What that means is that much of the time the pundit is on Fox News is not spent on giving opinion, but on hawking the latest "I hate liberals" tome. At the FNC, even filler needs filler.

But sometimes pundits do actually give their take on current events, and Fox News heavily relies on these characters: how would viewers know what to think about things without consulting Ann Coulter or Dick Morris? Their penny dreadful takes on life and their *Reefer Madness*-type messages help shape the FNC product.

In many ways, these defenders of ideological extremism are given a free ride at Fox: on the whole (though there are exceptions), they are not seriously challenged or criticized by Fox hosts or anchors. There is no "Yeah right, prove it" to contend with. If the pundit is lucky, Sean Hannity or Bill O'Reilly will plug their new book. Television exposure, pleasant questions, opportunities to get frustrations off one's chest and free advertising: who could ask for anything more?

Some of the characters that grace Fox airwaves on a regular basis include:

Ann Coulter: A constitutional lawyer and well-known crotchety commentator by trade, Coulter has found marketing nirvana by becoming a regular pundit at the cable newser, though she doesn't seem interesting or versatile enough to hold her own show. Though known for her frequent (and on cue) baboonesque outbursts, intellectually Coulter is—at her best—a crabbier, bossier, shriller and more fragmented Lucy Van Pelt and, at her worst, a scrawnier version of G.G. Allin with better hair. Coulter's on-air persona has touches of Sissy Spacek's dark, crimsony and gooey homecoming scene in Carrie. It's gruesome to watch a possessed character exact her revenge on her stunned, random targets—but her fans sure do love it.

Though Fox's Christmas Queen has made a career of slagging and nagging progressives, strangely enough, she herself is the right's own middle-aged fuzzy den mother, assuring her fellow extremist righties that their bunker mentality and self-indulgently vindictive worldview are entirely justified, while simultaneously hen-pecking those left-wing party poopers. Not surprisingly, her schtick (though grating, limited and predictable) works wonders for her career.

Though Coulter has managed to sell her books on her own, Fox News hosts seem compelled to serve as her publicists on their programs. As Bill O'Reilly duly noted to viewers on his May 27, 2004 program:

O'REILLY: With us now is Ann Coulter, the author of the book *Treason*, which will be out in paperback this fall.

You did very well with that *Treason*. How many did you sell? Half million, more than that?

ANN COULTER: More than that.

Sean Hannity also turned enthusiastic Coulter book pitchman on his August 2, 2002 quasi-advertorial program:

> *In many ways, these defenders of ideological extremism are given a free ride at Fox.*

HANNITY: We're joined by constitutional attorney Ann Coulter. She's the author of the best-selling book *Slander*, number one on the *New York Times* list. Great buy. And defense attorney Lynn Gold Bikin is with us tonight.

Regular viewers would hear a similar pitch (akin to, "Hey kids, don't delay, order your copy today: operators at Fox are standing by!") almost a year later on Hannity's June 25, 2003 program:

HANNITY: We are now joined by *New York Times* best-selling author Ann Coulter. She is now the author of a new book just released yesterday, *Treason: Liberal Treachery From the Cold War to the War on Terrorism*. You could have, by the way, delayed the—the date of the publication of this book, give a little space between you and Hillary. You didn't do that?

ANN COULTER: Well, I think it's an important book. And I wanted to get it out.

The professional newsman Hannity showed America what a fair and balanced person he really was by killing air time discussing his hopes for Coulter's tome:

HANNITY: On time, taking on Hillary. Because I think you have a chance to knock it off of the bestseller list, more than any other book that I see out there right now. And I think it's a very strong possibility. Maybe not in week one or two, but certainly in a couple weeks I wouldn't be surprised.

COULTER: Thank you for your confidence. I'm confident that—sublimely confident—that more people will read my book than Hillary's, no matter how the sales go.

If there are those who complain that the line between commercials and programming is becoming increasingly blurred, that might be because these critics have been exposed to Sean Hannity's numerous "buy-Coulter's-book" endorsements:

◆ On June 4, 2004: "...and the author of the No. 1 best-selling book *Treason*, Ann Coulter, is with us. And congratulations on the great, successful book... Did you read her book? Did you read it?... Did you read it?... Wait until you read my book."

◆ On July 15, 2002: "I told you when I first got ahold of it from you, this is a book that needed to be written, because conservatives have been maligned, besmirched, their character assassinated by liberals. You find this funny, Colmes?"

◆ On June 25, 2002: "I love that title. I love that title."

Yet there *are* times when the topic of conversation is not about what a great author Coulter is; sometimes Hannity or O'Reilly do discuss other important breaking news topics with the attorney, such as Coulter's professional missteps—and when Coulter has a bad day, Fox hosts are there to hold her hand. *USA Today*, for instance, asked Coulter to write about the 2004 Democratic Convention in Boston, but then spiked her piece (apparently completely unaware of Coulter's schtick; and obviously editors were unable or unwilling to actually read or listen to her before they signed her on). The abrupt firing made news and Coulter seemed genuinely bummed out over her public rejection on the July 26, 2004 edition of "Hannity and Colmes":

COULTER: [The spiking of the column is] a great disappointment to me. I was hoping to create a buzz in hotel lobbies and airports across America.

It was a very different buzz that Coulter received: instead of being outraged or bemused by Coulter's petty logic, people discussed why a bland and middle-of-the-road newspaper would agree to let an honors graduate from the Overkill School of Writing such as Coulter pen the story in the first place. But nothing helps feelings of dejection more than insulting others, and little Annie and her friends did just that:

HANNITY: Let me ask you this. I've been having fun and calling this the reinvention convention. One of the things, especially on tone, I mean, Howard Dean, didn't get a chance to ask him but he advanced the theory that the President knew about 9/11 ahead of time. Dennis Kucinich accused the President of targeting civilians for assassination. He's called a liar regularly. Used the brown shirt comments of Al Gore, but now everything is controlled. This is the happy convention.

Are we seeing real Democrats here? Is this the real party?

COULTER: In a sense, because it's real for Democrats to try to fake out the American people.

COLMES: Ann, thank you very much. We'll be looking for your columns wherever they appear. We'll be right back. By the way, you're watching the network America trusts for real journalism, fair and balanced.

Yes, with the well-choreographed Coulter as a regular guest, how could Fox be anything but real journalism?

Newt Gingrich: This Congressman from Georgia was once the mighty and outspoken speaker of the House and a GOP darling who led the Republican Revolution straight into controlling the House in 1994. Newt Gingrich was the architect of *Contract With America*: one of those sound bite-friendly blueprints with catchy names that make certain right-wingers swoon and feel more secure in the world. A decade later, Republicans controlled the House, the Senate and the White House, but Gingrich left for greener pastures, including a regular stint as a commentator on Fox News, as do all other faded right-wing politicos, who will always find a welcome mat at Rupert Murdoch's Resting Home for Redundant Republicans.

Newt Gingrich's book, published by Murdoch's HarperCollins, was reviewed on Murdoch's FNC by Neil Cavuto:

"It's a great book."

Gingrich and Murdoch's ties go back even further. In 1994, Murdoch offered Gingrich (who had significant power and clout in his role as speaker) a whopping $4.5 million dollar advance for a two-book deal (which coincided, incidentally, with NBC's complaint to the FCC that News Corp was a foreign-owned company and that by owning Fox, the company was violating U.S. foreign ownership rules). Though Gingrich had to decline the generous advance (but still had his book published by Murdoch's HarperCollins), his ties to News Corp remain visible to this day.

The former speaker of the House now spends his time writing books and dropping in on various FNC programs to wax Republican on almost any issue—and to promote his books. Hannity does a fine job of promoting Gingrich's tomes, as he did on August 12, 2004: "But joining us now is the former speaker of the House, Fox News political analyst and author of the best-selling book, the great new book, *Grant Comes East*."

Newt's writing was great, agreed Neil Cavuto, who not only interviewed the former speaker of the House, but also implied that a Democrat in the White House may spell economic trouble on his July 23, 2004 program:

> **NEIL CAVUTO:** Are stocks getting hit hard of late because Republicans are about to get hit hard in the November election? To hear some traders tell it, and the reason why we're under 10,000 is, well, the four-digit Dow, people [are] concerned that there will be a [Democratic] President. That might seem extreme. Are people getting a little bit ahead of themselves?
>
> Who better to ask than former speaker of the House, Newt Gingrich. He's also a Fox contributor and author of another great book, *Grant Comes East*. I think he's written about 500 books, something like that. But he's a busy guy.

When Gingrich's books didn't need endorsing, Hannity was busy endorsing the former Speaker's mentions in newspaper articles, as he did on the July 14, 2004 edition of "Hannity and Colmes":

> **HANNITY:** As we get right to our top story tonight, joining us from Washington, the author of *Grant Comes East*, former speaker of the House, Fox News political analyst Newt Gingrich.
>
> By the way, did I read the *Washington Post* this week? Did they say something nice about you in that piece? What was that?

Gingrich then praised the article for its fairly nice portrayal of him, while Hannity enthusiastically concurred:

> **NEWT GINGRICH:** There was actually a terrific article on healthcare that was in the *Post* health section yesterday. It was very nice, very—very positive. A lovely article.
>
> **HANNITY:** They took a little shot, but that was it. I said this is impressive; Newt has come far. We're going to have to start questioning your credentials now.

GINGRICH: No, no, no. I think if you're trying to save lives you can actually get people on both sides of the aisle to agree that saving lives is a good thing. I wouldn't—I wouldn't carry it, as you'll see in the next ninety seconds—I wouldn't carry it into a broad bipartisan future.

HANNITY: I'm hoping. I like the old Newt, the Newt that was the revolutionary.

Gingrich, as usual, showed viewers how he was capable of seeing all sides of an issue with a level head:

GINGRICH: I am happy to watch on television. I will be glad to call in to the radio show. I hope to be allowed to come on the show with you and Alan. I'm sure Alan will be thrilled defending the convention, and explaining the various whacked out liberals that are on all day.

Gingrich wasn't called on the carpet for his unpoetic harangue by Colmes, nor was he challenged on his assertions—but why question his extremist views when he writes such *great* books?

Alan Keyes: A self-obsessed dilettante who has never learned to turn the other cheek, Alan Keyes piddles and putters around in various careers (nothing modest or humble mind you, Presidential candidate, ambassador, media personality), while giving new meaning to the phrase "using the Lord's name in vain." He thrives on cultivating a pontifical attitude, and his mindset is best described by the lyrics of the Austin Lounge Lizards song "Jesus Loves Me, But He Can't Stand You."

The list of his various manipulations and misuses of the Christian religion is long and appalling: when he unsuccessfully ran for a Senate seat in Illinois, he claimed that Jesus Christ would not vote for his Democratic opponent Barak Obama (Earth to Alan: Jesus did not cast his vote for *you*, either). It was Keyes who said with a straight face in a 2004 speech in Utah that the September 11 attacks on the U.S. were a "warning" from God about the "evil" of American women having abortions.

However, how Keyes knew that this alleged "deity-instigated" terrorist attack was a punishment for abortion, as opposed to His disdain for child molestation or the disturbing number of teenagers who have been kidnapped, tortured and murdered for kicks—or why Keyes thought that terrorist-piloted planes that targeted the ultimate symbol of capitalism would be an unequivocal sign that God frowned on abortions was never fully explained. Though Keyes' speech had espoused a satanic version of a Creator, it hasn't clued in Fox hosts to critically question Keyes about his uninformed and twisted worldview.

But being deliberately uninformed didn't seem to prevent Keyes from declining to appear on the September 19, 2003 edition of "Hannity and Colmes":

COLMES: Joining us now, former Presidential candidate, no stranger to the hustings, Ambassador Alan Keyes. Ambassador, I'm guessing you're not going to like any of the Presidential—any of the Democratic candidates.

You're not going to praise any of them, I'm guessing. So what's your take on [former Presidential hopeful Wesley] Clarke?

ALAN KEYES: Well, I'm not going to praise any of them. I guess I haven't been paying that close attention to them either. Right now I think this election is for G.W. Bush to win or lose. Right now I think it's pretty clear that he's going to win.

Months later, Fox News' hosts still hadn't learned their lesson when Bill O'Reilly nearly reenacted the September 19 broadcast with Keyes on his January 21, 2004 program:

O'REILLY: Anybody impressed you on the campaign trail thus far, ambassador?

KEYES: Well, to be honest, Bill, no. But I also have to be honest in saying that I haven't paid that much attention to the Democrats. I know that to a man, they all stand for things that I believe are deeply harmful to this country—abortion, the promotion of homosexual unions and marriage, socialism. I don't agree with any of them...

In both cases, hosts didn't challenge Keyes or at least follow up with questions about why Keyes chose to remain deliberately ignorant, but then have the nerve to come on a show that was slated to cover that very topic? Why was he wasting viewers' time? Why didn't Keyes do his homework? How can he ignore the other side during an election? What kind of informed citizen chooses to listen to only one side of the political spectrum—and then go on national television to boast about his political illiteracy? Apparently one who can count on an encore invite from the FNC.

Dick Morris: Morris' fame goes back to two eyebrow-raising incidences: his pivotal role as advisor to former President Bill Clinton and his cavorting with a loose-lipped and rather used-looking hooker named Sherry Rowlands who cashed in on her tawdry encounters with Morris by selling her story to a tabloid. As to which of these two well-publicized episodes was the bigger affront to conservatives, opinion seems unanimous: his association with Clinton.

Perhaps Morris learned the value of signed airtight confidentiality agreements, or the tabloids were simply cutting down on "political advisors-turned-pundits who are caught with old, used-up hookers" stories, but these days he is known as a regular fixture on Fox News.

Pundits may be asked to predict the future, but that doesn't always mean that they will be right. Morris certainly didn't earn his keep as an oracle on the January 28, 2004 edition of "Hannity and Colmes":

MORRIS: I think now that Howard Dean is clearly not going to be the nominee, there's a very good chance that Hillary will be the Vice Presidential candidate.

I will flat out predict that whoever wins this nomination will make the first phone call to Hillary to ask her to run. And the reason I think Hillary might accept it is twofold. First of all the chance of winning.

And if a Democrat beats Bush in 2004, the only way for her to stay fresh is to be Vice President. If she's a Senator, she's out of it.

And if a Democrat loses to Bush, the guy who ran for Vice President will be her opponent in 2008. So it might as well be her.

HANNITY: She can't find—is the ambition that blind she can't find any satisfaction in just being a Senator from New York?

MORRIS: No.

Of course, a psychic sage such as Morris probably predicted that there would be ample opportunities for the obligatory Hannity book plug. Hannity delivered the goods on October 20, 2003:

> **HANNITY:** ...Fox News political analyst Dick Morris is here. Also author of the best selling book *Off With Their Heads*. Congratulations on the book.

Not to be outdone, the quick-thinking Colmes also added a more dexterous double plug on the same show, turning the entire program into the Fox Book Club:

> **COLMES:** I want to—Dick, I want to ask you about—congratulations on your book, by the way.
>
> **MORRIS:** Thank you.
>
> **COLMES:** Mine is out tomorrow.
>
> **MORRIS:** I look forward to reading yours.

O'Reilly pitched another Morris book on July 1, 2004:

> **O'REILLY:** "Unresolved Problem" segment tonight: who will run with John Kerry? Fox News political analyst Dick Morris is on the record saying it will be Hillary Clinton. I say balderdash and have bet Morris a dinner.
>
> He joins us now, still counting the money he's making from his new bestseller, *Rewriting History*, big *New York Times* hit. OK?

Whatever you say, Bill.

Michelle Malkin: Malkin, a somewhat bland and forgettable (though right-leaning) syndicated newspaper columnist and author, has also made a variety of FNC appearances and, yes, like Coulter, Morris and the rest of the Fox A-listers, Malkin got a book plug on the September 12, 2002 edition of "Hannity and Colmes":

> **COLMES:** Our next guest says the nineteen hijackers on the planes that attacked America, it's a very powerful help to the U.S. government. In her book *Invasion: How America Still Welcomes Terrorists, Criminals and Other Foreign Menaces to Our Shores*, Michelle Malkin says our government made it too easy for the terrorists to enter this country.
>
> Michelle Malkin now joins us. I know your goal is to knock Hannity off the bestseller list for the book. That's why you're here.
>
> **HANNITY:** It's a great book.
>
> **MALKIN:** The more the merrier, right?
>
> **HANNITY:** Great book.

But a regular guest cannot expect unconditional effusive praise without delivering the goods—in her case, blunt, if simplistic commentary aimed at putting down various left-leaning individuals. Or offering a stern, if unoriginal opinion after talking down to a show's left-leaning host, as Malkin did on the May 1, 2002 edition of "Hannity and Colmes":

> **MALKIN:** You know, Alan, I'm always glad to hear you questioning the role of government intervention.

COLMES: I always do.

MALKIN: And you know, I'll tell you what I think is proper. It is proper for parents to exercise their vote with their credit card, and put pressure on these companies to be responsible.

Hannity and Colmes tend to be pussycats around the confident, if somewhat unworldly Malkin—a courtesy that would eventually come back and slap her in the face when she tried the same schtick on a host who did not work for the FNC.

The problems with kissy-faced pseudo-interviews is that they can skew a guest's view of the true nature of this nasty world: when "Hardball" host Chris Matthews gruffly questioned her about her views on then-Presidential candidate John Kerry in August 2004, a rudely awakened Malkin threw a pouty fit over a journalist refusing to handle her with the same pampered pussycat treatment as she was accustomed to on Fox. Malkin came on Matthew's show, expecting to hawk her book and defend another tome, *Unfit for Command,* and seemingly set her mind on autopilot—with disastrous results. Not being used to tough questions, the formerly sheltered Malkin launched into an August 20 diatribe on her website with the childish, snooty and overly defensive title "Ambush Journalism... Or My Evening With Caveman Chris Matthews":

> Despite the show's basement ratings, [I] figured it's a good opportunity to reach out to a new audience. Fox News, with whom I have a contract, has generously allowed me to appear on some competing networks to talk about the book.

> [...]When I tried to make a point about how the mainstream media ought to subject John Kerry to as much skull-pounding interrogation as private citizens such as Swift Boat Vet Larry Thurlow had endured from Matthews and the *Washington Post*, Matthews cut me off...

> [...He] frantically stuffed words down my mouth when I raised these allegations made in *Unfit for Command* that Kerry's wounds might have been self-inflicted. In his ill-informed and ideologically warped mind, this transmogrified into me accusing Kerry of "shooting himself on purpose" to get an award.

> [...]Only someone who had not read *Unfit for Command* would interpret what I was saying the way Matthews did. The book raises questions by vets, many of whom were with Kerry...

Yes, and many of whom have an axe to grind. Sadly, that wasn't the last word Malkin (who obviously uses old *Calvin and Hobbes* cartoons in lieu of a thesaurus) had to say about her displeasure that Matthews hadn't fawned over her on his news program and didn't call her book "great" like Sean Hannity always does. In her immature rage, Malkin even resorted to the traditionally leftist argument that Matthews was sexist just because he wouldn't give her a lollipop. So what if he was a raging misogynist? If she were a capable debater and truly his equal, she could still get her point across. Life is full of obstacles, opposition and interference. Besides, don't right-wingers like to fancy themselves as the toughest street fighters in town? What happened to Malkin besides reality?

Fox News hosts had spoiled Malkin—as they do to most of their right-wing guests—hence, her introduction to a purer model of hard journalism where guests aren't enabled or given free reign to spew their underdeveloped opinions without concrete proof from multiple sources was obviously more than she could handle. Malkin fantastically blew the interview, but did not have the courage to admit it; she opted for the traditional "it's someone else's fault" cop out.

The episode just goes to show that though many right-wing pundits may seem strong, aggressive and tough on Fox News, if they are thrown into the ring with an equally aggressive adversary who is ready for a fight, suddenly their façade and their stamina quickly crumbles, and a more honest version of their true selves starts to emerge. There is a dishonesty in the way Fox News pairs off guests—the leftist guest will usually be intellectually weaker, less seasoned and less aggressive than his rightist counterpart. The fact that Fox hosts will ask softer questions of the right and be more belligerent to the left further skews the issues the speakers are addressing. Simply change the venue and properly match the opponents, and a far different picture unfolds.

Laura Ingraham: For those who think that familiarity breeds contempt, they obviously never met a Laura Ingraham fan—no matter how well-worn her observations and quips, her fans will still stick with this rightie radio talk show host and hack. If you are a right-leaning shut-in or amnesiac, Ingraham's witticisms may seem fresh and original to you.

Stale or not, Ingraham's mug can be regularly seen on Fox News. She will give her insights and may try to be clever with her answers, but viewers can expect tired views repackaged with a conservative slant. For instance, on the June 24, 2004 "Hannity and Colmes," Ingraham quipped, "have we ever seen Michael Moore and Al Gore in the same room together? That's the first thing I want to say. Because they seem to be, in their physicality and their ideology, melding into the same person." Viewers may have been waiting for the funny, clever or even original part (updating the ancient Michael and LaToya Jackson joke by changing the names still gives you a clichéd contrivance), but Ingraham never delivered.

Nor does she seem to exert sufficient mental effort to think her positions through or use the services of a dialogue coach. Her blasé and seat-squirming replies are both pedestrian and unoriginal. Among Ingraham's more uninteresting observations:

◆ On January 9, 2002: "The reality is, is news has turned into entertainment."

No kidding.

◆ On June 15, 2004: "I think it's great. I want Teresa Heinz to be out there on the campaign trail every day saying exactly the kinds of things she's saying today... I think the more she speaks the better for Republicans, because it shows that John Kerry doesn't have the personality to eclipse his wife."

Perhaps Ingraham's mental apparatus isn't as sharp as she thinks: if the sophisticated and understated Kerry is secure enough to marry someone who is more flamboyant than him, and has no qualms about his partner in life speaking her mind, doesn't that actually point to someone who in fact has an equally strong, but different personality than his wife? If he isn't obsessed with the childish desire to be the center of the universe, it is a good indication that his priorities will not be chasing media attention at the expense of running the White House.

- ◆ On December 13, 2002: "Have we lost all sense of humor in the United States? [...T]he idea that someone from the National Organization for Women can come in today and say that Trent Lott is sexist for a joke at a party... And now they're saying that a joke about a 100-year-old man rises to the level of sexist behavior?"

The feminist as the humorless shrew is an old argument, but that didn't stop Ingraham from making a first-run show seem like a rerun.

- ◆ On January 22, 2003, about Hollywood entertainers who do not support George W. Bush's war against Iraq, particularly about the Dixie Chicks' comments that they were ashamed of their President: "That's anti-American."

So is stifling free speech and differing opinions, Laura.

- ◆ Her dazzling Spoonerism on October 22, 2003: "Until we win the war against terror, we haven't won the war against terror..."

Cribbing from Yogi Berra to describe violent, searing, life-altering events? Isn't there any other rightie pundit out there who could offer something a little more insightful and less embarrassing instead?

With all the banal deadwood falling from her lips, do FNC hosts ever point out Ingraham's uninspired slacker sophistry? Bill O'Reilly came close when he once replied somewhat tersely to one of her remarks: "Baloney, Laura." In most cases, she goes unchallenged.

Of course, just like any other enterprising right-winged ideologue, Ingraham got the official Sean Hannity book blessing on December 13, 2003:

HANNITY: [...A]nd from Westwood One Radio and she's nationally syndicated, also the author—this is a great book, by the way, of *The Hillary Trap*, the definitive book on Hillary Clinton, is our good friend Laura Ingraham.

Hannity's book-peddling on Ingraham's behalf was similar on September 15, 2003: "I love this book. I'm not kidding. I really hope everybody gets a copy of this thing, because you say things that I have often thought, you do it succinctly."

Heck, Bill O'Reilly's endorsement of one of the creatively-stifled yapper's tomes bordered on an infomercial on his June 14, 2004 program:

O'REILLY: With us now is radio talk show host Laura Ingraham, whose syndicated program is heard on 230 stations. Ms. Ingraham is also author of the book *Shut Up & Sing: How Elites From Hollywood, Politics and the UN are Subverting America*. It makes a good Father's Day gift.

O'Reilly didn't mention whether viewers who ordered Ingraham's book would also receive a free can of spray-on hair to give dad on his special day.

Very Special Guest Stars

Some other people (and issues) on the other hand, can't rely on marketable surliness to get regular face time: these poor souls actually have to either have an impact on a significant portion of society in order to get their mugs on television—or, less often, they have to have big, bouncy breasts. But cleavage seems to be an anti-requisite: rarely will an important policy maker with big bouncy breasts find herself on Fox.

Fox News doesn't reach very deep in the Pool of Life to find people to interview: journalists, analysts, jurists, militarists, capitalists and politicians are the usual professionals who are considered to be worthy newsmakers. Though these are the people (usually white Republican men) who clearly have the edge when it comes to face time, there is one exception to the rule: Fox News will occasionally sprinkle their shows with porn stars just to keep the crowds titillated.

Politicos: Like other television news outlets, Fox News heavily relies on interviewing politicians. Like other news outlets, it will ask tough, abrasive questions to Democrat politicians. Unlike other network news outfits, the FNC doesn't always ask them of conservative politicians. For example, Vice President Dick Cheney got a free ride with Neil Cavuto's loaded, but positive questions on June 25, 2004:

> CAVUTO: First, on the economy, you were talking it up here today in a speech. We got more good economic news today, existing home sales at a record pace after yesterday, new home sales at a record pace. Does it bother you, though, that in the media it is still not trumpeted that much?

> CHENEY: Well, I think the evidence is overwhelming that the economy is doing very well. We've come through the recession and the aftermath of 9/11. I think it's —it's beginning to sink in with the public as well, too.

> You know, in this business, you don't have any control over what the press says and how they portray things. And that's their prerogative. But I think anybody who looks at it objectively has trouble making the case that somehow this is a bad economy.

For Fox News hosts, there is no question too easy, too flaky or too positive to ask a GOP politician, especially one that is associated with the country's most recent leader.

George W. Bush

For a man who is the epitome of the patronizing "papa spank" attitude toward world events and leaders, Bush is made to seem tough, but fuzzy; genial at play, but take-charge when provoked. Fox News' coverage of Bush looks more like an exercise in thumbing through a thesaurus, looking for any adjective that carries a positive connotation. Is Bush determined or stubborn? Is he tough or tyrannical? Is he flexible or a flip-flopper?

On Fox, the connotation is always positive. As John Nichols observed, "during the Bush presidency it has been almost an idol worship sort of coverage and an image of George Bush as a President who is completely in charge, competent, attractive, appealing as a person, intellectually far more sound than all the people who work with him say he is. Remember Paul O'Neill, Richard Clarke and others have portrayed the President as disengaged, not functional, yet with Fox you would think this guy is waking up at five in the morning, going on his computer, making calls around the world, getting Israel sorted out, then moving quickly to Iraq and then there's a problem in Malaysia; I'll take care of that... sort of Superman." Nichols added, "Fox portrays

George W. Bush: Delicious comedy.

his every action as a heroic move, as something dramatic or significant. I imagine it's very hard for the Fox producers. Some days George Bush doesn't do anything interesting, and yet they've got to find something that makes him heroic that day... the comedy of it is, at times, sort of just delicious."

Fox News hosts and guests do seem to think Bush has courage. In typical Fox News fashion, Focus on the Family founder James Dobson opined on July 15, 2004: "George Bush is one of the most conservative Presidents we've ever had. He is the strongest pro-life President we've ever had. He had the courage to stand up for family and for marriage and no one else has, to this point. He rolled back taxes on the family. He's done a lot of very, very good things, and I believe—I believe this is going to play a major role in November."

When Bush was photographed with the sign "Mission Accomplished" behind him, Fox News used that clip in their promos. As Nichols observed, if the Bush administration "dress him up in flight suit drag or whatever outfit they want to put him in, Fox will cover it not in a way they should, in a way serious journalists would, which is to say, 'look, it's just Michael Dukakis wearing the helmet in the tank; this is silly.'"

According to Fox logic, on Dukakis it looks silly; on Bush, it's smashing.

When Bush sat down with "Factor" host Bill O'Reilly, the interview was played for three consecutive nights: though O'Reilly brought up unpleasant issues, he framed them in a way that seemed uncharacteristically sympathetic for the gruff and insulting host. O'Reilly's soft interview started with this deferential icebreaker on September 27, 2004:

> **PRESIDENT BUSH:** Well, there's, it's a big gamble on my part.
>
> **O'REILLY:** No, it isn't, not really though. You, we talked four and a half years ago...
>
> **PRESIDENT BUSH:** I'm teasing.
>
> **O'REILLY:** Uh, yeah, when you...
>
> **PRESIDENT BUSH:** I, I enjoy, I enjoy how you interview people, and I appreciate you giving me the chance to come on and have what we say in Texas, just a visit.
>
> **O'REILLY:** Yeah. We're going to have a visit here. I've got fifteen questions for you. If they're dumb, tell me they're dumb. Because the audience will like that.

The same interview O'Reilly warned the President about a tough question that didn't turn out to be so tough at all:

O'REILLY: This is really a tough one.

PRESIDENT BUSH: Okay. (CHUCKLE)

O'REILLY: Iran. Uh, said yesterday, hey, we're going to develop this nuclear stuff, we don't care what you think. You ready to use military force against Iran if they continue to defy the world on nuclear?

PRESIDENT BUSH: My hope is that we can solve this diplomatically.

O'REILLY: But if you can't.

PRESIDENT BUSH: Well, let me try to solve it diplomatically first. All options are on the table, of course, in any situation. But diplomacy is the first option.

The second part of the interview, aired the following evening, was interesting in that while O'Reilly played journalistic puppy, he still tried to insert one of his more famous insults—of course, they weren't lobbed at Bush, but at one of the President's antagonists who did show support for the U.S. War on Iraq:

O'REILLY: Not [French President] Jacques Chirac?

BUSH: Well, he voted yes at the Security Council.

O'REILLY: Yeah, but he stabbed you guys in the back, you thought he was going to help you and he didn't... do you have any theory on why college professors pinhead press people?... And I'm in one of those, by the way—I'm a pinhead press figure—why they go into the liberal realm?... And they're all pinhead liberals over there, right?

The final night of the interview had O'Reilly make this loaded comment to the American prez: "One of the big propaganda things against you is the classroom in Florida after 9/11 when Andrew Card came in and whispered in your ear." Those at the FNC, of course, content themselves with whispering sweet nothings in Bush's ear instead of distressing news.

The Spirit of Ronald Reagan

It has been recounted elsewhere that Rupert Murdoch was an adoring fan of Ronald Reagan. Reagan seems to be considered a Fox News deity: when there is an opportunity to glorify the former President, on-air talent will oblige. Though Reagan had made numerous controversial decisions during his eight year tenure in the White House, viewers would not know it from watching an FNC broadcast. Former Fox News reporter Jon Du Pre recalled a skirmish he had with John Moody when his assignment was to "do live shots throughout the day [for] Ronald Reagan's 90th birthday":

For Fox News Channel viewers, though, as I was instructed, this was something akin to a holy day—this was Ronald Reagan's birthday. My assignment was to go to the Reagan Presidential Library in Simi Valley, California and to do live shots from before dawn until dark to report on Ronald Reagan's birthday. That was pretty much the sort of broad-based assignment I had that day.

The soft news assignment was going smoothly until Du Pre was confronted with a common reality with museums—people don't really like to go there on a weekday:

> It wasn't anything specific until they saw my first three or four live shots early in the morning and Mr. Moody called in to say, "What is he doing out there?" Apparently my live shots weren't meeting the expectation of what the importance of this day really was. I wasn't giving those live shots the energy and the enthusiasm that I should have been giving those live shots. And so the criticism wasn't necessarily over content as much as it was over presentation with respect to that story assignment.

Feeling the heat for reporting the less than spectacular reality, the former Fox News journalist tried his best to give his superiors the story they wanted:

> **I knew I was being watched very carefully;** so I attempted as the day went on to put more energy and more enthusiasm into my live shots. I was told that just because there weren't more than maybe fifteen or twenty people at the Presidential Library that day, I was not to mention that. I was not to mention that there was no celebration planned that day.

In fact, only a fourth grade class had visited the museum that day—the endless, adoring crowds that Moody was banking on just weren't there—why would they be? People don't even celebrate their *own* birthdays, let alone the birthday of a current or former President, regardless of political orientation. Few recognized holidays bring any significant uptake in museum visits on a national level—though movie theaters do seem to reap the benefits of larger audiences on holidays, patriotic or otherwise. No one was getting Reagan's birthday off. Du Pre says he felt the sting of Moody's wrath at the end of the day: "I got in big trouble for that one. In fact, I was suspended for a week."

Du Pre may have been the victim of Moody's blind miscalculations, but Reagan stories still continue to get prominent play, even though the late President hasn't been in office since 1988. If only other 80s icons could get the same gushing A-list coverage decades after their last high profile gig.

Pornos: Believe it or not, Fox News moralizers have a furtive eye on any man or woman whose place of employment happens to be Vivid Entertainment. Porn stars may not be on Fox every day, but they will make guest shots when things get a little too staid around the set. In fact, one Fox News visual that railed against the business had actually shown hardcore porn in the background. In short, Fox News may pretend to look down on the porn business, but their on-again off-again interest raises some interesting questions.

If no porn star is available for an interview, a porn-related story will suffice. Bill O'Reilly showed off his street cred on his October 23, 2003 program when he informed viewers that one of former Iraqi kahuna Saddam Hussein's deceased sons was making his posthumous film debut:

> **O'REILLY:** Even though Qusay Hussein is gone, he is not forgotten. Some porn video

OUTFOXED

sites are selling a sex deal called "Qusay and His Whores," showing him in orgies at his luxury Baghdad villa. We assume this was before he was shot in the head, but, on the Internet, one can never be certain.

We are certain, however, that it is ridiculous. Maybe Ludacris could sing a song about it.

Porn stars such as Jenna Jameson and Tabitha Stevens have also given interviews for Fox hosts and anchors to discuss such newsworthy events as getting an endorsement deal with a shoe company and hosting an X-rated reality program, respectively; however, other lesser-known sex trade twinkies have been interviewed on the FNC. Serious journalist and moralist Bill O'Reilly got to get down with two X-rated starlets on his August 8, 2004 program:

> **O'REILLY:** Vivid Entertainment is a porn company that grosses more than a billion dollars a year, most of it in the USA. Now, many of us object to this industry, and I respect your opinion about it, whatever it is. So you might not want to see this next segment.
>
> The video sex business is now going mainstream into your local bookstore with a tome entitled *How to Have a XXX Sex Life*. A short time ago, I interviewed two of the authors, Sunrise Adams in LA and Savanna Samson in New York.

O'Reilly's clear and articulate questions were dutifully answered by one of the book's authors:

> **O'REILLY:** If people watch your movies, OK, why would they need to read the book? You see what I'm talking about here? If they're watching you do this stuff, why do they need to read about it?
>
> **SAVANNA SAMSON:** Well, you know, it's funny. If you can read about it—because in the book, it has examples of what we're talking about. And with the book, there's so many suggestions of what couples can do together.

Though some more sensitive viewers may have had some vague suspicions over the host's motives for conducting the interview, O'Reilly assured his audience that researching that evening's subject was a very difficult thing for him:

> **O'REILLY:** I'm a very busy guy. But anyway, I would imagine that the movies have a lot of suggestions too. Do you have more suggestions in the book than there are in the movies?

Just in case slower viewers did not catch his drift the first time, O'Reilly made sure everyone was aware that though he was *not* that kind of guy, he would still do research like a serious journalist:

> **O'REILLY:** OK, so you're just telling folks, "Here's what I like, and these guys forced me to do this in the movie... I don't particularly like it." All right, Ms. Adams, do you agree with that? See, my dilemma is this. I've got my $25, OK, and I—this is hypothetical, because I haven't seen any of your movies either, but I promise I'll try to go. I've got to get through "Shrek 2," then I'm right on to you.

Those who are associated with adult entertainment are likely to be profiled or interviewed on Fox News. Greta Van Susteren interviewed *Playboy* titan Hugh Hefner on his magazine's fiftieth aniversary, while Neil Cavuto interviewed Hef's daughter Christie. Larry Flynt made it onto "Hannity and Colmes." An attorney for the creators of *Girls Gone Wild* was interviewed by Van Susteren.

If someone somewhere is associated with on-camera sex, the vixen network will, at the very least, do a story about it. That means that even inadvertent pornographers can find themselves in the Fox News spotlight. Bill O'Reilly let viewers know how far the "Factor" crew were willing to research for this November 12, 2003 story:

Greta Van Susteren does some of the "anti-porn" interviews.

O'REILLY: "Factor" alert, this next report is not for kids.

In the "Personal Story" segment tonight, the powerful Hilton family, the hotel people are threatening to sue various people and websites in conjunction with a video showing twenty-two-year-old Paris Hilton having sex.

The "Factor" has obtained that video, but we're not going to show it to you because of taste issues.

Two days later, O'Reilly still felt compelled to report on Ms. Hilton's faux pas while simultaneously jabbing a left-wing politician for good measure:

> **O'REILLY:** In the "Personal Story" segment tonight, this may sound insignificant, but it really isn't. Sex scandals can ruin people's lives. Say somebody accuses you of sexual harassment or even worse and you're innocent. Well, the stigma of the accusation is going to be around your neck no matter what you do.
>
> Now, earlier this week, we told you about twenty-one-year-old hotel heiress Paris [Hilton] who was foolish enough to record a sex video, which is now all over the country. Her wealthy parents have threatened to sue the man in the video and now that man, Rick Solomon, has filed a $10 million lawsuit against the Hiltons, claiming they have slandered him.
>
> The question: are Americans numb to all of this in light of the Clinton-Lewinsky situation and a number of other cases out in Hollywood?

Reporting on debauchery in front of rolling cameras may seem out of place in a Foxified world, but these players are key figures: viewers can dress these characters down while still managing to steal a peak or two at the heaving cleavage and heavy breathing. It's the best of both worlds, and the FNC delivers both.

Capitalists: Since the Fox News Channel represents values that Republicans hold dear, it is no surprise that business leaders get generous FNC airtime. Capitalism is the hallmark of American society, meaning that those on almost all sides of the political spectrum have some positive feeling toward the entrepreneurial spirit. The FNC isn't overly critical in its business coverage, making its news items play like advertorials for Fortune 500 companies.

Any semblance of detachment is thrown out the window: one of Neil Cavuto's segments on his

program is brazenly entitled "Neil's Heroes." Yet questioning the "Heroes" portion of the show is treading into dangerous territory: the people profiled are those who have "made a difference" outside the boardroom. Cavuto himself became inspired after he was diagnosed with multiple sclerosis (he had battled cancer a decade earlier). Conventional wisdom dictates that news coverage about people doing good can be just as effusive without fear of criticism.

Yet the profiles seem too uncritical to be considered anything but ad copy. Cavuto's June 7, 2004 introduction was a case of a journalist falling for a source:

> **CAVUTO:** Well, you know, never underestimate the simple power of a smile or the persuasive power of a laugh. Who knew that better than Ronald Reagan, who could charm even his sharpest critics? And who knows that better than my next guest, an early Reagan backer and one of his most trusted business confidantes, and as luck would have it, one of my heroes in my book as well, *More Than Money*. The man they call Mr. Salt Lake City, and so much more, Jon Huntsman, whose own battles with cancer and difficulties show he has a bit of a touch of that Reagan grit.

The introduction was remarkable for several reasons:

◆ Praise was lavished on someone who was deeply connected to Reagan—and could afford to pay for his own public relations firm to come up with that kind of copy;

◆ A shameless plug for Reagan and Republicans was weaved into what was supposed to be a legitimate news story;

◆ The host managed to plug his own book (published by News Corp) when he was supposed to be reporting the news.

What Cavuto claimed to like about Huntsman was that he was nice to the hired help and, as Martha Stewart would say, "the little people":

> **CAVUTO:** You know, one thing we were talking [about] earlier today when we were doing a book-signing, and you were saying that how important it is to connect with people. And I noticed that the smallest people on your staff, you give them a hearty hello and you treat them very well. Remember they say Ronald Reagan knew the smallest people in the White House, down to, you know, the ushers, to the cooks, he knew them all. And I tend to believe that that is what makes a leader, not how you treat the big boys like yourself, but the folks who serve.

Cavuto managed to slip in yet another Reagan analogy:

> **CAVUTO:** You have very little turnover at your company, which is amazing. And I don't think it owes to what you pay your people, but how you treat your people. Ronald Reagan, in his administration, had very little turnover; similarity?

Cavuto also asked one guest this loaded question: "One of the inspirations for this book for me was to show that not all CEOs are rich guys or bad guys. Does it bug you [that] a lot of people lump success with bad?" In the same interview, Cavuto made certain he plugged his book: "For those who have been watching this show, I have been profiling modern day heroes from my book *More Than Money*, which is out in bookstores everywhere." Whatever you do at Fox, remember to plug your book first.

Virgin founder and CEO Richard Branson is a particular favorite of Cavuto; Branson was even dubbed one of Cavuto's "heroes" for being Branson. Cavuto's admiration of the Virgin honcho sometimes got the better of him, as it did on October 15, 2003:

> **CAVUTO:** He's one of the most successful and outrageous businessmen on the planet, building the Virgin empire, creating over a hundred companies that offer everything from music to air travel.
>
> Today, Sir Richard Branson is at it again, launching the newest company in the Virgin family. It is called Virgin Pulse. It's an electronics line that will offer top-of-the-line products for low prices. How will they weigh in with the competition?

Cavuto continued with his air kissing, though he seemed somewhat aware of it:

> **CAVUTO:** But do you worry a lot of that caché—and this isn't false praise your way—is because of you? That if there were a less hip, cool guy running the firm, maybe Virgin wouldn't carry that caché, maybe all the hot chatchkas in the world wouldn't make a difference? Let's say you've got a nerd running the firm. Then you'd be in deep trouble, right?

Months later, Cavuto would interview Branson again, but this time the Virgin founder had a direct connection with Cavuto's employer. The May 20, 2004 program not only plugged Branson, but previewed Branson's upcoming show for the Fox Network that was a near-copycat program of Donald Trump's serialized game show "The Apprentice" (though the segment made it sound as if it were way cooler than Trump's):

> **CAVUTO:** Well, think that Donald Trump knows how to pick an apprentice? Not my next guest, who is launching a new show on Fox and is doing everything Trump did not do. It is called "The Billionaire: Branson's Quest for the Best," where sixteen contestants will travel around the world to compete in physical and intellectual tasks. Earlier I spoke with Sir Richard, the founder and the chairman of the Virgin Group, and I asked him if this show is a different version of Trump's?

However, there are people and issues who can never hope to receive air kisses and lavish praise from the likes of Sean Hannity, Neil Cavuto or Bill O'Reilly—why would they? They don't fit in the Fox News mold.

Chapter 8

Enemies of the Murdochian State

"We're just having a little fun."
Roger Ailes, chairman and CEO of Fox News,
on Fox placing a billboard on top of CNN's

Hatred and anger have never been good traits for the white collar professional to possess: an angry teacher may traumatize or physically assault a student, an angry prosecutor can make errors or make a jury sympathize with a guilty defendant and an angry doctor obsessed with his personal vendettas can disable or inadvertently kill his patients. Strong emotions can not only cloud your judgment but can also make you a danger to the same people you're being paid to help.

There is a certain bitterness to the tone of some of Fox News Channel's stories. While George 43 may go into a Presidential debate looking unprepared, sneering and acting defensive, his image will get the spin treatment on the FNC and he will come out looking more certain and positively Presidential. The FNC will lovingly conceal the unsightly blemishes and enhance the image of their favorite Republicans with a few deft masterstrokes.

On the other hand, for Kerry and other Democrats and progressives, FNC prefers to put away the airbrushes and air-kisses and instead smear these folks with grease paint; the hostile coverage of the left-of-center is littered with obnoxious and snide remarks. Professional reporters don't rely on cutting remarks and rudeness in lieu of research, but rudeness is encouraged at the FNC. In one March 23, 2003 Fox News memo, John Moody warned Fox's anchors and hosts to knock it off with the pleasantries:

ON AIR TALENT: COULD WE MAKE AN EFFORT TO CUT DOWN ON MOUTH CANDY WHEN GETTING OUT OF GUEST SEGMENTS, SUCH AS, "WE APPRECIATE YOUR PERSPECTIVE."

The "mouth candy" ban seems to only apply to those whose perspective isn't quite appreciated at the FNC. After all, why remind the viewers at home that what they just heard is only a "perspective" and not fact? But playing favorites isn't exactly a new phenomenon: teachers do it, coaches do it, even parents do it. The kiddie question of who Mom really likes best goes right to the main problem, that the FNC is a "fair and balanced" news outfit; while brass can claim they treat all newsmakers the same way, their behavior says otherwise. George W. Bush may be on top of the vixen network's heartthrob list, but not everyone gets the kid gloves treatment. For example, one of Bill O'Reilly's "Talking Points memos" in February 2003 revealed that one "Villain of the Week" was none other than:

> [...A]uthor Norman Mailer, who, once again, [is] promoting a book by bashing anyone who disagrees with his left-wing point of view. On the publicity circuit, Mailer has compared President Bush to a drug dealer. Isn't that nice? He has praised the sexual shenanigans of President Clinton and generally attacked American policy from soup to nuts.

In case anyone wanted to accuse O'Reilly of being an uneducated and ignorant boor who did not know what he was talking about, the "Factor" host cut his critics off at the pass with this little add-on:

> You know, Norman, *The Naked and the Dead* was a great book. *Ancient Evenings*, unreadable. Grandstanding your highly permissive views is fine. Calling the President a dope dealer is irresponsible. So you are the Villain of the Week.
>
> Congratulations.

So, who are the unlucky souls who can expect to be harassed, ridiculed and teased by FNC bullies on the television playground, and what exactly are their crimes? For some, their crimes are very real: the FNC doesn't like terrorists or child molesters. However, for others, they are mixed in with the degenerates even though they have done nothing to harm or degrade another being. As John Nichols noted, "if you watch Fox on a regular basis, you will come to the conclusion that America is teetering on the edge of a collapse into a Sodom and Gomorrah disaster that would really pretty much be the end of the country. It's just moments away from child molesters, gays and lesbians, abortionists and Democrats taking power."

And even audiences of progressives are subject to insults and dismissal. Bill O'Reilly gave his own description of the "Daily Show" host Jon Stewart's demographic on the September 17, 2004 edition of the "O'Reilly Factor":

O'REILLY: Come on, you do the research, you know the research on your program.

STEWART: No, we don't.

O'REILLY: Eighty-seven percent are intoxicated when they watch it. You didn't see that?

STEWART: No, I didn't realize that.

O'REILLY: Yeah, we have that there.

O'Reilly must have thought his audience was too dense to remember that Stewart's audience should be roundly dismissed, so the considerate O'Reilly reminded them:

O'REILLY: You can't stop them.

STEWART: Yeah, I just don't know how motivated they would be, these stoned slackers.

O'REILLY: Yeah, it just depends if they have to go out that day.

STEWART: What am I, a Cheech and Chong movie? Stoned slackers?

As if two reminders were not enough, O'Reilly then asked Stewart: "Do you think that Kerry does himself any good talking to you? Because I think most of your audience is going to vote for him anyway, aren't they?... The stoned slackers." Whether O'Reilly believed his viewers suffered from Korsakoff's amnesia wasn't explicitly mentioned, but the fact that he repeated the "stoned slacker" bit several times pointed out that the "Factor" host had a low opinion of his audience, as well.

When the Name Doesn't Fit the Goods

While journalistic objectivity didn't exactly fulfill its role as an emotional or ethical check, it did at least remind those in the profession to try to observe their surroundings with a critical eye, and to remember that every issue has at least two sides. Where journalistic objectivity failed was that journalists decided that most issues only had two sides, and that they were opposed to each other in every way: a capitalist had to be opposed by an activist, a Democrat had to be opposed by a Republican, a hero had to be opposed by a villain. It became easy for readers and viewers to dismiss the side they disagreed with, since reporters offered a forced choice in their stories. After all, the two had to be at odds with each other for a reason: they had opposing values and goals. Though many journalists tried not to present the sides as in conflict (or if they did assign blame, they used the standard "a plague on both their houses" approach), in many respects, some stories inevitably became tales of us versus them, right versus wrong, good versus evil.

It is this little tenet of journalistic objectivity that the FNC seems to love best: it can present only two sides to an issue and then assign the opposing labels as the network sees fit. That way, the fair and balanced network can almost live up to its motto: balance implies weighing two sides and fairness implies leveling the playing field at the expense of the person who has the advantage, meaning that any and all natural or earned blessings are taken away. What's left is a distortion of the real picture.

While the FNC is exceedingly fair to right-of-center politicians and pundits, it is fair at the expense of moderates and progressives. In the Murdochian kingdom, the valiant Fox News knights in shining armor have decided that righties are the weaker side and have a disadvantage in the media, and now have taken it upon themselves to balance out the coverage by overprotecting their ideological damsels in distress. But why does this supposed Republican damsel need protection, and from whom? Since the damsel is one side of the story, it stands to reason that the "other" side is the villain and the dragon the FNC knights need to slay, or at the very least, keep at bay. By convenient default, the "other side" are the progressives and Democrats. Norman Mailer and stoner slackers who watch Jon Stewart may be on the FNC hit list, but they are in good company: everyone from former two-term Presidents to civil rights leaders also finds themselves the enemies of the Murdochian state.

Those Damned Democrats

Affirming that your ideologies lie left-of-center is a dangerous declaration to make in the Murdochian kingdom. In fact, Fox News is wary of those who lean anywhere away from the right, even if they are merely resting their left shoulders against the wall. They never know if that is an act of political defiance or mere physical convenience. Democrats' every action is scrutinized and ultimately declared to be unacceptable in a Foxified world. For example, a December 7, 2001 roundtable discussion with Brit Hume included the standard issue Republican kudos:

> **MORTON KONDRACKE:** I must say that I don't see the give here, on anybody's side. And the longer time goes on, the more in deadlock they become. And you know, on the Republican side, I think that they're looking at some favorable indicators aside from the unemployment numbers, that purchasing orders, or their purchasing managers have said that inventories are down, therefore there's reason to think that the economy will be back earlier next year.

...but then Beltway boy Fred Barnes was his typical anti-Democrat self when he discussed the "other side" of the issue:

> **FRED BARNES:** No stimulus. And I thought before [that] there would be one. I mean, and look, I took it as good news that it broke up today. We already [have] plenty of stimulus from the unprecedented rate cuts by the Federal Reserve. This enormous tax cut across the board for everyone. Gasoline prices are sinking like crazy—I got some down in Virginia for 95.9 the other day. I thought that was pretty good. You get outside Washington and gas doesn't cost that much.
>
> So we really don't need one. And Republicans—Mort's exactly right.
>
> Republicans now realize we don't need it. Why do we have to accept all that Democrat spending? And they don't.

He then ended by declaring that the Republicans were in the right, if the facts were interpreted to his own liking:

> **BARNES:** I'm not sure politically it's needed. I mean, you cited the unemployment figures. Unemployment is always a lagging indicator. What is a forward looking indicator is the stock market. Now, the stock market is rallied, not on the basis of spectacular economic news. I think it's the leading edge in this recovery, which may come sooner than we thought.

Unfortunately, Democrats do not get such thoughtful considerations; Democrats are just plain wrong, and their arguments have to *appear* wrong to the FNC viewer. One way to ensure that those arguments sound wrong is by making certain less persuasive Democrats are allowed to open their

mouths on FNC, as one former Fox employee recalled:

> My experience with guests is that if a guest is a Democrat [who is] very sharp, very aggressive, Fox management tends to not like them because it's somebody who essentially can compete, or it's somebody who makes their point so effectively that they come across as annoying or irritating to the guest bookers or to management; whereas if it's somebody who is a "nice" Democrat; somebody who can sort of see the other side's point of view, but can sort of quietly and calmly make their point of view known, that's a terrific guest for Fox News because they're a Democrat, they're a liberal and they're nice and polite. Never mind that the Republican or the conservative they're put up against is a pugnacious rabble-rouser, a beat-him-over-the-head Ann Coulter-type [...] If you're a Democrat, you got to be nice and polite; if you're a Republican, it makes for better TV if you're an attack dog because that's what [Fox] viewers want.

Another former Fox employee recalled how the Fox News Channel's choice of stories also helped contribute to the negative view of the anti-Republican:

> [...] Certain stories that made fun of "flaky" Democrat types... Anything like that would be assigned or encouraged. Make fun of certain type[s] of Senators, reinforce certain stereotypes.

The Democratic stereotype is simple: a weak, flaky flip-flopper who loves to increase taxes and embrace the lunatic fringe. The FNC uses several permutations of the cliché for several of the DNC's most prominent politicos.

John Kerry: Impeccable cuticles.

John Kerry:
When Hard Military Service Makes You a
French-Looking, Weak and Flip-Flopping Pretty Boy

Most military veterans can expect a warm welcome on Fox, complete with effusive praise and deference. Fox News loves a good general or decorated soldier. These people are the symbol of a country's strength and dedication, and thus they are readily exploited by the FNC to help maintain their patriotic image. Even U.S. troops serving in Iraq will be repeatedly praised by both reporters and anchors alike. As a general rule, warriors are the FNC's shorthand for American greatness.

War heroes are a special breed of warrior: these are the men and women who looked death in the face and still managed to do something more heroic than their comrades. The FNC loves a war hero— unless, of course, the war hero in question happens to be a Democrat. Further marks are docked if the Democrat war hero is running for President. John Forbes Kerry may have fought in Viet Nam and even have come home with some lovely parting gifts in the form of medals, but he still couldn't get a fair shake from the FNC when he decided to go up against their heartthrob, George W. Bush.

The FNC's differing approaches to both Bush and Kerry during the 2004 Presidential race were most evident in the curt way they dealt with the Democratic contender. As James Wolcott observed, Kerry couldn't manage to get the same FNC face time as his competitor:

> [Fox News] will give you almost the full Bush stump speech no matter where it is and no matter how many times they've shown it. They cut live to these campaign rallies as if there was going to be real news in them, as if Bush was going to say anything earth-shattering. And it's always the same thing, "we believe in freedom," "we love freedom," "Americans love freedom," "terrorists hate freedom; that's why they hate us." And we get this two or three times a week because Bush is always doing fundraisers. It's true, Kerry gets a sliver of time...

Kerry's speeches didn't seem particularly important to Moody, at least that's the impression one gets from reading his memos:

◆ On April 6, 2004: "Kerry's speech on the economy at Georgetown is likely to move onto the topic of Iraq. We should take the beginning of Kerry's speech, see if it contains new information (aside from a promise to create ten million jobs) and see if other news at that time is more compelling. It is not required to take it start to finish."

◆ On April 29, 2004: "[...] John Kerry addresses the Black Mayors conference in Philly. We should take some of that live, until it reverts to stump stuff."

Kerry could do no right: sure, he may have shifted his position on certain issues, as do most politicians, but he would be singled out for his waffling while Bush's waffling was dismissed as merely a change of mind. As Moody mused to his minions in a March 16, 2004 memo:

> Kerry, starting to feel the heat for his flip-flop voting record, is in West Virginia. There's a near-meaningless primary in Illinois.

Reporters, hosts and anchors took Moody's "flip-flop" cue to heart, particularly militarily inexperienced news dandy Sean Hannity who seemed to be the worst FNC offender. Some of the low lights of the "Kerry as gasping fish analogy" included the following gems:

◆ Sean Hannity on March 30, 2004: "How could John Kerry first of all flip-flop from just two years ago. He's flip-flopped on every major issue."

◆ Morton Kondracke on February 14, 2004: "Kerry is trying to deal with two flip-flops on this issue, saying that he's against gay marriage while opposing a ban on them, and saying that it's up to the states to decide, but then voting against the Defense of Marriage Act, which would do just that."

◆ Sean Hannity on March 22, 2004: "Here's what he said, and it just characterizes what a flip-flopper he is."

♦ Sean Hannity on April 16, 2004: "John Kerry has flipped and flopped on just about every issue. Here's a guy who's had seven different positions on Iraq."

♦ Hannity on July 22, 2004: "And here's what bothers me. You have a candidate, John Kerry, who has flip-flopped all over the place, not only on Iraq, but on every other issue. He does not have a core."

♦ On May 21, 2004: "Does John Kerry lie? Does John Kerry flip-flop?"

♦ On August 25, 2004: "After the first Trade Center bombing, he proposed those $6 billion in cuts in the intelligence community. And then the flip-flopping all over Iraq."

♦ On July 30, 2004: "You know, it was amazing, too, that you talk about Kerry the flip-flopper. You know, he says 'We have to get away from the politics of personal destruction' and repeatedly insinuated or suggested the President's a liar. Which is just in true Kerry form. I want to run this tape. He's trying to, in spite of a record that is weak on national defense, Pat, he has been voting against most major weapons systems we used."

♦ Tony Snow on March 1, 2004: "John Kerry is... a guy who really doesn't know who he is. My theory is the one authentic period of his life were those four months in Vietnam, where he seemed to find himself. Otherwise, a lot of his life has been cautious posturing. And so you're going to find him on both sides of just about every issue, I guarantee you. The flip-flop is also going to be a hardy perennial in the Republican strategy for this year."

♦ Bill O'Reilly on July 29, 2004: "But is Kerry just—is he a flip-flopper, or is he just a guy who sees every side of the problem and votes whatever the situation ethic is?"

♦ John Kasich on February 11, 2004: "Senator Kerry's, you know, he's flipping and flopping."

Sean Hannity on January 27, 2004: "He has flip-flopped on Iraq, on No Child Left Behind, on a whole series of... the Patriot Act, supports it, criticizes it, supports it, criticizes it."

♦ On September 2, 2004, Brian Wilson included this kicker from the Republican convention in New York City:

WILSON: Then I learned something I didn't know. One Republican explained this is actually political commentary aimed at Democratic opponent John Kerry. It's the...

UNIDENTIFIED MALE: Flip-flop dance.

WILSON: Oh, well, maybe that explains it.

John Gibson may not have used the word "flip-flop" on August 18, 2004 to describe Kerry, but the sentiment was clearly there:

> John Kerry couldn't manage to get the same FNC face time as George W. Bush.

GIBSON: Senator Kerry explained why he is against the President's plan to withdraw 70,000 troops from Asia and Europe. Kerry also announced he'd like to add 40,000 troops to our forces worldwide. But two weeks ago, Kerry said, quote, "I think we can significantly change the deployment of troops, not just in Iraq, but elsewhere in the world, in the Korean peninsula, perhaps, in Europe perhaps." Sounds a bit like the President's plan, which he's now criticizing.

Joining me in Portland, Oregon, retired U.S. Air Force General Merrill McPeak. He is an advisor to the Kerry campaign. So General, that does sounds a little bit like two weeks ago, Kerry was more or less for what the President's proposing now.

Gibson's military guest, not surprisingly, was more than glad to concur with the Fox News host:

GENERAL MERRILL MCPEAK: Well, John, this administration has a real talent for doing the right thing in absolutely the wrong way. I think what the Senator has said is that this is the wrong time to do this and the wrong way to do it even if, in principle, some of it may be right. But he's also indicated that it's not right. I mean, you figure out why we're reducing our troop strength 25% on the Korean peninsula.

Various Republican guests on Fox—from failed Presidential candidate Elizabeth Dole ("I think that's a rather big flip-flop on the part of the head of the ticket") to right-wing pundit Laura Ingraham ("I think this is just one of a myriad of flip-flops that John Kerry is having a difficult time explaining") to even Bush's Chief Political Strategist Matthew Dowd ("So no longer is he just flip-flopping from day to day. He's flip-flopping in a fifty-two-minute speech") all described Kerry as a flip flopper without challenge from the Fox News kids. The "flip flop" brigade all sounded as if they were reading from a prepared script, just as a group of neighborhood thugs pick a mark and then all chime in with the same put-down. The "flip flop" tag may not have been the most creative put-down, but the snowballing effect would stick to the Senator.

Yet Kerry would face other insults from the GOP Fan Club. The word "weak" was also linked to Kerry on numerous occasions:

- ◆ Sean Hannity on February 18, 2004: "Tell me if you think my interpretation is wrong on what happened in the results last night in Wisconsin. I think this shows that John Kerry is weak in the party. Because first of all, I don't think he would have won this nomination or would be winning these primaries had Howard Dean not imploded first."

- ◆ Carl Cameron on June 1, 2004: "Republicans... say John Kerry is weak on security and has laid out a series of goals that everybody agrees to without any concrete plans to get there."

- ◆ Sean Hannity on April 28, 2004: "One of the—one of the criticisms the President and

Vice President and the Republicans are making against John Kerry is that he's weak on defense and he's weak on intelligence."

◆ Guest Rep. Duncan Hunter on August 11, 2004: "John Kerry has had a very weak voting record on national security."

◆ Sean Hannity on March 1, 2004: "John Kerry will raise taxes. John Kerry is weak on intelligence, and on military issues. And here are the specific votes. Here is where he was throughout history."

Kerry was also seen as dishonest or, as Hannity opined on March 11, 2004, "The Kerry, you know, Kool-Aid people that just lie and say anything, like we just heard, frankly, it was just a total misrepresentation." Kerry was also considered to be something of a dandy to those homely Foxians who seem to prefer slobs to those who take some pride in their appearance. During the first Presidential debate between contender Kerry and Fox News favorite George W. Bush, the consensus was that Kerry won the debate, while Bush seemed defensive, bored and unprepared, but did the FNC see it that way? Well, they saw something, alright: Kerry's fingernails.

Apparently, those ADHD sufferers over at Fox News were too busy scrutinizing Mr. Kerry's cuticles and made comments about their deep and relevant observations, as serious news anchor Brit Hume did to flighty moderate Susan Estrich on September 30, 2004:

HUME: And the manicure.

ESTRICH: The manicure! Help me with the manicure. (LAUGHTER)

HUME: I've had a manicure in my life. It was a rather pleasant experience. But do you think it was the thing to do today, perhaps?

ESTRICH: No! No! No! Look, I get my nails done all the time. I mean I'm a fool for manicures. But obviously, what John Kerry needs to do tonight, among other things, is make a connection with average working people. And probably the way to start doing that is not with a manicure. Now, you've had them. But my guess is most men don't stop on their way to an important event with a manicure.

Oh, and he apparently doesn't look at all like your typical New England native. According to some FNC anchors, Kerry looks French but, then again, due to the vanity or economic hardship of being an FNC employee, they may not be able to buy themselves badly needed prescription eye glasses. But any real or perceived chink in Kerry's armor was fair game for Fox News. When there was controversy swirling over Kerry's antiwar activist past and its consequences, the FNC made sure to give it prominent play. In one April 2004 memo from John Moody, he asked this question to his underlings:

Ribbons or medals? Which did John Kerry throw away after he returned from Viet Nam? This may become an issue for him today. His perceived disrespect for the military could be more damaging to the candidate than questions about his actions in uniform.

Kerry's medals were the topic on the April 26, 2004 edition of "Hannity and Colmes":

> **HANNITY:** [...T]his is an important issue for me, because it goes to the heart of whether or not he's an honest man. And I have every belief—he said in the *Los Angeles Times* just this past week, John, he said he never claimed to have thrown his own medals—his own medals. "I never implied that. I never implied that I did that." Clearly contradicting himself. And he has several other stories in between. What do you make [of] all of these contradictions?

This was again the topic of conversation on "Hannity and Colmes" the following evening:

> **HANNITY:** I'm not going to ask you about George W. Bush. I want a direct answer. Here is my point. John Kerry said last week in the *Los Angeles Times*, that he never said he threw his medals. And then this tape emerges from "Good Morning America" that contradicts that. In between we found that he gave four separate, differing versions on the medal controversy.

Why should Americans believe him when he so contradicted himself?

> **No matter what Kerry did or didn't do, he's a shady figure who is not to be trusted in the Fox News world.**

Bill Clinton: The Anti-Bush

If what the Fox News Channel portrayed was true, then former President William Jefferson Clinton was, as John Nichols referred to him, a "sex criminal... Fox found something he was doing wrong every day and they savaged him." Dave Korb, a former freelance news writer for the FNC, recalled that staff were only "to take stories about Clinton when he makes an ass out of himself." Hannity and Colmes had the pleasure of interviewing Gennifer Flowers a year after Clinton admitted to having an inappropriate relationship with Monica Lewinsky. When he faced impeachment over his alleged perjury over his denial of his affair with Lewinsky, the FNC was there, bringing viewers the latest intimate detail and then throwing it in the President's face. For example, on the March 8, 1999 edition of "Special Report," the roundtable discussion focused on Clinton's apparent truth dyslexia:

> **HUME:** All right. That's certainly true. What does everybody think is sort of the net political effect here now of the post-impeachment events? You've had the Juanita Broaddrick charges, which, as Michael Barone was noting earlier, a lot of people found quite credible, followed now by the Monica Lewinsky interview, in which she seems generally to have gotten negative reviews from the public if the polls can be believed. Now you have this—these declarations by George Stephanopoulos that, you know, he thought the President was a liar. Has it—has this affected the atmosphere in any way? Has it changed since the impeachment trial ended?

> **JEFFREY BIRNBAUM:** Yes, I think—I was expecting that after the President was acquitted in the impeachment trial that there would be, in effect, a round of applause for him in the polls, and that he would benefit greatly by being vindicated, finally, after being...

HUME: I would say, quote, "vindicated."

BIRNBAUM: Quote, "vindicated." At least relatively...

HUME: He was cleared, sort of.

Even though Clinton's second term was completed by 2000, his character still got a whumping from the Fox News kids. When his 2004 autobiography *My Life* hit bookstores, Sean Hannity had no kind words to offer. From his June 21 program:

> **LANNY DAVIS:** But nobody that I knew was interested in impeaching Bill Clinton because of a personal relationship or personal failings. It had to do with...
>
> **HANNITY:** It had to do with lying under oath as the chief law enforcement officer, Congressman. Good to see you again. Thanks for being with us. And Lanny, Lanny, Lanny, how are you? You just left Bill Clinton, didn't you?
>
> **DAVIS:** I just left a big audience where he was speaking on the book party launching this great book.
>
> **HANNITY:** He loves this. It's all about me; it's all about me. He loves this. This is great for him.
>
> **DAVIS:** An autobiography is, by definition.
>
> **HANNITY:** *My Life*, me, me, I, I, I. All right. Let's forget about what the right-wing conspiracy thinks. Let's go to the *New York Times*, your beloved *New York Times* that reviewed Mr. Clinton's book. Let's put up on the screen some of what it said.

Hannity then went on to tell a "crazed" Davis that the *Times* panned the tome. Interestingly, if the *Times* had lauded the former President's literary efforts, Hannity would have most likely claimed the positive review was a direct result of the paper's "liberal" view, yet its thumbs down didn't seem to show that the *Times* was an objective paper. But just as the *Times* can't win, neither could Clinton: he, too, was vain like Kerry, according to the FNC—and neither could he be trusted.

Hillary Clinton

The former First Lady and New York Senator was also a regular target of scorn and derision on the FNC, both in and out of the White House. Like her husband, her credibility is considered nonexistent according to Fox News. Her 2003 autobiography *Living History* was fodder for criticism on various FNC programs. Bill O'Reilly began his strategic attack on Bill Clinton's better half on his June 5 program:

> **O'REILLY:** [...T]his is an important story because Senator Clinton is the most powerful Democrat in the country right now, and is very hard to define because she's so guarded about everything. It's not like the press has access to Hillary Clinton. We don't. She answers to no one. So, when she writes a book, it is fodder for the press, especially because there are doubts about the woman's honesty and because she may be elected President in five years.

Persistent rumors that O'Reilly himself is toying with eventually running against Clinton in the

New York Senate race makes his set up particularly interesting. But before viewers could ponder their hero's motives for his "Talking Points" memo, he went on to discuss his latest complaint against the Senator:

> **O'REILLY:** Hillary Clinton claims to have been shocked when her husband admitted the Lewinsky episode. She paints herself as a betrayed wife and a victim of Bill Clinton's lies and deceits. But just one day before Senator Clinton says her husband confessed, a front page *New York Times* headline glared, "President Weighs Admitting He Had Sexual Contacts." In the following article, this statement, "President Clinton has had extensive discussions with his inner circle about a strategy of acknowledging to a grand jury that he had intimate sexual encounters with Monica S. Lewinsky." Surely Mrs. Clinton would have been alerted to that article.

He then went on to discuss the apparent discrepancies between her words and what he saw as proof that she really knew:

> **O'REILLY:** So, it's kind of hard to imagine her being awakened by her husband a day later and her being shocked. Also, the dress scandal had been... out [... I]t speaks to honesty. You remember that Senator Clinton testified she did not remember key elements of the Whitewater mess or the Travelgate debacle, yet she has enough to recall to put out a 500-page book.

Finally, O'Reilly connected the dots for his viewers:

> **O'REILLY:** So, once again, "Talking Points" must conclude that Senator Clinton is not a truthful person. I could be wrong. I can't read minds. I simply know that I want the President of the United States, whoever it is, to be an honest person. And so should all-Americans.

Those who defend or refuse to besmirch Clinton also find themselves the target of FNC scorn. David Brock, one time right-wing journalist darling who made the mistake of not tearing Clinton to shreds in his biography, recalled how he tackled his book:

> The approach of the book, which was to treat Hillary Clinton like a human being and, from my point of view, being inside the conservative movement, there was no toleration for any fairness or balance or any kind of accuracy toward Hillary Clinton at that time, and we're talking 1996.

Brock's appearance on O'Reilly's program was not the trouble-free interview he was expecting:

> He was grilling me in a hostile fashion... I don't know that I was treated much differently, and this seems to be his manner of interviewing, but certainly, even though I was still working at the *American Spectator* and had a conservative reputation, he was very skeptical about the book and grilled me about that.

Though O'Reilly still didn't have the attack dog reputation he enjoys today, Brock recalled that he "was taken aback a bit by how challenging and hostile he was." When it comes to the former First Lady, the Fox News kids won't see her as anything else but a clay pigeon.

Al Gore

The former Vice President has also been an unwelcome guest in the Murdochian kingdom, particularly since his controversial 2000 White House loss to FNC darling Bush. Gore is an unfriendly reminder that the forty-third President of the United States wasn't the decided choice among voters; in fact, Bush won the presidency even though fewer voters cast their ballots for him than Gore. The FNC seems to go out of their way to portray the former veep as an unstable airhead who deserved to lose out on the presidency. For instance, Sean Hannity once scolded one guest that, "You ought to be ashamed at a former Vice President while we're at war talking about the President betraying the country."

When Gore criticized Bush's handling of Iraq, he was accused of acting like an extremist ideologue, on the May 26, 2004 edition of the "O'Reilly Factor":

> **O'REILLY:** I do think that Gore's making a fundamental mistake by allying himself with the far left. Moveon.org and a lot of the bomb throwers that hang around in that area [are] using words like "betrayed his country," Gore actually called Bush a "moral coward."
>
> Now that's offensive to a lot of people, not just Bush supporters. The commander in chief in the middle of a war on terror, you're getting Al Gore saying he's a moral coward. That is Michael Moore kind of stuff. And I think that Gore has gone way to the left.

Gore's mere presence is a rude reminder that Bush, Jr.'s rise to power was decided in a courtroom and not at the ballot. To ridicule him is the FNC's way of trying to airbrush the ugly and bleary beginnings of the Bush 43 presidency.

Jesse Jackson

Though he is not a politician, activist Jesse Jackson is strongly aligned with the Democratic party. His bid to become President ended in failure, but his outspoken nature has not endeared him to the FNC, and the network seems to take pleasure in humiliating him. Former FNC reporter Jon Du Pre recalled how the newsroom viewed Jackson:

> Fox News Channel's stated practice was to embarrass, humiliate, challenge or disrupt whatever Jesse Jackson did. But we were told by our bureau chief on many occasions that the Reverend Jesse Jackson was one of our targets.

And a frequent target at that. Jackson's strong antiwar views got him a Hannity harangue on the April 27, 2004 edition of "Hannity and Colmes":

> **HANNITY:** A speech in Boston earlier this month has landed the Reverend Jesse Jackson in the middle of another controversy.
>
> According to the *Boston Herald*, Jesse Jackson said that the United Nations should consider sanctioning the U.S. for the decision to "murder all of these

people on faulty information" by waging war in Iraq.

Jackson went on to say that the U.S. invasion of Iraq is a crime against the Iraqis, because they're human beings, too. And we killed them and we executed people on this flawed policy.

And has Jesse Jackson finally gone too far?

O'Reilly also got his digs in on his January 16, 2003 program:

> **O'REILLY:** In fact, if Americans are forced to pay reparations, the racial backlash would be tremendous against blacks. That backlash would fuel bigotry and divide the country. But Jesse Jackson doesn't care. He wants the country divided. The only thing he has to offer is the promise of entitlements to a poor constituency.

A couple of months later, O'Reilly also ridiculed Jackson for his remarks regarding recalled California ex-Governor Gray Davis on April 13, 2003:

> **O'REILLY:** Time now for the "Most Ridiculous Item of the Day." Our pal, Jesse Jackson, has weighed in on the California recall. Says Jackson, quote, "Governor Davis is guilty of no crime, no malfeasance in office, nothing that would warrant impeachment or removal. If anything, he is a victim of circumstance and of George W. Bush." So, according to Jackson, who's supposed to be nonpartisan because two of his organizations are tax exempt, President Bush is the reason Davis bankrupted California.
>
> Ridiculous doesn't even come close.

O'Reilly must have liked this tirade against Jackson so much, he used a similarly worded one on April 26, 2004:

> **O'REILLY:** "Unresolved problems" tonight, we continue to get reports that our pal, Jesse Jackson, is using his power in dubious ways. As always, we like to speak with the Reverend, but he remains elusive.
>
> The latest controversy concerns the Coca-Cola company's continued monetary support of Jackson. Joining us now from Washington, Peter Flaherty, president of the National Legal and Policy Center, a conservative watchdog group.
>
> All right, let me set this up. Jackson has had innings with Coca-Cola before. In the year 2000, it was a $1.5 billion discrimination class action lawsuit filed on behalf of African-American Coca-Cola employees.
>
> Jackson got involved. Coke settled for $192 million. You figure Jackson got a piece of that. Do you know how much, Mr. Flaherty, that he got out of that?

> **PETER FLAHERTY:** No, I don't.

Jackson has been dodging FNC cream pies for years; but with each taunt, the cumulative effect makes him seem that much more controversial and embattled. He is roundly dismissed by the Fox News kids, and he may have a hard time gaining credibility from regular FNC viewers because of it.

Monica Lewinsky

The former White House intern and Clinton mistress may be old gossip in the news world, but she is still an object of ridicule at the FNC, not because of her political beliefs or that she yields an ounce of influence, but because she dallied with the married Bill Clinton. Since Lewinsky fooled around with a Democrat, Fox News brass consider her to be a woman with absolutely no taste in men and hence she deserves all the psychological ribbing she gets. The April 21, 2003 edition of the "O'Reilly Factor" yet again threw the former intern's past in her face:

> **O'REILLY:** Time now for the "Most Ridiculous Item of the Day." Our pal, Monica Lewinsky, has a new program on the Fox network. Does that surprise you? Ms. Lewinsky is the host of a dating show called "Mr. Personality." I have nothing to do with this. And it begins this evening.
>
> Now I don't wish ill for Monica. I don't know her. She looks like a nice person. That's not her kissing a guy. I don't know who that is. I don't know who that is.
>
> But come on. The only reason she's on television is because of her oral skills, and those have nothing to do with speaking, if you get my drift.
>
> So this is just another example of how tawdry behavior is rewarded in our society, which, of course, is ridiculous.

Though Lewinsky is not a powerful or influential force, she can still expect to get a punch in the teeth at the FNC: she is a fantastic reminder of Bill Clinton's shame, and she serves as a living maxim that girls who show their thongs to Democrats will be swiftly spanked by the gods for finding a Democrat arousing. Even though Lewinsky was employed by another News Corp property, her association with a Democrat makes her prime fodder for FNC taunts.

The Hollywood Scuffle

Even though the Fox News Channel is owned by the same company that owns Fox studios and the Fox network, they don't seem happy in the presence of Tinsel Town denizens, probably since many of them are outspoken about their progressive beliefs. Left-wing actors, singers and directors are particularly galling: they're rich, beautiful, talented, adored and successful—and they're not Republicans. The shame and the horror! That the world's most admired and desired people go against every FNC rule doesn't seem to clue in the Murdochian minions that perhaps their theories may be flawed. Fox News still tries to make the beautiful people seem less attractive. One former Fox employee recalled that there were "certain stories that made fun of 'flaky' Democrat types [such as] Barbra Streisand kind of actors. Anything like that would be assigned or encouraged."

Of course, it is completely outrageous that entertainers, who pay taxes and vote, would express their political beliefs in a public forum. On the one hand, citizens are encouraged to get involved in the political process; on the other hand, when entertainers get involved, the FNC demands that they keep silent, as if they weren't American citizens. Fox News slags off actors for wanting to engage themselves in the Democratic process, but never dares to ask whether the reason those very entertainers and directors were successful in their professional lives in the first place was precisely because they were alert and passionately cared about the world around them.

When one of the Dixie Chicks made comments that she was against the U.S. war in Iraq and that she was ashamed of President Bush, the April 3, 2003 edition of the "O'Reilly Factor" relished the backlash:

America's last line of defense from the Dixie Chicks.

O'REILLY: After that controversy, record sales for the Chicks went way down.

There have been some demonstrations against them.

Now we offered a forum to Ms. Maines to explain the situation, you know, come on the "Factor" and talk to you, and she said, no way, which was a very foolish thing for her to do.

Joining us now from Atlanta is country singer Travis Tritt, who sees things differently than Ms. Maines and knows her and knows the situation.

I—you know, if I were [Natalie] Maines, I mean, just from my own image, I would come on this program and other programs and say, look, here's what I meant. I'm sorry. She did issue a statement, but that's not good enough. Why doesn't—why is she doing that?

The presumptuous Tritt assumed Maines was a politically illiterate little girl:

TRAVIS TRITT: Well, you know what? I think one of the reasons that this whole statement was made and things were handled the way that they were has a lot to do with, first of all, the age of Natalie Maines. She's a fairly young person.

She's probably not ever spent any time following politics, following foreign policy, following this administration at all and, you know, it's very easy when you're in an entertainment position to get caught up in the moment and, obviously, she was overseas, and, you know, the statements were made.

The fact is—I think, had she just come out and said, look, you know, I'm very young, I never really have followed politics...

O'REILLY: Sure.

Actors who have spoken out against the war were also caught in the FNC crosshairs: whether these performers may have a legitimate point and the right to express it isn't an issue in a Foxified world.

Damn Foreigners

Non-Americans, for the most part, don't fare well on the FNC: for one, they, by Fox News' definition, will always be inferior to Americans. Second, they are outsiders who may not hold the same values as the intellectually limited FNC. Third, there is always a chance another country may exploit or

harm U.S. citizens. Outsiders may be more or less tolerable, depending on how closely they agree with Fox News dogma.

If it looks as if an outsider might be leeching on the U.S., they are fair FNC game, as shown on the January 9, 2003 edition of the "O'Reilly Factor":

> **O'REILLY:** In the "Unresolved Problem" tonight, the "Factor" continues its investigation into crimes committed by illegal aliens.
>
> In the State of California, 12% of people behind bars are undocumented illegal aliens. In Texas and Arizona, 8% are illegal aliens.
>
> Most of those criminals are Mexican nationals. The Center for Immigration Studies estimates there are more than three million of them currently in the United States, and 31% of Mexican immigrants receive some kind of welfare from the United States government.
>
> And, in major cities like Los Angeles, New York and Chicago, local authorities do not inform the INS when an illegal alien is arrested, if you can believe it.

When one former Fox News reporter wanted to do a positive story on immigration, he found out the hard way that a Foxified world does not allow for the praising of outsiders:

> I did a piece on immigration... and how inspiring it was because these folks had to go through a lot to get their citizenship earned, not born, suggesting that they really want citizenship because they got to go through all these motions. It's not an easy thing. Well, the guy who was managing editor at the time called me from New York and he said very angrily, "What have these people earned? They haven't earned a thing. They're just here for the free ride; they're just here trying to take advantage of all our freebies."

The former FNC journalist was left shaken by the encounter:

> I had put a lot of time and energy into this [story] and I thought it was poignant to tell the stories of these people and all the things that they had to go through to get citizenship and how we take for granted how really blessed we are to be born with it. Nonetheless, I was really blown away by the approach he took.

Canadians are also untrustworthy creatures in the Fox News world (why they're so calculatedly reviled is discussed in Chapter 16). They are considered too leftist, lackadaisical and lippy to be trusted, as shown on the April 16, 2003 edition of the "O'Reilly Factor":

> **O'REILLY:** Canada is utterly dependent on the USA for its economic well being, as we know. Nine million Americans cross into Canada more than 40 million times each year. We spend at least $10 billion [on] this annually and [are] taxed billions more by the socialistic government. So, if we stop going north, Canadians will fall into a depression, not a recession, a depression.

O'Reilly's rant against the nation's former Prime Minister, who he mentioned by name, proved that the "Factor" kahuna can Google like a pro:

Jean Chretien will leave office in February 2004, and the world can only hope a more responsible leader will emerge. Canadians are generally good people. The country has been a loyal ally of the USA in the past, and perhaps Chretien is simply a misguided soul.

But then again, maybe Canada has changed its worldview and cannot be considered a friend any longer. If that's the case, I will make this forecast—it will get much colder up there.

France's opposition to the Iraq war and its refusal to play along got the European nation into the FNC's permanent bad books. In a March 12, 2004 memo, John Moody made his anger toward the nation known:

Spain's neighbor, the ever-superior France, had its own spate of railway terrorist warnings last week, though it's not clear that those were in any way related to the Madrid bombings.

The memo framed the war in a way that not only justified the invasion, but also cast a wary eye on outsiders:

The continuing carnage in Iraq—most recently the deaths of seven U.S. troops in Sadr City—is leaving the American military little choice but to punish perpetrators. When this happens, we should be ready to put in context the events that led to it. More than 600 U.S. military dead, attacks on the U.N. headquarters last year, assassination of iraqi [sic] officials who work with the coalition, the deaths of Spanish troops last fall, the outrage in Fallujah: whatever happens, it is richly deserved.

Ironically, for a news channel that was created by a foreigner, foreigners are treated with disdain and disrespect. But Fox News' xenophobia runs deep in stories: most foreigners will not get a fair hearing, nor will their motives be taken at face value.

The New York Times

The paper of record is considered one of the Murdochian kingdom's biggest villains, and jabs against the paper are numerous (a discussion of the FNC feud with the *Times* is detailed in Chapter 13). For the FNC, the *Times* represents the "liberal" point of view, and thus cannot be trusted. Brit Hume warned his viewers about the paper's shenanigans on Fox's "All Star Panel" on May 21, 2003:

HUME: Well, we have a couple of other developments now. We have this remarkable speech made over the weekend at a graduation exercise out in Rockford College out in the American heartland, out in Illinois by Christopher Hedges. Which was a speech in which no word was ever spoken to or about the graduates by Hedges. The speech was an antiwar argument and anti-Iraq war in particular. One might argue anti-U.S. foreign policy from beginning to end.

And in the meantime, another time *Times* reporter Robert Worth was seen by

the *New York Sun* filling out an information request form for Greenpeace, the environmental—militant environmental group. But he acknowledged when asked about that, maybe under the *Times'* new regulations, that wasn't such a good idea.

But what does this suggest, Ceci, about the *Times* and its ad Tuesday towards political views and advocacy?

Anyone who is willing to throttle the paper is a welcome guest on Fox News. One of Bill O'Reilly's "reliable sources" who could justify his *Times*-bashing was disgraced journalist Jayson Blair (who was fired for plagiarizing and fabricating numerous stories at the paper, sending it into a tailspin). Blair enabled O'Reilly's delusions on a March 10, 2004 program:

> *Anyone who is willing to trash the New York Times is a welcome guest.*

O'REILLY: With us now is the aforementioned Jayson Blair, the author of the new book *Burning Down My Master's House: My Life at the New York Times.* You know, this is going to make you feel good, I think. I don't care what you did. You don't have to apologize to me or anybody else on this program. That's between you and the *New York Times* and the people who read that newspaper. I don't care what you did. I don't care if you took drugs. I don't care if you're bipolar. I don't care.

What I do care about, though, is the nation's most powerful and influential newspaper and what is happening over there. As you know, we have issues with the *New York Times.*

Blair told O'Reilly everything he wanted to hear—never mind the fact that Blair had vested interests in slamming a paper where he committed numerous acts of journalistic fraud. Blair was promoting his book, and it didn't hurt to endear himself to O'Reilly's audience:

BLAIR: Well, one of the problems—and I don't necessarily agree with this notion—[with] Howell's reign at the *Times* was he—you know, I believe that the *New York Times* newsroom does have a social change agenda, and it's very liberal, it's certainly anti-conservative.

You could make the argument that it's a pro-liberal, anti-conservative social change agenda, and Howell didn't just push it, but he made it obvious. It's normally more subtle and more hidden and... masked and cloaked.

O'REILLY: So they wanted a new society, more secular society, more liberal society. Is that fair to say?

BLAIR: That is fair to say.

O'REILLY: And if you didn't buy into that, what would happen?

BLAIR: I can't think of anyone there who didn't buy into that.

O'REILLY: All of them—all right.

O'Reilly's vanity got the better of him, but his self-referential question got the answer he seemed to have wanted:

> **O'REILLY:** If you walk[ed] into the newsroom and you said that "O'Reilly Factor" is my favorite program, I love that O'Reilly guy...
>
> **BLAIR:** Well, look at what...
>
> **O'REILLY:** ...what would happen to you if you were a *New York Times* reporter?
>
> **BLAIR:** I'd be laughed out of the newsroom. I mean, people would brand me as a neo-con and, you know, they'd stop talking to me. They would...
>
> **O'REILLY:** Really?
>
> **BLAIR:** It would hurt my stories. People would say that I—you know, there are a handful of people who have conservative...

Blair reinforced the notion that right-of-center journalists don't get a fair shake at the *Times*:

> **O'REILLY:** Yes, they've got a couple of token—Safire and these guys.
>
> **BLAIR:** Right. But they're outcasts.
>
> **O'REILLY:** All right.
>
> **BLAIR:** They're outcasts inside the...
>
> **O'REILLY:** So the prevailing wisdom inside the nation's most powerful newspaper, all right [...] It's a very sharp agenda that they push, not only in their editorial pages, but in their news pages.

It doesn't matter how discredited and unreliable a person may be: so long as they toe the party line, they can speak nothing but the truth for the Fox News Channel.

A Friend of Dorothy's is No Friend of the FNC

The controversy surrounding gay marriage was played prominently on the FNC. Though gays and lesbians weren't necessarily attacked outright, they were nevertheless portrayed as somewhat underhandedly on the March 3, 2004 edition of the "O'Reilly Factor":

> **O'REILLY:** In the second "Personal Story" segment tonight, anarchy continues to reign on the gay marriage issue.
>
> In ultra-liberal Multnomah County—that's Portland, Oregon—officials have begun marrying gays after finding a loophole in the law there.

The gay population were also seen as aggressive and unlawful in their tactics:

> But, in Ulster County, New York, a more conservative area, the mayor of New Paltz has been charged with nineteen counts of criminal behavior for marrying homosexuals in that small town. He could go to jail.
>
> [...]All right. I'm going to be the advocate for the gay marriage crew, all right, and I'm going to put forth their point of view, and then you answer [as to] why it's fallacious,

OK?

WILLIAM BENNETT: All right.

Finally, they were being psychologically isolated from the rest of country:

> **O'REILLY:** Now they've been very effective, I believe, in putting this forth as a con-
> stitutional issue, a violation of the Constitution. They say gay Americans are
> entitled to the same rights as straight Americans.
>
> Therefore, you cannot deny them the right to marriage. Where are they going
> wrong?
>
> **BENNETT:** Well, they do have the right to marry. Every guy has a right to marry a wom-
> an. Every woman has a right to marry a guy. But I don't think they have the right
> to change the definition of marriage, and that's really the fundamental issue.

In a brilliant "hitting two liberals with one stone" approach, O'Reilly managed to slight both gays and the *New York Times* on the July 15, 2004 edition of the "O'Reilly Factor":

> **O'REILLY:** According to a Fox News Opinion Dynamics poll taken in May, just 25%
> of the American people believe gays should have the right to marry. A CBS poll
> has the number at 28%.
>
> [...]"Talking Points" has said over and over that if Lenny and Larry want to get
> married, we don't care, but we do care that the will of the people is being over-
> run by activists, judges and an unbelievably biased press.
>
> Today the *New York Times* proves once again that it uses its news pages to pro-
> mote its editorial point of view. The *Times* ran two articles about the gay mar-
> riage amendment. [...] Now if you read the articles, it's obvious what the *Times*
> is doing. Anyone who opposes gay marriage is labeled a conservative, which is
> the worst thing you can possibly be at the *New York Times*.

Just as being a liberal is the worst thing you can possibly be at the Fox News Channel.

Baby Slappers and Other Perverts

If Fox News only picked on progressives, then their grumpy worldview could be easily dismissed: so, they don't like left-leaning people? Don't right-wingers need a news outlet to call their own? To each his own, right?

Wrong. The problem with the FNC is that it doesn't merely thrash liberals, but that they put progressives in the same boat as terrorists and child killers. Putting liberals in the same category as rapists is a slimy tactic that is meant to discredit the left by implying that they are of the same untrustworthy stock as child killers. The "O'Reilly Factor" is probably the worst offender, mixing liberals with real sickos in O'Reilly's "Villain of the Week" segment. If O'Reilly mixed Republicans with child molesters, posters on the freerepublic.com website would have to resort to wearing Depends while ingesting heart medication: the shouts of "political outrage!" and "left-wing propaganda!" would never stop.

Any kiddie or puppy molester is virtually guaranteed a mention on the "Factor," as was one who got some press publicity in a January 2003 edition of O'Reilly's "Villain of the Week":

> **O'REILLY:** As you may know, one child was murdered, two others were horribly abused in Newark, New Jersey. Authorities have the adults involved in custody. But state child protection agents simply didn't do their jobs. And the fate of these children is partially on them.
>
> And so caseworker Katherine Davis, who allowed the case to be closed, despite not having seen the children in a year, her supervisor, Donna Wells Tucker, who went along with it, and their boss, Victoria Amaroso, are the Villains of the Week.
>
> I'm sure they all have excuses, but excuses walk. Davis and Tucker should be criminally charged with negligence.

In the same month, O'Reilly had this villain to condemn after two teenagers were caught having oral sex in full view of their peers on a school bus:

> The incident shocked Americans, but the principal of the high school involved, Richard Kelley, still refuses to say how he has disciplined those students, citing their privacy, if you can believe it.
>
> Now nobody's asking for names, but I believe everybody in the Silver Lake school district knows who these kids are. But what clear-thinking Americans are demanding is that a message be sent that this kind of conduct is not acceptable, and that message includes a publicly stated penalty of those students.
>
> Since Kelley refuses to do that, he becomes our Villain of the Week and a shameful example of public school leadership. He should be fired.

When one Florida girl was abducted and murdered by a repeat offender, O'Reilly went after the judge who gave the previously convicted criminal a light sentence.

But hey, liberals, rapists, terrorists—what's the difference on the Fox News Channel?

Chapter 9

The Predators

"They have a tactic, a single tactic. Attack the President, attack the President, assassinate his character and make a big deal over nothing, like landing on an aircraft carrier."

Sean Hannity on President George W. Bush's critics

I n its short history, Fox News has spawned several popular news shows that generate buzz and solid ratings. With very few misses, the cable newser has managed to cultivate a roster of popular news programming: "Hannity and Colmes," "On the Record," "Special Report With Brit Hume" and "Your World With Neil Cavuto," just to name a few of the shows that are in little danger of facing cancellation in the near future.

CNN has seen the ratings for most of its programs slide; MSNBC has seen many of its highly publicized new offerings register a 0.1 or even a dismal 0.0 rating (meaning less than 50,000 people watched the program out of a potential audience pool of three hundred million). Yet Fox News' lead over its rivals is comfortable and consistent. The question is, what is Fox News' formula for steadfast success? What does Fox have that CNN or MSNBC doesn't?

Fox News doesn't rely on having more facts than its rivals; in fact it has *less* information, yet the network finds itself the cable news channel that viewers turn to for their information. Even more fascinating, is that though both MSNBC and CNN have more resources and more scoops than Fox, they both lag behind their data-sparse competitor in total viewers. There is something about Fox that gives it an edge with viewers; something that CNN and MSNBC cannot replicate for the time being—but what's Fox's key to success?

To understand the Fox formula, it's important to understand what makes a news show a hit or miss.

How to Be a Successful News Personality Without Really Trying

Most journalists either fancy themselves as tenacious scouts who will stop at almost nothing to uncover the elusive and treacherous Truth, or humble pencil pushers who fairly and objectively report the facts as they come; the choice is between defining oneself as a excavator or a conduit. For those who align themselves with the former, many dream of carving themselves a more public and lucrative niche as a news personality rather than a mere reporter or anchor.

Not that anyone could blame those journalists for wanting to somewhat "sell out" for a more glamorous and less investigative calling: in a profession that is marked by mediocre pay, questionable job security, high stress and abusive bosses, sources and audiences, the journalists who thrive best in the profession are not the ones with the thickest skin or the best ability, but the ones who have the audacity to abuse back. Those who have the most forceful of personalities will find themselves getting further ahead than their neutral milquetoast colleagues.

Yet news shows are a dime a dozen on both network and cable TV and the genre has spawned countless permutations; how to get the attention of a bored audience who has already been exposed to the likes of "60 Minutes," "Meet the Press," "Crossfire" and "20/20" becomes increasingly difficult every year and the ambitious host and producer knows this. The pressure is on both the network and the talent to come up with a program that a sizable audience will want to see for years to come; for many reporters, that one failed show will be their only chance at perceived immortality.

Of the chosen few who are responsible for anchoring a primetime news program, most hosts do not capture either a broad audience or viewers' imaginations enough to make a strong and lasting impression. Shows come; shows go. Some of these newsmagazines or talkfests may have been innovative—or at least somewhat different than the standard news show fare, but viewers either stayed away or merely faded away. "CNN Newsstand," "The Crusaders" (a syndicated Disney news magazine that had its correspondents try to "make a difference" by meddling in the news stories they covered), "Day One" and "Pozner and Donahue" were all trying to find an audience with a distinctive twist or look, but all of these shows either faded or crashed out of sight and memory.

What makes a news show a hit, flop or bomb depends on a number of factors, such as the show's format and even the quality of its graphics—but neither quality can ensure a show's popularity. The short-lived "Day One" was considered edgy for its time, but it could never compete in ratings or longevity with the stylistically minimalist "60 Minutes," a show that doesn't even have its own catchy opening music. Though that CBS news program features three stories per episode, other less successful shows have followed its well-worn formula. Style and format may be important, but it's not enough to secure solid Nielsen numbers.

Contrary to common sense, a show's success does not hinge on having more timely or interesting topics than its competitors, since most news programs will cover the same breaking events at the same time. If there is an explosion in a crowded building, a political convention in a major metropolitan city or an election to determine the next President, the chances are nil that any news

show is not going to report on or discuss these events. A spelling bee will never trump the attempted assassination of a major political figure.

Getting a seasoned source or interviewee to agree to an interview is also no guarantee of grabbing a substantial audience. A savvy interviewer's oldest tricks will have all been done before on numerous occasions; if a newsmaker is media savvy and has had media training, he will know how to answer the questions without worrying about making a fool of himself or saying the wrong thing at the wrong time. He will know how to dress, how to behave and what to say. The answers will be prepared, rehearsed and pat. The odds that a self-respecting journalist can extract a startling, novel and newsworthy response from his subject are against him.

On the other hand, boring guests equal a bored audience: the anchor, reporter or host has to provoke the guest, and make unpredictable comments and questions. If that fails, it's up to the producer to ensure that at least the guests are either naturally outrageous and unpredictable, making the talent's charismatic and professional deficiencies less important, or that the guests already have a devout, considerable and built-in audience who are willing to tune in regardless of the host's interviewing skills or presence. This means that the expertise and knowledge base of the source are sacrificed for carny tactics. Fortunately, there is no shortage of guests who are attention-seekers and who will adjust their schtick to ensure themselves frequent airtime.

Here, Fox thrives on having childish guests doing all sorts of childish things: throwing tantrums, ranting, pouting, hurling random insults and acting like a seemingly untamed cabal of smug monkeys trained to make spectacles of themselves in convenient and pithy sound bites. Coulter, Gingrich and the rest can nail "perpetually outraged Republican" in one take. If the guest isn't snickering at his progressive or moderate opponent or accusing another guest of being weak or unpatriotic, something has gone seriously wrong.

Yet even here, producers and talent are faced with an unnerving dilemma: if the guests are left unchecked and are free to overshadow the talent on every program, the host becomes lost in the noise, making it difficult for that show to hold a steady and regular audience. The entire point of having a regular host or anchor is to attract a regular audience who all seek the same distinct combination of qualities in their news programs. The talent is the draw and the foundation; the guests are the stimulation and entertainment. The host has to attract viewers: the guests are there merely to amuse regular viewers and give them water cooler fodder for the next day. The talent must define the show no matter what.

What Makes a News Show

If a show's success or failure largely rests on the shoulders of its host and talent, then we can expect that certain types of journalists and anchors are more likely to get rewarded with hosting duties than others. Intelligence, expertise, knowledge and interviewing skills don't necessarily translate to big ratings. What a news program's success boils down to is the strength of the host's personality.

This is hardly an earth-shattering revelation: no one wants to hang around a droning dud. Current events are already dry and heavy: any more *Sturm und Drang* from a monotonous talking head and the viewer will be perilously close to entering Leonard Cohen territory. Why would a viewer—who may even be acquainted with Prozac—want to relapse into a depression (dysthimic disorder or even getting "bummed out")—by watching a painful topic with an equally painful-to-watch host?

The personality of the host may be the drug that hooks the viewers, but a host that can be described as deferential and modest isn't quite the personality type that can hold a show together. If a sunny disposition isn't enough to lift viewers' spirits, then what is? If Fox's ratings are any indication, the draw for the viewer is how well the talking head has cultivated an abrasive, in-your-face style that is equated with toughness and truthfulness.

A Fox News talking head is going to behave as if he isn't going to take any guff from anyone: he is going to confront anyone who espouses a worldview that differs from his own. It helps if the host blasts his random thoughts in a powerful and pontifical manner: yes, he knows what you're up to and, no, you're not going to fool him. A tough guy who can't be fooled is an ideal persona for a news host to perfect. The Fox News host appears streetwise enough not to be taken in, humble enough to not seem as if he is an untrustworthy egghead and refined enough to engage in dialogue with experts and politicians without drooling or misusing big words in public.

At other networks, the anchors and hosts, conversely, are supposed to be above that sort of churlish behavior: they are the knowledgeable moderators who referee both the liberal and conservative guests with their startling insights, forceful presence, vast knowledge and irreproachable sense of fairness and balance.

That's the theory, though the application is somewhat less than ideal at the FNC. The "boys" Hannity and Colmes overtly represent the "fairness" and "balance" of Fox News, though Hannity looks like he could beat Colmes in a thumb wrestling match every time. Brit Hume can be counted on to bring a veneer of bona fide objective journalistic credentials to the FNC, even if he does interview a disproportionate number of Republican newsmakers. Greta Van Susteren is the cosmetically-enhanced refugee from the "left-leaning" CNN. Even tainted journalistic commodity Geraldo Rivera is known for being a hormonally-charged, controversial joke standing behind a bushy mustache—but one who nevertheless can still get a scoop or two along with negative press coverage.

With the exception of the left-leaning and becalmed Alan Colmes, these are some of Fox's most popular and recognizable predators: they are the talent who circle their progressive prey before they pounce and tear them to shreds. Fox News may claim to be fair and balanced, but the ideological breakdown of its various hosts points to something a little less fair and a little less balanced.

Sean Hannity and Alan Colmes

Opposites may attract, but they can also help prop up an editorially weak program. Sean Hannity and his co-pilot Alan Colmes have managed to get decent ratings using a familiar genre—the opposites taking polar views approach is nothing new; shows such as "Crossfire," "This Week" and "The McLaughlin Group" are all past permutations of this tired approach. They compete against

the solo Larry King, and the two lesser-known talking heads have not only managed to join forces to overthrow King, but they have on occasion had the top-rated cable news show—even the title sounds like that of a jovial, if featherweight buddy movie. Nevertheless, they have staked down their primetime territory with their routine. Mission Accomplished.

Hannity and Colmes aren't on the air just to win their time slot, though: they are Fox's token effort at proving to their critics that Murdoch's partisan channel is capable of being a "fair and balanced" news outfit. Fox brass have publicly pointed to Colmes to let the world know that left-leaning journalists can find employment at News Corp. Colmes is essential—not for ratings, but for professional credibility. Hannity is essential to keep viewers happy. Each man serves an entirely different purpose for the FNC.

Hannity and Colmes are opposites of each other in every other way imaginable, as well. Hannity is quick, strapping, forceful and right-winged, while Colmes is more plodding, wiry, wispy and left-winged.

Yet "Hannity and Colmes" was not News Corp's first foray into the alpha-male-Republican-paired-with-courteous-liberal-sidekick territory, as former WTTG producer Frank O'Donnell noted:

> The "Hannity and Colmes" show for example, really got kind of a trial run on our show, years earlier with different people doing it. [Fox executives] were kind of feeling their way along about the kind of thing they wanted to do. Typically, what they'll do now, of course, is try to put on the appearance of being balanced, but really [are] kind of a mismatch. You'll have a "Hannity and Colmes" show where Hannity is really a good-looking, kind of clean-cut all-American kind of guy, and his counterpart is a little squirrelly-looking, frankly[...] It sends a subtle message, I think to the viewers that the conservative guy has got to be right because he's better looking.

There are other differences between the two diametrically opposed prime-time hosts, as well. Hannity looks well-tended and sturdy (as Fox News talking head Neil Cavuto quipped, not every host can succeed in "trying to get that Hannity hair"); Colmes is scrawnier and paler than his cohort and is facing male pattern baldness. The last name "Hannity" sounds more striking and harsher than the balmy-sounding "Colmes." Even Hannity's dark, bushy eyebrows are more expressive than Colmes', giving the neo-con a better chance of winning audience empathy and support over his left-leaning antagonist. On the other hand, Colmes is at least an amiable gentleman, while Hannity seems to have been an indulged child with conduct issues who was raised by parents who did not believe in disciplining their offspring.

The program's underlying scheme is self-evident enough: the hosts will talk about the issues that would interest the far-right, ideologically-driven guests are thrown into the mix to give the hosts people to spar with and the hosts question their guests from the right (Hannity) and the left (Colmes). While Hannity is busy hamming and mugging it up for America, Colmes is fighting for some meaningful face time.

While the title implies that the show is a group effort, the program is really Hannity's vehicle: it is his outrageous remarks that drive the show. He liberally equates progressives with most of the world's evils; he is one step away from kneeling in front of any guest who represents the Republican establishment; he is belligerent to anyone who holds views that differ from his. Hannity may be the biggest Republican fan boy in the west; Colmes is not as passionate. Hannity's books *Deliver Us From Evil* and *Let Freedom Ring* throw his views in readers' faces with reckless abandon, while Colmes' tome is called *Red, White & Liberal*: even when Colmes is off the air there is a need to justify his political stance. Hannity feels he needs to make no apologies, explanations or excuses for his extremist views.

Colmes is not always the most aggressive or passionate debater, making it harder for him to win the hearts and minds of his FNC viewers and, as Wolcott noted, "Sean Hannity would say the most grotesque, outrageous things and Alan Colmes would just sit there, and he was supposed to be the liberal." Colmes' delivery is too tepid compared to the overwhelming Hannity; his words merely get overshadowed by whatever liberal-phobic invective Hannity disgorges. After all, it is Hannity who gets top billing, proving that, at least on Fox, nice guys really do finish last. Even foxnews.com shows Hannity's picture first with the tagline "Sean Hannity's Bio," while his partner's picture is below him—with the tag "Meet Alan Colmes." As Wolcott noted, "people on the Internet would refer to the show as *Sean Hannity and that other guy.*"

The "other guy" tried to put his left foot down with Senator Orrin Hatch on his October 23, 2003 program, with less than progressive results:

COLMES: ...Her race has nothing to do with why Democrats oppose her.

HATCH: Oh, come on. Look, you saw the cartoon that was done against her. It wasn't done by my colleagues but it was done by many of these outside left-wing groups.

COLMES: It was done by one radical group.

HATCH: Fine, but that's typical of what we're getting.

COLMES: No, it's not, sir. With all due respect...

HATCH: Oh, yes it is. Oh, yes it is. Let me tell you with regard to just a couple of weeks ago, one of the top civil rights leaders, a very liberal man, head of the ACLU in Mississippi, a minister told me, he said, "Senator, you're right, it's all about abortion." But he said, "I'm pro-choice," he said, "but it's despicable." He said, "It's all about abortion." And it really is.

COLMES: I'll agree with you there.

Not only does Colmes have a tendency to back down on key points, but he could also use some assertiveness training as well:

HATCH: And let me tell you, it really does make a difference that she is a conservative African-American woman jurist, Supreme Court Justice from California, who is on the fast track to the Supreme Court. And if they're not liberal, then just look at the Congressional Black Caucus.

Automatically, knee-jerk came out against her even though they didn't listen to

her. Democrats were condemning her without having heard her say one word of testimony.

COLMES: Well, the issue...

HATCH: Now let me just sum it up. I just was on the floor tonight with one of the leading Democrats on the committee. I said, "What did you think?" He said, "She's terrific. She was really, really good." I said, "Well, then, are you going to let her go through without a filibuster?" And I got kind of just a kind of a sad look.

The segment ended thereafter with Colmes barely uttering another word. Colmes' penchant for agreeing with guests he is supposed to challenge assures that his right-winged antagonists go unscathed and unchallenged. His debate with the verbose Ann Coulter on December 13, 2002 was anything but rigorous and unpredictable:

COLMES: [...D]o you feel that Trent Lott should step aside? Is it better for the Republicans if he steps aside?

ANN COULTER: If you would have asked me ten days ago, I would have said absolutely, I'd send a check to anyone that would run against him as Majority Leader. But I think people are getting a little sick of these gotcha moments. I don't think any honest person can say that his remarks at an old-timer's birthday party [were] his idea of announcing a statement for the Republican party of bringing back segregation... I think people get tired of these gotcha games.

COLMES: I agree with you. I'm tired of the gotcha stuff. I honestly don't want to... and I normally agree with Reverend Sharpton. I'm very sensitive to racial insensitivity.

But I think all this piling on, now, is getting to be ludicrous.

What was ludicrous was the way that a two-sided debate suddenly turned into a mediation, with both sides coming to a consensus without much give and take. If the progressive side is supposed to challenge the conservative, then why isn't the progressive faction not putting up a bigger challenge or resistance? Why not question Coulter's self-admitted flip-flop? Why would she let someone off the hook just because she has become bored with the offensive party's detractors? Should we let someone off the hook because there are people out there who are persistent and consistent with their grievances? Should someone who utters racist sentiments be absolved of wrongdoing because we feel his antagonists have been outraged too long? What if they were outraged because action wasn't taken? Does she think time heals all wounds for people whose pain has not been acknowledged and properly remedied? What if Lott's sentiments were ones that affronted her directly and put her nose out of joint? Would she just take it?

These were only a few of the many weaknesses with her comments, yet Colmes chose to agree with her rather than push further. Would Hannity be as chivalrous with his ideological opposite? Hannity pounces; Colmes retreats.

Colmes' pathological deference reared its meek head again, this time with Newt Gingrich on April 1, 2003:

COLMES: I disagree with you vehemently. We have a free press in this country.

GINGRICH: Wait a second, wait a second. I didn't say he didn't have the right to go. You can have the right to do something and it can be the wrong thing to do. That's actually a quote from Edward R. Murrow's producer, who for years ran PBS roundtables that I used to participate in and would argue again and again having the right to do something doesn't mean it's the right thing to do.

COLMES: Well, I agree with that concept.

While Colmes may make an excellent empathizer and consensus-builder, he wastes valuable airtime making nice with those he should be challenging and confronting. Colmes used some of his disarming tactics on his February 19, 2004 program:

COLMES: Joining us now, John Podhoretz, author of the new book, *Bush Country: How W. Became a Great President While Driving Liberals Insane*. John, nice to have you with us.

JOHN PODHORETZ: Thank you.

COLMES: It's not Bush that drives me insane, but your book a little bit, because I don't agree with it. It's a well-written book, by the way.

PODHORETZ: Well, look—listen, if I weren't driving you insane, then I wouldn't be doing my job.

COLMES: That means you're doing your job. Exactly right.

Colmes' lack of hunting or stalking instincts contrasts sharply to his co-host's more predatory and diva-like inclinations. Hannity is by far the more aggressive of the boys: he is the muscle-bound beach bully kicking sand in the face of his less combative companion. For instance, an April 16, 2004 segment may have seemed jovial and courteous on the surface, but was typical of the dominant-submissive dynamic between the two hosts:

COLMES: You got treated so nicely by the media.

HANNITY: They could not have been nicer to me. Lester Holt. Katie Couric was as nice as could be.

You know, I think everybody that has kids, you've got to realize that the one thing that is true is there are groups of people. And there are millions of them, animals out there with no conscience and no soul and they want to destroy us. And this is not liberal or conservative, Republican or Democrat.

COLMES: I agree with that.

HANNITY: We have got to unite and fight these people and defeat them.

And George Bush and the Bush doctrine is the way to go.

COLMES: Wait a minute. We're allowed to disagree with that. We're allowed to be-lieve that Bush is not the way to go, and that there is another policy that could be better. That's what I would call - what I would call America.

HANNITY: Because I'm celebrating, I'm going to give you the last word this week.

COLMES: Have a nice weekend, Mr. Hannity.

HANNITY: That's all the time we have left this evening.

And by the way, you're not going to want to miss Monday night's show.

I will have Monday night an exclusive interview with Attorney General John Ashcroft.

So much for Hannity giving Colmes the last word.

Hannity makes no secret of his cult-like adoration for George W. Bush, or anything else that resembles a far right-wing ideology. His cheerleading has become somewhat over-the-top on his show of late. Unlike the grounded Colmes, Hannity is smug, rigid and underhanded in his debating tactics. Hannity's popularity rests with his ability to seemingly get away with making harsh and unfounded accusations while maintaining a patina of purity and goodness. Hannity gets to insult the dregs of humanity, all the while pulling the strings and trying to make his hostile guests seem frightening to his audience.

Sean Hannity also seems to be the most obedient to John Moody's memos: when Moody issued certain sentiments about Iraq in his numerous decrees, Hannity made similar statements on his program, both in content and tone. If nothing else, at least Hannity can follow orders from management to the letter.

Yet Hannity's disdain for progressives never ends. On the February 17, 2003 edition of his show he asked, "Now, if you don't think there is enough liberal bias in the media, like my good friend Alan Colmes, well you'll be thrilled that a group of wealthy Democrats are planning to start a fourteen-hour a day liberal talk radio network. Now they say liberals are overshadowed by conservative radio hosts like me and our very good friend Rush Limbaugh. So do liberals really need a radio network of their own?"

Ten days later, Hannity was at it again: "Why was Phil Donahue's television show canceled after just six months on the air? The liberals, with the exception of our very own Alan Colmes, have a tougher time getting ratings."

If news producers are supposed to be levelheaded observers of the world around them, then someone hadn't passed along that factoid to Hannity. His running schtick throughout 2004 was his open desire to see his hero George W. Bush get another term in the White House:

◆ On January 22, 2004: "And only 285 days until George W. Bush gets reelected, so—at least according to me."

◆ On June 21, 2004: "There you have it. Only 134 days until Americans go to the polls and reelect President Bush."

◆ On July 6, 2004: "You have only 119 days until we go to the polls to reelect George W. Bush, right, Alan?"

◆ On July 20, 2004: "Just 105 days to go until George W. Bush is elected for a second term as President. But some in Hollywood are trying their hardest to go beat up on the commander in chief."

The Other Fox Players (minus O'Reilly)

Sean Hannity	Host of Hannity and Colmes	Aggressive
Alan Colmes	Token on Hannity and Colmes	Passive
Brit Hume	News Anchor	Serious
Tony Snow	News Personality	Authoritative
Neil Cavuto	Business Correspondent	Optimistic
Carl Cameron	Political Correspondent	Subtle
Greta Van Susteren	Legal Correspondent	Moderate
Geraldo Rivera	Gonzo Correspondent	Nuts

◆ On August 3, 2004: "There you have it: just ninety-one days until Americans rush to the polls to reelect my President, George W. Bush."

◆ On August 4, 2004: "There you have it; just ninety days until Americans across the country go back and reelect George W. Bush in a landslide, right Pat?"

◆ On August 17, 2004: "There you have it, just seventy-seven days left until November 2, when Americans go to reelect our commander in chief for another four years."

Although Colmes did manage a few jabs to counter Hannity's declarations (for example, Colmes started off one broadcast quipping, "Well, 246 days to go until President Bush finds out if he's headed for early retirement") it is Hannity's version that viewers remember. Unfortunately for Colmes, he is playing the patient, overtaxed father; Hannity seems to be his out-of-control son. The problem is—as most brides and actors will tell you—children and animals always upstage the adults.

Brit Hume

For any news outlet to have credibility, it needs a veteran correspondent or anchor that has established impressive roots with another media outlet: respected newspapers or networks will entrust the most important stories and duties to him. Strictly relying on untested commodities or second-rate journalists won't carry much weight with news consumers. Familiarity is important, but so are impressive credentials. Without the elder statesman, a news outlet cannot be taken seriously.

Fox News' most valuable bargaining chip with its viewers is Brit Hume. Hume's roots in serious

journalism are impressive; among other duties, he worked as both a Capitol Hill and White House correspondent at ABC News. Whatever you say about Hume, he has a sterling track record in his chosen profession, which is why he is one of the FNC's most crucial on-air employees: they would not have gained the prominence they have without him.

Hume knows how to comport himself with dignity[4], Hume is not as obnoxiously conservative as his younger colleague Sean Hannity. He doesn't call his guests boobs or idiots. As Alexander Kippen, former Washington bureau reporter for the Fox Network, noted about Hume:

> [FNC had] several false starts that didn't really work... Now I wasn't privy to many of the details of the false starts. I know that there were two or three occasions, where we would learn about the bureau and what was going on inside. Needless to say, none of it succeeded. It really wasn't until Kim Hume [and] then Brit Hume came on. They were really the first heavyweights from an administration point of view to come on board that... could really make the network as we know it today work at all.

Yet that doesn't mean Hume is the avatar of unbiased reportage: he, like his fellow Fox News kids, lobbed soft questions to Republican bigwigs and concentrated on interviewing right-of-center guests. His June 14, 2004 exclusive interview of former President George Bush Senior (or George 41) on his 80th birthday mainly consisted of a shameless publicity stunt: Hume went skydiving with George 41. The gambit got Hume press, but why he was willing to jump out of a plane to interview a retired politico and not jump out of a plane to interview a soldier in a war-torn country makes his ploy seem less heroic than it was supposed to. The fact that the interview coincided with George 43's reelection campaign also called into question why the interview was conducted in the first place.

But take place it did, and Hume's leanings became evident in his questioning of George 43's pop:

HUME: Do you think the criticism of your son has been harsher and more unfair than you felt the criticism was of you?

BUSH: Pretty good question. I don't know. But yes, I do. I honestly do.

HUME: How so?

BUSH: It depends what outlet you are talking about. Well, there's a confluence of events. The problems on his shoulders are bigger than the problems I faced. You know, the Taliban. Of course, the biggest is 9/11. Something happened. Something bad happened to our country. And we brought home the fact that we can no longer depend on the Pacific and on the Atlantic to keep us safe. And all of this it fell on the shoulders of the President, having to go and fight against international terror, in [a] way that... hadn't been done before.

Hume doesn't have to be overtly Republican; he is the FNC's window dressing. Just as Alan Colmes is the FNC's "proof" of balance, Hume is their evidence of fairness. Hume may be fair; it's just that he's more fair to some people than others. Would he have ever warmly interviewed Bill Clinton's late mother while she indulged in her reveries?

4 Unless he is in the same room as NPR correspondent Mara Liasson.

Tony Snow

A former Ronald Reagan speech writer, Snow has found a second career as a news personality, as do many other former employees of politicians from both sides of the political spectrum (such as Newt Gingrich's press secretary Tony Blankley and Bill Clinton's advisor George Stephanopoulos). Snow was a newspaper columnist before he landed a stint on the FNC.

Snow's take on domestic and world events has a strong GOP slant; he is not known for moderate views. Snow's spinning of the facts will inevitably land on the right side of the room. For example, he gave O'Reilly his take on director Michael Moore on O'Reilly's June 30, 2004 program:

> **SNOW:** Interestingly, both political parties think it's going to be good for them. Democrats think it's going to supply some of the passion that John Kerry has so far failed to whoop up.
>
> Republicans think it's going to strengthen a view that they have tried to make in an Internet ad, which is that some Democrats have lost their minds —you get Al Gore screaming, and so on.
>
> So both sides are hoping it's going to be to their benefit. But I'm with you. I think in the end, it's not going to be of much consequence, except that Michael Moore is going to make a lot of money.

No matter what the situation, Snow's authoritative stances make it seem as if he is analyzing, and not merely opining. Right-of-center actions are framed in a positive way; left-of-center are framed in negative ones. Snow asked these loaded glass-is-half-full questions on August 24, 2003:

> **SNOW:** Last week's bombing of the U.N. headquarters in Baghdad raises a host of questions about U.S. policy in Iraq: Are we winning the peace? Who is responsible for the recent mayhem? And what role should the U.N. play in bringing liberal democracy to Iraq?
>
> For answers, we turn to the U.S. administrator in Iraq, Ambassador L. Paul Bremer. Ambassador Bremer, first, I want to get your sense of the reaction within Iraq to the bombing. Has it created new sympathy for the United States and the coalition forces?

Snow's "do they pity us now" question was as loaded as his May 11, 2004 interview with Dick Cheney:

> **SNOW:** [T]he latest Gallup poll indicating 56% of the American public now thinks the invasion of Iraq was a mistake. What do you tell them, those doubting Americans, to assure them that this was the right thing to do?

It doesn't matter what the GOP faction does, Snow will make certain the questions won't offend or make Republicans look bad. His take on Bill O'Reilly's interview with George Bush was framed this way on September 29, 2004:

> **SNOW:** [W]e're going to see in the debate, and as we saw on the interview, a lot of what happens when candidates are speaking to the public, they are giving people an opportunity to take their measure. How do they react to tough

questions? How do they react to the unexpected? And I think what you saw there was a President who was composed and somebody also comfortable with himself. I like the last answer—the answer in the last segment where he said, you know what, I weep when you weep, I laugh when you laugh. That's a good human touch.

So long as Snow's on the FNC, Republican guests can always expect an easy ride and good press without the effort.

Neil Cavuto

Fox's official capitalist chronicler does his best to counter CNN's version of Lou Dobbs, Captain Corporate America. Cavuto is the obligatory resident business host who heaps on lavish praise to the people who earn millions with their power lunches and trendy buzzwords. "Your World With Neil Cavuto" is not necessarily all about your world; more accurately, it is all about the corporate world and how it sees itself: as infallible, indispensable and always informed. He interviews suits in a way that conforms to this lofty self-view of the industry.

Cavuto isn't the only such reporter to engage in fluffy reportage: business journalism in North America tends to sound like press releases: while corporate titans such as Ken Lay and Bernie Ebbers racked up accolades from the business press, they weren't exactly living up to the hype. Cavuto is pretty much from this faction of the business press, only his style is a more exaggerated version of others in the field.

Deferential treatment isn't just reserved for the suits; politicians who also like to keep up appearances get to control Cavuto's interview, as was the case on his August 27, 2004 program:

> **CAVUTO:** Senator John Kerry [was irate] after the U.S. Census Bureau announced that the number of Americans living without health insurance has increased. Is this a dose of bad news for the Bush campaign? Joining us now, Health and Human Services Secretary Tommy Thompson. Secretary, thank you for coming. Good to have you.

> **TOMMY THOMPSON:** It's always a pleasure, Neil. And let me just respond very quickly to what Senator Kerry has said.

> **CAVUTO:** Sure.

Thompson then went on at some length about why he thought Kerry was off base in his criticism:

> **THOMPSON:** He is absolutely wrong. In twenty years in the United States Senate he has never really pushed for any major health reform package whatsoever.
>
> Since President Bush has been in office, he's done several things. We have used the administration to expand waivers to allow for an additional 2.2 million people to be covered under the Medicaid system. He has absolutely increased community health centers by over 600, serving an additional three million low-income Americans.

He has cut taxes so that we could get the economy moving. And these figures are in fiscal year 2003, when we were at the height of the recession, which was, of course, from the Clinton administration.

Cavuto's next question pretty much left Thompson unchallenged in his assertions; in fact, the question reinforced what the Health and Human Services Secretary asserted:

CAVUTO: So you think we're up from those levels?

THOMPSON: Oh, absolutely. This is 2003.

Cavuto's next question may have used a trendy buzzword, but it did allow Thompson the opportunity to answer a different question—one that disparaged the Democrats in the process:

CAVUTO: So if you had to guesstimate how many more would be without health insurance, are you saying it's a net gain or a net loss?

THOMPSON: Oh, I'm saying that we would certainly [see] a reduction in the number, for these 2004 numbers, because we've had 1.2 million additional new jobs in 2004. And this, of course, indicates that the economy is improving. Therefore, people have more money and would be able to have more insurance.

But, truly, Neil, the problem has been that the President has advanced many new proposals, tax credits, association health plans and many other ways in which we could get people covered, such as health savings accounts. But the Congress, especially the Democrats in the Congress, have been opposed to every proposal the President has advanced.

Cavuto's air-kissing interviews with CEOs can be over-the-top, as with Orin Smith, the President and CEO of Starbucks, on the July 22, 2004 edition of his program:

CAVUTO: Let me ask you something. Have you been to a Starbucks lately? The lines are out of this world, and so are the third-quarter earnings.

The company [posted] $98 million, or twenty-four cents a share, up from $68 million, or seventeen cents a share, in the same period a year earlier. Better than expected. But why is the market not responding to all of this good economic news? Let us ask Orin Smith. He is the President and the CEO at Starbucks, and he joins us from Seattle.

Mr. Smith, good to have you.

SMITH: Thank you very much. Glad to be here.

CAVUTO: You know, you're growing at an alarming rate. You are bucking, by and large, the Wall Street trend that tends to shrug its shoulders at even great news. But what do you think collectively is going on with the market, where it ignores great news?

Lobbing leading softball questions seems to be a Cavuto trademark: corporate titans aren't going to be asked the hard, skeptical questions. It is their world Cavuto is presenting: one where there isn't a cloud in the sky or a pothole in the road. Everything is smooth sailing and the business elite can rest assured that Cavuto will not challenge their delusions.

Carl Cameron

Fox News' chief political correspondent doesn't have a show to call his own, but he is entrusted with the important task of finding new information for his colleagues to ruminate over on their respective programs; in other words, he's a reporter.

Cameron's credentials are not as lofty as Brit Hume or Bill O'Reilly's: he worked at a New Hampshire television station before coming aboard Fox News at its 1996 inception. Yet it's not his credentials as much as his demeanor that makes him an interesting study. As one former Fox News employee noted about his then-colleague:

Carl Cameron: GOP handyman.

> Carl Cameron is an interesting guy, very smart, perfect for the Fox model in that he's somebody who plays at the edges. He's not going to smash you over the head with a Republican bias; it's going to be much more sort of subtle and much more creative than that. He's perfect at the flippant one-liners, very witty, very creative. The problem is there's no sense of integrity as far as having a line that can't be crossed.

Cameron's reports tend to quietly remain true to the Republican view of life. In one of his reports, aired on August 30, 2004, Cameron's comments echoed GOP criticism of the Kerry-Edwards ticket:

> **CAMERON:** Kerry and Edwards have been pounded by the GOP for months as weak on terror. Edwards tried to use the President's own words to turn the tables.

The old Kerry-as-flip-flopper refrain crept into Cameron's report:

> **CAMERON:** But the Democratic ticket may have taken an inadvertent hit from Senate Democratic leader Tom Daschle, who is in a tough reelection fight in conservative South Dakota. Daschle associates himself not with Kerry but with the President in his latest ad and touts his vote for the $87 billion to fight the war on terror, something Kerry voted against.

Even a fellow Democrat seemed to prefer Bush to Kerry, according to Cameron:

> **CAMERON:** Of course, Daschle aides say the ad is not meant to give more favor to President Bush than Senator Kerry. But for Daschle, who is Kerry's Democratic leader in the U.S. Senate, to be cozying up to the President in ads, and talking about his support for the troops when Kerry voted against that $87 billion funding, is perhaps not exactly what they wanted on a day that the Republican convention is beginning, and they hoped to cast Kerry as the stronger leader.

Though it was well established that Republicans accused Kerry of being "weak" on defense, that didn't stop Cameron from reiterating the point on a June 1, 2004 story:

> **CAMERON:** For months, Democrats have accused the President of both hyping the

Cameron interviewed President Bush during his reelection campaign while his wife was working for the same reelection team.

terror threat for political advantage, but not doing enough about the problem. Republicans, in turn, say John Kerry is weak on security and has laid out a series of goals that everybody agrees to without any concrete plans to get there.

Kerry was also portrayed as hypocritical by the senior correspondent. Though some people do not wish to speak ill of the dead, apparently it was a sign that Kerry could not be trusted—or at least that's the impression one got from Cameron's June 8, 2004 report:

CAMERON: Never a Reagan fan, Kerry long boast[ed] that he led the fight against Reagan's, quote, "illegal war" in Central America. And when Republicans slammed Kerry as weak on defense in the war on terror, they cited Kerry's opposition to the very weapons systems that were approved under Reagan that are now in use in Iraq and Afghanistan. But at a Michigan high school graduation [this] weekend, Kerry offered only praise for the former President.

Kerry seemed pretty thick, too, if one listened to one of Cameron's April 30, 2004 reports:

CAMERON: While Kerry makes a distinction between the war in Iraq and the war on terror, President Bush says they are synonymous. And just four days ago in that same auditorium, Vice President Dick Cheney blasted Kerry by name more than thirty times as weak on defense and unable to even comprehend the war on terror.

Throughout his tenure at the FNC, there have been other signs that Cameron may not be as detached from the GOP as a political journalist should be: in 2000, his then-wife Pauline was working for George W. Bush's campaign team during the 2000 Presidential election, though he was allowed to continue to file stories about the election. During the pre-interview chatter with Bush, Cameron seemed quite chummy with his interviewee and spoke in a voice that did not quite match his usual on-air enunciations:

CAMERON: Tell me when you're ready, guys.

BUSH: And things are good. Your family?

CAMERON: Very well. My wife has been hanging out with your sister.

BUSH: Yeah good. My country... (LAUGHTER)

CAMERON: Dorothy has been all over the state campaigning and Pauline's been constantly with her. Um...

BUSH: Yeah, Doro's a good person.

CAMERON: Oh, she's been terrific. I mean, to hear Pauline tell it. When she first started campaigning for you, she was a little bit nervous.

BUSH: She's getting her stride.

CAMERON: Now she's up there. She doesn't need notes. She's going to crowds and she's got the whole riff down.

BUSH: She's a good soul.

CAMERON: She's having fun, too.

BUSH: She's a really good soul.

CAMERON: OK, you guys ready?

BUSH: That's great. (LAUGHTER)

CAMERON: See, it's the little things that get disclosed.

BUSH: I like that.

CAMERON: Thanks for joining us, sir.

BUSH: Yes sir, thanks Carl, it's good to see you again...

While other media outlets would normally require connected journalists to step off certain assignments lest there be a conflict of interest, the FNC simply kept the reporter on his beat, without worrying whether someone whose wife was working toward a Bush victory might consciously or unconsciously tilt his stories to help her. A former Fox News employee noted, "the idea that his wife is working for one of the campaigns... not having that sort of line becomes very tempting for somebody who's that creative, who in a sense is that narcissistic and that becomes very easy to self-promote by crossing the line, saying something funny you would never dare say if you were stepping back and looking at it from the sense of a journalism school, and 'is this the right thing for journalism?'—it would never happen."

As another former Fox News employee noted about the FNC's conflict of interest policies:

> It was known in the summer of 2000 that Fox's lead political correspondent covering the Bush campaign, that his wife was campaigning for Bush. And in any other news organization, in fact, in CNN that very summer there was a producer whose husband was a lawyer for the Gore team. And this was a producer who would've naturally covered Gore, who was immediately told you're not to have anything to do with campaign coverage, either covering Bush or covering Gore because of the possible conflict of interest, or the perception of a conflict of interest.

> At Fox, they didn't care. The fact that the senior political reporter, his wife is actually campaigning for the Bush campaign at a time when this guy is covering them, that didn't even register... That's their lack of having some sort of basic journalistic integrity that is just missing from that organization.

But the Bush episode wasn't the last time Cameron's action would raise eyebrows. When John Kerry debated George W. Bush in the first of three Presidential debates, the following article, penned by Cameron, was posted on foxnews.com on October 1, 2004:

> "Didn't my nails and cuticles look great? What a good debate!" Kerry said Friday.

> With the foreign-policy debate in the history books, Kerry hopes to keep the pressure on and the sense of traction going.

> Aides say he will step up attacks on the President in the next few days, and pivot somewhat to the domestic agenda, with a focus on women and abortion rights.

"It's about the Supreme Court. Women should like me! I do manicures," Kerry said.

Kerry still trails in actual horse-race polls, but aides say his performance was strong enough to rally his base and further appeal to voters ready for a change.

"I'm metrosexual—he's a cowboy," the Democratic candidate said of himself and his opponent.

After the first Presidential debate, Cameron put a fake article up on the Fox website that falsely quoted John Kerry.

The article was presented to readers as fact, but Cameron had allegedly written the article in jest, never intending for it to be made public. The gaffe was quickly spotted, the article was yanked and the FNC's website posted a retraction that read, in part, "We regret the error, which occurred because of fatigue and bad judgment, not malice." Had someone else made the same "error" against Fox News, the FNC would have pounded relentlessly at their disparagers. Cameron's mean-spirited and uncalled for "joke" was unprofessional and revealed yet again that Cameron's beliefs about both Republicans and Democrats are too strong for him to be a credible political reporter. But even after his lapse in judgment, he was still filing stories about Kerry. If Cameron ever got bitten by the politics bug, the FNC would undoubtedly allow him to file stories about his own campaign. It's a thought.

Greta Van Susteren

A lawyer by trade, Greta Van Susteren is best known for her two programs on CNN—"Burden of Proof" and, later, "The Point." Though she is an award-winning host who can more than hold her own, before she became a Fox News personality she was mostly known for her distinctive voice and messy hair. Worse, it was the O.J. Simpson trial that gave her a boost in her TV career.

When Van Susteren moved to Fox to host her own show, "On the Record With Greta Van Susteren," she made the cover of *People* magazine: no, she wasn't considered newsworthy because of her journalistic or legal talents, but because she had had a lot of plastic surgery. Hey, new network, new show, new face.

Her purpose on Fox is less defined than that of Alan Colmes. She's supposed to be the left-of-center voice, though her program is supposed to deal more with legal stories in the news than political ones. When Rupert Murdoch was asked about the FNC's political balance, he cited her and Colmes by name as his left-of-center foot soldiers. Van Susteren has disclosed during interviews that her husband John Coale raised money for John Kerry's Presidential campaign.

However, even though Van Susteren's tilt is more left than right, she has often reined in her tendencies and opted to wear kid gloves when interviewing high profile Republicans, something Sean Hannity has yet to do when interviewing Democrat ones. In the segment dubbed "America's Mayor," she

placidly interviewed former New York City mayor Rudolph Giuliani. The segment title was an interesting description for a former mayor of New York City (there may be some grain of truth to the exaggerated title, since New Yorkers see themselves as being the center of the world; calling him merely "America's Mayor" seems somewhat humble). The September 1, 2004 interview hardly hinted at Van Susteren's true political stripes:

> **VAN SUSTEREN:** Live from Madison Square Garden for the last night of the Republican national convention. And joining us here is former New York City mayor Rudy Giuliani. Mayor, you're the big hit in the audience here coming up to the set.
>
> **GIULIANI:** Well, it's been a great convention. I mean, I think it's exceeded all expectations. There was some nervousness about a convention in New York, and I think it turned out to be the perfect place at the perfect time.
>
> And President Bush's speech tonight was a combination of a State of the Union speech and an acceptance speech. It had both. It [had] a lot of stuff [on] policies, domestic policy, but also a great deal of inspiration.

The same interview had Van Susteren asking this not-so-tough question from the program's host:

> **VAN SUSTEREN:** All right, I think everyone would agree you brought down the house with your speech. How much work went into this thing? I mean, it looked like a tremendous amount of work.
>
> **GIULIANI:** It was a lot of work. I wrote it about three weeks ago, rewrote it, went over it with some of my advisers and people. And it just worked. You know...
>
> **VAN SUSTEREN:** Did you practice in front of a mirror?

A few days earlier, on August 25, Van Susteren interviewed Senator John McCain with similar softie questions:

> **VAN SUSTEREN:** All right. I read in the *New York Times* this morning, your mother is in town.
>
> **MCCAIN:** Yes, indeed. Ninety-two-years old, she and her identical twin sister.
>
> **VAN SUSTEREN:** Does she know you told her age on the air?
>
> **MCCAIN:** Oh, yes. I don't know. But she and her identical twin sister are in town and they're having a great time.
>
> **VAN SUSTEREN:** Did they come here tonight.
>
> **MCCAIN:** Yes, they were here tonight. Yes. They're very active. They're very active. Two Christmases ago, I got a call from my mother. And I said where are you? She said Flagstaff. I said what are you doing in Flagstaff? She said I'm driving across the country. Drove across the country by herself—she was only ninety then. (LAUGHTER)

The interview was hardly hard-hitting nor particularly useful:

> **VAN SUSTEREN:** Did she critique your speeches?
>
> **MCCAIN:** Does what?

VAN SUSTEREN: Does she critique your speeches?

MCCAIN: Well, one time I wrote a book… depicting my experiences in prison. That book was excerpted in a Washington magazine, the *Washingtonian*. Part one of those excerpts was the language, foul language that I used yelling at the guards in order to help the morale of my fellow POWs. Phone call, "Johnny?" I said "Yes." She said "I just read that excerpt from your book in the *Washingtonian* magazine." I said "What do you think?" She said "I'm going to come over there and wash your mouth out with soap." (LAUGHTER)

Van Susteren may be Murdoch's cosmetic ace in the hole, but her softball questions to Republican leaders seem to show that she isn't going to rock the boat at Fox. She isn't an ideological opposite to Sean Hannity and she doesn't even host a political show: she mainly talks about the court case *du jour*. She's tolerable, she's watchable, she may even be described as reasonable—but she is not the ideologically balanced host that she is presented as being.

Geraldo Rivera

What can be said about a man who used to be a red hot buzzworthy reporter on ABC News who got the scoops, but then left it all behind to host a low rent tabloid talk show—and got his sorry butt whipped by his thug "guests"? *Spy* magazine compared his then-bandaged-up mug to Bozo the Clown's. He's best known for courting media hype for a live TV special that culminated in opening Al Capone's near-empty vault. The title of his autobiography, *Exposing Myself*, made it sound as if he was busted for being a flasher. More recently, during his stint on the vixen network, he was in hot water for giving sensitive U.S. military information to his viewers. He's supposed to be a left-of-center voice just because he didn't condemn former President Bill Clinton for lying about his debauched affair with Monica Lewinsky. He's done enough damage all by himself; let us leave the man alone.

While most of the Fox personalities mentioned have seen a decent following, respectable ratings, lucrative book deals and the standard perks of being an in-demand B-list quasi-celebrity, none of these hosts and personalities are the main attraction at Fox: none of them alone can define the heart and soul of the heartless and soulless network, nor do they have enough presence, persona and vision to personify the FNC. Despite their well-practiced demeanor, carefully measured words and ability to win their time slots, none can come even close to matching the sheer authority or magnetism of one particular colleague who knows how to work a crowd. And none of them are complex or complicated enough to shape modern thinking. No, none of these other FNC employees can be rightfully called the king of prime-time cable news programs.

That title is strictly reserved for an excitable, raw gentleman by the name of Bill O'Reilly.

Chapter 10

O'Reilly—The Rabid Fox

*"Now we're going to have a nice intelligent
discussion here, gentlemen, and
I'm going to moderate [it]."*

"O'Reilly Factor" host Bill O'Reilly

To be respected in modern Western culture is not to be polite, persistent, hardworking, useful or caring, but to "tell it like it is"—or at least to have the appearance of telling it like it is. It helps to deftly contort and mold your face into a convincing scowl while wagging a wrathful finger at your audience, all the while telling them about the abuses they are allowing themselves to be exposed to. Or telling them about the various evil and nefarious nogoodniks who are skulking around waiting for an unsuspecting victim. Or, perhaps, telling an audience: "Caution, you're about to enter a No Spin Zone."

Fox News' biggest star is Bill O'Reilly: former nomadic TV reporter, one-time anchor of the syndicated tabloid program "Inside Edition" and current feral philosopher king with a nightly opinion slugfest called "The O'Reilly Factor." No other news host can touch his ratings or his clout, nor can any news show title—on cable or network TV—come close to sounding as cool as the "Factor." He makes headlines, writes books, gives speeches and ensures his undisputed place in pop culture history. Professionally, at least, O'Reilly is at his prime.

Though he is mightily educated (a master's degree in Broadcast Journalism from Boston University and a master's degree in Public Administration from Harvard, no less) and had toiled for years as a reporter (as an on-air correspondent for ABC's "World News Tonight," O'Reilly won two Emmys for his reporting), O'Reilly's success doesn't come from acting or sounding like a journalist. He liberally litters the ends of his sentences with "OK?" and "all right?" yet he doesn't get called on the carpet for his borderline-Valley girl tags. He uses crude insults to describe people he doesn't like. He copiously spews his severe sentiments as if they were edicts issued from the heavens. In other words, Bill O'Reilly behaves like an edgy and arrogant warrior-prophet and is handsomely rewarded with a legion of devout, protective viewers who will buy his best-selling bibles and attend his nightly tele-sermons. It's a nice job if you can get it, and Bill O'Reilly's got it in more ways than one.

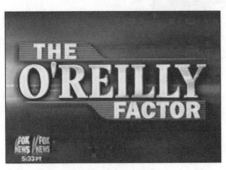

Fox's highest rated program, and the cornerstone of the network.

Yet despite the clear, decisive and regal success for this uninhibited roughhewn character, there's something about the Hamlet-esque O'Reilly that reeks of frustration and misery—something that goes beyond the clichéd and profitable Angry Middle-Aged White Male Conservative schtick that is prevalent in American culture. For someone who's at the top of his game, O'Reilly seems too bitter, and a man who is ill at ease with his surroundings.

At rare times, his outbursts don't seem targeted at anyone in particular, and if those outbursts are focused on an identifiable target, they certainly go over and beyond whatever verbal spanking the person seemed to deserve. O'Reilly seems to be a genuinely melancholy man. He is sympathetic because he seems to be a conflicted individual: while he may rail against various injustices, his routine helps contribute to others. Why can't he be satisfied with what he has? Why won't he be a good sport and smile for America?

It's A Bird! It's A Plane! It's "The O'Reilly Factor"!

The problem is that the incessantly irate "Factor" host is in the wrong place and, unfortunately, he can never get to the place where he could truly shine and be fulfilled. O'Reilly is constricted and stuck in a studio, having to tone down his energy, when he could unleash his mojo somewhere else. So where is it that O'Reilly ought to be? Network television? Wall Street? The White House?

No, none of those places are big enough for him and his ego. The truth is that Bill O'Reilly is a comic book character stuck in the mundane real world, forced to do battle with mere out-of-shape and less-than-swift mortals, most of whom, quite frankly, suck at even rudimentary verbal combat, let alone challenging someone as deft and unpredictable as he is.

The hints of O'Reilly's secret ambition are everywhere: from the self-referential title of his show to the choice of words he uses to describe his various enemies. Unlike most people, famous or otherwise, he actually has a rogue's gallery to battle, and an A-list one to boot (Al Franken, Bill Moyers, Michael Moore, the *New York Times*), and O'Reilly also has a quirky and high-profile menagerie of one-shot caricature opponents with comic book-ready names, such as the obligatory vixen (Jenna Jameson) and bad-ass purveyors of the gangster lifestyle (Ludacris and Eminem, whose mother was on the "Factor") to keep the show interesting. If the segment name "Villain of the Week" doesn't clue you in that O'Reilly may be aware of who Jack Ryder and Vic Sage really are, then you haven't been paying attention to the fact that the "Factor" is a young fan boy's dream come true.

Yet the secret superhero signals go beyond the title and the feuds. O'Reilly uses simple catch phrases that can be easily transformed to have a funny book appeal: *"Stars and stripes! We're entering the No Spin Zone!"* He's a tall guy who has stared down and intimidated seasoned adults who thought they were used to hard, grilling public interviews. He seems as if he's always itching for a fight. His own birth name sounds like the alter-ego of a spunky comic book character. He could even transform a nowhere job in syndicated tabloid-TV hell into an enviable prime-time career with benefits and spin-offs galore. If that isn't a superpower, then nothing else is. Make no mistake: he is a resilient comeback kid who can take it as good as he can give it.

Say what you will about O'Reilly: he may seem boorish, intellectually promiscuous and ethically vexatious, but he's got both powerful energy and a flamboyant persona that are helplessly trapped in the confines of a human body. He seems desperate to put on a cape and cowl and fight menacing aliens to save the world from certain destruction. Life can be so unfair at times.

Regardless of what his detractors may think of him, O'Reilly is brave, alert, ambitious, daring, capable, intelligent and persistent. He has taken strong moral stands that are hard, if not downright impossible to disagree with: he does rail against child exploitation, he does seem to have a real sympathy toward the victimized and the misused. Unlike his employer's sheltered children, O'Reilly has had to claw and crawl his way to the top in a ruthless business with no protectors: he went from market to market, working slowly to the top while taking calculated risks—the level of his success to date was truly earned.

When his career was in limbo, through no fault of his own—always the most frightening and panic-inducing prospect for any journalist who understands the callous nature of his business—he not only refused to give up or wimp out, but he went back to university to better himself. He has a TV show, a radio show and a newspaper column; he gives speeches and writes books (nonfiction and even a novel). Obviously O'Reilly isn't afraid of hard work. Nor does he flaunt his hard-earned wealth. He may be a controversial figure thanks to his outrageous views and behavior, and he may have hurled some despicable and hurtful comments on his show, but as a person, he isn't a villain.

And that is precisely what makes him the most dangerous on-air figure at Fox News today: he is fully aware of all his redeeming qualities and doesn't seem to think he's doing anything wrong. It is his awareness of his good side that makes him utterly impervious to criticism: he desires to right wrongs and his critics rail against him, ergo, his critics must want injustices to continue. Worse, O'Reilly's critics refuse to acknowledge his obvious and numerous positive traits, making it that much easier for O'Reilly to ignore them. People don't look as if they have a legitimate grievance with his one-sided or faulty views—O'Reilly merely accuses them of being out to get him. Some reports accuse O'Reilly of being paranoid, which seems a tad melodramatic and inaccurate: what seems more likely is that he takes too much comfort in his blessings to see what the problem is.

People who work hard and become outraged at injustice aren't immune to being unjust tyrants themselves—in fact, they are more likely to use their morals and their personal travails to justify their severe views and actions. He may have done ample stories on abused children and have found monster success through his perseverance, but O'Reilly is still abusive, disrespectful to the differing life requirements of others and has been chronically sloppy and manipulative with his facts. He plays dirty, he misuses his show to settle childish scores and he throws fits whenever the mood suits him. It is his tendency to gleefully play God with his guests which hints that O'Reilly's troubling dark side has neither been properly inhibited nor fully acknowledged by him.

Regardless of what his admirers may think, O'Reilly isn't a hero: he fancies himself as an outsider, not to mention one who has let his anger get the better of him one time too many. Though O'Reilly isn't a bad guy, he would still be problematic if he were to be left unchecked.

Unfortunately, his keepers at Fox News—particularly his savior and enabler Roger Ailes—blithely and recklessly unleashed O'Reilly's righteous rage onto an ill-equipped public for ratings and buzz, seemingly unconcerned about the extent of the damage and pain that O'Reilly's unchecked anger can bring to innocent people. Boffo ratings at the expense of societal cohesion and compassion is irresponsible, but Ailes' marching orders were to defeat CNN, not to preserve American values or dignity.

Whether viewers want to see him as a hero, anti-hero or villain, O'Reilly can be relied on to consistently summon Fox's core constituents to Murdoch's GOP love-fest night after night. As mesmerizing as his viewers may see him as, O'Reilly seems to see himself as the stern, but pragmatic and moral leader the rest of the country desperately needs. O'Reilly seems to be readying himself for bigger and better things: why else did he enroll at Harvard University's John F. Kennedy School of Government in 1995? He has managed to find his success by fostering a take-charge persona, but could his schtick translate to a political career?

Speculations about O'Reilly's political ambitions are too far ahead to matter at the moment. What makes him a formidable television force is his presence, charisma and persona. As journalist David Brock noted, "he has a lot invested… in the idea that he's giving real, truthful, solid information. He denies it's spin; I believe he says he's not a conservative." There may be some truth to that assessment: Bill O'Reilly has done a splendid job of looking after Bill O'Reilly. Ideologues usually can't land on their feet the same way as pragmatists. What O'Reilly does do is blur opinion with outrage without letting facts and decorum get in the way of a good show.

Manners Are for Losers

O'Reilly's success has been credited to his ability to "tell it like it is." But what does "telling it like it is" really mean? And does he really tell his viewers how it is, or does he actually tell them something else?

Much of what O'Reilly says isn't how it is at all: he assured his viewers Iraq was teeming with sub rosa WMD (it wasn't). He warned them that Canadians were indoctrinating their children to despise Americans (they were too busy going about their Canadian lives to bother). He told his viewers his call for a boycott on France was a success, but it turned out to be more of a bust. Oh, well.

What he tells his viewers "it is" is what they hope it is: someone else's fault. He presents his followers with a highly identifiable list of people and nations that he assures them are responsible for their suf-

ferings and personal failures in life. This is the pinhead who is preventing you from realizing your dreams! This is the idiot who is responsible for your misery at work! Here is the boob who is stopping you from having a good time on a Friday night! Here is the nut who wants to raise your taxes! This is the creep who wants to corrupt your children! Get a load of the thug who wants to kill you! They want to steal your money! They want to imprison you! They want to castrate you and make you feel impotent! They must pay! Come on troops, let's get 'em!

To whip the audience into fighting form, the "Factor" emcee has to know what issues are going to trigger a strong emotional response from his viewers on a nightly basis: he has to offer his audience more than objects of scorn, he has to associate those targets with problems his audience can relate to. O'Reilly also offers brazen insults and observations that are too emotional and slanted for a serious news program to permit. As he warned his viewers on July 13, 2004:

> **O'REILLY:** The smearing of America continues... While the federal government is punishing lewd behavior on the public airwaves, something far worse is going unchallenged by the Feds. Slander, libel and defamation have now become profit centers with weasels putting out vicious falsehoods and running to the banks with their blood money. The latest atrocity is a rap song by a guy named Jadakiss, who is just a pitiful pawn being run by the huge Vivendi Corporation, a French company that's distributing some of the most vile entertainment [we at the "O'Reilly Factor" have] ever seen.

O'Reilly has made it no secret that he dislikes the French for not supporting the U.S. war in Iraq, as well as rappers for promoting an outlaw lifestyle. The fact that he can connect the French with rappers gets him giddy: he can hit two enemies for the price of one.

Because he will go outside traditional journalistic boundaries of decorum, O'Reilly can and will cut the microphone of elected public officials. He will call his recalcitrant opponents demeaning names. He will tell his adult guests to shut up. O'Reilly is the boss from Hell, and his hostile guests are treated as if they were his incompetent subordinates who had the audacity not to agree with him. Labor laws aren't going to save any guest who finds himself getting an abusive tongue-lashing in the No Spin Zone.

In other words, O'Reilly is allowed to be as rude, unthinking and hurtful as he wants to be—or more importantly, be as hurtful as the audience wishes they could be toward others. There is an underlying acrimony to almost everything O'Reilly says, yet he doesn't turn off viewers with his depressing and bitter worldview. His behavior mimics the divorced man who was forced to pay an exorbitant alimony to his greedy ex-wife or the divorced woman whose husband left her for a younger and prettier model. He's angry, bitter, unforgiving and trying to use that unresolved and boiling rage to make others feel as miserable as he seems to feel. Usually a useless personality like that is an excellent people repellant, but O'Reilly seems to defy logic and has found himself a large and devoted audience.

If O'Reilly's success is any indication, parents are continually making the same mistake with their children: they insist that children "mind their manners" and "be polite." O'Reilly doesn't do anything of the sort and yet he's rewarded for his behavior. He has rewritten the rules of prime-time news talk shows: a host is now expected to challenge certain guests by way of stinging personal attacks, not necessarily by using facts and research to expose their factual and logical flaws. Etiquette is treated as if it was reserved for the servant classes who have to learn to hold their tongues in order to maintain their meager wages. O'Reilly's in charge and he doesn't have to dance around another's feelings or self-esteem.

His interview style is one that can only be described as staccato: he repeatedly interrupts his hostile guests in the middle of their sentences, thereby not allowing them to complete their thoughts, as he did to one guest on June 5, 2002:

O'REILLY: But Harvard does agree with [the] Arab Holy Land Foundation raising money for terrorists. They think that's fine.

WRIGHT: No, I think you're conflating...

O'REILLY: Well, then, why aren't they banned?

WRIGHT: Well, let me finish, and I'll tell you. I think you're conflating two issues that aren't related in any way.

O'REILLY: Sure I am. No, I'm not. Not at all. Mr.—look, you got groups coming on...

WRIGHT: The fundraising...

O'REILLY: ...campus, you got—Miss Wright, you got groups coming on campus, OK? It's the same thing. One's allowed, one isn't.

WRIGHT: No, the...

O'REILLY: You see my point?

WRIGHT: I see your point, but I'd like to get a chance to share mine.

Why inconvenience someone by inviting them on a program to inform and debate, but then not let them inform or debate? Yet many invited "Factor" guests find that they can't even express their most rudimentary thoughts because their combative host won't let them. Somehow, regular "Factor" viewers don't seem to mind that they are watching others gasping for air in the No Spin Zone. It's what makes O'Reilly an apt icon of his era: in a time where fear and distrust prevails and a crude 'tude is more important than thoughtful and constructive analysis, O'Reilly seems to be the poster child for disruptive behavior and having the ability to make niceness look like stupidity. Anyone trying to disarm O'Reilly with civility will find himself struggling to get his point across and will be trying to ward off O'Reilly's verbal attacks.

O'Reilly's critics see him as an unthinking boor; his admirers see him as someone who is willing to stand up for wholesome values and tradition. Both sides still can't grasp the nuances and complexities of the O'Reilly Enigma—both sides are right and wrong at the same time, but both don't quite see the big picture. The most frustrating thing for O'Reilly must be that not only do his detractors underestimate his canny, powerful genius and his subtle intellectual dexterity, but that even his most diehard fans fail to see it, too. Both sides hear the harsh tone of his raised voice and his brusque putdowns and think that that's all there is to him. Ironically, that across-the-board underestimation is precisely what gives O'Reilly the edge.

There are, and have been, other attack-dog hosts—from Rush Limbaugh and Michael Savage to Wally George and Morton Downey Jr. They all had their fifteen minutes, but none had the same dignity, credentials or head for strategy as O'Reilly. Downey was a joke and a jerk. George was known to hire actors to play left-wing lunatics. On the surface, Limbaugh may seem to be in the same league as O'Reilly, but the portly former pill-popping talker's tirades lack the style and brilliance that has made O'Reilly a television draw. If it came down to an intellectual duel between Limbaugh and O'Reilly, Limbaugh would be mortally wounded within seconds.

O'Reilly is nothing like his fellow combative talking heads; for one, he publicly denies any political affiliations. For another, his arguments are not usually based on simplistic, standard-issue Republican snaps. If they were, O'Reilly wouldn't be commanding the attention that he does. He is in a league by himself: he has created a persona that is utterly unique, yet feels like a well-worn cliché. He's familiar, but novel. He's a strategist who resorts to insults. He can debate, but keeps interrupting his hostile guests. O'Reilly is a living pastiche of contradictory elements.

> O'Reilly can be relied on to consistently summon Fox's core constituents to the GOP love-fest night after night.

Yet O'Reilly's contradictions work for him. Who else could proclaim his program to be a No Spin Zone, but then refer to his guests as "liberals" and "pinheads"? Who else could accuse critic and reporter Jack Matthews of "hiding under" his desk for not wanting to be a guest on his radio program, but then ignore other critics who are willing to challenge him? Who else could spend decades cultivating envious journalistic credentials, but at the height of his career gossip and ask guests about the mental condition of others with a blunt "Is he a nut?" or calling suspected murder suspects "bizarro"? He has no tact, and yells at many of his guests, but then tells one of his guests "You made your argument, and I'm going to rebut the argument. Then you can rebut my rebuttal. That's how gentlemen behave." Who else can read out fan mail on his show, but then claim that certain unknown masses are "always mad at me"?

Many of O'Reilly's detractors don't *get* him and do not have a full appreciation of his craft, wit and resourcefulness. O'Reilly does not mindlessly and indiscriminately disembowel and devour his nightly opponents, he disembowels and devours them with *style*—there is a certain finesse and aesthetic appreciation to what O'Reilly does. There is a method to his madness, and he has elevated unpredictable and ruthless ad hominem attacks to a craft, even an art form.

Those shouts of "Shut up!" and "Cut his mike!" are well-timed and directed at a very specific audience: O'Reilly was a working class boy, and with that upbringing comes the special knowledge that the "take no bull" approach is highly respected within certain blue collar circles. While the bourgeoisie may shake their coifed heads in disbelief, the Coors crowd grew up with many of their closest loved ones shouting similar commands, and like what they hear. It's palatable dysfunction.

O'Reilly is not trying to be all things to all people, and this cagey strategy works for him. Unlike the compassionless and insipid Rush Limbaugh, who justified the humiliation and torture of Iraqi soldiers, O'Reilly's strength lies in his ability to stand up to the P.C. set without seeming callous to his chosen audience. O'Reilly has a sense of timing and understanding of when to throw down his full weight on his opponent and when to hold back. For the most part, he can read his target and decide on an effective strategy. He can use his working class bravado and his marketable worldview to endear himself to his audience.

O'Reilly doesn't run rough-shod over every progressive, and not every conservative gets the kid glove treatment from him: he gave Whitewater figure Susan McDougal such a walk on his program that she openly expressed her relief and gratitude ("You are so nice. Thank you very much... I was so afraid. I think you are fair"). His interview with U2 front man Bono about the AIDS crisis in Africa was both professional and educational. Though he generally gives a hard time to progressives, there is still enough unpredictability to keep his opponents from regaining their balance.

On the other hand, not every conservative has gotten an easy ride with O'Reilly. To dismiss O'Reilly as some senseless and raving automaton or thug is missing the point: he is a natural-born hunter who knows how to hunt and stalk his prey with flair. Anyone who thinks otherwise is underestimating O'Reilly's intelligence and skill at their own risk. His is a rare, misused talent, though his keen senses have left him alone with, and at the mercy of, his primal rage when he gets sucker-punched by one of his guests. It is these moments that critics erroneously grab on to, even though these incidences don't paint an accurate picture of why O'Reilly needs to be reined in.

An Unpredictable Trek Through the No Spin Zone

For those who can stomach the ride, the No Spin Zone is supposed to be the one, true place where Truth and Justice can be uncovered. The implication is that Bill O'Reilly's tough interviewing style can immediately strip away a guest's mask and force the interviewee to present himself and the situation as it really is: no window dressing, no sentence parsing, no spin. The amazing O'Reilly will cut through the lies and exaggerations to separate the virtuous from the villainous, and the latter will be exposed and brought to task for their misdeeds. In brightest day, in blackest night, no evil will escape O'Reilly's sight.

That's the official theory, but of course the truth is a little more mundane. O'Reilly has opinions about people, events and ideologies, and he shares them with his like-minded viewers. There are people that O'Reilly tolerates, and those he has no qualms disparaging. Some of those villains include world leaders, while others fall into the "Page Six" category, such as entertainers. Singer Whitney Houston was referred to as a "degenerate." Ludacris was deemed to be a "rap thug." Eminem was called a "vile rap star," "thug" and "major villain." Bullies on the playground can always aspire to ply their gift of hurtful put-downs to a lucrative career on a cable news show.

Of course, Houston and Eminem are easy targets, and their bad-ass behavior makes them vulnerable to O'Reilly's cold admonishments. But bullies pick the easy targets; they don't take on people who are stronger and more powerful than they are. Picking on singers with colorful and controversial

lifestyles isn't new, but it's still a reliable way to get attention and a reputation as an upstanding citizen. Eminem may have immortalized his childhood tormentor D'Angelo Bailey in one of his songs, but if he thought his success would shield him from future browbeating, his tactic backfired.

So if picking on entertainers is predictable, then what's the O'Reilly advantage? One of the "Factor" host's strengths lie in his disarming demeanor. O'Reilly doesn't seem so intimidating when he casually introduces his program with a simple, "Hi, I'm Bill O'Reilly." In fact, at the beginning of his programs, he often sounds laid back and non-threatening. He doesn't look like an attack dog; in fact, he looks as if he could be your favorite high school teacher.

Which is precisely what he used to do before he took the plunge into a journalistic career: O'Reilly taught high school in Miami. That job alone must have prepared him for his "Factor" stint—and helped him learn a few good put-downs from his students. You can always rely on a cabal of cocky, mouthy teenagers to teach you a thing or two about how to insult and snap at someone in order to elevate your status among your jaded peers.

Insulting and snapping are two activities at which O'Reilly excels. Unlike most news hosts, who refrain from school-yard taunts, the "Factor" emcee revels in them. He also has the ability to shoot a series of unpleasant statements at his opponent in rapid succession, then make it seem as if the person suddenly agrees with O'Reilly's side. This method is deceptive and difficult to achieve, but the spry and swift O'Reilly has the key gifts of quick thought and forceful energy. It seemed as if O'Reilly did just that with director Michael Moore when they debated the merits of the U.S. invasion in Iraq on O'Reilly's July 27, 2004 program:

> **O'REILLY:** Any government? Hitler, in Germany, not a threat to us at the beginning, but over there executing people all day long—you would have let him go?
>
> **MOORE:** That's not true. Hitler, with Japan, attacked the United States.
>
> **O'REILLY:** From '33 until '41, he wasn't an imminent threat to the United States.
>
> **MOORE:** There's a lot of things we should have done.

O'Reilly's next comment may seem innocuous on the surface, but it would work in his favor:

> **O'REILLY:** You wouldn't have removed him.

In a slight tactical error, Moore answered the question in this way...

> **MOORE:** I wouldn't have even allowed him to come to power.

...allowing the shrewd O'Reilly to deliver his finishing move:

> **O'REILLY:** That was a preemption from Michael Moore. You would have invaded.

Of course the implication was that an "honest" Michael Moore would have also invaded Iraq the way President Bush did (but O'Reilly did not take into consideration that the two situations were vastly different—there was no pile of millions of tortured and starved innocents in Iraq, nor was Saddam expanding his empire or acquiring WMDs). Though Michael Moore also managed to score points against the "Factor" host during that verbal match, O'Reilly held his own and maintained control throughout the interview. The interview was classic O'Reilly.

The carnivalesque ride through the No Spin Zone also includes a heavy dose of personal and professional score settling. Any person of note who criticizes O'Reilly can expect to be the subject of a "Factor" segment. When the *Source*, a hip-hop magazine, chastised O'Reilly for his strong anti hip-hop stance, O'Reilly brought the lashing down on his February 18, 2003 show:

> **O'REILLY:** [...The *Source*] personally attacks me in an article called "Five Reasons Bill O'Reilly Can Never Come to the 'Hood." The piece is the usual propaganda, that I didn't have a working class upbringing, that I'm against blacks, that I'm a bully, blah, blah, blah.

During the segment, O'Reilly framed the issue in a way that dismissed his opponent before he ever had a chance to present his point of view:

> **O'REILLY:** Now the reason this kind of personal stuff is put out there is that those who sell and condone the selling of mind poison in the form of antisocial rap cannot win the argument. The stuff hurts unsupervised children, many of whom are poor.

O'Reilly was also canny enough to introduce his guest this way: "...the founder and CEO of the *Source*, David Mays, a Harvard graduate. So, you know, two Harvard men here. You know. Let's have a civil discussion." O'Reilly let his viewers know that the editor of the hip-hop magazine was an Ivy Leaguer and not some genuine, street-smart tough. During the tussle later on, O'Reilly made sure to point out that his opponent was exploiting others with his magazine.

During the match, O'Reilly retorted to Mays that "I've done more reporting from the 'hood than you'll ever do, all right... I have twenty-eight-years reporting... in the worst neighborhoods in this country... I've seen more than you'll ever see." O'Reilly's underdog moral posturing endears him to his audience. He mixes the personal with the political; he isn't afraid to win an argument not by parading dry facts, but by bringing up snatches of his personal biography. He uses the feminization of debate to his advantage. O'Reilly doesn't limit or inhibit himself: he uses a pastiche of different arguing styles and techniques to throw his opponent off track and keep the folks back home satisfied. He doesn't debate to inform; he debates to win.

Invoking moral arguments is one of O'Reilly's pet debating tactics. More specifically, he frames the issue in such a way that he seems ethical while his opponent seems depraved. For example, when one set of O'Reilly's guests were arguing about Pepsi's flip-flopping over their association with O'Reilly's nemesis Ludacris, they defended the rap star's lyrics by insisting that young children are supervised and therefore will not be harmed by the content of the lyrics. O'Reilly merely retorted, "What if the nine-year-old is unsupervised? You don't—see, you guys are willing to throw those kids away."

As a retaliation, it was a cunning masterstroke and typical of the way O'Reilly operates. He valiantly takes the high moral stand protecting the women and children, while simultaneously making his opponent look like the defender of the reprehensible. The pigeons may object, but O'Reilly strikes first, and as most spinmeisters will tell you, it is the first message that people will remember. Rebuttals have no effect. O'Reilly will quickly frame the debate with his strategic sucker punches, while his perpetually stunned and defensive targets can only offer angry, disjointed and impotent denials.

For O'Reilly, it must be like shooting fish in a barrel.

His guests continually fall and trap themselves in O'Reilly's sticky and vertigo-inducing No Spin Zone—they may expect a grilling and personal attack, but they don't seem entirely prepared for exactly how O'Reilly will strike at them. Most hostile guests don't look as if they truly grasp the O'Reilly method of personal combat: he sizes up his targets, he assesses their intellectual weaknesses, the strength of their on-air presence and their potential image problems—and then he takes the most salient of their vulnerabilities to paint them as immoral and dangerous. It is here where O'Reilly almost always has the upper hand: most people are generally poor self-judgers and self-critics.

Bill O'Reilly as a guest on C-SPAN.

As a rule, most of us don't see ourselves as immoral, and so we do not fathom that anyone else will see us that way, either. It is hard to admit that others can see our most routine actions and deepest beliefs as being utterly despicable. We get angry at mean people who hurt cute little bunnies and we read *Curious George* to our children with all the funny little voices; so how can anyone accuse us of being immoral monsters and be effective? How does O'Reilly get away with it?

Since the Western world is one where raw, primal debating and personal moral criticism are frowned upon and individuality is encouraged, O'Reilly has his targets right where he wants them. Who's used to receiving these types of eye-popping accusations and knowing how to anticipate them before they happen? O'Reilly's No Spin Zone is really a "no-control zone"—his targets have no control over their carefully managed image, nor how they will appear during the interview, because they come ill-prepared to defend their worldviews and the very stuff of their flawed, fragile souls. When everything is sterilized and sanitized, even the smallest bacteria to pass through can cause serious damage to the system. When certain guests naïvely enter O'Reilly's no-control zone with no protection, they are exposing themselves to a fast and fierce contagion with no mercy.

Few guests seem to have been savvy enough to anticipate and ward off O'Reilly's ingenious attacks, such as U2's Bono, who had grasped that praising right-wing heroes would prevent a confrontation with O'Reilly. The sage Irish rocker also seemed careful to give ample credit to Americans in their fight against AIDS worldwide, making his time in the hot seat more than bearable. Most other hostile guests can never grope their way out of the "Factor" glass house of horrors; no matter how visible the floor plan and routine are from the outside, the guests always trap themselves right in front of the distorting mirror as they're trying to get away from the taunting and intimidating O'Reilly. Those hapless Watsons never realize they're going up against someone who has the strategic genius of a Professor Moriarity.

Some Watsons still think they understand O'Reilly's methods. *Slate*'s Jack Shafer thought he did when he offered his readers some advice on O'Reilly's methods, including to be larger than life, to agree to go to the "Factor" studio to debate and to kill him with kindness. But Shafer is missing the point: O'Reilly knows his targets' weaknesses and knows for the most part what buttons to push and how to twist their words. If Shafer used those methods, confident that he'd beat O'Reilly, he'd find that he had just set himself up as a perfect "Factor" patsy.

O'Reilly playing cat and mouse in his own studio simply makes for more riveting television. You can't fake or bluff your way out of the No Spin Zone: you either have the intellectual mettle and strategic shrewdness to challenge him, or you don't. Shafer's advice to approach O'Reilly in a "low voice, reassuring tenor, respectful tone" is bemusing, but underestimates O'Reilly's intelligence and hunting instincts: lordosis is a posture of submission, not confident aggression. Unfortunately for those peddling snarky instant analysis, O'Reilly is not an easy mark to read.

An O'Reilly Primer

O'Reilly presents himself as the proverbial working-class boy done good. He has a blue collar sense of pride, and he proves that the old school version of the American Dream is alive and well in the 21st century. As his online biography on foxnews.com proudly proclaims:

> The "O'Reilly Factor"… is the most-watched program on cable news and has caused the powerful in America to duck for cover as the rigidly enforced "No Spin Zone" deals with the nation's most important issues in a straightforward and provocative manner.

> From humble beginnings on Long Island, NY, Bill O'Reilly has risen to become "the new pope of TV Journalism" according to television critic Marvin Kitman.

Yes, his parents were so poor they couldn't afford the soap they needed to wash out his mouth. His father was an accountant, not quite blue collar, but not privileged, either. The Fox News crib sheet also went on to paint a picture of a down-to-earth everyday boy unaware of his true destiny:

> While growing up O'Reilly had no idea that journalism would be his calling. He lived in a modest house with his father, mother and sister in the Westbury section of Levittown. O'Reilly began working in his early teens mowing lawns, which evolved into a house painting business.

Who could fault a man who grew up mowing his neighbors' lawns? Finally, a scrappy talking head pontiff for the Coors crowd. Last, but not least, the biography assures Fox viewers that success has not spoiled Bill O'Reilly:

> Bill O'Reilly continues to live on Long Island where his best friends are guys with whom he attended first grade.

Does O'Reilly's working class charisma ever end? A real man doing real journalism; not like those self-adoring pretty boy anchors and hosts who preen and blather in front of the camera, no sir. He's just a good old boy who shoots from the hip, according to his employers, and that is O'Reilly's appeal. Good old boys trust other good old boys. Ergo, they can trust O'Reilly.

Though many of his detractors dispute that O'Reilly came from a working class background, there is no denying that he fully comprehends the blue collar mindset, making the "did-he-or-didn't-he"

arguments petty. What many critics from this line of questioning do not understand is that the working class set do not automatically embrace every person claiming a modest background; poseurs can be quickly spotted and dismissed. It takes a certain mindset and experience to understand what it's like to be denied opportunities and advantages in a person's career and personal life because his parents couldn't afford to stop for an hour to socialize or make the right connections for him. He's young, willing, able, capable and ready to set the world on fire, and the door to better things is promptly shut in his face. It can be a rude awakening that blinds some people from noticing that everyone, including the well-heeled, also have struggles to face. Spending the next couple of decades banging and tearing down those doors unleashes a certain anger and resentment that is hard to ever shake. O'Reilly's post-success bitterness seems genuine.

In that regard, O'Reilly represents the working class ideology: go for the simple explanation, be unpretentious and take no bull from anyone you disagree with (people you agree with get a free walk since they're obviously not giving any bull). Psychological or philosophical explanations are too complicated and sound wishy-washy, so they must be wrong. Life is hard, there are dangers everywhere and outsiders demanding a piece of the action can't be trusted. It's this know-it-all pool hall wisdom O'Reilly espouses every time he rails against child killers, gangster rap and the "liberal elite print press."

Except that O'Reilly isn't a working class guy anymore, and he hasn't been for years. He has more than one university degree to his name (there's nothing blue collar in having an undergraduate degree in the humanities); he has trained his mind to think in terms of hypothetical constructs and theories. He wasn't a factory worker who had to break his back and lose his health to put food on his family's table; he started his family late in life when he was wealthy and had already established himself professionally. He was always a white collar employee. He was a teacher and a news producer: two careers that deal with being exposed to raw information that has to be evaluated, analyzed, processed and disseminated to a generally intellectually naïve crowd. No dirt or grease blemishes his hands.

No, O'Reilly isn't one of them, even though he curries favor with the party boy set. O'Reilly hasn't been a laborer or a discontent working stiff, and the day you are pulling down a multimillion dollar salary, you cease to become a good old boy. O'Reilly has the biggest audience share of any cable news program: that alone makes him the Establishment and part of the conservative elite television press. He has reportedly mused about running for the Senate, where in his own private paradise he resoundly defeats Hillary Clinton and brings justice to his fellow New Yorkers. His is not the life of a worn-down grunt, but he still knows how to speak to them.

The World According to Bill

Getting paid to be opinionated sounds like an easy and fun job, but it still is hard work: how do you develop an opinion for everything—even topics you don't qualify to have an opinion on? Researching and analyzing takes too much energy and bogs down the opinion-spewing process: an audience does not want to be bored with dry details, nor do they want to hear a complex or thoughtful argument about how a tolerant and centrist approach is the best way to understand the situation. The opinion has to be strong, simple, punchy and one-sided.

On some days it's just too hard to come up even with a simple and punchy opinion, so the next best thing is to hurl an insult at one side of an issue. For a professional "news channel" such as FNC, empty put-downs flow freely from the mouths of "serious" hosts. The "Factor" host's frequent use of name-calling is par for the course of the FNC; it's just that O'Reilly happens to be the worst offender.

To justify the numerous put-downs, O'Reilly needs to dig up reasons why his targets of scorn deserve to be dismissed and ridiculed. People are either mentally sound (if they agree with him) or raving idealistic morons (if they don't). There are no shades of gray or complicated explanations O'Reilly needs to account for when he issues his edicts; he simply dismisses with a quick and devastating explanation. For example, he introduced the results of a survey this way on his November 21, 2002 show: "A new study by the National Geographic Society said most American students are dunderheads when it comes to geography."

O'Reilly must have been in one of his moods when he cast this pearl of wisdom to his viewers on a January 27, 2003 edition of the "O'Reilly Factor":

> **BILL O'REILLY:** You can say you're standing with the people of the world, but if they believe this, you're standing with the pinheads of the world who don't know anything.
>
> To basically say that the United States government, removing Manuel Noriega...

Whether O'Reilly thought this evil organization known as the Pinheads of the World were out to dominate and destroy civilization wasn't made entirely clear but, suffice to say, O'Reilly has a quaint tendency to talk in comic book clichés that can be annoying at the worst of times and mildly endearing at best. O'Reilly would continue to make his point using ungentlemanly and unjournalistic terms:

> **SOLAY:** Who was an ally of the United States.
>
> **O'REILLY:** I don't care. It doesn't—so was Stalin, OK? I mean, you have no idea how history unfolds and how it's different. It fogs in, it fogs out. It depends on the circumstances.
>
> Manuel Noriega, running a cartel, a drug distribution cartel out of Panama and we don't have the moral right to go in there and remove him?
>
> That's insane.

The villainous pinheads would pop up again, this time supporting another one of O'Reilly's baddies, namely William Jefferson Clinton:

> **O'REILLY:** So listen, I didn't hear a word from you, Miles, or any of your organizations, when President Clinton initiated the regime change in Yugoslavia. You didn't say a word about it. And none of these pinheads would have signed it, because they like Clinton.

If Solay did not know his motives for his antiwar stance, O'Reilly would outline them for him in the exchange; however, O'Reilly's psychoanalysis would be liberally peppered with a string of insults:

O'REILLY: What this is about is, you don't like Bush, you don't like the Republicans and you're going to use this shoddy, cheap and denigrating propaganda, offensive to the families of lost people, to make your point.

But this time it would be O'Reilly who would get a surprise, not with cruder and cooler insults, but with a juicy and unexpected plot twist:

SOLAY: There are family members from September 11 who had signed...

O'REILLY: Nobody signed this from September 11.

O'Reilly's overconfident assertion would be resoundly disproved by the steady Solay, who seemed to have an ace in the hole:

SOLAY: Jeremy Glick, who lost his father in September 11, has signed this statement. As well as a group called A Peaceful Tomorrow.

What? Fresh meat? A new adventure? A new member O'Reilly could add to his ever expanding rogue's gallery? A baddie with a twist? Someone new to battle and conquer in the arena? No way! An intrigued O'Reilly could not quite contain his happy hunter's heart:

O'REILLY: We'll get that guy Jeremy Glick on tomorrow if that's the case. I'm not sure it is the case.

It must have all sounded too good to the seasoned O'Reilly, but the relish of the thought of someone new to take on seemed to get his adrenaline going—yes, taking on this new villain was going to be fun, and a top priority:

O'REILLY: You know that. And there's a reason they have. All right. Jeremy Glick. OK, we're going to get him.

That triple-entendre cue "get him" probably sent his underlings to instantly and frantically scour the Internet for this new opponent, but their boss quickly went back to the current battle at hand, such as laying down the law to Solay:

O'REILLY: Listen, again, you want to be against the war, fine. I respect that.

You want to say that we are the moral equivalent to terrorists...

SOLAY: That's not what we say.

O'REILLY: Yes it is. You read that. That's exactly what it says.

The haughty and trifling "did-not-did-too" exchange would prove less than exciting, but it did prove that O'Reilly always stands his ground:

SOLAY: Read the quote. Read the quote.

O'REILLY: I read the quote.

SOLAY: It's a different quote.

Always ready to decimate his opponent's standing in the community, O'Reilly will be ready with any evidence he believes will deliver a decisive death blow to his hostile guest's message. Few viewers could feel some sympathy or accept Solay's point of view, but just in case a few viewers started to waiver and tolerate Solay's point of view, O'Reilly ended the interview by providing both concrete evidence of his opponent's perceived misdeeds and context:

> **O'REILLY:** It's right there in black and white. And everybody can read it on billoreilly. com, if you want to read it again.
>
> All right, Mr. Solay, we appreciate you coming in, but this is disgraceful.

Jeremy Glick: O'Reilly's personal nightmare.

The backhanded ending was vintage O'Reilly, insulting to the opponent with a hint of begrudging niceties—sure, the host appreciated his guest coming in; so much so that he called his actions disgraceful. O'Reilly opens his segments by framing the terms of debate, then closes recapping what he thinks of his hostile guest. No matter, O'Reilly could now salivate over his upcoming battle with this new guy named Glick.

However, the battle with Jeremy Glick would not go according to plan for O'Reilly, making it one of his few unmitigated failures in the No Spin Zone arena (for a more detailed account of the Glick episode, see Chapter 16).

Fox's motto *du jour* may be "we report; you decide," but the "O'Reilly Factor" leaves little room for viewers to make their own decisions without feeling some serious cognitive dissonance for disagreeing with the host's point of view. Ideological rivals are stupid, immoral, even insane according to O'Reilly. The "insanity offense" is an infrequent, but trusty tool in O'Reilly's utility belt. When O'Reilly discussed the issue of rabid hate mail from Rush Limbaugh fans (who had sent hate mail to Limbaugh's various detractors), he used method head-shrinking on his November 21, 2002 program:

> **O'REILLY:** ...once it crosses over into the insane realm, it's not the responsibility of the radio or television commentator.
>
> I'm going to give you another example. The danger swings both ways.

O'Reilly didn't think hosts should be held accountable for the ravings and actions of their more strident and malicious fans. Limbaugh's fans may have wished death on an MSNBC ex-President's disabled son because the former executive criticized Limbaugh in a newspaper column, but those were the breaks. O'Reilly continued to play armchair psychiatrist, making tasteful and sensitive diagnoses of Limbaugh's various overzealous critics:

> **O'REILLY:** Everybody, including Rush Limbaugh—you know, Rush Limbaugh is the target of nuts all the time, you see? Because of what he says about Tom Daschle and what he says about Osama bin Laden and the others. People want to do him and his family harm as well.

O'Reilly skirted around the issue of whether certain current events hosts attract and incite certain unstable characters; instead, he flipped the issue around and bridged his reply toward a more sympathetic and self-serving topic (well, we get malicious mail, too). "Bridging" is a popular tool used by the media-savvy to avoid answering hard questions. O'Reilly then discussed how his life was af-

fected by these nasty letter-writers, and his stoicism in the face of adversity certainly put the likes of Mandela and Gandhi to shame:

> **O'REILLY:** But you don't hear Rush Limbaugh complaining or even Bill O'Reilly on the air about the danger that we face just by speaking out.

Insult-laden interviewing and churlish ranting isn't just a job for O'Reilly, it's a calling. His comic book thought processes continually creep up in his product: he talks about the inherent dangers of his job, he melodramatically cautions his readers about the enemies who are out to destroy him and democracy. Though O'Reilly may believe he never complains on air about his problems with his critics, that's pretty much a big part of the O'Reilly routine. It's not as if he never mentions Al Franken or Bill Moyers on a regular basis. If by "danger" O'Reilly means criticism, then perhaps he is not as rugged as he appears.

The mere thought of admonishing comments caused O'Reilly to digress into a superhero's soliloquy:

> **O'REILLY:** So my point is this, anyone who speaks out, anyone, is at risk in America. We live in a dangerous place. We live in a dangerous world. Anyone who gives an opinion on any side is in danger. Is that not the truth?

Not getting a standing ovation for every pearl of wisdom that is cast or being called on the carpet for appalling worldviews is hardly lethal, but O'Reilly's aside was worthy of a Batman graphic novel. There is a certain *je ne sais quois* about O'Reilly's dark, gritty and dramatic speeches, *non*?

When O'Reilly isn't openly complaining about the dangers of being a superhost, he resorts to using childish insults to describe people he doesn't like. Nothing fancy or heroic with O'Reilly: you won't be catching him trying to think up subtle and clever put downs—he just uses ones that will get the job done without having to worry whether he will be fined by the FCC. One of those more juvenile episodes transpired on his July 1, 1999 program:

> **O'REILLY:** See, Hunter's an incompetent. We all know that. He's a boob, OK? So if you want to solve the case, you remove him, right?

Easy insults; easy answers. Just malign and clean house and everything will be all right in the end. For viewers looking for a quick solution, they've found their man in O'Reilly.

What is Bill O'Reilly?

What is Bill O'Reilly to his fans and critics? Figuring out O'Reilly may seem simple on the surface. His fans think he's the man, while his detractors think he's an overbearing jerk. He's someone who either needs anger-management training or who has little patience for positive self-presentation. He's either unprofessional for calling people "pinheads," "boobs" and "idiots" or he's a breath of fresh air for doing it. He is either the man who redefined the rules of television news programs or destroyed the genre entirely.

And yet none of those descriptions give a satisfactory answer. Literalists may define him as a "star," a television personality, a host or even a journalist, but all those well-worn labels are missing the point.

O'Reilly's success doesn't stem from being professional in the traditional sense. There are countless talking heads spewing news, analysis and opinion, but none have achieved the same success or loyal following as O'Reilly. You're not supposed to cheer or boo for the guy who's presenting or analyzing the news. You're not supposed to notice him or care. You're supposed to watch these programs to get informed, not psyched. Making a strong positive or negative emotional investment in someone who interviews newsmakers sounds ridiculous, but that's exactly what O'Reilly has working for him. Loving him or loathing him is irrelevant and doesn't throw light on his function.

There is something more to the man, obviously. Off camera, he is mortal and common. On camera, his humanity is discarded by his audience, who transform him into a symbol. To understand O'Reilly's success, it's important to not ask "Who is Bill O'Reilly," but "*What* is Bill O'Reilly?" More precisely, "*What is Bill O'Reilly when he is on his program?*"

Bill O'Reilly represents what the toiling classes would say and do if only they had the courage to. They can't tell off those who hold power over them or those who made it further in life than they did, but they'll do it vicariously through their hero. The bosses, the cops who gave them speeding tickets, the war protesters who have the courage to thumb their noses at authority and the gay activists who won't stand to be treated like second class citizens, are all galling to those who fool themselves into thinking they have to swallow their pride just to get by.

O'Reilly represents a deep-seated outrage at people who don't conform to society's rules. He stands for the repressive and blind adherence to authority and majority rule. Sometimes those who break rules are dangerous, such as murderers, and O'Reilly vehemently opposes them. Good for him. But then anyone else who decides to break the rules for the betterment of society gets thrown in the same boat as those who physically harm others. People who either profit from the old rules or who need those rules to stay in place in order to justify their failures and complacency will look to O'Reilly to punish those challengers.

Yet he's more than the keeper of Old School Dogma; he represents freedom and success within those confines. He is allowed to be an angry, insulting and simplistic fighter who can stare down the bad guys who want to break away from the rules. He can get his way and win every match. He can even have a cool comic-bookish name for his show ("The Factor!"), and—get this—he can even have his own name attached to it. O'Reilly is the hero of those who didn't live up to their American Dreams— he gives them the hope that it is possible to be free and strong and cool in a cage. He is the seething man's hero. He is the caged man's hope that their hero will break all dissent so that no one will be reminded of their fear of breaking out of the cage.

O'Reilly's success is also dependent on him melding juvenile antics, blue collar bravado, poor manners and disembodied anger to create a new breed of commentator. He's deftly put all the wrong ingredients in a cooker to come out with a truly terrible dish that he can force feed to his various detractors—his audience has the pleasure of watching the contorted facial expressions of those who are forced to swallow O'Reilly's unwholesome concoction. In other words, Bill O'Reilly is an icon of punishment against those who'd rather try it another way.

A No Spin Zone Road Map

O'Reilly Rex rules the cable news race with his brand of opinion and persona. With his iron fist guiding his show, the "O'Reilly Factor" is a forum where people with an opposing opinion can come on and get their collective asses whupped. Hostile guests get thrashed, bashed, abused, manipulated and ultimately humiliated just so the folks back home have something to gossip about at the water cooler the next day. Getting an appointment on O'Reilly's show is not as difficult as surviving through the grilling with your dignity and reputation intact. Those hostile guests who have been grilled on other shows may think they know how to handle O'Reilly, but those rules don't apply in the No Spin Zone: it's like trying to find your way home out of Boston reading a New York City map.

O'Reilly has said of his special zone: "So now the No Spin Zone has come through once again, and cut through the spin that you've been hearing all day long. And that's what's going on here." More jaded critics may think that "No Spin Zone" is a bloated and empty catch phrase. They are wrong in their assessment. The No Spin Zone is a real and vast place: it is a psycho-geographical location that begins in O'Reilly's mind and extends to the minds of his hostile guests and O'Reilly's viewing public. It's an intricate and booby-trapped place where the layout changes according to the host's needs and goals. It is a special area specifically designed for O'Reilly to conduct brutal psychological warfare, and it is elaborately rigged so that the Zone's architect will win every bout. He warns both guests and viewers alike to be careful before entering his domain, effectively guaranteeing that they'll come in to see what the fuss is about. Even though the No Spin Zone seems chaotic, there are enough stable landmarks and roads for someone to map out a fairly accurate floor plan of the place.

> The No Spin Zone is where O'Reilly conducts brutal, elaborately rigged warfare on his guests—minus any rules of journalism.

Ironically, for someone who is the unofficial guardian of old school rules, the "Factor" host himself has an utter disregard for the traditional rules of journalism. Because he is not confined to being a traditional journalist and news host, O'Reilly has the leeway to set up his show to ensure he can best his hostile guests and maintain his gritty, combative image. But it's hard to have a combative image unless you have someone to fight with: no problem, O'Reilly can use his show and other open outlets to cultivate feuds and grudges that he can use for later fodder on his show. Take, for instance, his battle with the *New York Times*. Instead of telling his viewers or readers about the important issues of the day, he can instead tell them all the reasons he thinks the paper sucks, as he did in his June 21, 2004 column in the *New York Daily News*:

> Somewhere along the line, the *Times* got out of the news business and into the nation building business. Its primary intent is no longer to provide objective information and fair-minded analysis to its readers, but to convince them to support a brave new world in the U.S. The power of the *Times* is being used to promote the formation of a new America, a bright, shining progressive city on a hill of steep government entitlements.

Got the general idea that the *Times* isn't O'Reilly's favorite reading material? Maybe you only *think* you do: perhaps you actually think that maybe he only pretends to hate it, but really, deep down, he actually kind of likes it. Why else would O'Reilly go on discussing the point in the same column:

> In almost every section, a *Times* reader is confronted with liberal ideology. Even the feature sections are skewed. *Times* business reporter Geraldine Fabrikant wrote an article on me a few months back and described your humble correspondent as a "conservative" four times. I guess the label was used the fourth time in case you might have missed the other three.

Just in case some people still don't catch his drift, O'Reilly gladly repeats the point in his writings, his TV show and his radio program. Cud chewing is a regular part of the "Factor." If he taught high school the same way he conducts himself on his program, then his classes must have been a real drag. The No Spin Zone may be a large, scary and unpredictable place, but it's not as complicated as it seems: there are circles and loops that will take guests and viewers right back to the starting point. You can only lose yourself if you don't pay attention to the noises around you.

For the timid, the No Spin Zone is also blessed with a certain stability: the show is divided into high-concept sections with cutesy segment names such as "Most Ridiculous Item of the Day," "Back of the Book," "Talking Points," "Villain of the Week," "Personal Story" and "Unresolved Problem." The titles are simple and descriptive, and knowing where a guest or topic is slotted can give clues as to how O'Reilly will interpret them. Ridiculous items are to be scoffed at and dismissed as frivolous, villains are to be reviled and vanquished, personal stories are ones that affect O'Reilly directly, unresolved problems need O'Reilly's meddling to be solved and Talking Points are O'Reilly's platforms on various political issues. It's all lively, yet predictable. These self-contained vignettes could very well be panels in a comic book: while each panel is separate from the rest, they are meant to be read together to give the audience a story about the hero.

The No Spin Zone has one other identifiable landmark: the type of topics likely to be discussed by the "Factor" host. Happy news isn't likely to be found here, meaning the No Spin Zone's fun house will be a grotesque, newsy "It's a Small World" ride. As John Nichols noted, "O'Reilly has a nightly child molester, or some [similar] sort of story." Perverts at carnivals can always be expected; in that regard, the No Spin Zone fun house is no different.

With everything that is predictable, there are parts of the No Spin Zone that aren't so easy to find. Logical fragmentation is part of the "Factor" charm. Ideas do not flow smoothly, and topics on the show aren't themed. Insults are mixed in with serious news, as they were on the March 24, 2004 edition of the "O'Reilly Factor":

> **O'REILLY:** All right. Well, we wish you the best. We think this law will be passed, and we appreciate you taking the time to lobby some of these pinheads on Capitol Hill here who really need a dose of reality.
>
> Thank you very much. We appreciate you coming in.
>
> Plenty more ahead as the "Factor" moves along this evening. Is Canada persecut-

ing physicians who refuse to perform abortions? We'll be right back with that story.

Bizarre irony and hypocrisy also mars the Zone. While O'Reilly is free to liberally label people and then denigrate them, he does not like his opponents to do the same. He seemed to get his briefs in a knot when the American Psychological Association defined conservatives, on the August 7, 2003 edition of his program:

> **O'REILLY:** In the "Impact" segment tonight, if you read a lot of elite media publications, they go out of their way to label people conservatives.
>
> Yet you rarely see the word "liberal" attached to people such as Bill Moyers or Walter Cronkite, for example.

O'Reilly, a former (CBS and ABC) and current (Fox, *New York Daily News*) elite media employee, then told his viewers what the fuss was all about:

> **O'REILLY:** That's because the elite types feel conservatives are, well, limited thinkers, and that false perception has been reinforced by the American Psychological Association, which has legitimatized a study by U.C. Berkeley…

The man who seconds ago railed against labeling people, began labeling others:

> **O'REILLY:** …a bastion of liberalism that diminishes conservative thought.
>
> And here's the kicker. It cost the taxpayer $1.2 million to have that study done.

Then came the obligatory insult:

> **O'REILLY:** [...]This is outrageous, isn't it? You got a bunch of pinheads from Berkeley. Let me just read you—this is incredible. We're not taking this seriously, folks, so don't get angry. We take it seriously—the money.

O'Reilly's illogical logic was the driving force that set the layout for the No Spin Zone: doors that only open one way, blustery winds that knock certain guests off their feet but elevate others high above the dangers and crooked stairs that descend straight to nowhere are all part of the Zone's landscape. The ground keeps shifting, and the ceilings rise and fall depending on who walks under them. Distorting mirrors are strategically hidden and placed in unexpected and secretly dangerous areas. At the control room is the main attraction—O'Reilly, manipulating the landscape to suit his needs.

In 2003, when France decided to pass on the opportunity to sacrifice its soldiers to oust Iraqi leader Saddam Hussein, O'Reilly was furious at the snub. The No Spin Zone's strange layout was laid bare for viewers at his old alma mater of Harvard University, where O'Reilly taped one of his programs, that later aired on May 6, 2002:

> **O'REILLY:** Well, I'm not eating any more french fries, number one.
>
> OK? Croissants, they're out. OK?
>
> It is insulting. I mean, I understand the French passion for, you know, not wanting the death penalty. I mean, they used that same passion when the Nazis invaded. Any history majors here? I think that the French have—are jealous of America, you know, generally speaking.

Harvard students also found out that in O'Reilly's No Spin Zone, complexities to people's motives are nonexistent:

> **UNIDENTIFIED MALE:** There was an article in this Sunday's *New York Times*. And it was listing the European community's reaction to the acts of terrorism in Israel. And basically summarized—it condemned the Israeli response to the terrorist activities. I wanted to know if you thought that there was a bias in European...
>
> **O'REILLY:** Bias in Europe? No.
>
> **UNIDENTIFIED MALE:** Well, why?
>
> **O'REILLY:** Because they're pinheads.

O'Reilly, the holder of three different university degrees (History, Broadcasting and Public Administration) offered this illogic as to why Europeans thought differently than Americans:

> **O'REILLY:** I mean, these people—I mean, look, say you're in Belgium, all right? There's nothing to do in Belgium, all right? So you're sitting around. And you know, five guys come on Belgium television. Oh, yes, the Israeli—they live in a world that's totally divorced from the rest of the world.
>
> You know, we have trouble with these people in Europe all the time, trying to convince them that there is evil. Talk about moral relativism.
>
> My God. And if you look at the history of Europe, I mean, the amount of horrible, terrible things that have taken place just in this little area where they—it's something in the water. That's all I can say.

But O'Reilly did have more to say on the topic, and gave America a simple explanation as to why Americans were targeted by foreign terrorists:

> **O'REILLY:** But Americans make the mistake, [Europeans] don't like us, generally speaking. All right? We're just way too much for them. We're obnoxious.
>
> We're loud. If you go over to Europe, you see Americans in the yellow and orange pantsuits and that's enough. You know, if I lived over there, I'd hate these people. And we're—our culture takes over. It's our music, it's our movies. America, America, America.

So what was the end result of wearing colorful clothes outside the United States? Apparently it sparked nothing less than savage acts of terrorism, according to O'Reilly:

> **O'REILLY:** That's why Osama bin Laden has the strength that he has, because he plays on it. These Americans are corrupting everything. Look at Puff Daddy. You know, I mean, that's enough to get fifteen guys to blow themselves up. Puff Daddy. All right? It's a—we have a culture here that's so free and so powerful, that it just overpowers other people.

In other words, tacky rappers gave Bin Laden his mandate, since the terrorist mastermind just didn't have the backbone to tell his kids to turn the down music in their rooms. The notion is simply Ludacris.

Ludicrous or ridiculous, the No Spin Zone has a surreal carnival quality that defies geographic logic. If the layout doesn't make sense, it's because it's not supposed to: a predictable layout would give hostile guests too much control and security, and the No Spin Zone's landlord has no desire to relinquish his power so easily.

But for those that O'Reilly agrees with, the No Spin Zone be an easy ride where they can finish their thoughts without fear of incessant interruption, especially if they agree with him, as was the case on an April 22, 2004 program:

> **KRIS KOBACH:** Well, let me give you another example of reasons I encountered working in the Justice Department. Sometimes you get [a] push back from the State Department, because certain countries start complaining, specifically here it'd be Canada and Mexico.
>
> But you're absolutely right to highlight the need to do this. You know, the terrorists realize we're starting to close down the gaps in our ports of entry. And now overland entry into the United States is a real possibility.
>
> **O'REILLY:** Absolutely. Everybody knows that.

O'Reilly's guest managed to make his case with the blessing of the show's host:

> **KOBACH:** There's a case of Mahmoud Kurani. On January 15th of this year, he was indicted by a grand jury in Dearborn, Michigan. Why? He had been raising money for Hezbollah in the United States. How did he get in?
>
> He went from Lebanon, where he'd been training with Hezbollah. He bribed a Mexican official in Beirut, then went to Mexico City and then traveled overland, smuggled across the border.
>
> **O'REILLY:** Right.

The allegedly serious conversation then took a slightly surreal turn, thanks to a bad-mannered O'Reilly:

> **KOBACH:** We've got to close these gaps in our border[s].
>
> **O'REILLY:** So you tell these pinheads on the Senate Judiciary Committee all this, I assume today, doctor?

The guest did not skip a beat, and behaved as though a serious news interviewer calling others pinheads was perfectly normal:

> **KOBACH:** Well, actually, today the focus was more on interior enforcement, about not only—there's kind of a parallel strategy here. On the border, we've got to augment the 10,000 border patrol agents by deploying more National Guard, in my opinion. And on the interior, we've only got 2,000 interior enforcement agents for the DHS. And yet there are eight to 10 million...
>
> **O'REILLY:** I know. Isn't that a joke? And in 2000, you almost have to come in and show them a machine gun before they'll do anything.

The sound of the word "pinhead" must fill O'Reilly up with glee since he uses the strategic insult to make his sworn enemies look ridiculous, as they must have appeared to viewers on May 21, 2003 when O'Reilly fired off one of his on-air "memos" to no one in particular:

> **O'REILLY:** Once again, the "Factor" was right. We called this early. We told you the U.N. was not honest, was not looking out for Americans, and did not care about right and wrong. It's good to be right, but it's frustrating as well. The U.N. will continue to be a corrupt institution. American pinhead media will continue to support it. And there's nothing any of us [can] do about it. That's the memo.

The "one-step-away-from-dork" put-down was used again days later when he asked one guest on his May 28, 2003 program: "Well, who's going to do it? Are you going to get a little pinhead panel together, or what are you going to do?" O'Reilly also used the insult on his January 2, 2003 show, when he said of antiwar activists that they "wouldn't even have a country if it wasn't for us, and our soldiers died over there, and these pinheads are out there, you know, spitting on American flags and setting them on fire. They can you-know-what."

If someone O'Reilly disagrees with isn't a "pinhead," then they are probably an "idiot" (which of the two is the bigger put-down is anyone's guess). The No Spin Zone is littered with outrageous insults that stick to the careless people who don't watch where they are going. The biting and juvenile barbs are meant to effectively dismiss guests and enemies alike. The following exchange, on November 22, 2002, seemed ordinary:

> **CURT SMITH:** It's just beginning, Bill. I think many people in Bloomington are aware of what's happened. But across the state, there hasn't been a great deal of awareness. A news story or two about what happened [and] the university's announcement it's going to investigate.
>
> But it is only beginning to sink in, what's really happened, and the lack of response.
>
> **O'REILLY:** Now, why has it been so slow? We did—this is our third story on it, and we just think this is outrageous.
>
> **SMITH:** Well...

But then O'Reilly spewed his usual invective, thereby ending all possible disagreement with him:

> **O'REILLY:** And the reason is, I don't really care about the dopey porn movie. I mean, these students signed a paper. If they want to be idiots...
>
> **SMITH:** Sure.
>
> **O'REILLY:** ...and ruin their lives, I can't help them.

If these amateur pornographers are a bunch of immoral idiots who are beyond help, as O'Reilly claims, then there's no point in dragging the issue any further, is there? The No Spin Zone is full of these abrupt dead-end roads; O'Reilly drags these dregs out, thrashes them about and then unceremoniously throws their limp remains against the wall. The end.

An interesting side note: O'Reilly didn't say that "nobody" can help these students, or that their "parents" can't help them, but that *he* can't help them. Why would anyone expect a news talk show host

living in another state to help fully-grown adults he is not in any way related to? Is he a registered psychologist or psychiatrist in charge of their case? He's not a youth counselor or teacher anymore. Why on earth do they need O'Reilly's help at all? Did they even ask for it? Did they plea to him? Who asked him?

Nobody asked him, but that's not the point: the "Factor" host is the king of the No Spin Zone and he is the one who is looked to by his audience to make everything all right in the world.

Except that most of the time O'Reilly is too busy bandying about his various insults, as he did on December 12, 2002, when he glibly stated that one "judge is an idiot. You know that." He continued to belabor his point:

> **O'REILLY:** In the "Back of the Book" segment tonight, Orlando, Florida sex crimes detective Ed Mann, also the president of the Cops for Christ organization down there, has pled guilty to having an affair with a 14-year-old girl, a freshman in high school. That's statutory rape. But Judge John Adams has sentenced Mann to house arrest and probation. How could that happen? Joining us now from Orlando is Marc Lubet, the attorney who represented Mann… All right. Let me read you some of the things that he said, all right? This judge is an idiot. John Adams.
>
> **LUBET:** No, he isn't.
>
> **O'REILLY:** And he should change his name. All right. Here's what he said. And you were there, Counselor, and I don't know how you…
>
> **LUBET:** Yes, I was.
>
> **O'REILLY:** …you didn't laugh. "Compared to the relationship"—he—the judge compared the relationship of Mann and the girl to Clinton and Lewinsky, saying…
>
> **LUBET:** That is—that is absolutely taken out of context.
>
> **O'REILLY:** Out of context? Well, tell me what it was.
>
> **LUBET:** What he said was people in power…
>
> **O'REILLY:** Yes?
>
> **LUBET:** …have had relationships where they weren't punished when they had a…
>
> **O'REILLY:** So what does that have to do with this? So what?

O'Reilly's guest would try to tell him so what, but had little success getting a full thought expressed:

> **LUBET:** Because—because Ed Mann had a relationship with a woman, and he—a girl, and he had power in the relationship…
>
> **O'REILLY:** Yes.
>
> **LUBET:** …over this fourteen-year-old girl that…
>
> **O'REILLY:** So—and he says, quote, "A lot"…
>
> **LUBET:** He's not…
>
> **O'REILLY:** …"of powerful people do bad things, and nothing happens to them." So what?

LUBET: Well...

O'REILLY: So what?

If O'Reilly could keep his mouth shut for more than three seconds, perhaps his guest could properly answer his question, but O'Reilly couldn't help but amuse himself with calling the judge another puerile name:

LUBET: That's—it's an example of what he thought and why...

O'REILLY: Yes, it's an example that this judge is an incompetent boob. Here's another one.

LUBET: He is...

O'REILLY: Here's another one.

LUBET: He's very competent.

Perhaps the guest was so flustered that he didn't see that O'Reilly was carefully luring him full speed ahead to one of the No Spin Zone's sudden dead end roads:

LUBET: There was also a clinical psychologist who testified that—who was a specialist in sexual deviation...

O'REILLY: Yes?

LUBET: ...who testified that...

O'REILLY: Did you pay him?

LUBET: Did I pay him?

O'REILLY: Yes. Did you pay the psychologist?

LUBET: Sure. Yes.

O'REILLY: Yes. Of course you did. So he's going to say anything you want. Come on. Don't...

LUBET: Oh, that's absolutely untrue.

Though O'Reilly's argument was flawed (as always, both sides of the law pay for expert opinion because experts, like Bill O'Reilly, don't work for free), but in the minds of many viewers, the argument was about to close, with O'Reilly once again victorious:

O'REILLY: Oh, stop it. Come on! I can get fifteen guys to tell—pay them tomorrow and tell them your client should get ten years in prison. Don't give me that.

LUBET: So, if I pay an expert, that means the expert is going to say what I want.

O'REILLY: You pay—you pay an expert to say what you want him to say. We all know...

LUBET: Well, that's not what the law is, and you know it.

Too late; the guest seemed to justify his actions, making O'Reilly seem like the winner, exposing a guilty party of wrongdoing. Some guests may not be in O'Reilly's cross hairs, but they still are somewhat naïve as to his methods, as one guest was who seemed to be taken aback during this exchange on February 23, 1999:

O'REILLY: In the "Impact" segment today, Project No-Spank here in California. The idea is to pass a law that would make it illegal for parents to spank their own children. Heading up the effort is Jordan Riak, the executive director of an organization called Parents and Teachers Against Violence in Education. Mr. Riak joins us from Oakland, California...

RIAK: Children are being brought into the children's hospital with welts and burns, and...

O'REILLY: Yeah, sure, and that's abuse.

RIAK: ...invariably, the perpetrator said, "Oh, I was only disciplining her. I didn't..."

O'REILLY: And they're idiots.

RIAK: Well...

O'REILLY: They're idiots. I mean, quite flat out...

RIAK: But the government says it's OK.

O'REILLY: ...they're idiots. No, no, no.

RIAK: Our traditions say it's...

O'REILLY: It depends. It depends. The government doesn't always say it's OK.

O'Reilly seems to subscribe to the theory that the world is crawling with "experts" all equally qualified and willing to go on the take of the highest bidder:

RIAK: He should see how his peers have voiced their opinions on this subject. Overwhelmingly, the mental health field, the child development field, the American Academy of Pediatrics, the American Academy of Child and Adolescent Psychiatry—I can go down the list [...] organizations such as these have overwhelmingly come down against hitting children, and you've managed to find one...

O'REILLY: No, I can find fifty.

RIAK: ...academic who's out of step. I'm sure you could find...

O'REILLY: I could find fifty. I could find fifty.

RIAK: Well...

O'REILLY: I could find fifty, and we're going to have him on the broadcast in—not this week but—I can find 150. Basically...

RIAK: Oh, I guess if you work at it...

O'REILLY: ...it's a debatable situation.

What is also a debatable situation is whether O'Reilly treats all his guests in a fair and balanced way. There was a certain decided coziness in the air when he interviewed professional kvetching grump Ann Coulter on May 27, 2004. The interview began with O'Reilly pointing out the robust sales of her "*New York Times* best-selling" book *Treason*[5], but after Coulter got her allotted brag, she also received a cookie and an easy question from the "Factor" host:

5 It's ironic that for a man who gripes about the *Times* as much as he does, O'Reilly repeatedly brings attention to the fact that his books and those of his favorite guests are *Times* bestsellers—if the *Times* is too biased and can't be trusted on any account, then why sully one's reputation and those of your comrades by drawing attention to it?

O'REILLY: Wow, good for you. Why has Bush fallen in the polls?

COULTER: I suspect a lot of people aren't paying attention right now and, basically, the same 500 people are being polled and you'll see them go up and down and up and down until the election gets closer and then I think people will pay attention, we'll have more of a sense.

The No Spin Zone is only a dangerous place for those who do not support ideological reaction and stagnation. Fresh air is not welcome in the Zone, and guests who wish to contribute to the stale verbal smog are free to pollute the airwaves as much as they wish. It doesn't matter that thousands of people are surveyed by numerous polling outfits and not "the same 500," but the clichéd "wait and see" fence-sitting reply wasn't challenged by the allegedly gruff O'Reilly. Coulter, who was presumably placed in front of rolling cameras to give a definite opinion and analysis, went wishy-washy when it counted the most. It must have been naptime for both Annie and Billy in the No Spin Zone.

A Psychic Invite to the Zone

The No Spin Zone reaches out beyond the "Factor" studio, and O'Reilly excels at making most of his viewers feel like a strong part of his program. He reads and responds to their letters on the air, and he tries to get them to participate in everything from charities (he has several links to them on his website) to boycotts. They can be happy when he has good tidings to bring, and feel outraged when he brings bad news, sometimes within moments of each other. As O'Reilly announced on his November 2, 2001 program:

O'REILLY: Well, it's been a very good week for the "Factor."

First of all, the Red Cross has changed its game plan and will donate at least $26 million more directly to the grieving families. We're happy about that.

But then O'Reilly had some bad news (complete with requisite insult), and some encouraging news, if viewers could keep up with this emotional roller coaster:

O'REILLY: Out in Hollywood, while some nitwit publicists are trying to organize a boycott against the "Factor," a few big-name stars are breaking ranks and are angry about the mess.

The Zone isn't just a gladiatorial arena: it also converts to a lecture room when the situation calls for it. The high school teacher in O'Reilly has never truly left him, and he has lectured his "Factor" students on occasion. In one April 15, 2004 show, role model O'Reilly gave his viewers this piece of sage advice:

O'REILLY: Don't be a Kool-Aid person... In 1978, more than 900 people committed suicide in Guyana by drinking cyanide-laced Kool-Aid at the behest of a religious nut named Jim Jones. Thus the term "Kool-Aid people." They are folks who do not think for themselves. They are true believers committed to a political ideology or other belief system. And no matter what evidence is presented to them, they are incapable of change. You see, Kool-Aid people [are] most often in the political arena, on both the right and the left. Don't be one. Think

independently.

That's right: think independently, so long as you're thinking whatever Professor O'Reilly believes. Why did O'Reilly feel compelled to nag his audience on this particular point? He disagreed with 100 people whose loved ones perished on September 11 (whom he dismissed as "less than 1% of the folks directly affected by 9/11") for joining the antiwar group Families for a Peaceful Tomorrow, a left-of-center organization opposed to the U.S. war on Iraq.

Not all of O'Reilly's messages are directly pointed at the audience but, nevertheless, his chatty style sounds as if he's talking to his buddies, not his viewers. He gave his opinion on international laws in such fashion on his May 31, 2002 show:

> **O'REILLY:** Many Americans disagree with me on this, but I think in this war, the Geneva Convention and due process laws are out of date and actually harmful to this nation. I mean, come on! Are we supposed to wait for a cataclysmic attack before realizing that these fanatical terrorists will use weapons of mass destruction if they can?
>
> In the *New York Times* today, there was the predictable left-wing reaction to the FBI's new mandate of investigating possible terror activity without probable cause. I looked hard at the new policy and found that none of my rights will be violated. I don't care if somebody wants to watch me come out of church.

If the *New York Times* endorses it, then it must be wrong, kids. For someone who has cultivated an independent and hard-as-nails image, O'Reilly was espousing heavy government intervention, dependence on a father figure and naked cowardice. Where's the freedom? Where's the bravery in the face of adversity? Where is the understanding that there is no such thing as absolute security?

Countless Americans have suffered, sacrificed and died defending basic human rights and freedoms not only for their own country, but for the world; yet O'Reilly seems eager to desecrate what made the United States the land of opportunity, individuality and, most importantly, the absolute and greatest bastion of freedom and democracy in the first place. Land of the Free? Home of the Brave? Forget it: you won't find either in the No Spin Zone. How can you? Fear is whispering to and taunting both hostile guests and credulous viewers in every corner of this confounding, guileful land.

Psychological Prestidigitation

To market yourself as someone who is absolutely right, you have to market others as being absolutely wrong. There's no room for charitable notions such as "to each his own," "one size does not fit all" or even the most annoying of all, "maybe it works for them." It has to be a forced choice; otherwise, any room to disagree and you give others room to go against your opinion and feel confident in their choices.

Bill O'Reilly has put the "rant" back in "tolerant"; that is, he is surpassingly proficient in creating false forced choices. "Sink or swim" may be a common logic error, but in O'Reilly's agile hands, it seems perfectly logical. Though he can make appeals to authority, the straw man argument and the personal attack seem rational—it is the forced-choice sleight of hand that is his forte. His arguments will start with a slickly packaged argument flaw, and then draw viewers in with evidence supporting his view.

When O'Reilly took offense to other networks allowing his fellow Americans to exercise their First Amendment right (the one their ancestors fought and died for so that future generations could live in freedom)—particularly those others who did not have the same opinions as him, the pompous "Factor" pooh-bah would have none of it on his April 8, 2004 show:

O'Reilly did his best to link Kerry to "morally corrupt" Hollywood.

O'REILLY: ...I don't mind, you know, Hollywood stars going out and saying, "I love whoever," but to inject it into a storyline—you know, it seems almost Joseph Goebbles-ish. You know what I'm saying to you?

The old "detractor-as-fascist-sympathizer" is a sneaky if now overused argument, but O'Reilly managed to discredit his opponents in the eyes of many viewers. Though it was not one of the most original smear tactics to ooze out of O'Reilly's lips, it was still an effective way to make his targets look like flaming Nazis without him having to actually prove anything:

> **O'REILLY:** Get that message across subliminally, little dabs here and there?

This is a common tactic that O'Reilly employs on his show: he paints the so-called "enemy" as cunning, using subliminals on a helpless audience. That way, the more gullible members of the "Factor" peanut gallery won't dare try to listen to arguments from the other side: heck, are those un-American Americans just trying to brainwash them or something?

If there were viewers who failed to catch O'Reilly's drift that all networks not owned by a certain Australian media conqueror may be trying to brain-bomb them, O'Reilly gave them something that they could construe as proof while conversing with Alan Schroeder, billed as a professor "who teaches journalism at Northeastern University and is author of the book *Celebrity in Chief: How Showbusiness Took Over the White House.*"

> **SCHROEDER:** But see, I don't think it's all that subliminal. They're pretty out [in] front with it. I don't see what's subliminal about it if the media...
>
> **O'REILLY:** Let me give you an example. Jesse Martin, who plays a black detective on "Law and Order," goes—it's just in a throwaway line.
>
> He goes—refers to Bush as "that dude who lied to us." You know, come on. There are a lot of people who don't follow politics and they watch these entertainment programs. They might like this Jesse Martin guy. They think he's saying it. You know?

First, O'Reilly assumes television viewers are automatons who buy anything they see on television. Second, to prove a point, the chronically offended O'Reilly has taken a single quote from a single show and taken it out of context. So what if a character knocks the President without a politically

OUTFOXED

correct rebuttal on the same episode? Never mind that realistic characters are created by giving them realistic qualities. If all of television required scrubbing content for some viewers who might be offended by what someone uttered on the air, Mr. O'Reilly would have been unemployed a long time ago.

It was ironic that O'Reilly picked on "Law and Order," then a popular NBC program. For those who aren't familiar with producer Dick Wolf's venerable show, "Law and Order" made an effort to showcase not only fictionalized accounts of real high-profile crimes, but also had a motley crew of diverse and complex characters. Martin's predecessor Benjamin Bratt portrayed Reynaldo Curtis, a conservative character, and Angie Harmon's character Abbie Carmichael was also a conservative. Former Mayor Rudy Giuliani played himself in a cameo in one episode. And what about current "Law and Order" regular and former Republican Senator Fred Dalton Thompson? Why have a card-carrying member of the Republican party play a good guy—or play any role on the show, for that matter?

Wolf's programs have also taken on Bill Clinton—one 1999 episode referred to oral sex as "getting a Lewinsky." O'Reilly doesn't state whether he is a regular viewer of the show—if he isn't, the comment revealed his ignorance of the program, and thereby weakened his argument. O'Reilly's guest tried to reason with the host, but the counter-argument seemed to fall on offended ears:

> **SCHROEDER:** Yes, but you know, there are people in the country who feel that way. And so if a character on the TV show makes that point, how is that different from how a lot of just ordinary folks feel?

> **O'REILLY:** If that were balanced and then they have Sam Watterson come on saying, "I really admire President Bush. He's got a lot of courage." I wouldn't mind it.

To top off his argument, O'Reilly revisited his subliminal seduction theme:

> **O'REILLY:** But it seems it's all one way. And I predicted this was going to happen, that they're doing it in a sneaky—it's sneaky, professor. Sneaky.

A classic O'Reilly comic book-ism: a covert conspiracy is afoot and it has been uncovered by none other than O'Reilly himself. Don't trust the shows on any other network, lest they trick you into having un-American thoughts such as critical thinking and skepticism. If the line "it's sneaky, professor. Sneaky" doesn't belong in a superhero's word bubble, then what does?

Kettle Black, Pot Says

Most strong and captivating personalities are a study of contradictions, and Bill O'Reilly is no different: he can flog his enemies for the same intellectual crimes he is committing. Despite the fact that most of his followers think of their superhost as a simple, straightforward guy, O'Reilly is complicated and contradictory. It's those qualities that make him unpredictable and a force to be reckoned with.

One of those incidences of blatant contradiction happened when he frowned on the practice of outing, while he himself outed an alleged lesbian. The first salvo came on the November 13, 2003 edition of the "O'Reilly Factor," with guest Philip Moran, described by O'Reilly as the General Counsel for the Catholic League in Massachusetts:

O'REILLY: Here's why I don't believe it. One of the judges in the Supreme Court, you correct me if I'm wrong Mr. Moran, is lesbian, all right?

PHILIP MORAN: That's the rumor, yes.

O'REILLY: And she apparently voted against gay marriage? Is that true?

MORAN: That's what we hear. She's one of the...

This piece of juicy gossip would serve O'Reilly's interest: if a bona fide gay person in authority didn't want her kind to have the right to get married, then of course it stands to reason that they shouldn't. Note another classic O'Reilly logic flaw: he appeals to authority as if it were an infallible edict.

O'Reilly continued to let his gossipy busybody side rule his argument:

O'REILLY: Right, that's what we hear, too. Because she said I don't have a right to make this law.

MORAN: That's right.

O'REILLY: All right? So she voted against it. She was the swing vote. A lesbian was a swing vote, which is another public relations nightmare for the pro gay marriage jurists, you know, who want to go around, look, if the folks of the Commonwealth of Massachusetts vote, you know how they're going to vote, don't you? You saw the polls.

Since there was only one female judge on the panel, guessing who O'Reilly was referring to was no difficult task. It was a gossipy way to win the fight, but O'Reilly is not above using a variety of unconventional and unpredictable techniques to do it. A few months later, O'Reilly again outed the so-called "lesbian judge" in a July 13, 2004 broadcast:

O'REILLY: Does it bother you at all, Mr. Wolfson, as an American citizen that in the State of Massachusetts, the activist judges there found a loophole. And even the lesbian judge on the Supreme Court who dissented—she loves me and you know her—she said in her dissent...

WOLFSON: I don't know what you're talking about.

Gossip isn't cool unless your audience is ignorant about the salacious or surprising tidbit, but even here O'Reilly's victory was bittersweet: if Wolfson was in the dark about O'Reilly's lesbian judge, then it meant Wolfson didn't watch his show—or at least not on a regular basis. O'Reilly didn't keep his disappointment bottled up:

O'REILLY: OK. So, you—I'm shocked that you don't know this.

WOLFSON: I don't know this.

O'REILLY: It's supposed to be your area of expertise.

Granted, it may have been Wolfson's expertise, but if he was a regular "Factor" viewer, he would have already been in the know, shame on him. In any case, O'Reilly's bossy instincts took over and he drew Wolfson a diagram:

WOLFSON: Well, I...

O'REILLY: All right, let me explain it to you.

WOLFSON: ...that I don't know what you're talking about. But I have to say...

O'REILLY: No, you're not going to say anything. I'm going to explain this to you...

Good to his word this time, O'Reilly explained away, though he seemed vexed at his guest who obviously didn't do his homework by regularly tuning in to the "Factor":

O'REILLY: And in her dissenting opinion, the judge said—the lesbian judge said that my colleagues—the four who voted against it—actively looked for a way to circumvent the law. That is her dissenting opinion.

Now just the fact that you don't know that dissenting opinion exists, you know, tells me that you just don't know the case.

Perhaps Wolfson wasn't aware of his faux pas of not being a rabid Fox fan, but O'Reilly's guest would get a dressing down for coming to class without doing his homework:

WOLFSON: No, the part I'm contesting is you're saying that she's a lesbian judge, and I'm not sure what you're talking about there. But what I'm saying...

O'REILLY: Well, maybe I can explain it. She's a lesbian judge.

WOLFSON: OK, well, obviously it's your show. You can say what you want to say.

The finishing touch was O'Reilly putting money where his loud mouth was:

O'REILLY: That's public. What, would you like to make a wager on this? Because I could use $10,000.

WOLFSON: I told you I don't know anything about that.

O'REILLY: Absolutely.

Wolfson did not take up the wager, making O'Reilly victorious once again. Yet it wasn't the last time the phantom lesbian judge would make her appearance on the show. In the phantasm's next appearance, she would show that even though the "Factor" host may have outed a judge, that didn't mean he approved of the practice, since he chastised gay activist Michael Rodgers, who partook in the same pastime a few days later, on June 19, 2004:

O'REILLY: But somebody's personal sex life should have nothing to do with any kind of a policy, and let me give you an example. We reported on a judge in Boston, OK, who dissented from the...

MICHAEL ROGERS: Correct. But you outed her on your show.

O'REILLY: But we didn't, because her...

Rogers may have done his homework, but O'Reilly was ready for him:

ROGERS: Well, nowhere in Lexis-Nexis does it talk about her sexual orientation.

O'REILLY: But interestingly enough, our guests—our guests were the ones that mentioned the fact that this was...

ROGERS: But these gentlemen appear as cover boys in local gay magazines. They go to gay and lesbian organizations...

In a classic bridging move, O'Reilly sidestepped his apparent hypocrisy and turned the subject around to something that worked to his benefit:

> **O'REILLY:** OK, I'm not disputing the fact that they may be gay. But let me just make my point, and then you can rebut. I'm not disputing the fact that they might be gay and that they might have the gay lifestyle.
>
> But you can be gay and be against gay marriage. See, that's the thing.

O'Reilly's incredulous guest wouldn't escape the show without a serious verbal spanking from O'Reilly:

> **ROGERS:** And if they live an out gay life, we have the right to tell people that here are people in your community who are doing this.
>
> **O'REILLY:** But I think that—I don't think that you have the right to do it. I think it's a sleazy tactic.

Don't ever go into the No Spin Zone without a map: you never know when one of those one-way doors might throw you into the mouth of a spinning tunnel that spits you out right in front of a distorting mirror.

Bill's Bible

O'Reilly seems to like the sound of certain insults more than others. "Pinhead" and "idiot" sound cool in O'Reilly's world, but put-downs, such as "coward," are less often used. He likes put-downs that have a juvenile connotation to them: calling someone a coward won't evoke the same laughs from a vindictive crowd that "boob" will: the choice of slurs seems deliberate. Any slur with a "bwah ha ha" quality is usually chosen over a more mundane one.

Yet O'Reilly would dust off and use the "coward" slight toward another object of his derision (namely, Ted Kennedy) in a May 9, 2002 edition of his program:

> **O'REILLY:** ...Patrick Kennedy, who's a congressman from Rhode Island, all right, is— he says the sex scandal is inexcusable, and urged that abusive priests be fully prosecuted. So Patrick Kennedy we don't have any problem with. But I can't—I mean, he's a kid compared to his uncle.
>
> And his uncle's a coward. Ted Kennedy's a coward.

Those were strong words, but O'Reilly refused to back down from his accusation, much to the chagrin of his guest Laurence Leamer, the author of *The Kennedy Men*:

> **O'REILLY:** He's a coward.
>
> **LEAMER:** ...Listen, that's inexcusable, Bill, to call him a coward...
>
> **O'REILLY:** Oh, it is, huh?
>
> **LEAMER:** ...because he's not speaking out at that moment.
>
> **O'REILLY:** That's inexcusable? Well, then you tell me why, where I'm wrong.

The abuse of children is a sensitive topic with O'Reilly, and anyone who does not feel as strongly as he does about exploited and hurt children will feel the sting of his wrath:

LEAMER: ...is Senator Kerry, is Senator Kerry a coward? Is every politician in America who hasn't said that [Cardinal] Law should resign a coward?

O'REILLY: Here, let me define it for you. Every politician who's not out front on this issue in protecting children in a public way is a coward. How about that?

For those who feel that every one of O'Reilly's outbursts are disingenuous, remember that in his younger days he was a teacher, and his original life choices most likely reflect his beliefs. O'Reilly seems to have a genuine compassion for children; what he doesn't seem to have is much respect for his fellow grown-up citizens. When asked whether television viewers were aware that the federal government owned "one span of [the] spectrum, and they don't own another," O'Reilly replied, "No, I don't think the consumer knows anything, but why is that important?"

Adults are untrustworthy in other ways, too. Some of them are just plain unstable, according to O'Reilly on April 26, 2004:

O'REILLY: I mean, both of those guys—McDermott we know is a longtime nut. And the people of Seattle who vote him in should be ashamed of themselves. He's irresponsible. He shouldn't be in the Congress. He shouldn't even be working at—well, anyway, he's just awful.

There are countless ways to be awful in O'Reilly's books, and criticizing the United States in any way, shape or form is a biggie. O'Reilly didn't beat around the Bush when he began this diatribe against his old nemesis, an evil organization known as the *Los Angeles Times*, on his March 11, 2003 program:

O'REILLY: In an absolutely disgraceful column today, Los Angeles writer—*Times* writer Robert Scheer says the United States will join the ranks of, quote, "war criminals," unquote, if we attack Iraq.

Scheer is perhaps the most radical journalist writing in a major newspaper today, and his moral indignation and blatant anti-Americanism is revolting.

Sometimes it's so revolting that the "Factor" host is just too disgusted to listen. O'Reilly's patience can wear preternaturally thin with his guests, who may be a little more controversial or pugnacious than he cares for. He liberally uses his power to silence those he disagrees with, making dissent on his show difficult at times, as it was for Lance Williams, who found out that his views on inner city violence were just a little too provocative on August 5, 2002:

O'REILLY: I want to go over to Mr. Williams, who's an expert on gang warfare. And were you surprised at this when you read about this case? Did you immediately link it up to the gangs? Because I didn't. And then when I heard it was gang-related, then I knew why nobody came forward.

WILLIAMS: Well, what I would say firstly is that we—it's very important for us to look at this particular incident in the context of a larger systemic way in which we can understand the factors that may influence such type[s] of behavior. And I think that—I can't speak to the specifics of why young people or these young people did what they did, if they were involved in this situation at all.

The above statement ran counter to the world according to Bill O'Reilly, but it would be the guest's next remark that blasted up O'Reilly's blood pressure:

> **WILLIAMS:** I'm very, very uncomfortable with talking about how young people are perceived in our society today, particularly when we know, at the Center for Inner City Studies, our research shows that in order to really understand this, we need to look at about five basic factors. We need to look at the institutional racism that causes young people...

Big mistake: Williams suddenly found himself being silenced by O'Reilly, who had taken offense with the experts' view on the motives of gang members:

> **O'REILLY:** Yeah, but you're making excuses for this stuff.
>
> **WILLIAMS:** ...to respond...
>
> **O'REILLY:** All right, Mr. Williams, I'm going to stop you, I don't have time...

O'Reilly's first warning was met with the following reply:

> **WILLIAMS:** ...if you really want to understand...

O'Reilly's patience was wearing thin for his hostile guest:

> **O'REILLY:** Mr. Williams, look, I don't have time...
>
> **WILLIAMS:** ...the situation, what you need to understand...
>
> **O'REILLY:** ...for a diatribe—Mr. Williams!

The schoolteacher in O'Reilly may have burst into the open, but his unruly guest was still trying to get his controversial point across:

> **WILLIAMS:** ...that the violent nature of America...
>
> **O'REILLY:** Mr. Williams! One more time...
>
> **WILLIAMS:** ...pathetic federal government...

That did it:

> **O'REILLY:** Cut his mike. All right. I don't have time for a diatribe on why gangs do what they do. I'm dealing with a very horrendous crime here, and if you don't want to answer the question, we're not going to talk to you.

Why does O'Reilly play "Mike God" with his guests? Because he can, and because his audience tunes in to live out their fantasies vicariously through him: the power to oppress and vindictively humiliate others on national television has its appeal. After the Williams incident, at least one viewer wrote to O'Reilly praising his authoritarian solution to a dissenting opinion. At least O'Reilly gives the people what they want.

Yet the Williams incident was hardly the first or last time O'Reilly exercised his power to deny guests the right to speak their minds. O'Reilly's style of censorship is quick and certain:

◆ On March 12, 2002: "Mr. Mayor, I'm going to have to cut your mike off if you... don't let me get a question in here, OK? [...]I'm going to have to cut your mike off if you

don't let me get a question, because I want to be fair here."

◆ On April 17, 2003: "Cut his mike. All right, Doctor. Now, you either going listen to me, or you are going to get knocked off the air right now. OK? That's the deal. Put your mike back on. All right, Doctor? I talk, you talk. That's the way we do it. You say we've been given false information. That's your opinion, and you're entitled to it. I don't believe that. And I'm as smart as you are."

◆ On July 15, 2002: "Counsel, hold it. One more thing, counselor. Cut her mike. Cut her mike."

◆ On August 6, 2004: "Mr. Gillespie, I'm going to cut your mike now because you've had your say."

Censorship is a powerful tool: it not only allows the gatekeeper the ability to prevent ideological pollution by introducing foreign ideas and concepts, but it also indirectly maligns the silenced. After all, why would they be yanked unless they were saying something yank-worthy? O'Reilly is the king and tyrant of all he surveys and he exercises his right to silence those hostile guests who try to present their unwanted views. On the whole, right-leaning guests don't seem to get their mikes cut off as often as their left-leaning counterparts.

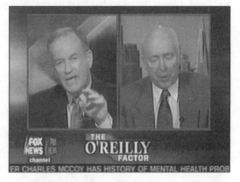

The "Factor" is so predictable that there is a drinking game based on O'Reilly's catch phrases.

But cutting off a guest's microphone isn't the only regular staple on the "Factor": there is a laundry list of regular quirks and features that make O'Reilly's program comforting and predictable to his believers. Viewers can count on him to use particularly hurtful insults to particular people who espouse particular views. They can count on O'Reilly to cover specific topics and say specific phrases. While the host's temper may be unpredictable, there is no doubt that it will be unsparingly unleashed.

In fact, the "Factor" is so predictable that it is possible for viewers to amuse themselves and quickly destroy their livers by playing a simple drinking game based on O'Reilly's guaranteed phrases and routines. At the most basic level: viewers can drink one shot (of whiskey sour, naturally) for every "OK?", "All right?" and "No Spin Zone," not to mention one drink for every other predictable utterance such as "our pal," "boob," "idiot," "pinhead," "villain," "memo," "Talking Points," "personal story," "disgraceful," "ridiculous" and three shots for every reference O'Reilly makes to "Stuart Smalley" and "cut his mike"; two shots for references to "far left" or "liberal media" and multiple drinks when O'Reilly slags Bill Moyers, Michael Moore or the *New York Times*. Bonus shots for his griping over various vast conspiracies aimed at him, any utterances that sound as if they came from a superhero comic book, any complaints about slights against his employers and insults toward viewers who complain about his stances. The fun really never ends with O'Reilly.

The Inevitable Deathwatch of the "Factor"

Some people have already gotten a head start on counting down until O'Reilly's studied schtick inevitably becomes passé. After all, O'Reilly does represent an era where the culture of fear rules, and makes deliberate acts of self-confinement and repression seem as if they're the only way to survive: if it means your enemies are restricted as well, restricting yourself and abandoning your own freedoms are a small price to pay for ensuring that you breathe for one more day.

But sooner or later an era's set of beliefs are challenged and destroyed by a new generation, technology or just a bad case of mass common sense. Being stir crazy isn't just confined to the physical: people can feel claustrophobic in their own minds. When life has passed the fearful by, only then do they realize that their invisible walls have done them more harm than good.

For others, the most frightening realization of all will hit them: that just because they chose to live in a bunker willingly, doesn't mean others will be as complacent or gullible as they are. There comes a point when the danger spreads not in the empty open, but in the dark nooks and crannies where there is easy and stunned prey to be found. But then where will they run and hide when the danger has trapped them in the very prison they helped their enemies create? Those who live in freedom are faster, more alert and more cunning than those living in cages.

O'Reilly's No Spin Zone feeds off fear, and that is why it succeeds. Without those who are scared of terrorists, closeted lesbian judges, child molesters, television programs with snarky African-American cops, pornographers, rappers, *New York Times* newspaper reporters, gangs, pinheads, french fries, idiots, the public school system, boobs, Democrats, liberal comedians who can't be pushed around and antiwar activists, O'Reilly would have no natural energy to fuel the Zone. Fear has paralyzed many who think restricting freedom has something to do with being brave or practical. His abusive "I'm OK, but you need work" attitude seems reassuring—after all, he's looking out for you. He's the one who strips away the golden patina of his opponents—but he isn't your father, dammit, and he isn't your boss; he is your guardian and your hero.

There will always be a couple of million people who need a gruff hero; hence, there will always be a need for the tough-talking cowboy in the white hat. Those who think this psychological weakness can be permanently eradicated are being naïve. There will always be a fan base for such an archetype. In this regard, O'Reilly himself has nothing to fear.

However, his brand of schtick can be easily imitated and updated for younger audiences. The new upstart will be vying for the same audience share as the current reigning champ. Here, O'Reilly's future success is on much shakier ground.

When a copycat enters the picture, he is the fresh face and breath of fresh air everyone has been waiting for. He can upstage the old guard with even less than a new twist on the established genre: the new kid is novel just by being himself and will grab some of the audience away by default. But the stakes will be higher and the young turk has to trump the old guard by pushing that envelope just a little bit farther and being just a little bit different.

The new guy will have to try harder and have to seem tougher and less trusting than O'Reilly. A new generation of Bill O'Reillys will go to just about any length to get some attention and buzz. How much pushing will still be respectable until a pathetic descent into Morton Downey, Jr. territory becomes inevitable? How long can O'Reilly Rex's reign last before a younger, more seething version of himself takes the crown? Will a more trenchant O'Reilly steal the original's thunder?

A younger, more wrathful O'Reilly model seems probable, but a shrewder version of the "Factor" firecracker isn't ever likely to happen: his talent is a rare one, and most people, fan or detractor, don't appreciate the subtleties of his craft. He has an innate feel for psychological combat and a talent for knowing how easy it is to take advantage of an opponent's mental laziness and naïveté. The next generation of Bill O'Reillys will ignore the grace, and calculate that they simply must out-shout their mentor. Most of the copycats are going to try to imitate him without comprehending that it's his sub rosa tactics that are the actual, unconscious draw. The new breed is always less refined, innovative or studied than the master. They will out-scream him, but never out-think him.

For O'Reilly, this inevitable fact is probably a moot one: he is close to the point of needing a bigger challenge. Unless the fallout of his former producer's sexual harassment lawsuit against him (which was quickly settled out of court) proves to be his undoing, O'Reilly may still weather the storm and retain much, if not most, of his fan base, who appreciate his bravado and admitted libido. Yet that still doesn't mean that he'll stay on top forever. Hannity and Colmes have flirted with being crowned co-kings of the cable news ratings race; they will most likely be the Next Big Thing, while O'Reilly sets off using his well-honed skills for a newer, more challenging goal. O'Reilly's been practicing, squaring off with liberal opponents in the public eye for years. He's told his viewers his various platforms on a diverse range of issues from foreign policy to domestic crime. All he needs now is the right opportunity to put those specialized skills and his Harvard degree to proper use.

> O'Reilly's No Spin Zone feeds off fear, and that is why it succeeds.

Because a strategist of O'Reilly's caliber is always itching for a fight,
it won't matter who he takes on, or how—just so long as he wins.

Chapter 11

Guest Shots

"Fox is supposed to be the fair and balanced network, so I thought, well, we're going to have lots of opportunities to cover other sides of the story, but those opportunities didn't come."

Clara Frenk, former Fox News producer

Filling airtime is a news outlet's biggest headache: new words, sounds and images must be displayed on a flickering screen without stop. Popular guests have to be coaxed into giving repeat engagements while fresh blood has to be brought in to amuse viewers with short attention spans and picky and intolerant standards. Those hard-to-please audiences must be stimulated and entertained with both novelty and familiarity. If a guest can help a network fulfill all those obligations and can impart some information in convenient sound bites, then the network can consider that a job well done.

In this regard, bookers are the unsung heroes and baby-sitters of the television industry. Bookers continually have to find new stuffed toys to shake in front of their attentionally-fragmented charges while keeping tabs on of what parentally-sanctioned older toys have a good track record of keeping the children amused. Bookers scour the Internet and keep their rolodexes up to date: if a guest can offer pithy sound bites on short notice, the booker's job is made that much easier.

Not surprisingly, not all guests are created equal. Some of the tele-guests, while amusing, have not much to offer in terms of first-hand knowledge of the subject area in question. These guests, used mostly as rent-a-quotes, will go on all the networks and offer a diversion, but not much else. Other guests may offer knowledge, but their delivery stinks. They are boring, wordy and get their points across without once offering a snarky one-liner. For Fox News, the latter category has no place on their programs. Everything uttered has to be done with attitude.

Though some of the choices of guests seem as if Fox has taken a dip in the shallow end of the pool,

there is logic to who gets access on the show: on the one hand, certain viewers are attracted to specific elements of a program, such as a show's host or format. Formula is an essential ingredient to a program's success; if a show or network's popular features are changed, the core audience vanishes. The root elements cannot deviate from the script, since it was those very elements that attracted that audience in the first place. For a network like Fox, one of those key ingredients is the guests who interact with the hosts.

But if every guest behaved the same way, or if the same three guests appeared on every show every day, those same viewers would quickly change the channel in boredom. New stimuli must be presented at a steady pace; even research in infant psychology shows that babies bombarded with photographs will turns their little heads away in boredom if the same images are shown for prolonged periods of time. For television, the new stimulus can't be radically different than its predecessors, or the viewer will feel alienated.

Fox News has reached a compromise: they will regularly showcase their viewer's favorite righties, but they still need new fodder to keep things fresh. While a news show's host can be expected to remain constant (as long as the ratings are in top form), he or she needs new friends to play with for a fixed amount of time before the viewers don't want to watch the same friends poke each other in the eye anymore. In the news world, those friends are called guests: hosts will interact with them for a while, but then the novelty or the naïveté wears off. For friendly guests, the air-kissing act will wear thin; hostile guests aren't likely to want to come back for another whumping. Fox News knows to make the act seem fresh.

While guests are an important factor for any news channel, this type of fodder is particularly important for Fox News. Fox likes to cultivate a tough street fighter image, and it's not enough for hosts to scowl at the camera: they either need a guest who will scowl along with them, a guest they can scowl at or guests who will scowl at each other. FNC hosts tend to be combative, but they cannot be combative all by themselves: they either need an enemy to thrash about or an ally to gossip with.

It's the adversarial mode that viewers want to see: watching Ann Coulter jab Susan Estrich or Bill O'Reilly slapping some "liberal elite" journalist is the main attraction at Fox News. Lobbing snarky comments at the expense of one's dignity is the name of the game and no one sets confrontations better than the FNC. In the arena, guests shout *Ave Murdoch, morituri te salutant!* right before the cameras roll. It's a great schtick, except that, of course, on several levels the fighting is rigged.

The News Corp style of choosing guests is intriguing: people are chosen to speak for others. For example, on a local level, News Corp's local Fox affiliates don't always get their information straight from the horse's mouth. Youth Media Council director Malkia Cyril recounted one study her group conducted on a local Fox News affiliate:

> We studied about three months of Fox News coverage in the Bay Area and what they had to say about young people... [and] one thing we found was that white adults speak on behalf of people of color nine times out of ten. So prosecutors, police and politicians tend to be the primary spokespeople in coverage of youth of color. We found

that problematic not only in that young people don't get to speak for themselves, but because they're portrayed so often as criminals, they're not even perceived as deserving to speak for themselves.

A local affiliate is one thing, but a national network is quite another—and even then, the choice of guests used is still troubling in the same ways: guests aren't fairly matched, and some guests do not represent the individuals, groups or ideologies that the network implies or claims they do. Other studies have also found problems with how FNC guests are chosen, such as studies conducted by

Clara Frenk
Former Fox News Producer

Clara Frenk, one of many "former" Fox producers.

the media watchdog group Fairness and Accuracy In Reporting (FAIR)—more on that in Chapter 17. If Fox News were about fairness and balance, they would take the most care of any news channel to ensure that all sides of an issue had decent representation. Yet when right-of-center guests continuously slaughter their left-of-center counterparts day after day on Fox News, but do not have the same in-the-bag-odds anywhere else, the silent skeptical alarm begins to sound off in one's head.

How to Rig a Gladiatorial Fight

So how are guests chosen? How are guests treated on air? Those are two separate questions, but they are not unrelated. You have to know who you are looking for in order to find the right guests to fit the bill. There is no point in finding an aggressive street fighter to willingly play the wussy punching bag—he isn't going to risk his reputation and livelihood for your benefit and your audience's amusement. He is going to fight dirty and give your hosts a run for their money. This scenario is too unpredictable and potentially damaging: image control is crucial for Fox, they cannot leave anything to chance.

For a news channel that prides itself on being a "fair and balanced" information conduit, one would assume the never-ending hunt for new guests would be a fairly straightforward and vigorous process: just find the most qualified, relevant and powerful guests from all sides of an issue, then let them duke it out on air. That process seems guaranteed to build both suspense and ratings. Which guest had a better argument or was the most competent debater would be the hook to reel viewers in.

But that assessment seems naïve. Clara Frenk, a former producer and booker who worked at the Fox News Channel, and was responsible for booking many of the guests on various Fox programs, started working at the network with the same assumptions, as she recalled: "I thought, 'Well, I'm going over there as a booker and being a booker, I always thought that... was a fairly neutral position. A story breaks and you get somebody on the air to talk about it.'"

Her assumptions didn't exactly turn out to be correct. What Frenk thought she'd do turned out to be vastly different to what her marching orders would be; however, she remained optimistic over what she would be allowed to do:

[...]I started [working at Fox when] the Monica Lewinsky story had already broken and the mood in Washington was one of complete and utter frenzy. Every single channel was covering the Lewinsky story almost exclusively, and I was really concerned about it because I thought to myself there was a lot to this story that's not being said that really needs to be brought out. I had come from booking shows, so when you're booking a show you're limited by time. I thought maybe working at a cable channel where you've got eight hours or so to fill will give us more of an opportunity to do more of an analysis of this story.

New employee Frenk would soon learn the ways of the Fox. Her job orientation would immediately rouse her suspicion that all was not fair and balanced at the Fox News Network:

When I first arrived there, I was given a folder, a little binder that had the names of all the Fox News consultants, the people who were paid to come on the air to give their opinions. The first thing that I noticed was that I recognized all of the conservatives who were in the roster. They were very well known people who had come from radio or from some sort of political background, and so I knew all of these people, and they were very, very strong people.

Strong conservative guests would need strong progressive guests to engage in any balanced and intriguing debate, but Frenk would see that that's not how things worked at the cable newser:

But when I looked at the liberal roster, there was only one person's name which I recognized, and that was Bob Schrum, who is a very well known speech writer and political consultant in Washington. The other ones, though, were people I had never heard of, and I was very worried about that because I thought to myself that if, indeed, there was an attempt being made by the channel to present both sides of an issue equitably, that at least they would have somebody on the left who I would have known, and believe me, I grew up in Washington, and my entire background was in politics and political journalism, so I pretty much knew all the players in D.C. and I had never heard of these people.

Frenk was a bright young woman, and it wouldn't take her long to decipher Fox News' methods of pairing gladiatorial combatants in the arena:

I got a chance to meet some of [the left-wing Fox on-air consultants], [and] whilst they were very good and very knowledgeable, their credentials did not match up, necessarily, to the people on the right. And I noticed over a period of time that this was a pattern at Fox, that what they would do was take a very well-known, a very combative, very well-prepared conservative, and they would pair the person up with somebody who was very unprepared, or a person who was very reticent; a person who was more conciliatory. It seemed to be a pattern that went on and on, whether you were watching "Hannity and Colmes" or even the daytime programming.

A quiet and polite weakling paired with a rude and screeching powerhouse won't make for a fair

The conservative guests were more experienced and better prepared than the liberal consultants with whom they were matched.

fight: the weakling will try to appease his aggressor, mediate and find common ground because he knows there is no other way he can win the fight. He can't win on his charisma, presence or cunning; the best he can hope for is that the stronger opponent will not throw down his full weight on him. On the other hand, the more aggressive fighter will have no reason to compromise since he has no benefit from seeming benevolent: he will mercilessly crush his opponent and flex his muscles to impress his audience. The weakling will base his strategy on fear; the aggressor will base his on brute force and carny tricks. The weakling will not make his point seem incorrect and indefensible, but because he was chosen as presumably the *best* representative to argue his side, the audience will erroneously assume that the weakling's point has to be wrong: he's backed down for a reason, hasn't he?

Just as local Fox affiliates chose representatives who did not actually speak for a group of people, News Corp's prime jewel conducts business in a similar manner, except that their misalignment is ideologically based. Frenk described many of Fox's guests as "faux liberals" who "essentially agree… with the person on the right in a lot of cases, but because of their background, [are] still considered to be liberal… [Fox] would just bring on people who were very weak [and] were not well known…" She went on to describe how faux liberals were used on Fox:

> [One thing they would do…] that would irritate journalists to no end, is they would get a right-wing pundit, a right-wing talking head and then they would get a regular journalist, somebody from *Time* magazine, for example, to come on. I remember getting some very irate calls from some of these people saying, "I don't want you to put me on as someone on the left; I am a journalist; I am objective, and the problem was that at Fox, if you were working for a publication like that, then you were, by definition, on the left. That was the first indication [to me] that something was odd.

In 1999, when former President Bill Clinton was facing the business end of an impeachment because he denied having an affair with tartlet intern Monica Lewinsky, the stacking of guests became even more evident to Frenk. She noted that some producers at Fox "made no secret of the fact that they were very big fans of the Republicans on the Judiciary Committee and of the Republicans in Congress who were driving impeachment." If that's the case, Fox must have a unique interpretation of fairness and balance.

In an attempt to clarify to her employers that fair and balanced did not mean engaging in biased practices, Frenk made futile overtures to her recalcitrant superiors:

> I had made some suggestions because I certainly knew of some people who would be very, very strong and very good and the suggestions went nowhere. I believe that those decisions were made in New York and the problem was that you had to pay these people. So the suggestion had to come from New York because somebody had to approve the budget, and somebody had to decide that yes, this person was indeed worthy of receiving some kind of compensation for [his] opinion… It was just interesting that on this list

of paid people, there was such a tremendous discrepancy in terms of background and recognizability… on the left and the right.

Her efforts didn't work.

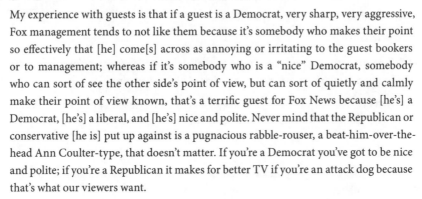

Frenk isn't the only former Fox News employee to see and be bothered by the rigging of guests. As one former Fox News employee noted:

> My experience with guests is that if a guest is a Democrat, very sharp, very aggressive, Fox management tends to not like them because it's somebody who makes their point so effectively that [he] come[s] across as annoying or irritating to the guest bookers or to management; whereas if it's somebody who is a "nice" Democrat, somebody who can sort of see the other side's point of view, but can sort of quietly and calmly make their point of view known, that's a terrific guest for Fox News because [he's] a Democrat, [he's] a liberal, and [he's] nice and polite. Never mind that the Republican or conservative [he is] put up against is a pugnacious rabble-rouser, a beat-him-over-the-head Ann Coulter-type, that doesn't matter. If you're a Democrat you've got to be nice and polite; if you're a Republican it makes for better TV if you're an attack dog because that's what our viewers want.

Choreographing Spontaneous Jousting

If the process of booking is less than straightforward and sporting, the question to ask is: what does Fox News have to gain by stacking the cards right? At Fox, certain guests need to fill certain needs. Righties are supposed to represent strength and righteousness; Lefties are supposed to be the wrong-headed comic relief.

The questions guests are asked also seem to depend on not only a guest's ideological leanings, but also on whether the guest is considered a friend of Fox or a foe. Certain guests will be showered in positively loaded questions, while hostile guests feel the lash of negatively loaded ones.

Welcome guests do get the fuzzy introductions, as Michael Reagan did on the June 22, 2004 edition of "Hannity and Colmes":

> **HANNITY:** […] And our exclusive first television interview with Michael Reagan. The son of the former President shares his memories of his father. It's very emotional. You don't want to miss this.
>
> But first, *My Life*, it hit stores today. And everyday Americans, they got their first look at Bill Clinton's much-awaited memoirs.

But Hannity wouldn't be Hannity if he let a mention of Clinton go without a nasty accusation leveled at the former President:

> But is it really revisionist history?
>
> Joining us now, former Clinton advisor, Fox News political analyst, author of *Rewriting History*, Dick Morris. And by the way, six weeks on the best seller list,

Dick. Congratulations to you on that.

Numerous conservative guests get a gushy howdy-do from Fox's own version of Walter Monheit, as Newt Gingrich did on the March 25, 2003 edition of "Hannity and Colmes":

> **HANNITY:** And we're glad you're out there. We continue our discussion about the war in Iraq. Former speaker of the House, Fox News political analyst and our good friend, speaker Newt Gingrich is joining us. How are you, sir?
>
> **NEWT GINGRICH:** Doing very well.

"Sir"? How deferential.

Hannity's "gee sir" attitude would continued unabated; he let viewers know just how qualified his guest was by giving Gingrich a five-monocle review of his credentials:

> **HANNITY:** First, we were showing images earlier, Mr. Speaker, of just what has gone on today and how far we have gone. And we're getting north, west, south, fifty miles outside of Baghdad. You're a historian. This is an extraordinary military effort and success.

Unlike hostile guests who get continually interrupted, Gingrich was allowed to speak at length about his take on the situation:

> **GINGRICH:** Well, I mean people need to put this in context. Desert Storm was a forty-six-day campaign, of which the first forty-two were an air campaign. But we tend to forget it was a forty-six-day campaign, and its only job was to liberate Kuwait.
>
> Now you're into the sixth day of a campaign. You already have an Army sitting within fifty miles of the dictator's capital. You have the second largest city rising in rebellion. You have a tremendous amount of effort both from the Jordanian side, where H2 and H3, the airfields, have been seized by the allies and you have a tremendous front opening up in the north, where American Airborne Forces are working and Special Forces are working with the Kurdish elements. I would say for six days into a campaign, this is an extraordinarily successful effort so far.

Hannity would underline Gingrich's points by adding more one-sided commentary to boost the former speaker of the House's comments:

> **HANNITY:** Yes. And if you read some of the more liberal newspapers, *New York Times* among them, you would think we're in great difficulty and this was almost a disaster as an effort. How important is this civilian uprising in Basra earlier today?
>
> **GINGRICH:** Well, I think it's primarily important—I mean, first of all, our hearts have to go out to the human beings who are involved, because Saddam's militia, which you ought to think of as the equivalent of the SS or the Gestapo in Nazi Germany in 1944, or '45, these are the militant hard core fanatics. They have no future. They're the rapists, the torturers, the killers.

However, military guests can also expect an easy ride on the vixen network, particularly if they believe their home team will win the big game. The No Spin Zone's Hard Question Generator must have been malfunctioning that day, since O'Reilly was only lobbing all his guests the same patronizing softball question on the March 25, 2003 edition of the "O'Reilly Factor":

> **O'REILLY:** Joining us are Peter Brookes, former deputy assistant secretary defense under Donald Rumsfeld. He's in Washington. Also in DC, Fox News military analyst and retired Navy Captain Chuck Nash. And Fox News military analyst, retired Army Captain David Christian here in the studio. What's the most important thing to happen today, David? Captain?
>
> **CAPTAIN DAVID CHRISTIAN (RETIRED):** A shocking thing for U.S. troops, I think, is the weather. The weather did what the Iraqi army couldn't do. It stopped us in our tracks. So we are regrouping while the sandstorms blow through here.

O'Reilly would repeat his question again to his next guest, though it was interesting that the normally gruff O'Reilly put away his trademark fangs for the evening:

> **O'REILLY:** That may be good. Gives everybody a breather, you know.
>
> **CHRISTIAN:** Gives us a break. Gives the whole army a break. And I think they need a break. We've moved faster and fiercer, if you want to use the word fierce, but we moved faster, historically speaking, than in modern military history under Colonel Parker. He's really moved an army here.
>
> **O'REILLY:** Yes. I mean, a sandstorm is a sandstorm. I mean, you've got to expect that kind of thing. Captain Nash, what's the most important thing to happen today?
>
> **CAPTAIN CHUCK NASH (RETIRED), FOX NEWS MILITARY ANALYST:** I think all the evidence started clicking in, what the United States has been saying about Iraq is pretty much right on target. I mean, they've got people dressed in U.S. uniforms shooting their own troops. They're hiding tanks in hospitals, and when given the opportunity, the town of Basra revolts against the Saddam Hussein regime.

The schoolteacher tendencies in O'Reilly could not be flogged down as he repeated his patronizing questioning to another one of his dutiful guests:

> **O'REILLY:** OK. It's hard to get—you know, we don't have anybody in there. A couple of Sky TV reporters from Britain, but they're out with the British troops; they're not in the middle of it. But if true, I mean, this is a turning point.
>
> Mr. Brookes, what was the most important thing for you that happened today?
>
> **PETER BROOKES:** Without a doubt, I think it was Basra. This is another fissure in the crack of the regime. And we are hoping for this sort of uprising [that] we can have something south. If we [act] more quickly and cautiously, we may be able to sustain this and see the same thing in the North with the Kurds.

Guests with happy news can expect warm, fuzzy questions from Fox's allegedly hardened hosts. If a guest can report that an American war goes well or the domestic economy is humming, there is no need to wear the skeptical journalist's hat.

Or at least it seems that way by watching Neil Cavuto's advertorialesque business programs. CEOs will get their enthusiastic air kisses and easy questions from Cavuto if the news they have to impart is good, as it was on the October 14, 1999 edition of the "Cavuto Report":

NEIL CAVUTO: And up, up and away for shares of Boeing, the airplane maker earning a lot more money than Wall Street was expecting, last year's production problems all but gone. Asia's economy looking a lot better as well, and news of an aerospace pairing in Europe that could mean more business for Boeing down the road, Boeing stock closing up… Joining us now from company headquarters in Seattle is Debby Hopkins.

Debby is Boeing's chief financial officer. By the way, Ms. Hopkins has just been ranked this week by *Fortune* magazine as the sixth most powerful woman in American business. Good to have you with us, Ms. Hopkins.

DEBBY HOPKINS: Oh, well thank you for having me.

It seemed as if Hopkins had Cavuto instead, but that's another story. Captain Capitalist himself just couldn't help but shower the executive with loads of kudos:

CAVUTO: And a twin congratulations there. Very nice company to be in.

HOPKINS: Thank you.

When the actual interview finally came, it was smooth sailing for Hopkins. After all, there wasn't an ounce of bad news she was giving America:

CAVUTO: Let me ask you a little bit about these numbers, which are better than expected, and momentum going forward. There were some concerns, as you know, ma'am, not too long ago about slowing orders. Is that still a worry going forward, or how do you see it?

HOPKINS: No, we're feeling very good about what we're seeing for the future… and feeling very confident about delivering our 620 airplanes this year and 480 next year.

Maintaining a Foxified reality is heavily dependent on the type of guests the network uses. Messengers of good tidings will never be asked a hard or uncomfortable question. The tones will always be pleasant. Most importantly, the guest will never be asked a question that he cannot answer. The same cannot be said for guests who are critical or bring news that counters the Fox way of life.

A New Meaning to the Phrase "Gotcha" Journalism

Sometimes progressive guests on Fox face a strange dilemma: they will be brought on the show to discuss a topic that they have an expertise in, but then the show's host will pull a surreal rope-a-dope and ask an irrelevant question or make a statement that is clearly out of the subject's league. Unless the guest is a Renaissance man or know-it-all, he cannot possibly answer the question with any authority. This manufactured ignorance seems deliberate and sneaky: the guest suddenly seems unknowledgable and naïve, making whatever else he has to say seem uninformed, even if he is qualified to make other assessments. But appearances are everything: even slight weaknesses are enough

for some people to discount someone else's analysis. It would be akin to bringing a doctor on the program to talk about surgery, but then throwing a fit because he couldn't answer your questions about fixing your car.

One instance of this ridiculous form of gotcha journalism was used on media critic Steve Rendall on the March 25, 2003 edition of the "O'Reilly Factor":

> **O'REILLY:** All right. Now the reason... is—none of us are oracles, but the reason is that we're fighting a political war, as we pointed out. We have twenty dead. That's—it's—by all military accounts, even you would have to admit that this war has gone very smoothly for the allies. Twenty dead.
>
> **RENDALL:** Well, I'm not—I'm not a military analyst.
>
> **O'REILLY:** No, it's obvious you're not.
>
> **RENDALL:** I'm a media...
>
> **O'REILLY:** It's obvious you're not...
>
> **RENDALL:** I'm a media critic.
>
> **O'REILLY:** ...because, if you think the war isn't going well, then you're in the land of Oz.
>
> **RENDALL:** The war is not the cake walk that it was sold to us as.
>
> **O'REILLY:** Sure it is. You've got twenty dead after five days.

If Rendall's specialty is the news media, then why bring up a body count? Besides, a low body count (which dramatically increased to over one thousand dead a year later, after the war was "officially over") doesn't mean a low physical or psychological casualty count, a low suicide count or that the war was a clean, clinical and cheap operation. Rendall's point was that the news media was not critical in its war coverage: was the war justified, and what would the physical, psychological, financial or environmental toll be? O'Reilly made it sound as if Rendall's lack of militaristic credentials made him an unreliable analyst. A death toll is only one factor that points to a war's success or failure, but dressing down a hostile guest is more important than taking more then one factor into consideration in a Foxified world.

Fox Dream Liberals

When a progressive guest does make the Fox cut on a regular basis, they are not the strong, snarky, scenery-chewing counterparts to the flamboyant conservative hosts and pundits one would expect. In fact, liberal guests tend not to be all that liberal or larger-than-life. These are wishy-washy liberals who will agree with the host's conservative views or won't present cogent arguments or rebuttals to a conservative pundit's wacky decrees. Fox liberals just sit there, nod their heads and placidly roll with the punches.

One such Fox dream liberal is pundit and lawyer Susan Estrich. She's like a "Saturday Night Live" alumni in that she never seems quite ready for prime-time, but she's Fox's liberal dream girl, as James Wolcott observed:

The most embarrassing [one] by far is Susan Estrich. Susan Estrich who talks like she's going to throw up. [It's] like, "Susan, there's a microphone there, you know; you don't have to yell 3,000 miles across the coast. If you have ever watched her, she is exactly what the Republican[s] would want a Democrat to be. She reviled Clinton for his philandering; she was pro-Arnold Schwarzenegger. One night I turned her on and she

FOX NEWS POLITICAL ANALYST
SUSAN ESTRICH

Estrich is a guest "liberal" that usually agrees with her right-leaning Fox hosts.

was complaining about how they were going after Rush Limbaugh and how unfair it was. So she's like a dream liberal for these people.

Estrich does tend to agree with her right-leaning hosts. On one May 5, 2003 edition of the "O'Reilly Factor," Estrich must have been in a too-good-of-a-mood, since she repeatedly went along merrily through the No Spin Zone:

O'REILLY: Some are criticizing Geragos because he blasted Peterson on television before Scott Peterson hired him. Now I don't care. Peterson can hire anybody he wants. But the case is now taking on political implications because a National Organization for Women leader in New Jersey said Laci Peterson's baby should not be the subject of a murder charge by the State of California, implying the California law that protects unborn children from criminal harm should not be upheld. That outraged many Americans. [...] I think that did damage to the far left. What do you say?

ESTRICH: I actually agree with you, Bill.

The on-again, off-again deference continued throughout the program:

O'REILLY: But here's the—here's the problem with the far left, OK? You've got this Laci Peterson case, which is tremendously emotional. That's why these cable programs are doing hour after hour after hour after hour.

ESTRICH: Right.

O'REILLY: It's just an emotional case. You've got a young woman about to give birth, disappears Christmas Eve, brutally murdered. The baby brutally murdered, OK?

ESTRICH: Right.

Perhaps it was the nice May weather that put Estrich in a good mood, since she was willing to concede point after point to the "Factor" potentate:

O'REILLY: But anyway—so American—you know, American—particular women— American women are really tied into this. Then this person over in New Jersey says this, and even people who are pro choice are just repelled, repelled by it, all right?

ESTRICH: I agree with you.

If Estrich was in an agreeable mood, O'Reilly sure wasn't, since he seemed sick of Estrich's easygoing antics altogether:

> **ESTRICH:** ...and gay rights, we're going to win that one. I mean that's what I don't get about the far right. They keep handing it to us.
>
> **O'REILLY:** What do you mean we're going to win? What is this "we're"? We're all Americans. We should root [that] the economy gets better for everybody.
>
> **ESTRICH:** Well, I agree with you. I agree with you. I am rooting for it because I'm a mother of two kids, but if you're going to give tax cuts to the wealthy, it's just not going to...
>
> **O'REILLY:** Oh, God. You know, can't you—can't you stop with that stupid mantra? It's ridiculous.

Yet Estrich isn't the only murky progressive Fox News displays for show. As Wolcott noted, "the most hilarious thing to me is when [Fox News] sets up people who are liberals who are clearly not liberals, but simply more sort of objective moderates. For example, on the Fox "All-Stars," I've had people tell me that Mara Liasson is supposed to be a liberal. She's on NPR; she's very moderate, but God forbid she ever says anything that disagrees with Fred Barnes or Brit Hume, they start snapping at her." Liasson is a particularly interesting "left-of-center" guest: she does a fabulous job of not standing up for or defending any left-of-center views. Her presence is something of an enigma—why have her on if she repeatedly gets cut off, as she did on the September 22, 2004 edition of the "All-Star" panel:

> **HUME:** The question I was trying to get Fred to answer, and he answered in a way that was sort of off the point, was is this enough to serve CBS' needs at this moment?
>
> **LIASSON:** Yes. At this moment? The question is...
>
> **HUME:** Excuse me. The question is should Mary Mapes be left on duty at this stage?
>
> **LIASSON:** You mean during this investigation?
>
> **HUME:** Yes.
>
> **LIASSON:** I don't know—I think this investigation...
>
> **HUME:** We also now know, based on our reporting today, that this isn't the first time she's been acting as a go-between, as she did with Lockhart here and the Kerry campaign.

But are Fox hosts really biased toward Republicans? Could the charges of favoritism not be a little petty and uncalled for by excitable progressives? Sometimes people perceive a bias even when it's not there, right? If the August 10, 2004 edition of "Hannity and Colmes" is any indication of the FNC's agenda, all moderates and lefties should get out their picket signs and start marching:

> **COLMES:** Joining us now for the exclusive first interview, the newest Republican congressman, Rodney Alexander.
>
> **HANNITY:** Woo-hoo!

We report. You decide.

Part Four:

THE Fox FACTOR

Chapter 12

Crazy Like a Fox

"Although the scene you are watching may appear chaotic, it is important to remember there is a government plan in place."

Fox News host Brit Hume commenting on
New York City images on September 11, 2001

Fox News Channel's game of partisan reporting goes much further than choosing certain guests, images, stories, wording and then grooming on-air talent and producers on how to present its processed information. When all those choreographed elements are mixed together, what comes out is an entity that takes on a life of its own. The net effect is that the whole is not only greater than the sum of its parts, but that the FNC almost becomes a living entity with its own beliefs, agenda, tactics, rules, vulnerabilities and thought processes.

The fact that the Fox News Channel has a distinctive voice and look makes it no different than other cable channels such as MTV, HBO, CNN, Spike TV and Nickelodeon. Cable channels are supposed to distinguish themselves in order to capture a regular audience. Even though they are both news channels disseminating breaking news and current events, CNN and Fox News could

not be confused with one another, and that's what allows each channel to survive in a crowded marketplace. However, what separates the FNC from its fellow specialty channels is that Fox News has an aggressive approach of being more than a news channel. It calls for boycotts against other countries that have not threatened or invaded the United States. It isolates, insults and makes accusations against people of a particular political affiliation. It can influence public policy and manipulate the Ortgeist. It's the power to change the destinies of both the guilty and the innocent that makes the FNC something more than a place to park and amuse your eyeballs for a few hours each day.

Getting the Fox on the Couch

Because of the power the FNC can wield, it at least helps if we can determine the figurative psychological mindset of the network: what are the FNC's strengths and weaknesses? How does it "see" the world around it? What's the FNC's agenda? What are its fears? What are its hang-ups? In other words, if a psychoanalyst put the vixen network on the couch and asked the FNC about its ego and id, what conclusions would that shrink make?

On the surface, it might seem that the psychoanalyst would find a brash, swaggering and snazzily-dressed dandy who has all the right put-downs and opinions. Fox News has a stable of hosts and reporters who have the ability to appear as if they ooze confidence and cynicism. The FNC seems to be a rich and uninhibited subject that can outfox the shrink: the flippant patient just tells the analyst that he merely exposes and breaks the weak-minded and the corrupt, consequences be damned. When former Vermont Governor Howard Dean lost the Democratic Presidential primary in Wisconsin in 2004, Bill O'Reilly said on February 18 that "we're not gloating about Dean. I'd like to talk to him down the road some time for the terrible way he treated Fox News Channel and myself, when it was totally unnecessary. And it certainly didn't do him any good." O'Reilly's moral of the story: badmouth O'Reilly and Fox News and get your comeuppance. The Fox News kids seem to think very highly of their place in the cosmic order.

At least that's the window-dressing the FNC presents to the outside world. However, if this cheeky, image-obsessed rogue has all the answers, why is it toiling in the information business? Why doesn't it prove its theories right by applying them in the real world? For example, if the FNC is ardently pro-war, why not put its money where its mouth is and show the rest of us how it's done in Baghdad?

Of course, the FNC isn't a boy of Baghdad, but the network's never-ending fighting words and intrepid images of stout soldiers and American flags make it seem as if it were. The reasons why Fox News chooses to cultivate a half-baked all-knowing, angry, tough and jaded Republican street fighter image are anything but simple; however, no matter how many leaks this manufactured image seems to spring, its audience still seems satisfied with the results and is blissfully unaware of any inconsistencies. Sure the FNC may be imperturbable on the outside, but it still masks its inner deficiencies: maintaining that Avatar of Truth and Might image is crucial because the FNC is playing a game and it is playing for keeps. Show any vulnerability and the game is up: its target audiences don't want to see it wimp out.

The seemingly forceful and patriotic messages issued by Fox News make it seem as if the network is telling viewers the way it is: yet the images of mangled American soldiers in Iraq are nowhere to be found, nor did U.S. forces find those WMD that the FNC warned were there. If the FNC has its finger on the world's pulse, why do they have so few foreign bureaus? If it claims to be a fair and balanced news outlet, then why are the left and right pundits consistently unevenly matched? Fox News claims to be an outsider to the media elite, yet it is owned by one of the biggest mainstream media companies on the planet. To take the FNC's bravado and image at face value would be to ignore the large chinks in its armor.

Slowly, when each layer in Fox News' façade is pulled back, a more accurate picture of our subject is revealed. The FNC is a person in need of controlling its image and environment. It is a simplistic, domineering, inflexible, paranoid, sadistic, narcissistic, manipulative, petty and deceptive entity—and those are just its good qualities. The FNC is an appealing-looking bundle of unpalatable contradictions: it consistently vacillates between self-adoration and self-loathing, and praises its audience while it talks down to it.

My Way or the Highway

The American political system was built on the Democratic model, meaning that there is an inherent acknowledgment that different and differing ideologies and beliefs are crucial for national progress; in other words, the entire American political and social systems were built on plurality and the assumption that divergent views weren't necessarily wrong or at odds with each other. Without the diversity of worldviews and opinion, the system can't function as well as it can when there is natural ideological diversity amongst its citizens. Democracy and capitalism can't function properly without fostering and encouraging a myriad of tastes, methods, views and beliefs.

If the FNC is supposed to be a microcosm or at least a reflection of the United States, it has failed miserably. Not only is the Fox News worldview decidedly one-sided and simplistic, and not only does it present only one side of America, but it goes against every tenet of the American Democratic system. It assumes that one size fits all, and that the size it wears will fit everybody else.

While it blatantly disregards those who don't fit its mold, Fox News will side with its favorites even before it gets all its facts. The 2000 Presidential election was marked with nail-biting uncertainty as to who won the close and deciding race in Florida; at least it was uncertain for everyone except the FNC. In fact, one Fox News employee other than Carl Cameron had a clear conflict of interest: John Ellis was not only the director of the Fox News decision desk, but he was also George W. Bush's first cousin, hardly someone who had a disinterest in the outcome. A Fox News employee since 1998, Ellis was responsible for crunching and analyzing exit poll numbers for the FNC. It was Fox News that was the first network to declare George Bush the winner in Florida, thereby declaring him the next President of the United States. The other networks then declared Bush the winner mere minutes later, though all later retracted their statements once it became clear that there was no clear winner. As

John Nichols, Washington correspondent for the *Nation*, recalled:

> Now the first person who made the call to say that George W. Bush had been elected President of the United States was the person in charge of Fox News; election analysis division, the people who crunch the numbers... [Ellis'] job was to take the raw data of exit polling, analyze it, county by county against the actual voting and make a serious reasoned judgment about who had won Florida.

> [...]At around two in the morning, a new set of data had come in and it was complex data from precincts all over Florida and John Ellis had a tough job. His job was to go over it and try to figure out who had won Florida. The proper answer in analyzing that data was you couldn't tell; it was too close to call, there was simply no clear winner. Instead, John Ellis called it as a clear win for George Bush. Fox News then interrupted its ongoing election coverage and announced that George Bush had been elected President of the United States.

That confident declaration didn't square with the turn of events at the Florida polling stations, but the FNC saw no need to exercise caution in declaring their odds-on favorite horse the winner of the race. As Nichols observed, "what's significant about that is not the intervention of the President's cousin to declare his relative the new President of the United States without a serious crunching of the data, it was the fact that within minutes, ABC, NBC and CBS also fell right in line calling Bush as the winner. There's no way that they could have crunched the data in that time to come to that conclusion. In fact, quite the opposite. They should have come to the conclusion [that] the *Associated Press* came to which was that you couldn't make the call."

But the FNC made the call, and with it, most likely changed the course of history.

As Nichols opined, "We live in a country of perceptions. Politics is covered in a very vapid manner these days and as a result, when Fox made the call that Bush had won and the other networks followed on, that created the perception that Bush was the winner, [when] in fact he wasn't. But that perception was what really held for the next thirty-seven days and I would suggest... that that call on election night had more to do with making George Bush President than any recount or ballot design issue."

It's not just a tight election call where Fox News' confident stubbornness overwhelms its product. Bill O'Reilly's program is built on controlling his message and his guests. He claims his show is a "No Spin Zone," meaning that any opinion other than his own is not going to be tolerated. He deems certain items as being the "most ridiculous item of the day," he decides what's an "unresolved problem" and he is the only one who is allowed to open his mouth. He has his "memos" and "Talking Points." He is the boss, and it is he alone who calls the shots. It's as if he doesn't consider himself to be the mere host of a current affairs show, but an official in a position of high power, such as the CEO of a multinational company or a leader in an oval office.

Off-camera decrees are equally domineering. Memos control how reporters are to cover their stories, meaning their natural instincts are suppressed in favor of predetermined beliefs. One of

John Moody's June 2003 memos stated: "We have FCC Chairman Michael Powell on Cavuto today (hosted by Brenda [Buttner]). Let's do a few hits on the commission's vote about media ownership rules." The June 2, 2004 interview started with one of the more loaded and self-serving introductions on Fox News:

> **BUTTNER:** [...E]ver since he took over as chairman of the FCC, Michael Powell has been causing quite a stir in Washington. His quest for free markets and less government intrusion led to harsh criticism and even harsher enemies along the way. But nothing like his latest move. He single-handedly paved the way for the biggest media shakeup you may ever see in your lifetime. Earlier today, the FCC [was] voting to throw out stodgy, outdated ownership rules for media companies.

The FNC feels the need to control not only the messages their viewers see and hear, but their foot soldiers as well. Why aren't journalists' natural instincts good enough for FNC brass? Why would they tell reporters how to cover an event before it happens? Is Moody claiming some sort of psychic ability or does he have so little regard for his charges that he must guide them by their noses?

Telling others where to go is a power the FNC relishes. O'Reilly uses the command "shut up" to dominate the guests he doesn't like. His ambush style of interviewing serves to annihilate dissenting opinion. Sean Hannity also practices the art of waylaying dissenting guests, though he is a paler version of O'Reilly. Because his on-air partner Alan Colmes is less forceful in temperament, Hannity seems even more overbearing than O'Reilly; but in fact, Hannity's style of attack is cruder and less cunning than big brother O'Reilly's. O'Reilly doesn't need a contrast or a foil to enhance his television persona: he can handle his opponents all by himself. Though Hannity gets top billing, he still needs a contrast to be noticed. Make no mistake—Colmes isn't an expendable part of the program; without him, Hannity's apparent forcefulness diminishes.

Nevertheless, Hannity still waylays his guests just as one pulverized, hapless activist discovered on a March 22, 2004 edition of "Hannity and Colmes":

> **HANNITY:** Is it right to call the President an assassin, as [he] was called? Is it right to have voodoo dolls in the image of the President?
>
> Was it right to call him the Dim Son and Pizza Dim Son or Bush Light?
>
> Was it right to have a toilet seat with the President's face put in it? That's what was going on.
>
> **REV. HERBERT DAUGHTRY:** I don't even know what you're talking about.

Well, that was no excuse, and Hannity pounded away:

> **HANNITY:** I'm talking about the events that took place in San Francisco. You organized one of them. The one in New York calls the President a liar.
>
> **DAUGHTRY:** I participated, as did others, in organizing. I don't know what you're talking about. But if you're talking about whether or not the President dealing with the American people had been aboveboard...

HANNITY: I'm asking you if it's appropriate that at your protests to have the picture of the President's face in a toilet bowl?

DAUGHTRY: If you're asking, did Bush mislead the American people...

HANNITY: Did he?

DAUGHTRY: The answer is yes.

HANNITY: Stop right there.

DAUGHTRY: If you're asking did he use 9/11—and did he wrap himself...

Hannity's self-righteous attack took a somewhat childish, if effective turn:

HANNITY: I want to test if you're an honest individual.

DAUGHTRY: Let me finish.

HANNITY: No, Reverend, I've got to ask a question.

DAUGHTRY: OK. You won't allow me to answer. You won't allow me to answer. No, I didn't.

HANNITY: I'll get you a chance to answer.

DAUGHTRY: Because you broke in on me.

> *Fox News will side with its favorites before it gets all the facts. John Ellis, director of the Fox News decision desk, is George W. Bush's first cousin.*

Turnaround was fair play and Hannity used a tried but true misdirection to take the heat off his hero and on to another American President he found to be icky:

HANNITY: Did Bill Clinton, is he as big a liar, when he bombed Iraq and said his job is to attack their nuclear, chemical and biological weapons? Did Bill Clinton mislead the American people?

DAUGHTRY: I'm dealing with Bush now...

HANNITY: You can't handle that question, because you have a double standard in the application against this President.

DAUGHTRY: No, no. Because you want to get me off the point.

HANNITY: You have a double standard in the application against this President. Try and see if...

Perhaps the good Reverend couldn't handle the question because it was an irrelevant misdirection, but refusing to answer a baiting question seemed proof positive that the activist was wrong in Hannity's eyes.

Stubborn as a Fox

Once a Fox News kid formulates a theory, it cannot be disproved. There is almost no room for reassessment or contrition when their theories prove to be not only wrong, but harmful to the reputations of others. The views of various FNC hosts tend to be rigid and absolute, as Bill O'Reilly demonstrated on his May 17, 1999 broadcast:

O'REILLY: I've got one more question. President Clinton just seems to be such a liar, just, you know, in public. He—lying bothers me. Is he that way in private?

MORRIS: Well, I'll leave it to you to judge. He has told me...

O'REILLY: Well, you know the guy.

Hannity also had an inflexible attitude toward author David Korn on June 17, 2004:

HANNITY: Here's my problem with you David. We're done with the speeches, thank you very much. Here's my problem with you and all you—I call you the Bush haters, and I say that affectionately.

Here's the problem. You go out there with your books. You accuse the President of being a liar regularly. And here's the problem. You mentioned it here tonight. "Well, the President lied when he said he had weapons of mass destruction." Bill Clinton said it. John Kerry said it in 2003. The French told us; the U.N. told us. Everybody. But the only one that's a liar is George Bush. Wait a minute. You know what this proves to me? Is that you have a political agenda to hate the President. You are one sided, and you're biased and you're so fundamentally unfair you can't even see it.

Perhaps if Korn wrote a book pledging his undying allegiance to George 43, Hannity would have thought the book was as great as those of his favorite pundits. Hannity could have disagreed with Korn or challenged him on his points, but he took the argument to a personal and superficial level. No facts are needed in the FNC; as long as you can strong-arm opponents with your insults and lung power.

Paranoid Conspiracy Theories

The FNC doesn't just take political sides; it seems to think people to the left of it cannot be trusted on any account. The phrases "separate, but equal" and "to each his own" do not exist in the Fox News world; however, the network's paranoid tendencies did not begin on September 11, 2001, though they certainly became more pronounced. Not only were terrorists out to get them, but so were the lefties. The FNC didn't like either; ergo both must be wrong—and cut from the same wrong cloth. The Clintons were always suspect to the FNC, even before the collapse of the Twin Towers. The *New York Times* also couldn't be trusted on any account, as O'Reilly opined on his September 14, 2004 program:

O'REILLY: [An article] by Michael Dobbs and Howard Kurtz is instructive because it methodically goes through the evidence. The *Post* has been trying very hard to be fair lately, although it did do a puff piece on Kitty Kelley, which was embarrassing.

The Old Gray Lady was an underhanded little hag, according to O'Reilly:

O'REILLY: On that same note, the *New York Times* continues to embrace defamation. Today, the paper published the Kelley dirt. While the *Times* book reviewer was skeptical, the deed is done. This is the game the *Times* plays. It often publicizes left-wing tracts which whack people the paper doesn't like.

The old shrew was sneaky and playing favorites by way of giving cookies only to her favorite grandkids, according to serious journalist O'Reilly:

O'REILLY: My book *Who's Looking Out for You* spent a whopping twenty-three weeks on the *New York Times* bestseller list, but the paper ignored it, even though it's about you, not about politics. *Times* also did not review Sean Hannity's two bestsellers. *Who's Looking* is out today in paperback. And I expect little mention of it in the elite media, which generally despises me. By the way, I am proud of that.

Considering O'Reilly works for the world's most elite media companies, we can all sleep soundly knowing his book got the pampering it deserved.

Boo Ya!

Fox News hosts seem to have the drive to want to dominate guests, but they also tend to try to scare viewers right out their pants. Fear is a powerful motivating tool that can be an effective way of preventing an audience from scrutinizing dubious information. When it comes to stories about terrorists, the FNC can present a terrifying picture of imminent danger to everyone: elderly farmers in backwater villages are as likely to be in danger as high ranking government officials if one were to believe the slant of Fox News stories. Bruce Page summed up Rupert Murdoch's role in media fear-mongering:

What one must think of is the sad psychological state of contemporary politicians. One of the French generals in the Second World War who refused to surrender when Petain called for France to surrender to Germany and insisted on fighting on for what was called the Free French, was asked what he thought of Petain and he said, "Petain is nothing but a hook on which men hang their fears." And that's what Murdoch is in politics. He is the hook on which contemporary Western politicians hang their fears. They have made a mess over the last thirty years of explaining the modern state to its voters, constituents and members. They're terrified of their public, frightened mostly, and Murdoch comes along as a convenient peg, a device on which you can hang these fears and once they're hung up, they don't frighten you as much. I think it's childish and irresponsible and deeply foolish, but it is for the moment the way things are going.

Fear is cultivated very carefully on the FNC—talk of terrorism, biological weapons and imminent danger is frequent and can pop up at any moment, as one "Fox News Alert" did on May 24, 2004:

VAN SUSTEREN: This is a Fox News Alert. New intelligence suggests that terrorists are here in the United States and they're planning a major attack for this Summer. Joining us with the details is *Washington Times* national security reporter Bill Gertz. Bill, well?

BILL GERTZ: Well, Greta, things are definitely looking bad for the summer. There are a lot of intelligence reports.

These must have been slacker terrorists. The summer came and went without incident in the U.S. of

A.: perhaps eating too many nacho chips and watching too many nostalgic '80s music videos made these hardened thugs too soft and spoiled to detonate bombs or release biochemical weapons in the water system. Fox News would rather chase after and spook the so-called "security moms" without bothering themselves to tell these ignorant souls that, statistically, they are more likely to die at the hands of their spouses or partners than those of terrorists. But then again, women were never known for being good at math.

We Are the Champions

Pontifical self-importance permeates throughout the Murdochian kingdom. When the FNC does well in the ratings, brass won't shut up about it. When someone, somewhere makes a reference to the FNC, one of the hosts will surely bring it up and gloat, as O'Reilly did on his September 8, 2004 program:

 O'REILLY: "Washington Insider" segment, tonight. Power brokers are shaking over the growing power of Fox News demonstrated last week during the Republican convention. In fact, CBS News is running commercials saying that if you want real fair and balanced news, watch them. Wow.

While discussing "winners" and "losers" of the U.S. invasion on Iraq, Tony Snow and company couldn't help but to brag to viewers on "Fox News Sunday" on April 20, 2003:

BILL KRISTOL: Well, I think, if you look at network news, network news has had a terrible time. (LAUGHTER) I mean, goodness gracious, cable just...

SNOW: With the exception of "Fox News Sunday"... (LAUGHTER)... right here on the Fox Broadcast Network. Our numbers are up. Go ahead.

JUAN WILLIAMS: You're OK. You're all right.

SNOW: Finish your thought, Juan.

WILLIAMS: But, I mean, if you look at what happened to Dan Rather and CBS News and the notion of the nightly news during this period, young people who are interested in the war went one place. They went to cable.

SNOW: They went overwhelming[ly] to one place, but we won't gloat.

Brag yes; gloat never.

If an FNC reporter gets inconvenienced or gets a lucky break from Rupert, the network will even launch into programming to share the news with viewers. One "Fox News Alert" on September 14, 2004 did its part in watering down the potency of the bulletins:

LORI DHUE: A radio outage has flights grounded all over the southwestern United States at this hour. Fox's Wendell Goler is one of the many passengers stranded on the runway. He's at McCarran International Airport in Las Vegas. Wendell, what's happening?

Wendell didn't have any earth-shattering news, just a gripe:

WENDELL GOLER: Lori, I've been sitting here watching plane after plane turn around and head back to the terminal. The radios, we're told, for the air traffic control's regional center in Palmdale, California, went out, came back, went out again, with hundreds of planes still in the air. The air traffic controllers couldn't talk to them, so they didn't want to add to the congestion.

Just as viewers would take out their tissues in sympathy, good soldier Goler assured them he was going to be all right after all:

GOLER: So this occurred after the President had addressed the National Guard here in Las Vegas. He left an hour and a half before the press corps [were] scheduled to, got back to Washington just fine. But as we were number two for takeoff on the runway at about 4:30 pacific time, 7:30 eastern, the air traffic control problems began and the flights have been grounded ever since. So it looks like, I'm sad to say, a night in Las Vegas for the White House press corps. Lori, back to you.

DHUE: All right, I suppose there are worse places to be spending the night than Vegas. Wendell Golder, thank you very much for that information. We might add that about 600 flights have been grounded so far. Of course, we'll keep you posted on that.

When Murdoch christened his baby the Fox News Channel, most viewers never realized that it was literally going to be all about Fox News.

Petty Vices

If there is one piece of advice anyone could give a progressive about the Fox News Channel, it is this: don't ever make the mistake of making a mistake, or one of the Fox News hosts will eat you alive. Inhaling too quickly can be just as discrediting as flying a plane drunk; no matter what a progressive does, the FNC will find ways of criticizing that action, as they did with then-President Bill Clinton on numerous occasions. When the rest of the country was focused on the senseless and tragic death of John F. Kennedy, Jr., Sean Hannity could not contain his personal vendettas—he seemed to have a score to settle with Clinton when he dredged up the President's disposable remarks on the July 26, 1999 edition of his program:

HANNITY: Well, it turned out that John Kennedy, Jr. had already been back to the White House during the Nixon and Reagan presidency. So was it a simple slip up on the President's part, or was Bill Clinton using the Kennedy tragedy to score some political points?

Did the former President know he was mistaken? Did Kennedy erroneously tell him that factoid? Was Clinton confusing Kennedy with, perhaps, another former First Kid? If Clinton was deliberately lying, then wouldn't he worry that the press would find out and call him on the carpet? Knowing that his right-leaning antagonists would pounce at his every utterance, would he really risk it if he thought otherwise? Did it matter? Weren't there other more important events unfolding in the world that day? Those questions didn't seem to pass through Hannity's stiffly-coiffed head as he articulated his not-so-vast conspiracy theory to Betsy McCaughey Ross, a former New York State Lieutenant

Governor under George Pataki:

> **HANNITY:** [...] All right, Betsy, I'm going to turn to you. First of all, I think it's very clear what happened here. The President knew that this wasn't true but didn't think he was going to get caught here. Here's the President hoping a little transference is going to take place here, that the good feeling that the American people had for JFK, Jr. will be transferred to him. I thought it was a little shameless.

> **BETSY MCCAUGHEY ROSS:** Sean, how unkind, how needless to impute those dishonest motives to the President. It's really such a minor issue in this national tragedy.

Dr. Condoleezza Rice: Never a tough question on Fox.

It was a minute point in the greater scheme of things, but Hannity, not one to miss an opportunity to attack a left-winged politician, shamelessly used the Kennedy tragedy himself to score points with his more small-minded viewers:

> **HANNITY:** Oh, I think honesty is not a minor issue. I think truthfulness—let me tell you why this is important, 'cause this—not only did he lie under oath in the whole Monica Lewinsky scandal, Betsy, but you know what it is? He said back [in] May 30, 1996—I'm going to quote him for you— he said, "In our country during the '50s and '60s, black churches were burned to intimidate civil rights workers." He said, "I have vivid and painful memories of black churches being burned in my own state when I was a child." Well, after some investigative reporters went back and they checked it out, it was a lie.

Hannity doesn't bother getting scoops or conducting deep research on important topics: he just scans the headlines until an offending quote pops out, then tears the speaker of the quote to shreds for it. Hen-pecking is a nice job if you can get it.

Masters of Delusion

But just as you think that the FNC is at least grounded in some sort of reality, the hosts can surprise even the most jaded of skeptics with their creative beliefs and observations. For example, macho man Bill O'Reilly was deeply relating to the television character Buffy the Vampire Slayer on his May 26, 1999 program:

> **O'REILLY:** ...and "Buffy the Vampire Slayer"—you know, I've seen it a couple of times. I like her. She's spunky, and—I know it's just crazy stuff and you say it empowers the kids, but is that good? Is it good to empower teenagers in the way that they're solving their conflicts in a—even though it's cartoonish, in a violent manner?

O'Reilly's comic book tendencies were flaring up again and his guest (Matt Roush, who at the time

was a senior critic for *TV Guide*) seemed nonplussed by this quirky little admission:

ROUSH: Well, they are fighting evil here, you know.

O'REILLY: They are fighting evil.

ROUSH: They're fighting demons and evil and, a lot of times, it's metaphorically about the demons within themselves, to take it to the next level, you know.

The next utterance to slip out of the "Factor" host's mouth would be nothing less than stunning and a fascinating insight into the mind of O'Reilly. How many tough as nails men would feel a kinship with a female character? A previously unacknowledged sensitive side would emerge, though the reasoning behind it would be something less than serious:

O'REILLY: But, you know, Matt, I do that all the time here on the "O'Reilly Factor." I...

ROUSH: You get away with it.

O'REILLY: I'm fighting evil all the time, but I do it with the pen and the mouth. I'm not doing it with the sword and the—but I see your point. I mean, any idiot would know that this is just a flight of fantasy...

O'Reilly didn't say whether, like Buffy fans, his viewers downed a shot whenever he exposed his bra strap on camera, but suffice to say, Fox's resident vampire slayer had a more grandiose view of his purpose in life than most people imagine. O'Reilly's fighting evil, just like a real superhero. His admission did beg the question—do O'Reilly's underlings have to covertly procure their boss the latest issue of *Birds of Prey* or *Nightwing* for his reading enjoyment or does he have a pull list at his local comic book store?

Fox Kids' Club

While the FNC may look jaded and hardened on the outside, it in fact is a shrine to childhood and innocence. Cool graphics, pining for scary stories, snarky put-downs and fantasies of crime fighting are firmly rooted in the realm of pre-pubescence. When star personalities are allowed to throw fits at guests, it becomes news that the bratty inner child can use.

And what child wouldn't be enticed into coming out to play with the other Fox News kids? The FNC playhouse seems like a cool place to hang out; for example, the "No Spin Zone" sounds like a rule from Calvinball, and the "Most Ridiculous Item of the Day" can certainly pique one's curiosity. Besides, the FNC doesn't have just any round table, but one that is surrounded by "All-Stars." What big kid could resist?

But overgrown children beware: the Fox clubhouse is also a place where the FNC in-set can bully the weaklings and the others that they deem as freaks. Howard Dean may have been targeted for the Fox News bullies to tear down so that Bush could walk over him to get back to the White House, but the premature sneering at Dean took its toll too early in the game, and Senator John Kerry ruined everyone's fun by winning most of his primaries and the Democratic nomination. Though Kerry's victories were decisive, it didn't stop the Fox News kids from turning their attention to knocking him down enough pegs to virtually ensure his defeat, but it just wasn't the same easy game as it was to shove around the maverick Dean.

The FNC clubhouse is exclusive: Kerry was not allowed in the club, Jesse Jackson was not allowed in the club, Al Gore was not allowed in and Bill Clinton wasn't let anywhere near it. That these newsmakers aren't allowed in the club is actually a good thing—newsmakers aren't supposed to be *in* media clubs in the first place. Journalists are supposed to chronicle newsmakers, not lick their boots. If the FNC were equally cool to Republicans, they could claim to be a fair and balanced network, but right-winged politicians are allowed in the clubhouse. George W. Bush was in the club: Carl Cameron's boyish patter to the President clearly showed that access has never been universally denied. The FNC is no Diogenes Club.

Viewers are also allowed in the playhouse, which should come as no surprise, nor is it a reason to condemn the FNC: a news channel's purpose is to report the news to an audience. But a channel's other purpose is to make money for its corporate lords, and it does that by filling a niche that needs to be served. The FNC is providing viewers with information in an all-news format.

That's all very well and good, but there are already two other all-news channels on the market and their ratings are measured by the thousands, not millions. If FNC viewers were just in the market for a national news channel, then one news channel would suffice. When the marketplace is littered with several all-news channels—the oldest having the largest news gathering resources of its direct competitors—the argument that people are looking for a news channel just for the news loses its punch. People are looking for much more than merely headlines or breaking stories. Headlines can be found everywhere: newspapers, radio, Internet, television, even elevators and cell phones. Finding news in Western society is like scouring a Las Vegas cathouse looking for a call girl: wait two seconds and one will pop up. Fox News doesn't even have more information than its rivals; in fact, it has less.

So why do viewers prefer Fox News?

Fox News' mandate isn't to inform. Disseminating information to the public requires more than parading B-list celebrities and celluloid nymphets while frightening viewers with campfire stories about real and imagined criminals and terrorists. While Fox News has more than its share of more useless news stories about porn actresses who peddle their face for a shoe company or who have an opinion on military spending, their images of these lovelies can't beat the money shot of these same women on the Internet or on DVD.

So the FNC not only has less news than its rivals, but it also has less skin than other media outlets. Worse, many of the stories they report are hardly worth mentioning. Getting informed isn't going to happen by watching Fox News; thus, the lure must lie somewhere else other than viewers wanting to get informed. By default, if the FNC isn't informing, then its pull with viewers is its ability to entertain.

But the abusive treatment of guests isn't exactly entertaining. The pull for the Fox loyalist has to be deeper than flickering amusements. After all, what's the true entertainment value of watching Tony Snow, Brit Hume, Sean Hannity, Neil Cavuto or Bill O'Reilly, none of whom are as amusing as

watching sixteen scantily clad game show contestants make out with each other as they are stabbing each other in the back for paltry cash prizes? Hannity and Colmes can't beat a World Series for excitement or suspense, and the "O'Reilly Factor" pales in comparison to a Spider-Man movie installment. Fox News may be visually stimulating, but it's not the Circus Maximus.

So what is the draw? What does Fox give viewers that no one else can?

The draw of the Fox News Channel is its unique ability to reassure its viewers. As Hart noted "you don't have to go very long to see a story on Fox, whether it's about Jesse Jackson's finances, whether it's about some PC outrage, things that aren't necessarily all that newsworthy, especially if you're trying to find the most important things that happened that day. But they will appeal to this audience that Fox is trying to keep happy."

Strangely enough, Fox is a comforting voice to a certain group in society: one that may have failed to reach their dreams, yet at least Fox has reassured them their failures are not their fault, but are the fault of criminals, foreigners, gays, Democrats and various other real or imagined outsiders. In other words, people who watch Fox aren't necessarily doing it for informational or entertainment purposes; they watch it to reassure themselves that their own personal or professional slumps are the work of evil outside influences.

Unemployed? According to FNC reports, foreigners are parachuting in, threatening the U.S.'s economic health. The dissolution of families is not the fault of the FNC's viewers, but that of gays and feminists. Democrats tax too much, that's why there's so little money in the bank—it couldn't possibly be because the FNC viewer isn't financially responsible. Fox merely gives its viewers a face-saving out: no one need feel low self-esteem, shame or guilt. Fox News tells their audiences what they want to hear: pornographers are corrupting youth, not lax and irresponsible parents. Feminists are breaking up marriages, not the spouses who are too self-absorbed in their own problems to try to connect with their mate. Terrorists are creating dangers, not neglected teenagers who haven't been disciplined by their disconnected parents. It's always someone else's fault. Why take the blame for your personal failures when there are millions of anonymous Canadians and French who could take the blame just as easily? And why not try to destroy their economies just for the hell of it—maybe the FNC can make those citizens feel as miserable as some of their own viewers. Misery loves company.

That Fox lying on the couch just doesn't seem as attractive once the makeup is washed off.

Chapter 13

Thin-Skinned Fox

"He treated Fox News Channel worse in his newspaper than he treated the terrorists who recently beheaded an American. But of course, he sees Fox News as more dangerous."

Roger Ailes responding to *Los Angeles Times* editor
John S. Carroll's criticism of Fox News

As children, we learned the first rule of Playground Survival 101: big bullies are big babies who will push all the weak kids around until the bully misreads his pigeon and the pigeon snaps and fights back. The end result is always a bully retreating, never to go near someone who will not only resist his attacks, but will teach the lout the meaning of the word pain. Unfortunately, if the bully is stronger than his mark or if the victim doesn't try to fight back, the bully only gets worse, gets stronger, gets meaner and gets more egocentric. An annoying bully with little resistance becomes an unbearable one.

Fox News has bullied, blustered and bellowed its way to the top: management, publicists and on-air talent seem quick to hurl biting insults at their competitors and critics alike. Real journalists are expected to do their jobs without the degrading name-calling; Fox employees thrive on it. A calm and professional demeanor is advantageous to the media industry for a reason: when the jabs become personal and emotional, less time is spent on professional analysis and observation and more on irrelevant and self-absorbed vendettas. Imagine a doctor yelling at and calling his patient a "pinhead" for questioning the physician's too-quick and unsound diagnosis. That action alone would be enough to call the doctor's competency into question. But at the FNC, firing away with cruel put-downs seems to be accepted as a normal part of the job.

The FNC's attacks can only be described as sneering and vicious. Both on- and off-air talent must spend a significant amount of time coming up with particularly cruel jabs to throw at anyone who dares point out the network's various weaknesses instead of assessing their network's editorial defects and trying to improve their product.

The Fox News kids gleefully go for their enemy's jugular, hoping to traumatize, frighten and destroy the critic's reputation and credibility in the process. If the sucker punch doesn't stop the critic from taking another swing at Fox, at least let viewers dismiss the critic as a jealous liberal lunatic. The effect is chilling, but if this method is repeated one time too many, the network runs the risk of looking paranoid. Though the FNC hasn't reached the point of no return yet, they have managed to disparage enough people to burn some fairly significant bridges.

We May Seem Heartless, But Deep Down, We're Really Shy and Insecure

Even though this is the same newser that employs a middle-aged man who liberally peppers his on-air tirades with insults such as "boob" and "idiot," those who work at the FNC feel a deep sense of humiliation when others respond in kind. As one former Fox employee mused about the cable newser's oversensitive tendencies:

> Strangely enough, what matters to [Fox management] is when somebody gets up there at a political rally and holds up a sign that says "Fox unfair and unbalanced." [They] get very embarrassed when the demonstrations are in front of other media. Fox management likes to be able to go to the same sort of elite parties and be celebrated as the toast of the town, and when somebody shows up and offers a stink bomb, that's what gets to them.

The Fox News kids seem to love to prove that they can come up with biting insults, but when their critics return the favor, they go sit in the corner to sulk. This unstable flip-flopping between superiority and inferiority complexes shows in the final Fox News product: tiresome barbs and insults are used on the air to chasten those who do not fit into a Foxified world—however, some of the skirmishes are self-serving.

When antiwar activists were picketing outside FNC's building to protest the network's coverage, FAIR's Peter Hart recalled that someone at Fox News "changed the ticker outside the Fox News building to make fun of activists." Do viewers want a serious news-gathering outfit stooping to name-calling of those whose virtually only recourse is to stand outside a building with signs to express their frustrations?

When "Nightline" anchor Ted Koppel devoted one entire show to reading the names of all the American soldiers, the FNC made their disapproval known. As Hart observed, "Chris Wallace on 'Fox News Sunday' would schedule an entire broadcast devoted to answering Ted Koppel for having the audacity to read the names of the American dead in Iraq." Of course it is easy for Fox to escape scrutiny for their own news coverage by critics: by having so little actual content in their newscasts to scrutinize, there really isn't much for critics to analyze. The Fox News Channel has very little to do with disseminating news: they are the anti-journalists who will throw every insult, scream and parlor trick in the book at those who threaten their Foxified worldview. Of course the FNC reacts badly to criticism: nothing hurts more than the truth.

Delusions of Competency

Fox may have ratings, but they don't have quality, hard-hitting or investigative journalism. That may explain why the Fox News kids don't like people who work harder than they do. In a way, the FNC is guided by high school logic: the "brainy" kids always get picked on by the snarky slackers

Peter Hart
Media Analyst for FAIR
(Fairness & Accuracy in Reporting)

Peter Hart recalled that Fox News changed the ticker outside their building to make fun of protestors.

who resented the target's work ethic and success. While the name-callers may have been cooler, they knew that down the road their lack of effort was going to come back to haunt them. Fox News may put down other media outlets, but this is the same network that had serious discussions on the state of John Kerry's fingernails.

The FNC is almost obsessive with its relentless drive to punish not only critics, but with anyone who dares to deviate from the FNC life script. That type of behavior goes right to the top: Rupert Murdoch thrashes back at everyone from columnists from rival newspapers to comedians. Roger Ailes railed against David Brock. Bill O'Reilly attacks the "elite liberal media." Fox's Unholy Trinity of attack dogs refuses to look the other way: retribution is the only solution. Like all bullies, the Fox News kids target their opponents carefully, find their weaknesses and then humiliate and discredit them in public. Unfortunately, it seems their own mothers have forgotten to tell their children that for every finger they point at their rivals, three fingers are pointing right back at Fox.

Fox and CNN

Direct competition seems to bring out the worst in people, but with Fox, their worst seems more pronounced than that of their rivals, particularly their ongoing spat with CNN. Even though both newsers may experience the same consequences of ratings warfare, each one will handle their rivalry differently. CNN wooed Paula Zahn; Fox News wooed Greta Van Susteren. Van Susteren left without incident; Zahn was sued and cruelly insulted by both Ailes and an FNC spokesman.

News Corp has no problem using its news properties to lash out at rivals. When Ted Turner likened Murdoch to Hitler (a rather severe admonishment to say the least), Murdoch's *New York Post* hit harder by running with the headline: "Is Ted Nuts? You Decide." But it wasn't the last FNC jab at Turner; Bill O'Reilly also played attack dog at his employer's behest on his April 25, 2003 program:

> O'REILLY: Back here in the USA, our pal Ted Turner is saying it doesn't matter that the Fox News Channel overwhelmed CNN during the war because CNN is better, and ratings don't count for much. Well, Mr. Turner, again, is entitled to his opinion, but that is simply nonsense. Ratings matter a lot, and millions of Americans now prefer Fox over CNN.
>
> And that's the crux of the matter. If we were not so successful here, the elite media would not care at all about our point of view. They would ignore it. Truth is,

> Fox News Channel is emerging as one of the most powerful voices in America, and the elites can't stand it. That's because we reflect the point of view they find offensive—traditional values, a skepticism of politically correct thought and a willingness to hear all points of view.

Even viewers who seemed to disagree with the "Factor" emcee for his rival-bashing were on the receiving end of an O'Reilly factor. One letter-writer got hers from a haughty and snippy O'Reilly on his June 19, 2002 program:

> **O'REILLY:** Paula Williams, Pensacola, Florida. "O'Reilly, I heard you call Ken Lay and Martha Stewart greedy and Ted Turner something else. What happened to the news reporting that allowed listeners to make up their own minds? Ah, for the good old days." First off, Paula, you must be a new viewer. The "Factor" is a news analysis program. Just because I have a point of view doesn't mean you can't decide for yourself. As for the good old days, they're alive and well on the other networks and nostalgia from the '50s.

In one fell swoop, O'Reilly managed not only to make his viewer sound like an uninformed neophyte, but he also got extra marks for jabbing other networks at the same time. His rivals can't be anything but antiquated and are just, like, so passé, unlike those kewl kids at Fox, who know what rocks. We can suppose Paula Williams did not get the free mug or book for her correspondence.

Nor can the FNC resist the urge to condemn their rivals for the same sins Fox News commits. For instance, even though Carl Cameron was covering Bush when his wife was working on the President's election campaign, that didn't stop Bill O'Reilly from pointing fingers at CNN for similar behavior (while conveniently keeping quiet about the then-exposed fun factoid) on his June 28, 2004 program:

> **O'REILLY:** CNN's most famous reporter is a woman named Christiane Amanpour, who roams the world and sometimes reports on political situations. Ms. Amanpour is married to Jamie Rubin, who is a big shot in the John Kerry campaign. Is that a conflict of interest for her? And what should CNN do about it, if anything?

When O'Reilly's guest objected to the above description, the "Factor" martinet retorted that CNN was "very reliant on this individual. And she is a very high-profile person. And she does speak her mind on politics. And her husband is Kerry's driver. So CNN, with a liberal label attached to it anyway, has an image problem, does it not?" It's the same image problem that Fox News has with Carl Cameron, is it not?

Fox and the *New York Times*

If CNN is the bane of Fox's existence, the Old Gray Lady comes a close second. Until the Jayson Blair scandal, the *New York Times* represented everything the FNC didn't: respectability, investigative journalism, credibility and quality. While the *Times* has suffered for its carelessness with Blair, the Fox News kids still attack the newspaper for being an elite and liberal publication.

Copy of Internal Fox Memo

DATE: 5/9/2003   **FROM:** Moody

Let's spend a good deal of time on the battle over judicial nominations, which the President will address this morning. Nominees who both sides admit are qualified are being held up because of their POSSIBLE, not demonstrated, views on one issue—abortion. This should be a trademark issue for FNC today and in the days to come.

The animosity toward the *Times* isn't exclusive to the on-air talent: their keepers also have a disdain for the *Times*. In one memo Jim Moody sent to his staff on June 8, 2003, he could not contain his feelings toward the paper:

> We have good perp walk video of Eric Rudolph which we should use. We should NOT assume that anyone who supported or helped Eric Rudolph is a racist. No one's in favor of murder or bombing of public places. But feelings in North Carolina may just be more complicated than the *NY Times* can conceive. Two style notes: Rudolph is charged with bombing an abortion clinic, not a "health clinic." and TODAY'S HEARING IS NOT AN ARRAIGNMENT. IT IS AN INITIAL HEARING.

If "no one was in favor of murder or bombing," as Moody claimed, then why do so many people do it? Some even take a perverted pleasure in harming others who do not conform to their way of thinking. Obviously, there are many people in favor of such crude and drastic measures. Human beings may just be more complicated and darker than Moody himself can conceive.

However, some of the animosity toward the *Times* is merely self-serving: Murdoch owns the *New York Post*, a rival newspaper that can neither boast of having higher circulation numbers nor a superior reputation. But that conflict of interest won't prevent those at the FNC from continuing their goading snipes, as Bill O'Reilly did on August 5, 2004:

> **O'REILLY:** [...T]he attacks on the Fox News Channel increase and so do our ratings. The more they attack us, the more people watch. But it is my opinion that some of these defamatory charges must be confronted. Others disagree.

His typical infantile rant against the *Times* gave away a lot more than many viewers realize: O'Reilly openly admitted that the fuel and secret to Fox's success is provoking more established outlets so that they will give the chiseler newser free publicity in return. It's not in O'Reilly's interest to simply let *any* criticism against him or Fox go unnoticed: by pointing out the criticism from other media outlets, he is ensuring that his show and channel continue to generate buzz and headlines. For the FNC crew to exploit their colleagues is a dicey, yet crafty maneuver that can either propel the FNC to pop culture wonder or footnote. That may explain why O'Reilly is an adamant slagger of the *Times*:

O'REILLY: Now, you may remember a couple weeks ago I called out the editors of *New York Times* because that newspaper is printing every kind of libel against Fox News. The editors hid under their desks. But far-left columnist Paul Krugman did agree to debate me on the Tim Russert CNBC program, and you can see that this weekend.

It's not just the shameless push for free publicity that seems to drive the endless attacks; the soap opera quality of the "Factor" is also a key ingredient of its success—O'Reilly often speaks in these sorts of recaps and plot summaries. He reminds viewers of one of his many feuds with another media outlet; he tells his audience what happened and what the latest plot twist is; O'Reilly also knows how to build up suspense. What did his critics say? How did O'Reilly respond? What kind of putdown did O'Reilly use this time? What outrageous comeback did he use to put down those wimps? Did O'Reilly manage to put his detractor in his place or will the villain come back to do battle with our hero again another day? Whether the viewer is a fanboy or a detractor, he will need a scorecard to keep up with the enterprising host. In either case, with each taunt O'Reilly uses, he ups the stakes and the ante: the jabs become increasingly personally cruel, ensuring that his show is both suspenseful and unpredictable.

But the true genius of the strategy is how O'Reilly has the gift of personalizing and to a degree endearing himself on his show—through it, people get to know him, relate to him and root for him. It is his show and it is all about him, how he sees the world around him and how it sees him. It is interesting to note that he feels that his public spats are more newsworthy than what's happening in war-torn countries, in the Senate or in the White House. Was it a slow news day? Or does he just think his personal problems are more important than a current piece of legislation that may alter the lives of millions of Americans? How much research does it take to talk about the fight you had with a colleague? His feuds are both fodder and filler for his show.

After bringing viewers up to speed on his August 5 imbroglio, O'Reilly had some fighting words about his latest detractor:

O'REILLY: All right, now, look, Mr. Krugman lives in a world of his own. He embraces propaganda of the worst kind, and that's why I have very little regard for his professional analysis.

An interesting choice of words O'Reilly used to describe Krugman. Why does Krugman "live in a world of his own"? Because he doesn't believe what O'Reilly believes? Because O'Reilly has him pegged as a liberal? Does the "Factor" host think that any of his critics are psychologically stable or have any redeeming qualities? If Krugman was disengaged from reality, then how did he manage to work his way up in a field that requires its workers to be tuned to their surroundings? What makes Krugman a propagandist? What are the specific misstatements and the factual and emotional manipulation that he has endorsed or disseminated? O'Reilly didn't bother with trivial details such as hard evidence, but he did manage to get his digs at more than one rival outlet:

O'REILLY: It is unbelievable, but you don't know what you're talking about. We put more liberals on the air than conservatives. We put more liberal voices on the air than conservatives, and we have a tally every day of what we put on.

> There [are] no Talking Points. There is no marching order. It doesn't exist. But these people, they want you to think that. But here's the bottom line. In the Democratic Convention, the "Factor" killed CNN and MSNBC from eight to nine.

O'Reilly's comments were a flagrant denial of the content of Moody's memos, which clearly had a Republican slant on domestic and international events. Downplaying FNC's daily edicts while besmirching critics clearly was meant to distract attention away from the damning smoking gun: when caught in the act, the best course of action is to deny, deny, deny.

However, Fox News milked that debate for all it was worth: on the August 18, 2004 edition of the "O'Reilly Factor," guest host John Gibson got to slag the usual suspects:

> **GIBSON:** Bill recently issued a challenge to the editors at that paper to step into the No Spin Zone. And not surprisingly, nobody at the *Times* volunteered.
>
> But NBC's Tim Russert got Bill and the ultraliberal *Times* columnist Paul Krugman to sit down and hash some things out.

The debate in question took an interesting turn when Krugman threw O'Reilly's famous bad manners in his face:

KRUGMAN: OK, you know, this is not your show. You can't cut my mike.

O'REILLY: That's a cheap shot. You know, you're a cheap shot artist and you know it.

Krugman could hold his ground, since he was debating in neutral territory:

> **TIM RUSSERT:** So the broadcasters and journalists on Fox News take marching orders?
>
> **PAUL KRUGMAN:** Of course they do. I mean, if your fantasy was that there was a memo every morning that told you how we're going to cover the news so as to slant it, your fantasy would be right. We've now got copies of the memo.

But no one said shots couldn't be taken after the debate was over, and the Fox News kids took full advantage of the First Amendment. The next day, "guest host" John Kasich referred to Krugman as "ultra liberal." O'Reilly himself stated on another occasion that the *Times* "has shamed itself. It does it almost every week." But still it is six days a week fewer than the number of times O'Reilly has shamed his profession.

But O'Reilly used his show on July 19, 2004 again to drag out the stale debate to suit his purposes: "Obviously, there was passion in the debate. It's not a shouting match. That's what we do here. Now, why is this important?"

Yes, why was the debate so important that the "Factor" kahuna deemed his personal vendettas were more newsworthy than other breaking hard news topics? O'Reilly, always one to have a handy excuse handy, proffered one: "Well, first, because the *New York Times* continues to misstate what happens on the 'Factor.' And second, because people who dodge us, like Howard Dean, for example, continually say they don't want to go on the shout shows. That's the image they want the uninformed to have of the 'Factor.'"

The digs at the *Times* keep coming, particularly from O'Reilly. On April 3, 2003 he declared: "We have been telling you the *No Spin Zone* paperback has been climbing the *New York Times* bestseller list. It was number eight last Sunday. This Sunday coming, it will be number three. And the following Sunday, it will hit number one."

Perhaps O'Reilly is addicted to *Times*-slagging and needs an intervention; why else would he obsess over the topic? His rant continues: "I'm especially pleased because this drives the *New York Times* just nuts. And if you think I'm being ridiculous, listen to this. My two books, *The O'Reilly Factor* and *The No Spin Zone* combined have sold well over two million copies. Two million. Yet the *New York Times* has not reviewed either of them." Pity that the *Times'* snubs are driving O'Reilly nuts.

O'Reilly exploits his pulpit to preach against the perceived sins of one of his employer's many rivals:

◆ On July 15, 2004: "Today the *New York Times* proves once again that it uses its news pages to promote its editorial point of view."

◆ On November 4, 2002: "You know, after I read this piece in the *New York Times*, Frank Rich, very liberal writer, I wanted to take Eminem to church with me."

◆ On March 6, 2003: "The *New York Times* is printing a story that uses Mel Gibson's elderly father to make him look bad. Not very nice."

◆ On September 19, 2003: "In the past few weeks... a bunch of... papers have... flat-out libeled us. [...T]he *New York Times* is the worst offender. Its behavior has been truly shocking. Now once upon a time, I didn't buy into the elite liberal news slant. I was a fool. Some far-left newspapers in this country are so dishonest, it makes me ill. They can't win the debate. They can't bring down our ratings. So they have to deceive and defame. I'm just very lucky I have a forum to get our side out."

The O'Reilly formula is simple: hammer the *Times* for the news it covers, hammer the *Times* for hiring the journalists that they do, hammer the *Times* for not reviewing your books. Just whatever you do, talk about the *Times* and not about the times: research takes too much time, effort and resources.

Regardless of the fact that the FNC's skirmishes are fought both on the air and off, one thing is certain: the targets of scorn are well-chosen and well-exploited to suit the ends of the cable newser. But there is another issue at play: these rivalries and fights are personal enough to warrant the FNC to use their access to public airwaves to air their dirty laundry. Regular viewers may be amused with the steady stream of insults, but what more important information did they not receive because someone at the network chose to address the criticism rather than a more pressing issue that's unrelated to the FNC?

But even when the airwaves are being clogged with score settling, some at Fox News have a penchant for protecting their reputations—or sullying the reputations of their critics—in some very militant ways. However, when it is not possible for an FNC player to attack directly, he can always rely on one of his publicists to do it for him.

Roger Ailes has had his share of skirmishes with those critics who have voiced their complaints. He has a gift of cutting dismissal when negative publicity hits him or the FNC. But, as David Brock found out when he wrote his piece on Fox News for *New York* magazine, Ailes is ferociously protective of his employer's crown jewel:

> My dealings with Roger Ailes were—he was amazingly aggressive with me when I was writing that article for *New York* magazine and very threatening. I had some... problems trying to shut down sources, calling people and telling them not to talk to me, Lou Dobbs told me that he was called by Roger Ailes and [said] that I was up to no good and [he] shouldn't talk to me, that kind of thing. Now, that's what a political operative type would do. I don't think it's something that you'd normally see in journalism. And so here's somebody who's considered one of the most influential figures now in American journalism, but the background, I think, is very much from a political campaign, and that kind of intimidation and those kind of tactics. He certainly threatened to sue me, threatened to sue *New York* magazine. I imagine this is par for the course for the way he deals with people.

Roger Ailes tried to intimidate sources when David Brock was interviewing them for an article on Fox.

Brock recalled the combative methods Ailes used to wear down his critic:

> He would call me from his car going home to New Jersey, and my role and my goal was to get him to talk to me; so this was what it was all about. It was all off the record, negotiation, would he give me the information I wanted, which was really just an interview. So there was a lot of drama surrounding that, let me put it that way. I would call him and tell him what I'm hearing, then he would try to get the people to call me back and tell me no, no, no, that was wrong, and damage control. This reminds me much more of what I've seen in politics than anything I would've seen in journalism.

But Ailes seems to have no problem acting as critic to other people's news products. His comments about rival cable newser MSNBC are interesting, considering that the network is owned by the same parent company as Ailes' previous employer, CNBC. When MSNBC hired Oliver North to host one of its shows, Ailes snorted, "If they think it would save them, they'd be hiring people from Lyndon LaRouche." Ironically, North would become a regular on Ailes' channel, but there is no word yet as to whether Fox has hired LaRouche. When MSNBC went overboard with its coverage of the death of Princess Diana, Ailes sniffed without a trace of irony, "MSNBC is under such pressure to get ratings, they've gone totally tabloid." But he's not bitter.

Bill O'Reilly, on the other hand, is bitter. He's gotten about a twenty-year head start on being a grumpy old man; but since he won't gripe about the government like a good old man should, he settles for over-the-top clashes with well-known celebrities. At least he feuds with style.

OUTFOXED

Spanking Bill Moyers: One of O'Reilly's favorite targets of torment is former PBS journalist Bill Moyers, who he has slagged on and off camera on numerous occasions, including on his December 4, 2002 program:

> O'REILLY: Moyers versus O'Reilly, round two. That's the subject of this evening's "Talking Points" memo. As you may know, we have asked Bill Moyers to come on the "Factor" gazillions of times, but he will not. I finally got to talk to him today on the phone, and he told me no way will he appear to tell you how I am full of beans.

Since he has done it so often, O'Reilly naturally assumes the viewer is up to speed as to why O'Reilly is feuding with Moyers. The soap opera quality of the "Factor" makes for addictive television: what did Moyers do now? How will O'Reilly strike back? Will Moyers agree to enter the No Spin Zone? However, one point does stand out: if O'Reilly's lackeys have unsuccessfully tried "gazillions of times" to get Moyers on the "Factor" and Moyers always says "no" gazillions of times, perhaps the reason Moyers has steadfastly turned down invitation after invitation is that he does not wish to encourage his stalker.

By January 20, 2003, even O'Reilly himself must have realized how obsessive he sounded when he began his regularly scheduled Moyers attack: "The continuing sagas of George Clooney and Bill Moyers, that is the subject of this evening's 'Talking Points' memo. Now, I know I run the risk of overkill here, but these guys continue to misbehave. And what they are doing is important, because it's part of a bigger picture." O'Reilly, ironically, had this to say about his antagonist: "'Talking Points' knows charlatans when they rant and rave. There is no shame in being a liberal or a conservative. The shame lies in playing fast and loose with the truth and celebrating other people's misfortunes." Too bad O'Reilly doesn't take some of his own advice.

Renaming Al Franken: O'Reilly's most famous feud is with comedian, actor, writer and activist Al Franken. The two have had their share of words, but believe it or not, O'Reilly and Franken weren't always feuding. In fact, things sounded downright jovial when Franken made an appearance on the February 12, 1999 edition of the "Factor":

> O'REILLY: In the "Back of the Book" segment tonight, Al Franken, who is selling lots of books with his new tome about him being President, called *Why Not Me?* Why not, indeed?

O'Reilly ended the energetic interview (where he and Franken had a vigorous, but not acrimonious debate over former President Bill Clinton's impeachment acquittal) on this pleasant note:

> O'REILLY: We only have fifteen seconds left. One thing. This is a great plot for "Lateline," what you just laid out for me. That would be a great plot for you guys to do. Al Franken.
>
> FRANKEN: Well, when we come back on, we'll do it.
>
> O'REILLY: The book is *Why Not Me?* And why not, indeed? Thanks for coming in. Always good to talk with you.

Well, not always.

These two may never have been friends, but over the years they have become bitter enemies. O'Reilly's sentiments must have rubbed off on his supervisors: one April 6, 2004 Jim Moody memo seems to show that Moody also likes to get his digs at Franken:

> "Air America," featuring Al Franken and other liberals, got on the air last week, but at what cost? Well, in New York, it took the place of an ethnic show. In LA, it knocked off a Korean program. And in Chicago, a Spanish language broadcast was replaced. None of these people are happy.

Not that O'Reilly needs any encouragement. On June 2, 2003, O'Reilly declared on his show that he, "your humble correspondent, me, had to get tough with Al Franken." The reason? According to Big Bad Bill himself:

> **O'REILLY:** I guess I have to deal with this Al Franken situation since it's in the papers, and our competitors will try to exploit it. Ordinarily, I would never deal with the likes of Franken, who is simply beneath contempt.

His was an interesting declaration, since O'Reilly has had numerous high profile spats, including those with Franken, that he's numerously mentioned on his own show. Though O'Reilly seems as if he is trying to discredit his critics and rivals by warning viewers that they will "try to exploit" O'Reilly's on-the-job problems, isn't he trying to milk the situation the same way by repeatedly bringing up these feuds on his program? Yet O'Reilly continued to discredit his rival:

> **O'REILLY:** A few years ago he almost got into a fist fight with Sean Hannity, and a few weeks ago, he verbally assaulted Alan Colmes in public at a Washington dinner. The man is a fanatic and not worth anyone's time.

If Franken is a "fanatic" as O'Reilly claims, then why encourage him by repeatedly discussing the man on the "Factor"? Besides, what makes Franken a fanatic? That he won't back down? Besides, if Franken "isn't worth anyone's time" then why is O'Reilly wasting time on his show to discuss this "fanatic" called Al Franken? Wouldn't O'Reilly's repeated shots actually encourage Franken and give him more publicity? If what O'Reilly said had a kernel of truth to it, wouldn't it be better if O'Reilly settled this matter in private?

The fact is, O'Reilly needs public rivals and enemies to cultivate a tough guy image: without a cast of highly recognizable enemies, O'Reilly is just a regular newsie. His comic book persona dictates that he needs a rogue's gallery of sorts. Keep the fires burning; stoke the flames of hatred and viewer curiosity, and make sure you give them enough ammunition to keep the spat public for as long as possible. It is a stroke of sheer brilliance.

This enterprising cultivation can't seem obvious; so it helps to blame a third party for prolonging the battle, as O'Reilly did in the same broadcast:

> **O'REILLY:** But I made a promise to my publisher, Broadway Books, to attend the Los Angeles Book Fair on Saturday, and Franken was on the panel. Everybody knew there would be trouble, but I keep my promises.

Of course, it was all the publisher's fault that there would be a new battle to fight, but the upstanding

O'Reilly would never break his word:

> **O'REILLY:** That's fine, OK? This is what he does. He's a vicious—and that is with a capital V—person, who is blinded by ideology. You make a nice living being a propagandist, and more power to you. But don't put yourself up as a truth teller, because you are not.

Finally, the standard issue I'm-not-vindictive justification served as an important coda to O'Reilly's soliloquy: "Now, if I sounded angry, I was. Imagine sitting next to somebody calling you a liar for that period of time. If that happened 200 years ago, there would have been a duel, and trust me, he would have lost."

By March 2004, O'Reilly's disdain for Franken had culminated in his calling the comic "Stuart Smalley"— a character Franken popularized while he was on "Saturday Night Live." Franken suddenly wasn't good

Al Franken
Air America Host

Al Franken: Not Stuart Smalley

enough or smart enough for O'Reilly who, doggone it, didn't like him. Infantile, vendetta-based name-calling is what serious journalists do all the time, obviously, but O'Reilly, being the "extra mile" kind of guy that he is, took Franken's new moniker to the limit:

◆ On March 22, 2004, O'Reilly spat: "Newspaper editorial boards have meetings all the time with candidates from both parties and, of course, that's legit. But, as you point out, this was—[the] meeting took place in Stuart Smalley's apartment. He's a radical activist."

◆ On June 1, 2004: "Kerry himself has a problem because he can only win if he gets the undecided independent vote. And as soon as the undecided independents see Michael Moore, Stuart Smalley, George Soros and these people, they go, we don't want any part of these people, we don't want—even Ted Kennedy. As soon as anybody south of the Mason-Dixon line who is white sees Ted Kennedy, they don't want him."

◆ On July 14, 2004, O'Reilly had a discussion with Tony Snow about John Kerry: "I don't know if he wants Hillary Clinton out there, because he needs independent voters, and she's a polarizer. I don't think you're going to see John Kerry with Michael Moore or Stuart Smalley or many of these Hollywood idiots."

◆ On June 30, 2004, O'Reilly again complained to Snow about Franken by saying: "Nobody's run with this like they did with the Stuart Smalley book, the *New York Times* in particular, and run with this as a way to bludgeon Bush. You haven't seen any of that in the press?"

◆ On August 2, 2004, O'Reilly rapped with the authors of the book *Michael Moore is a Big Fat Stupid White Man*: "[...t]he idiot Stuart Smalley put it in his dishonest book..."

◆ On July 12, 2004, O'Reilly whined to Newt Gingrich: "Stuart Smalley made millions on his defamation book, and people are seeing that they can say and do anything they want and profit from it. Are you as worried as I am?"

◆ Also on July 12, to Molly Ivins: "All right, last question. You sat on a panel with me in Los Angeles last year when I was viciously attacked by Stuart Smalley. Think that was fair?"

◆ On June 28, 2003, always thoughtful to viewers, O'Reilly made it easy for them to follow the latest installment of the "Factor" soap opera: "If you can't beat him, slime him. I hope you read the *Parade* magazine item on me and Stuart Smalley yesterday. It simply blows the defamation king away. It's available on billoreilly.com if you missed it."

Then, on September 2, 2004, a swift Bill Maher asked O'Reilly point blank about his code word for his arch nemesis:

O'REILLY: [...] the Soros websites have, for a year, for a year smeared every guy and gal with whom they disagree, and I'm one of them, so I know what I'm talking about here. Isn't the tactic mud, and we're just going to fling it as much as we can—Michael Moore, Stuart Smalley, whoever it is flinging the mud, hope it sticks.

MAHER: You've refused to actually even use his name, Al Franken. He's Stuart Smalley.

O'REILLY: He is, indeed.

These aren't even all references to the Smalley moniker O'Reilly used on his show. Is it payback for Franken's "O'Lielly" jab? Most likely, but Franken's a comedian by trade; O'Reilly is supposed to be a news producer and analyzer who is meant to conduct himself with a modicum of decorum on his program. In fact, the feud most likely would have fizzled out if O'Reilly didn't bring his personal problems to the job with him. All right, you don't like Al Franken. We know, O'Reilly. Get over yourself, OK?

 **Getting Michael Moore:** The Oscar-winning documentary director has also felt the tongue-lashing of O'Reilly on many occasions. Like Bill Moyers, Moore had refused to enter the No Spin Zone; however, after O'Reilly agreed to a live, unedited debate, Moore agreed to debate the No Spin Zone architect.

So on July 27, 2004, O'Reilly finally got his chance to battle with the progressive Moore with a few condescending digs such as this one:

O'REILLY: You're diverting the issue... did you read Woodward's book?

MOORE: No, I haven't read his book.

O'REILLY: Woodward's a good reporter, right? Good guy, you know who he is, right?

MOORE: I know who he is.

O'Reilly also managed to make Moore seem as if he was evading O'Reilly's tough questions:

MOORE: But that was your question…

O'REILLY: Just the issues. You've got three separate investigations plus the President of Russia all saying… British intelligence, U.S. intelligence, Russian intelligence, told the President there were weapons of mass destruction; you say he lied. This is not a lie if you believe it to be true, now he may have made a mistake, which is obvious…

MOORE: Well, that's almost pathological. I mean, many criminals believe what they say is true; they could pass a lie detector test…

O'REILLY: All right, now you're dancing around a question…

It was a highly anticipated battle that made headlines: in-your-face director versus in-your-face interviewer. The stakes were high, and both sides of the political spectrum may have declared victory, but since the bout took place on the "Factor," the biggest winner was inevitably Bill O'Reilly, who understands that epic feuds translate to healthy ratings.

It's a vast left-wing conspiracy: O'Reilly must thrive on feuds, since he evokes them often in his various media platforms. For example, on October 8, 2003, O'Reilly warned viewers with this ominous message: "I've been telling you for months that there are powerful people and institutions behind these smear merchants currently running around the USA. The culture war's very, very intense."

Realizing that he may have taken his enterprising free publicity tactic just a tad too far, O'Reilly qualified his position, "Now I've got mail saying O'Reilly, you're paranoid, things like that. But here is the absolute truth. Broadway Books, which is publishing my new effort, *Who's Looking Out for You?* wanted me to go on National Public Radio to talk about the book."

O'Reilly went on to talk about the dangers of promoting a book:

O'REILLY: I told them that NPR would try to smash me because along with some other major newspapers in this country, it has championed the defamation books. But I agreed to do the program called Fresh Air, hosted by a woman named Terry Gross. For half an hour, Mrs. Gross attempted to embarrass me. Well, finally it came to this.

The "this" O'Reilly was referring to was that O'Reilly stormed out of the NPR studio during the interview. The infamous interview ended this way:

O'REILLY: I am. I mean, I'm evaluating this interview very closely. Obviously you are. Now we've spent now, all right, fifty minutes of me being—defending defamation against me in every possible way, while you gave Al Franken a complete pass on his defamatory book. And if you think that's fair, Terry, then you need to get in another business. I'll tell you that right now. And I'll tell your listeners, if you have the courage to put this on the air, this is basically an unfair interview designed to try to trap me into saying something that *Harper's* magazine can use. And you know it. And you should be ashamed of yourself. And that is the end of this interview.

It really was, though O'Reilly would discuss the "ambush" on his program later on. Though he supposedly conceded that he made an error, he also managed to attack NPR this way: "all right, the problem here is not that interview. I should have known better. But it's that I paid for it. And so did you." He then reminded viewers that NPR receives government funds. But O'Reilly's unpredictable stunt had the reek of a savvy publicity stunt that worked: other news outlets quickly picked up on the story.

Playing up his tiffs is something O'Reilly does well. As he informed his viewers on his July 26, 2004, program:

O'REILLY: And on that subject, our poll question on billoreilly.com—more than 50,000 of you went in to answer the question, who's worse: Michael Moore or Al Franken, aka Stuart Smalley? 85% say Moore is worse than Franken. But that's not true. Believe me, I'm among the 15%, but I know these two guys, and Stuart is way worse than Moore.

But O'Reilly's spats work for him, unlike those of his junior colleague Sean Hannity. When a grown man writes a shallow propagandistic tome equating liberals with terrorists, he is desperately looking to get attention and reaction from his target. But somehow, Hannity's methods are just not working for him the way they do for his more popular and charismatic colleague. Hannity may have substantially less presence and cultural consequence than Bill O'Reilly, but he is trying his darnedest to compete with the larger-than-life host. He can't—Hannity is the kid who spent hours building up a caché of snowballs to hurl, but then discovered that none of the kids on the block wanted to have a fight with him because they all went to have an epic snowball blowout with the most popular kid in town.

The trouble is, Hannity is merely hurling spurious insults with no style or function, while O'Reilly has bona-fide feuds with equally flamboyant progressive and centrist A-listers. Hannity is stuck with his built-in antagonist, the mild Alan Colmes; hence he is thought of as part of a package deal. It's "Hannity and Colmes" and not "The Hannity Factor" for a reason.

To make matters worse for poor, anchorless Hannity, O'Reilly's spats are emotional, melodramatic and shrill, but are completely genuine, logical and, many times, even personal. His ongoing hatefest with Franken is grand, gossipy and legendary; they may passionately slag each other in their books and programs, but there is a certain suspense and mesmerizing quality about their mutual animosity. There is a bizarre operatic appeal to O'Reilly's feuds that captures the imagination of both conservatives and progressives alike, because love him or hate him, Bill O'Reilly matters—and so do all of his chosen enemies. The cast of characters are all firmly entrenched in the big leagues.

Hannity, of course, doesn't matter in the slightest. He is just another disposable, predictable and pedestrian by-the-numbers Republican ideologue who offers nothing new or different to the political discourse. Unlike the cagey and labyrinthine O'Reilly, Hannity is an intellectual lightweight with no defining psychological strategy, though we do know he is capable of counting backwards. He dutifully follows the script, and he issues the standard put-downs Republicans assign to Democrats. Ho-hum.

Because Hannity lacks both star power and emotional pull, he doesn't really have real feuds or any real reason to lob defensive insults. The closest Hannity ever came to having an honest-to-goodness public feud was with comedienne Janeane Garofalo, but her battle with him on his show didn't have the same interest level or primal pleasure as it would have if someone sparred with the more animalistic O'Reilly. Besides, Michael Moore readily appeared more than once on Hannity's vehicle without any fanfare; however, Moore was far more reluctant to enter the ring with O'Reilly. Moore's "Hannity and Colmes" cameos didn't generate any heat or buzz; but his face-off with O'Reilly made headlines. Hannity may be a fleeting annoyance, but his contribution means little to the cultural and political discourse.

But hey, you can't fault a guy for giving it the good old electoral college try. He really, really wants to matter. He doesn't want to be just another right-winged extremist with good teeth and good hair—but he can't be a legend, because in order to catapult himself into the same sphere as O'Reilly, he would have to suffer for his craft and be everything that he currently isn't.

Which makes his longevity questionable, even if his fan base tends to be loyal. In order for Hannity not to be another flash in the pan, he needs enemies. He needs drama. But he is too well-tended, vapid and soft for enemies and drama to look convincing on him. Hannity doesn't take chances and thus builds no suspense; O'Reilly does, even though he has much more to lose than Junior. There is a real, raw emotion with O'Reilly that his viewers either see as salvation or danger; Hannity just safely follows the party line.

Hannity is trying too hard and it shows. Preeners aren't worthy adversaries, and while critics will shake a scornful finger at Hannity, they save their best attacks for the "Factor" host. O'Reilly may look scruffier, but his appearance works for him. Hannity looks better, he wears better suits, heck, even his hair looks better than O'Reilly's, and yet... nothing. Sure, his books sell, but a Republican lullaby singer just doesn't cut it as the star. Even when it's a contest Hannity should have sewn up, he doesn't win: he could only muster second place in *Playgirl* magazine's reader survey of best-looking news personalities.

Hannity is always runner-up, never the legend or the winner but give the man credit for trying to reposition himself by throwing verbal Molotov cocktails at critics and rivals, most likely in the hopes of sparking a feud. Whether any progressive will be naïve enough to bite at the bait remains to be seen, but he has tried with Michael Moore: on his February 16, 2003 program, he referred to Moore as "fringe people"; on July 20, 2004, he claimed that Moore "frankly, is not very bright... he comes up with the most bizarre conspiracy theories without any proof or evidence or substantiation."

Hannity might use a few fighting words in the safety of his own studio to jab Moore, but don't expect him to get off his duff and do it somewhere else, as he did when he canceled a speaking engagement at Washington University in St. Louis on October 2004. Though he was to give a speech, as he said, "countering the propaganda and lies that Michael Moore will have created the day before," he pulled out when the thought of flying in a Lear jet wigged him out. Sure, he'll support the sending of thousands of young men and women into quagmires such as Iraq, but don't let his majesty risk flying on a plane that has a one-in-a-million chance of crashing and possibly spoiling his hairdo. Hannity did later promise to give a pro bono speech to Washington U—but by then, Moore would be long gone. Oh well, maybe one day you'll grow up to be as big and strong and brave as Bill O'Reilly, Sean.

Press Release as Primal Scream Therapy

Sometimes the on-air talent may be too busy or too uninspired to throw a few zingers at critics; so the vixen network recruits their publicists to come up with a few barbs on what we can presume are their long stretches of downtime. Since their publicists must have plenty of free time considering there is very little real news product to promote, hurling insults makes the day go faster. Over the years, several spokesuits have done their share to make the news world a crueler place to work:

Brian Lewis, Official Fox Attack Dog Number One

Brian Lewis, Senior Vice President of Corporate Communications, has not often sunk to the role of pit bull, but he has on at least two occasions stooped to ridiculing CNN. As Lewis said of the network when it revamped its morning line up, "Their numbers in the morning are so bad that I guess they have to try something, but it is not going to work unless they change the culture." He also said in another interview that "obviously CNN has never had a high regard for what the American public wants." So nyah, nyah.

Rob Zimmerman, Official Fox Attack Dog Number Two

Going down the corporate ladder we find Rob Zimmerman, Fox News' spokesman and Vice President of Media Relations, who has also served as official spoiler. As the *Wall Street Journal* reported, Zimmerman said of the organizations MoveOn.org and Common Cause, when they filed a complaint with the Federal Trade Commission against the FNC for deceptive advertising for claiming to be fair and balanced, that "If they can attack Fox News to this extreme, then all-news organizations are at risk to be targeted by similar attacks... It's best to ignore nuts."

Zimmerman is no stranger to throwing vitriol and slurs at real and imagined enemies. When the editor of an online parody magazine was asked to come on the FNC as an expert guest, he did so without correcting the unworldly producers of their mistake. When more swift individuals pointed out the FNC's colossal blunder, Zimmerman attacked: "It's a well-known fact that Ray Richmond is a media whore and this is him trying to extend his five minutes of fame." Yeah, but who gave those five minutes to him?

When NBC reporter Ashleigh Banfield gave a speech critical of the media coverage of the Iraq war, Zimmerman scoffed at her with this misogynistic reply: "Fox News considers her a lightweight... She's the Anna Kournikova of TV news." When Paula Zahn left Fox News for CNN, Zimmerman retorted with this bitchy reply: "Paula Zahn's supposed attempt at reinventing herself as a journalist is like putting a fresh coat of paint on an outhouse." If Zahn was such an "outhouse," then why did Fox employ her on the first place? Was this a de facto admission that the cable newser doesn't look for quality when hiring journalists?

When a former FNC employee made his grievances with his ex-employers public, Zimmerman spat: "These accusations are the rantings of a bitter, disgruntled former employee. It's unfortunate that Charlie's career ended the way it did, but we wish him well."

When CNN was the only network to have footage of the U.S. Navy's surveillance team boarding their plane for Guam (and did not share its scoop footage as pool material with its rivals), Zimmerman griped that CNN performed "a disservice to millions of Americans that don't get cable." Be careful when you criticize Fox News: Robert Zimmerman will be waiting for you.

Irena Briganti/Steffan, Official Fox Attack Dog Number Three

Fox News' Senior Director of Public Relations has also come up with invective against both rivals and critics alike. When MoveOn.org filed their complaint over the "fair and balanced" motto, Briganti/Steffan replied, "While this is clearly a transparent publicity stunt, we recognize all forms of free speech and wish them well."

When Fox News' lawsuit against comedian Al Franken was dropped, how did Briganti/Steffan respond? Did she admit that her masters jumped the gun? Did she try to offer a face-saving explanation? No, she merely responded with the sour grapes reply, "It's time to return Al Franken to the obscurity that he's normally accustomed to." Petty, petty, petty.

When CNN's Aaron Brown described Greta Van Susteren's plastic surgery as making her "look like a twenty-five-year-old cheerleader," Steffan snapped, "Coming from a self-described news anchor that has on wine tasters and hypes Liza Minnelli's wedding, people in glass houses shouldn't throw stones." Speaking of CNN, Steffan verbally slapped the newser by snorting, "It is hard for CNN to accept that Fox News Channel has become the destination for breaking news."

Zimmerman wasn't the only spokessuit who got a kick in at Paula Zahn. Steffan reportedly said, "Why don't you ask [Zahn] why she's making a mountain out of a molehill? [...] Why don't you ask why she's turning this around and why she's making herself into a victim?" She added that as "a former network star, it's sad Paula has sunk to this level, but we wish her well." Did Zahn leave an employer or did she flee from a vindictive and obsessive ex-lover?

Steffan's pathological taunting didn't stop there. When Fox News erected a billboard that read "Come Home Connie. CNN Needs You. Brought to You by Your Friends at Fox News," Steffan simply said, "We thought this would lift the morale and bring a few smiles to the faces of the CNN staffers in Atlanta."

When Fox News was accused of sterilizing its Iraq war coverage, Steffan replied: "Given the choice, it's better to be viewed as a foot soldier for Bush than a spokeswoman for Al Qaeda." Since when is it ever respectable for any news outlet to play propagandist to a government or corporate body? Why assume there is an artificial forced choice between two undesirable labels? Wouldn't it be nice and more professional if Fox News was known as being a brave, honest and investigative news channel that doesn't pick sides in the first place?

Paul Schur, Official Fox Attack Dog Number Four

As yet another FNC publicist, Paul Schur, once gleefully told an *Atlanta Journal and Constitution* journalist, the ratings leader FNC would erect a billboard near CNN's Atlanta headquarters that would read: "Now that CNN's ratings are Gone With the Wind, our work on this board is done. We love you Atlanta. Brought to you by your friends at Fox News Channel. Sign up with AMERICA'S NEWSROOM! Forward resumes to resume@foxnews.com." Schur crowed to the scribe: "This is the last billboard... We feel the war is over for now. CNN is closer to MSNBC, and we wish them well in the battle for second place." But the company that owned the billboard refused to erect the ad. Fox brass went ballistic, threatening legal action against a company that wanted to do its part to clean up verbal littering.

When Al Franken took on guest hosting duties on CNN right after Fox's unsuccessful bid to sue the comedian for copyright infringement, Schur vowed that the newser would appeal: "We don't care if it's Al Franken, Al Lewis or 'Weird Al' Yankovic... We're here to protect our trademark and our talent."

Finally, when the August 2004 Republican Convention brought a ratings bonanza to the FNC (it had at one point beat all the networks), Schur responded to network critics who claimed that Fox was an extension of the GOP: "It must be embarrassing to no end that they got beat by a cable news network." Whether Schur was embarrassed that he, as a grown man, had to resort to childish taunting wasn't discussed.

Tracey Spector, Official Fox Attack Puppy

Even one Tracey Spector, at the time a mere publicist for the FNC, has been proactive in insulting CNN on at least one occasion. When CNN made schedule changes, Spector called one newspaper reporter to gloat that CNN's attempt to revamp its line-up was "nothing more than rearranging the deck chairs on the Titanic."

There are sore losers, and then there are sore winners.

Chapter 14

If Wal-Mart Ran the News

*"I went to work for them for about $20,000
less than I could have at any local station
here. But I was looking ahead. And in the
course of that, it was a rude awakening."*

A former Fox employee

Loud corporations have a few traits in common with each other: first, they boast of monster profits. Second, their company and its image are closely linked with their founder—usually a Type-A personality. Third, the inner workings are never as spotless as the public relations department claims in their cheery news releases. Finally, profit comes before quality. Which means both employees and customers will almost always get, in the words of a sage old movie siren, the fuzzy end of the lollipop.

Yet somehow it doesn't feel as if news should have to be held to these same shallow and commercial standards: medication shouldn't be diluted, food shouldn't be tainted and information should be neither. Yet media companies do precisely that. The Hearsts and Hollingers were both media dynasties from different eras that were marked by larger-than-life owners who enjoyed both fat profits and ample limelight. In many ways, Fox News is no different from any other property owned by a media giant. Murdoch reigns; his minions are closely monitored and pennies are saved—not to improve the editorial content, but to give the owner and shareholders something to brag about at dinner parties.

Granted, News Corporation does make profits that would make most people proud; unfortunately, how News Corp properties churn out editorial dreck is another matter entirely. The FNC may get their stories from Silicon Valley, but most likely they will involve nubile and chesty adult entertainers, or, as one former Fox News reporter put it, "I think news has gotten to the point where it's almost more about promoting itself than it is about telling you the stories." As former Fox News employee Clara Frenk observed:

If you just look at what television news used to look like twenty, thirty years ago, and what it looks like now, it's certainly become more glammed up to be more palatable to the public. In other words, now news has to be sold like a commodity and you have to give the public a reason to tune in, as opposed to before, where it was just a purely informative exercise, now there is a certain kind of glamour element to it, and

David Burnett
Former Fox News Reporter, Washington DC

David Burnett, former WTTG journalist.

a tremendous competitiveness. There's a lot of tabloidization, also, that's happened over the course of the past couple of years to make news more attractive... to the public.

Frenk went on to describe how the FNC and other media companies have sacrificed resources for the bottom line:

It's called the news business for a reason: it is news, but it is a business, and you realize as you advance in any news organization, that the higher up you go, the less concerned you are with the news, and the more concerned you are with the cost, with issues of budgets and ratings. And sometimes there are stories that aren't that ratings-friendly. The war in Kosovo was not ratings-friendly; earthquakes around the world are not necessarily ratings-friendly. They're news stories, but they are not ratings-friendly, which is why, for example, in American news you don't see foreign news covered as much as it used to be [...] You see all these bureaus overseas being closed down and that's purely a matter of cost, there's no question about that. Cable news has also created an environment where you are able to produce shows so cheaply, that the networks are scrambling to catch up; and therefore, they're not devoting the resources to covering stories that they would've covered twenty or thirty years ago.

Like Frenk, David Burnett, a former journalist with Fox-owned WTTG, also had his apprehensions over the battle between corporate and journalistic values:

What I've noticed most is that money and ratings drive the product [and] that has really driven what we see on TV and the kinds of stories that are done [...] The thing that distresses me more than anything else is that a lot of the news content is not coming straight out of the newsrooms, particularly in television, but out of the promotion department, and the general managers' offices. The desire to get ratings, to have more ad revenue is tremendously great, and it just distorted what we see on television.

The FNC has found some unique ways to save pennies: by plagiarizing from their dreaded rival CNN, no less. One former Fox employee noted that the Fox News Channel has engaged in some very cheap and creative news gathering methods:

It's not just about appealing to Republican viewers, there's also a profit motive that manifests itself in how the reporters do their journalism. For example, at other cable news organizations where it's still important to double-check your sources [and] to get

information independently, there's a natural benefit by Fox reporters to [go] out and just steal information from NBC News, from the *National Enquirer.* I saw on several occasions where reporters and producers at Fox would steal information right off the other networks' evening newscast, put it on the air at Fox, and management didn't care.

The former FNC employee explained why management allowed their reporters to stoop to unethical journalism:

It was almost because it served a purpose for management to sort of look the other way; this is a way that Fox, which has fewer resources, can stay competitive journalistically with other news organizations, and that way they're not behind on the story... Reporters are not punished by any means.

This Napsterization of the news is troubling to say the least: should viewers one day expect Brit Hume to have a television set by his desk, turn it on CNN, point at the screen and then make snarky and pointed commentary as various CNN anchors read the news? Do the Fox News kids have to be reminded to keep their eyes on their own papers? Besides, if FNC brass keeps reminding the rest of us how they think that CNN is liberal, antiquated, manipulative and wrong, then why steal their material? Could it be because CNN actually has a better product? How could the FNC even consider using material from the allegedly "liberal" CNN? Obviously FNC brass should be careful: if they are successful in sinking CNN out of existence, then who will Fox crib for its news?

The Fear Factor

The Fox News Channel has always claimed to be a fair and balanced network, but they never claimed that the fair and balanced part applied to their treatment of their own employees. Communications of employees are monitored; at least one reporter was punished for not over-hyping his surroundings to John Moody's liking. Underlings are treated with disrespect, as former FNC analyst Larry Johnson recalled:

I've heard directly from folks both as correspondents and as bookers who have expressed very grave reservations, almost as if they're being monitored by a Stalinist system, afraid to be seen talking to the wrong person or having the wrong kind of e-mail exchange. It's very much an environment of fear. The irony here is that the networks seem to like to present themselves as totally committed to freedom and [being] fair and balanced, and it appears to be "fear and unbalanced."

E-mail and telephone conversations are monitored at the FNC, but other Murdoch-owned media outlets also felt the heat, as former WTTG producer Frank O'Donnell recalled:

It was made very clear to us that our activities were being monitored and if someone wasn't watching it live, they were at least recording it and they would review it after the fact to see what we did. And so when we were given the orders, "all right, carry this now," we knew we had little choice but to either walk out in the middle of our jobs, which nobody would really do, or to obey that order and then try to figure out after the fact what we do next. Some former employees who originally applied to the FNC had high hopes for a meaningingful career in journalism. As [a] former Fox News employee recounted his own experience when he applied to the News Corporation crown jewel, "A friend of mine [told me that there] was this new startup operation, and it might be good to—they're not paying as much as everybody else—but it might be a good place to get in on the ground floor."

But some employees find that the ceiling is far more dangerous than the ground floor. Staff, having fewer resources and supports than their rivals, are being overworked as they are being monitored by the same lords who only seem to care about ratings, profits and settling their various feuds. As FAIR's Peter Hart noted:

I think that's why there's a fairly high turnover at some of the shows because you really have to be a true believer to work there and if you're not, I'm not sure that they want you. So we've talked to... people who have left Fox over the years and they all say similar things that you know what's expected of you and if you're not doing that you're going to get in some trouble. Fox is run in a very peculiar way. It's not to say other newsrooms aren't progressive or there isn't a lot of pressure on staff, but at Fox I think it's a very peculiar kind of pressure and it's very political.

The fear of getting on the bosses' collective bad side makes reporters think twice about telling their supervisors to take that job and shove it. One former Fox employee recalled his fear of getting his employers upset: "Fox first of all is a large corporation; it owns several newspapers and television stations, and obviously could affect my chances of getting employed someplace else in the future." When one student reporter interning at *Editor and Publisher* tried to get FNC personalities during the 2004 Republican National Convention such as Shepard Smith and Greta Van Susteren to give him an interview, all declined, some instructing the student to clear his interview request with FNC brass; however, he had no problem interviewing CNN journalists on the spot.

Fewer resources, less supports, less money, more monitoring, bigger chance of facing a blacklist— what could possibly be worse? How about regular motivational sermons from your bosses? Dave Korb, a former freelance news writer for Fox News, recalled the Ailes' Motivational Love-fest:

[...E]very three months [Roger Ailes] delivered his quarterly "state-of-the-business" update. Generally it was things like, "rah-rah"; it was a pep talk you would hear from any CEO or chairman in a news corporation or any business operation. "We're beating CNN in the ratings and we're doing it at 25% of what CNN is doing, is paying to do the same job."

But Ailes' pep talks weren't just about ratings or money; they were also political and personal, as Korb recalled:

I remember though, that my second state-of-the-business update [in April 2003] and I recall Roger, after going through the statistics, and telling us that we're beating CNN

and beating just about every[one] else in the ratings, I think Roger kind of launched into what I felt was the mission part of the statement. [He] told us that it was time for—his word—"revindication." "Revindication" for thirty years of Americans beating themselves up. Of telling themselves they were bad. Of telling themselves that Americans had been wrong. And I remember wondering at the moment whether younger staffers realize that was a reference to Vietnam and to Watergate.

One of Fox's biggest drawbacks is its lack of original investigative stories that don't involve looking down a vixen's blouse. CNN has broken stories and covered war zones up close and personal; Fox News cannot claim the same. Without substance, the FNC is a tabloid with an attitude. But the problem is that investigative stories are too expensive to produce. When the FNC does make a rare venture out into the world of real journalism, it will inevitably be one with a heavy Republican spin—and one that FNC brass will push to the forefront.

One story the FNC covered was the U.N. "Food for Oil" probe. As John Moody wrote in a memo on March 12, 2004:

> Kofi Annan always defended the U.N.'s oil for food program in the runup to the Iraq war. Now, it appears his son may have had a role in the company that ran the program, which we now know was used by Saddam to buy cooperation from influential people. Eric Shawn is pieces [sic] together the puzzle.

Moody had already made up his mind about the story in his March 16 memo:

> Eric Shawn will take us through the labyrinth of the U.N. oil for food program, which is beginning to shine light on the role of SecGen Kofi Annan's son. Can the U.N. reach a consensus on a scandal in its midst?

Moody's capital spin continued in an April 6 memo:

> Eric Shawn will have another day of Oil for Food lives, to coincide with congressional hearings on the topic. It's possible Kofi Annan will offer some additional information on what was going on at the U.N.. Either way, Eric will have new, and possibly exclusive information.

> fyi, and thanks to the DC bureau, here's part of what senate foreign affairs committee chairman richard lugar will say:

> THIS CORRUPTION WAS NOT SOLELY A PRODUCT OF SADDAM HUSSEIN'S MACHINATIONS. HE REQUIRED MEMBERS OF THE U.N. SECURITY COUNCIL WHO WERE WILLING TO BE COMPLICIT IN HIS ACTIVITIES, AND HE REQUIRED U.N. OFFICIALS AND CONTRACTORS WHO WERE DISHONEST, INATTENTIVE, OR WILLING TO MAKE DAMAGING COMPROMISES IN PURSUIT OF A COMPASSIONATE MISSION.

Moody didn't always sound as confident of Shawn's abilities; for example, in another April 6 memo, "The oil for food story being fronted by Eric Shawn is potentially a huge development. We have to be sure of each step, but if it works out, it will be a lead story after Iraq." Moody also had to remind his less swift underlings about the story's significance. On April 20, Moody ordered in a memo that, "It should be obvious that we are working hard on the oil for food scandal story at the U.N. Please be disposed to use stories on this story, rather than not."

However, some of the players in the scandal were also on the FNC payroll, as Moody noted in his April 21 memo:

> Fox's one big drawback is its lack of original (and highly expensive to produce) investigative stories.

The Oil for Food hearings are a turning point in a story that Fox has been pursuing diligently for weeks. Claudia Rossett, a former WSJ writer who has become a paid contributor to Fox, is among the witnesses testifying today. Label her just that way: Former *Wall Street Journal* reporter/Fox News Contributor.

The FNC's team up with the *Wall Street Journal* was noted, but Moody added an air of pulp suspense in his April 23 memo:

Oil For Food, a story that Fox News and the WSJ alone have kept front and center, may be approaching a new critical stage. Benon Sevan, the former head of the program, has returned to New York from his travels. Jonathan Hunt will track the story and Mr. Sevan's movements. Be careful what we say here. He hasn't been convicted yet, but he is a central figure in a mysterious set of circumstances.

If an FNC reporter may have wished to challenge or question Moody on his preset ideas, they would most likely find themselves in the hot seat, according to one former Fox News reporter:

I think that if you don't go along with the mindset of the hierarchy in New York, if you challenge them on their attitudes about things, you're history. Journalism is one of those kinds of businesses where you're encouraged to challenge; you're encouraged to bring new ideas if they want to be fair and balanced. You want to bring a diversity of opinion, an attitude toward certain things.

Yet the FNC isn't a pure journalistic property: because it has an agenda and political slant, dissenting voices need to be silenced. Contradictory opinion and information weakens the voice of a partisan news outlet; therefore, messages have to be controlled through daily decrees, messages have to be monitored and the ideological heretics have to be rapped. Without the vigilance, someone might get it in his head to report on information as he sees fit, not the way his employers believe it is.

We Report, You Decide: Joseph Cafasso Finds Religion at the FNC

Joseph Cafasso was a paid consultant specializing in military and counterintelligence for Fox News for over four months before March 2002, helping the network in its coverage of the Afghanistan war. When he left, the *New York Times* reported that they could not substantiate his credentials: that he was a lieutenant colonel in the Special Forces, that he won a Silver Star and that he served in Viet Nam. Though he did have contacts in the military and the information he supplied to the network was true, his own personal résumé seemed padded. The FNC did not themselves double-check Cafasso's credentials when they hired him, though his information was for the most part sound.

According to Cafasso, his short stint on the FNC proved to be more ecclesiastical than he expected, as he recalled:

Joseph Cafasso
Former Fox News Military & Counterterrorism Editor

Joseph Cafasso noticed extreme religious views at Fox.

> The first time I was actually inside a newsroom— and Fox is a very conservative place, and I'm a conservative... there was this one gentleman that would come in and out of Fox that was just out of place, and he would sit with Brit, Tony, and it just caught my eye—I don't know why—it was just something about him that caught my eye. And I'm a practicing Catholic, not the best, but I'm Catholic, I believe in God; I believe in Jesus Christ, but I don't carry that to an extreme. Then I found out later on the gentleman was a minister who comes into newsrooms to talk about Christianity to those Christians inside the newsroom. I don't normally have much of a problem with that, but I do have a problem with how that interacts with what I call extreme right-wing religious views and how that interplays with the news.

Cafasso also recalled one interesting talk he said he had with Kim Hume:

> Every Wednesday morning, Brit Hume and a few others in Washington will meet for a bible study in the morning. It's that impact where that begins to bridge with what I consider a secular view of news. I had an interesting conversation once with Kim Hume who caught me totally off guard. She asked me in her office, "Are you an angel?" I didn't know how to answer; I was just totally caught off guard by the question. This is the bureau chief asking me if I'm an angel. I believe in angels, but I also believe that angels are much higher authorities than mere humans and for the bureau chief to be asking me that question, [that] set me back and began to make me think.

While the FNC is an ideologically controlled environment, recent revelations may prove that in other areas, the vixen network can also be an untamed environment, too.

It Ain't Just Leads He's Chasing

Former President Bill Clinton was Public Enemy Number One on Fox News in the mid-1990s for his fling with intern Monica Lewinsky: here was a married man, commentators and hosts fumed, who was having a steamy affair with his much younger employee—and misusing cigars in the process. That may well have been the case, but if one pending civil case proves to be true, one of the big guns at the FNC was trying to do the very same thing, with somewhat less successful results.

One could honestly say that Bill O'Reilly is a professional mass debater; it's his job to challenge and argue with guests in a public forum. But what O'Reilly does when those cameras aren't rolling was under much debate.

The first blow came when Bill O'Reilly filed a lawsuit in October 2004 against a lawyer and his client, who also happened to be an FNC employee who worked for O'Reilly for over four years. O'Reilly claimed that the pair attempted to extort $60 million from him by threatening to go public with claims that the "Factor" kahuna sexually harassed an employee, thirty-three-year-old Andrea Mackris, who was an associate producer on O'Reilly's show. In an FNC press release, O'Reilly was quoted as saying, "As a public figure, I have received many threats. But enough is enough... the threats stop now. I will not give into extortion."

However, Mackris had allegations of her own, as she filed her own sexual harassment suit against O'Reilly, the FNC and others hours later. In her suit, she claimed O'Reilly's definition of hard news was somewhat more profane than the industry standard: he had made lewd comments toward her both when she first worked at FNC, and then again when she came back to the network after six months working for CNN. Mackris alleged that her boss would call her at home and use profane language while he was pleasuring himself with a vibrator.

By the wording of the suit, it seemed that Mackris taped some of those phone calls. In court papers, Mackris claimed that O'Reilly boasted to her that "nobody'd believe 'em... they wouldn't [tell] anyway, I can't imagine any of them ever doing that 'cuz I always made friends with women before I bedded them down," and that "if any woman ever breathed a word, I'll make her pay so dearly that she'll wish she'd never been born." O'Reilly noted how he'd drag a woman's reputation "through the mud," "that he had more money to access better lawyers" and that he would "never make the mistake of picking unstable crazy girls like that." She also claimed that O'Reilly got worked up when he interviewed two porn stars on his show, which may explain why these girlies seem to make not infrequent appearances on the "Factor."

As an aside, Mackris' suit also alleged that O'Reilly is obsessed with his arch nemesis Al Franken—he reportedly told Mackris:

> **If you cross Fox News Channel, it's not just me, it's [Fox President] Roger Ailes who will go after you.** I'm the street guy out front making loud noises about the issues, but Ailes operates behind the scenes; strategies [sic] and makes things happen so that one day BAM! The person gets what's coming to them but never sees it coming. Look at Al Franken, one day he's going to get a knock on his door and life as he's known it will change forever. That day will happen, trust me.

Mackris alleged that O'Reilly said, "Ailes knows very powerful people and this goes all the way to the top[...] of the country." However, O'Reilly struck first with his extortion suit and began to spin his side of the story in an October 2004 "Talking Points" memo:

Just about every famous person I know has been threatened by somebody. Fame makes you a target. It is something that has to be taken very seriously. As I've mentioned before, I've received many threats over the years. Everything from death letters to some guy running around the country offering people $25,000 to sign affidavits accusing me of whatever.

The lawyers here at Fox News have been great in dealing with these situations, but there comes a time when enough's enough. So this morning I had to file a lawsuit against some people who are demanding $60 million or they will "punish" me and Fox News. $60 million dollars.

He also said of Mackris' suit that it was "the single most evil thing I have ever experienced, and I've seen a lot. But these people picked the wrong guy." O'Reilly also stated in his own suit that Mackris' lawyer was a Democrat and had a vested interest in smearing his good name—the suit included a September 7, 2004 e-mail message Mackris sent to her CNN acquaintance; "[...]to answer your question, things are: wonderful, amazing, fun, creative, invigorating, secure, well-managed, challenging, interesting, fun and surrounded by really good, fun people. I'm home and I'll never leave again." It was Mackris who asked to come to the FNC and she did return, receiving a raise in the process. Though O'Reilly's case is the shakier of the two, it was vintage O'Reilly and probably scored points with his audience, who feel the pugnacious host is the victim of the Democrats. Mackris' behavior—willingly returning to an employer she felt was an intimidating and threatening letch who honed in on her does not make the case straightforward, in any event.

An employer reportedly sexually harasses his underling. The underling willingly asks to return to her allegedly abusive boss after she has already successfully escaped his supposedly filthy clutches claims she was fearful, but seems to find the courage to take him on only when there's a chance to handsomely profit from it. If she tape-recorded the conversations, she didn't seem to take them to FNC first or file a complaint (though it will most likely be argued that she felt intimidated and that the management would take O'Reilly's side). However, both sides sat down and ironed out a deal: both Mackris and O'Reilly withdrew their respective suits. Predators and exploiters claiming both bravura and then victimhood at the most convenient times. The Murdochian kingdom is a place where cobras and mongooses run and chase and exploit each other for both libidinous and financial reasons.

In any case, the Fox News Channel seems to be anything but a serious workplace dedicated to professional conduct and a strong focus to gathering and breaking serious news.

Chapter 15

News for Sale

"I love capitalism..."

Sean Hannity

I f Fox News were merely a conservative news network, we could still trust that the facts for the most part were accurate, even if we may disagree on what the interpretation of those facts means. If the crime rate in a given town rose by 10% from the previous year, a conservatively slanted reporter or network may blame the breakdown of families, the lack of tough laws or even the need for a stronger police force. Viewers may completely disagree with the assessment, but they could safely trust that the crime rate has increased by 10%, though we may have alternative suggestions as to how to reduce those levels. In fact, since there is no one "right" way and one "wrong" way of doing things, there could be any number of ways to solve a problem: we just know the network is simply partial to one of those methods. There is nothing logically or ethically wrong with having a conservative or progressive worldview.

But Fox is a partisan network. It sees the world through conservative eyes. It presents skewed coverage and pushes a false package: that George W. Bush is a valiant, brilliant and brave man without flaws, that the U.S. economy is never in the doldrums and that the Iraq War was just a gay, madcap escapade. Suddenly, the rules changed: why would the FNC present blatant falsehoods like that when none of them are even remotely close to the truth? When Democratic Presidential candidate John Kerry handily took control of all three debates during the 2004 race, the FNC focused on how Bush came shining through in the last half of the third debate. Why focus on the positive when for the majority of the debates the President gave, on the whole, a less than stellar performance, smirking, snapping and never quite finishing any of his thoughts?

So why don't the Fox News kids report facts in a truthful and honest way? Why be so shamelessly partisan, then try to deny it? For appearances' sake, behemoth News Corp has chosen the path of least resistance and greatest profits, as David Burnett cautioned:

> What I've noticed most is that money and ratings drive the product. The desire to get ratings has really driven what we see on TV and the kind of stories that are done [...] The thing I think that distresses me more than anything else is that a lot of the news content is not coming straight out of the newsrooms, particularly in television, but out of the promotion department, and the general managers' offices. The desire to get ratings and more ad revenue is tremendously great, and it's distorted what we see on television.

Those who are partisan prefer to rely on opinion over fact; so why rock the boat by shattering their egos and beliefs? Those who whisper sweet nothings in their pigeons' ears do so because they hope to *get* something for their false, self-serving compliments. With a partisan media outlet, news is for sale. A network isn't going to risk charges of bias for no reason: there has to be something in it for them to be worth the risk.

But in an indirect way, the FNC does admit to being something less than a news outfit. As James Wolcott observed, "One of the things that Fox News does... [is] pretend that they're not part of the media. If you ever hear Bill O'Reilly [or] Fox News people talk, they all refer to the media as if it's something 'out there' that they have no part in; as if somehow they're separate. But of course, they are the media." Perhaps their confidence that they are not the news media stems from the network disseminating anything but the news.

James Wolcott
Former Staff Writer for the New Yorker/
Cultural Critic for Vanity Fair

James Wolcott: Debunking the "elite" myth.

But it's not only the FNC that suffers from the watering down of the news product. Mark Crispin Miller observed the obvious when he said, "Commercial journalism has always been answerable to its advertisers." That can restrict what networks are able to report, but it's not the only factor that controls the news product: when media companies merge, the focus becomes less on the editorial content, but on feeding an insatiable beast. One former Fox News employee noted how media consolidation has impacted the quality of the news:

> Nowadays journalists are being asked to do so much more with less time, especially in cable where you constantly have to feed the beast. There's less time for actual real reporting; so there's less enterprise reporting, [the] inability to actually knock down doors, or talk to sources. As a result, I think there's much more of a reliance on the handouts, the press releases, the inside information, the guest bookings. And when you have in a very competitive environment, so many cable channels specifically competing for "the get," the nugget that somebody hands out, I think there's natural inclination to want to not be the one who sort of shakes things up a little bit because if you shake

things up, you're the one [who's] not going to get the nugget or the piece of information that may help you down the road. For the most part, journalists don't have time to shake things up and knock down the doors.

The way the FNC tries to shake things up is by focusing on the sensational and the lurid. Grisly crimes and promiscuous women are used to grab attention and ratings (and if court-filed accusations are to be believed, give Bill O'Reilly a cheap thrill while interviewing these lovelies). Hard news on important issues is replaced with empty stories that appeal to primal instincts. The FNC claims to be a hipper network than their rivals because the FNC supposedly pushes the envelope; however, pushing the envelope doesn't have to mean falling into the gutter. If innovation strictly meant being more vulgar and obnoxious than the last guy, then cars, computers, medication and electricity wouldn't exist and we'd all be sitting in a cold cave trying to see who could pass the most putrid wind.

Fox has been very good to the Bush administration, and they have responded in kind.

None of Fox News' major on-air talent is either young or has a young view of the world. O'Reilly is your dad's champion; Brit Hume also seems to focus his attentions on older newsmakers. Sean Hannity doesn't have a fresh take on conservatism. Even the pundits have a tired take on life; Ann Coulter and Michelle Malkin, who are two of the younger opinion spewers, use arguments that are long past their "sell by" date. Despite the claim that the FNC thinks younger than their competitors, it is still a bunch of old grumps sitting around the table complaining about all those long-haired weirdoes. The mindset of the FNC is clearly and hopelessly stuck in the 70s, where questions swirled around whether Richard Nixon was an ethical President and the disturbing death toll of U.S. soldiers in Viet Nam.

Fox's attempts at attracting a younger audience may seem no more sincere than other media outlets' attempts, despite the hair highlights, plastic surgery and polished images. But there was a time when the pre-FNC journalists were encouraged to think about younger audiences. As Alexander Kippen recalled about the days of the Fox Network's morning news program:

> Fox in those days was looking for an audience and when I was hired by the Fox Morning News, the news director at the time would always hammer this theme that we are different, that we have to find different angles, that Rupert Murdoch wanted to see different angles on different stories, not the same old tired stuff that you would see on other networks. So I was in my twenties at the time. I would, for example, whether it was the U.S. Supreme Court or the federal budget, try and find some angle that would be different. If I was covering the budget... I would look for [an] element of the budget that affected single people, with student loans, but without mortgages.

The inclusion of the non-sensational youth-oriented stories would peter out with Roger Ailes at the Fox News helm. The FNC has made its name pleasing older, not younger audiences (for more on FNC demographics, see Chapter 17). Cable news skewed toward an older male audience and, as Kippen noted, Fox News has "attached itself to their loyal audience with its 'if it pays it plays' mentality":

I think what's interesting about Fox is that it has achieved every business' dream. It located an under served market, in many cases angry suburbanites, and it served them and it is getting rich doing it. Fox has done what CNN still can't, and that's find a distinctive profile. And I think what's interesting about Fox is not so much what it's doing, but whom it's influencing: it's influencing its competitors. That's why MSNBC hired Joe Scarborough. That's why CNN in recent weeks has taken to reporting pretty much anything the Bush White House tells them to report. Maybe that's why Peter Jennings all of a sudden decided in [2003] to take a U.S. citizenship. There is a sense now that there is money in the flag and Fox knows that and its competitors know that Fox is on to something.

That something the FNC seems to be on to is catering to a Republican audience.

Republican males tend to get their information from cable news, and the FNC can offer the party a friendly audience who are likely not going to find anything amiss with the slant or point of view as Wolcott observed:

> I think [Fox News] has a very close relationship to the Bush administration, and the Bush administration wanted [a pro Iraq war] story put out and [Ambassador and Special Envoy to Iraq] Paul Bremer would put that out with his briefings. He would accent the positive things. And this only worked as long as the violence seemed isolated. Once it gained momentum, you couldn't make that argument anymore. But I think part of it was that it was part of a whole PR campaign because there was also talk of making Fox essentially the main news source in Iraq; they were clearly getting preferential treatment.

During President Bush's 2003 Thanksgiving Day "surprise" visit to U.S. troops stationed in Iraq, it was a Fox News reporter who was allowed to phone headquarters with the scoop. Fox has always had a special little snug relationship and that only worked as long as they could keep up the façade of good news. Their Bush administration interviews lobbed softball question after softball question. The FNC has been very good to the Bush administration, and the Bushites have responded in kind. When Rumsfeld was slated to appear on the FNC, brass issued a memo telling staff to promote the "dickens" out of it, not what types of tough questions they might wish to ask. As then-FNC Washington Bureau Chief Kim Hume (wife of Brit) reportedly told Cafasso, "Joe, we know the government lies. And the government knows that we lie. Somewhere in the middle, we meet and do business."

But the FNC is also corporation-friendly. While Fox News obsesses over small town crimes, it does not give the same attention to small industry: big business gets the kisses and the kudos. As Wolcott quipped, "it's always a good time to buy. There's never a good time to sell stocks. You should always be buying. If the market's going up you should be buying, and if the market's going down you should be buying because they're cheaper. But what Fox does is it really integrates investing with patriotism because a lot of segments are about 'will there be a new war rally?' 'Will there be a rally if Osama bin Laden is captured?'" He added that the FNC combines financial news with the political to come up with some unique scenarios for the economy:

When the guests make their predictions at the end of the show, often the predictions take the nature of "Bin Laden will be captured by September; the market will go up a thousand points." "The war in Iraq will wind down, the stock market will breathe a sigh of relief, and we're off to the races." So they integrate this sense of American patriotism with investing, and being invested, being a bear on the market is really not in their eyes being a patriot because you're supposed to be positive all the time about America and the market.

This tenuous cause-and-effect speculation by the FNC has made for some biased and dubious reports as Wolcott noted:

When the market goes down, one of the things you often hear is the market is worried about a [John] Kerry victory. Now how they know this, because after all, the market goes down based upon decisions by millions of investors. And how they know that the market went down because everybody had Kerry on their mind, as opposed to everyone was worried about interest rates, or everyone looked at the earnings figures and thought they weren't as good as projected. But they love to pretend that... they can read the mind of the market. But it's always on the premise that a Democrat will be bad for the market.

Yet, according to Wolcott, turnabout was never fair and balanced play at the Fox News Channel when it came to praising Bill Clinton's leadership or criticizing Bush's:

Now one of the reasons this is so perplexing is, of course, the Clinton era was fantastic for the stock market... one of the most fantastic eras you could have in the stock market was the Clinton period, and the Bush period has actually not been very good for the stock market, and yet there is this notion embedded that Republicans are good for the stock market and Democrats are bad, but what they really mean is that Republicans are good for Wall Street because the assumption is Republicans will not police Wall Street the way Democrats will. But no, Kerry is not going to catch a break on any of the financial shows: any spending program that he proposes is going to be touted as socialism.

John Kerry's policies may be progressive, but they were hardly what anyone with common sense and knowledge in political science would deem as socialistic. While there were fair and tough questions a news network could have asked about Kerry, the FNC preferred the easier version of sticking stigmatic labels on the Senator instead. So why did the network choose to use name-calling and inaccurate innuendoes instead of asking thoughtful questions that were backed by equally thoughtful research? The answer is simple: because political ads have almost always been more effective when they resorted to smearing and name-calling, and not to the finer points of a candidate and his rival's policies.

Chapter 16

Fear of the Fox

"Shut up... Shut up... Cut his mic.
I'm not going to dress you down anymore,
out of respect for your father."

Bill O'Reilly to guest Jeremy Glick

Vigorous public debate and confrontation are both essential tools needed for the Democratic process to work—how else can truths be uncovered and injustices be exposed unless someone has the courage to challenge someone else's faulty worldview? Without sublimated righteous anger, slavery, oppression and other self-serving atrocities would continue unabated. Enabling someone else's childish, selfish or decrepit delusions doesn't help society to progress or improve in the long run.

Unlike other media platforms, television news can be the ideal arena for this type of raw give-and-take; words cannot always express the subtle nuances that a facial expression can, and a heated exchange allows viewers to empathize with foreign points of views. Some people say they don't like any criticism of any sort lest someone's feelings get hurt; however, not every jab stems from mere mean-spiritedness, jealousy, professional impotence, frustration or close-mindedness. There are times when some bully needs a hard and stinging slap in the face.

Yet too many times these jabs do stem from vindictive motives, and the Fox News Channel unfortunately has a certain talent for turning someone's differing life requirements into something more sinister and tainted. Insulting, yelling and screaming at guests may be cathartic and career enhancing, but they do nothing to advance society or improve public discourse. It's one thing to hound the careless and the callous, but quite another to ferally assail rivals or banal individuals in a supposedly credible public forum.

Worse, what seems unfiltered is in fact choreographed, edited, manipulated and stacked against the target of abuse. A network claiming to be a news channel should concern itself with producing the news. There shouldn't be room for petty fights or settling personal scores. Fox News has taken advantage of the airwaves to wage wars against certain people and groups who do not fit into the Fox way of life.

Hitting Below the Belt

No matter who the victim of an FNC hit is, Fox's attacks are almost always personal and savage. No one knows how to psych out an opponent quite like those executives who toil at Fox News. Every misstep of a rival or irritant will be fervently and sadistically unrolled in front of their audiences with all the pomp and circumstance the cable newser can muster. When MSNBC reporter and former CNN Boy of Baghdad Peter Arnett criticized the Bush administration's Iraq War strategy on Iraqi state-run television, Fox News used the situation to their own benefit. Criticism against the government is unspeakable, they haughtily sniffed, and then proceeded to exploit the incident to their own benefit.

Taking advantage of the controversy, Fox News used the following 2003 ad that was a throwback to those "Is your neighbor a Communist?" brochures that were all the rage with the paranoid and senile back in the 50s:

> He spoke out against America's armed forces. He said America's war against terrorism had failed. He even vilified America's leadership. And he worked for MSNBC.
>
> Ask yourself—is this America's News Channel? We report, you decide. Fox News Channel. Real journalism, fair and balanced.

If Joe McCarthy were alive today, he would have been proud.

The news shows mimicked the thrash Arnett ads. Bill O'Reilly had guests ready to try Arnett for treason. O'Reilly gave this assessment of Arnett on his April 3, 2003 program:

> **O'REILLY:** [Arnett] said the war plan is failing. That gives encouragement to an army fighting against the coalition forces, false encouragement because Arnett was wrong, he's a dunderhead, but encouragement nevertheless. That could be conceived as aiding and abetting.

How a reporter's pessimism could be in the same league as supplying arms or exposing classified information wasn't explained by O'Reilly, but such details weren't important when maligning a colleague made for edgier television. Yet the "Factor" host wasn't the only Fox News kid to harp on the Arnett faux pas; Brit Hume and friend also got their two cents worth on April 1, 2003:

> **HUME:** [...T]here was some further fallout from the controversy involving our friend Peter Arnett, ex of NBC News, ex of *National Geographic* who made some remarkable statements on Iraqi TV. We talked about this before. His firing, it turns out was not an automatic thing at all... despite the comments he made.

Fox News Contributor Morton Kondracke took his criticism even further than Hume's:

KONDRACKE: Well, this was not journalism. This was appearing on enemy television, state-run enemy television, declaring that the regime had quote-unquote "good discipline in the streets of Baghdad." I mean good discipline, it's called police state, it's called Gestapo.

The cable newser loves to pounce on their rivals in a way that defies explanation: accusing them of nefarious actions seems par for the course. In 1997, when ABC News was facing a civil suit over its controversial undercover investigation about the sanitary conditions of the Food Lion supermarket chain, it was Fox News that aired outtake footage supplied by the grocery chain. In 2004 when CBS' "60 Minutes II" (Wednesday edition) purported to have memos claiming that George W. Bush received preferential treatment thirty years ago in the National Guard, and those documents turned out to be forgeries, Fox News pounded reporter Dan Rather relentlessly over "Rathergate" for days, even repeating themselves at times:

◆ Brit Hume on September 15, 2004: "Newspaper editorials, meanwhile, are now weighing in on the controversy with even the reliably liberal *L.A. Times* concluding, quote, 'CBS News was had.'"

◆ Bill O'Reilly on September 15, 2004: "Even the ultra liberal editorial page of the *Los Angeles Times* says this. 'CBS News was had.'"

The Fox News method of dealing with other media is interesting in that they do not necessarily claim they are the superior news source outright, but that their rivals are ideologically suspect, as John Nichols noted about the FNC's assessment of its colleagues during the Iraq war:

It creates a pole out there on the edge that says this is reality and if you're not reporting it this way, it's not just that you disagree with us and have made a different journalistic judgment, it is that you are unpatriotic and you are actually seeking to undermine the war effort, perhaps even get American young men and women killed overseas. Now the logical unreality of that is staggering because if the war was going on so well there would be no threat, the Americans wouldn't be in danger, but they don't take it to that level of discussion. What is incredible is that on Fox now you will see regular and serious critique of the other networks.

Gossiping about the neighbor's tacky dress is easier than discussing why your children are spiraling out of control and hate you or why you are staying in a dead-end job and not reaching your full potential. Fox brass also live by this weak man's credo: it is much cheaper to slag the competition than to actually spend some time, energy and money conducting serious investigative stories. Reality and self-examination are too depressing, while degrading the competition is so much more satisfying.

However, the FNC doesn't just use its airwaves to rattle their rivals' cages: billboards will also do quite nicely. Since 1999, the cable newser has erected a series of small-minded jabs at its main rival CNN, as previously mentioned. In 2004, one billboard rubbed CNN's nose in Fox News' top ratings. Another billboard near CNN's Atlanta headquarters smugly sneered, "Come Home Connie. CNN Needs You." It was signed "your friends at Fox News." Fox News could have taken the high road and instead pointed out how much more quality information their newscast had than CNN's—but since Fox News has less news, it opted for the snarky remarks instead.

Do Fox News ads emphasize its superior quality of information? Does it emphasize that it gives more news than other networks? Don't be silly: executives know they are slinging out an inferior quality product and have to grab attention some other way. While the ads mock their comrades, they are also shrewdly designed to draw attention away from Fox's deficiencies.

A channel purporting to be an all-news network seems to have very little to do with focusing on news. Hosts mug and vogue in front of the camera, all jockeying for face time and book plugs. Anchors throw disparaging remarks and jabs as if they were used tissues.

But don't you dare make the mistake of pointing out Fox News' shortcomings. When one politician took on the FNC, he found himself in the hot seat instead. As Joel Barkin, Communication Director for Vermont Congressman Bernie Sanders recalled:

> We released a report that looked at many of the claims and statements that Fox contributors and Fox hosts were giving about the war and about Iraq, and basically we looked at these claims and said, "Here's what Fox is saying or here's what they said in the past, and here's what turned out to be true." And we titled it *Fact Versus Foxtion*, but what we were trying to do was really profile and highlight how Fox distorted and misled their viewers, and we called on them and we asked... in the report would they come forward and acknowledge these mistakes.

One of the "foxtions" the report pointed to was this Hannity pearl of wisdom on the December 9, 2002 edition of "Hannity and Colmes":

> **HANNITY:** And in Northern Iraq today, this very day, al Qaeda is operating camps there, and they are attacking the Kurds in the North, and this has been well-documented and well chronicled. Now, if you're going to go after al Qaeda in every aspect, and obviously they have the support of Saddam, or we're not.

Contrary to Hannity's assertion, intelligence actually indicated that Hussein and al Qaeda did not have ties to one another, in fact, Osama bin Laden had a disliking for the secular Hussein, while the former Iraqi leader also seemed to dislike the al Qaeda leader. Another "foxtion" the report noted occurred on the August 1, 2003 edition of "Hannity and Colmes":

> **HANNITY:** David Kay, who's the chief weapons inspector now, he's compiled what he believes to be the motherload of documents and evidence that we have the case, we have the proof. He's not coming out until it's all been verified and all been put together.
>
> And I think a lot of these guys on the left that weren't there to help us defeat this animal and this madman and his two raping, vicious, murdering sons, I think they're going to have an awful lot of egg on their face.

Kay had made statements to the contrary, according to the report. Barkin recalled the newser's lightning-fast reaction to the report:

After putting out the report almost immediately, maybe within ten minutes, I received an e-mail from the Senior News Editor on Capitol Hill for Fox News [who] asked me two very explicit questions. First one was the House Ethics Committee wants to know how many staff hours were spent working on this report, and secondly, which one of the shows that my boss, Congressman Sanders, appears on, would he like me to send the report first? [It was] implying that they were going to hold my office accountable, and really, come back after us for issuing that report. And to date, since we've released that report, we have yet to be asked to come back on [Fox].

Vermont Representative Bernie Sanders.

Barkin also noted that he had "heard of other instances where this same editor has intimidated and tried to muscle other press secretaries on Capitol Hill just like this." He added, "I work with a number of media organizations, both national and in Vermont and ones that we've been critical of in the past, and I have never received any kind of e-mail or response to anything we've put out like this."

If the FNC likes to dish it out, but yelps vehemently when it has to take it, we can expect critics, rivals and those who defy a Foxified reality to find themselves targeted for scorching and personal attacks. If outsiders must be properly punished and banished from the realm of the acceptable, then what chilling effect does Fox have on public debate and what happens when someone has been singled out by Fox?

Comedian, writer and personality Al Franken has been one of the few who have benefited from Fox News' attacks. His long-standing feud with Bill O'Reilly has spilled onto newspaper pages and even the courtroom: when Franken's 2003 best-selling book *Lies and the Lying Liars Who Tell Them: A Fair and Balanced Look at the Right* was about to be released, Fox News sued the comedian for copyright infringement for using the cliché "fair and balanced." Though the suit was laughed out of court and Fox gave Franken endless hours and pages of fabulous prime free publicity, the episode was a typical example of how the network deals with those who don't believe that the FNC issues decrees from the gods. For Fox, criticism is a one-way street: they are free to harangue and ridicule others with xanthippic venom, but others cannot respond in kind.

Even those who don't criticize News Corp's crown jewel can get slapped in the face with the Fox's tail, as former Bush administration's counter-terrorism advisor Richard Clarke did when he apologized to the American people for his failure and that of the federal government for not adequately protecting American citizens during his 9-11 commission testimony. As James Wolcott observed "When Richard Clarke made that apology and that it had that dramatic effect, they knew that they were in trouble and had to get him. And so they launched a major... smear campaign. And in some ways it worked... One of the things Fox does and conservatives do is they don't have to win every argument, but if they can muddy the argument enough, if they can turn it into a draw, that to them is a victory because it denies the other side a victory."

Wolcott also noted how Fox News used innuendo in their descriptions of Clarke:

> ...tried to make the argument that Richard Clarke had problems with a black woman in authority. They tried to imply that there was this racism and one of the reasons this was so hilarious was—I mean—I'm trying to remember the last time the conservatives stood up for a black woman. I don't recall them standing up for Anita Hill. I seem to recall the way they went after Anita Hill. But now with Condoleezza Rice, it's all of a sudden

Richard Clarke: Smeared.

> like they're the defender of the Black woman and liberals. They assumed Richard Clarke is a liberal, I certainly don't, but that liberals somehow have a thing about Black women.
>
> This is the classic way that they go on the attack. I really think the "fair and balanced" thing is a way of taking the knife and twisting it. Roger Ailes is a prankster; he knows what will drive liberals crazy and he knew that this would drive them crazy.

Because Fox traffics in vitriol, it is mandatory that they continually increase the severity of their attacks: once the marks (i.e., the audience) become adjusted to the current level of sullying, subsequent attacks become pedestrian. With each new attack, the Fox News kids have to up the ante.

But it isn't just competitors, Vermont politicians, glib comedians and disenfranchised White House advisors who feel the Fox's jaws clench their flesh: anyone who does not snugly fit into Fox's worldview of what is good and just can also feel the FNC's powerful wrath.

Jeremy Glick's Wild Ride
Through the No Spin Zone

For the most part, Bill O'Reilly knows how to unbalance and control his opponents on his program: he can spar, bluster, intimidate, insult, confuse and outwit with ease and efficiency. He quickly frames an issue, unnerves his opponents, shocks them with piercing and snickering put downs, and then he does not give them the chance to reply or the time for them to pull themselves together. They can't think or relax because they are too busy trying to get a word in edgewise or too busy defending their battered honor. His hapless guests easily play along with O'Reilly's impossible game, and most leave rattled and looking worse off than they anticipated. There's always lots of damage control to do after taking a ride in the No Spin Zone.

The Bill O'Reilly School of Verbal Sparring has reaped its founder bountiful dividends. What is most surprising is that most of his hostile guests still have not grasped the nature of his ingenious methods: they are too busy paying attention to the unimportant details (O'Reilly's perfected temper; protecting their image) and not concentrating on what will save them (the format and timing of the

debate, framing their message in an innovative way, owning up to a brutal self-awareness of their flaws and image).

O'Reilly is chaotic and brutal on the outside, but he is calculated and strategic on the inside. Yet his targets never seem the wiser. Week after week, the sheep apprehensively walk into the fox's den, and week after week the fox savors his easy conquests. Though O'Reilly is unpredictable because he tailor-makes his campaigns on a person-by-person basis, his choice of combat is relatively transparent and fairly simple to decipher.

Since the inception of his program, the cocky O'Reilly has gotten a free ride in this regard: because his antagonistic guests don't catch the subtle shades of his fighting style, he has managed to perfect his populist routine. This has allowed him to attract a loyal following of viewers who crave to watch this style of sparring, but it has also made O'Reilly somewhat complacent and overconfident in his chosen dueling method. He has learned to rely on this method alone and not worry too much about what would happen if someone broke his complicated code.

In February 2003 someone would do just that, and snap the venerable host out of his delusions of invulnerability. Unfortunately for the code breaker, a startled, pissed off O'Reilly is not someone who is to be toyed with that easily. Though this modern day Intrepid held his own in the No Spin Zone, he would soon discover the extent of O'Reilly's power—and that O'Reilly's fights extend far past the show's allocated time slot.

Jeremy Glick was a PhD student in Afro-American literature at Rutgers, an educator and an activist (concentrating on prisons and the antiwar movement) whose father Barry was one of the thousands of Americans who died in the terror attacks on September 11, 2001 (he met his fate at the World Trade Center). Not surprisingly, the event would compel Glick to make life-altering decisions. Like many other relatives of those who perished in the 9/11 catastrophe, Glick chose to go public with his feelings in order to deal with his shocking and senseless loss. But unlike some others who were directly affected by 9/11, Glick adamantly opposed the U.S. war against Iraq.

There is an old joke that a conservative is a liberal who's been mugged. This piece of conservative wishful thinking implies that liberals somehow don't live in reality or were ever exposed to pain: if those pesky progressives faced the wrath of a cruel world, they would harden their hearts and convert to hardened methods. Even though Glick was mugged in the worst way possible, he didn't let this crime change his perspective or close his heart. His beliefs were consistent to the point that he openly signed an antiwar petition. When Glick signed his name on that document, he might as well have said *Jacta alea est!*

Shortly after, a fellow antiwar activist who was getting verbally thrashed about in the No Spin Zone tried to defend himself from the reigning gladiator by telling him about the singular Glick (see Chapter 10 about Solay's "Factor" appearance). Though the news didn't stop O'Reilly from finishing his signature drubbing to his personal satisfaction, it did compel him to seek out this new potential opponent. O'Reilly's lackeys immediately had two jobs to do: find Glick (not a problem) and convince him to come on the program (problem).

It turned out coaxing Glick wasn't going to be easy—he was not a naïve man; why would he expose himself to O'Reilly's methodical rage? However, as Glick recalled about his fateful call from Fox News:

> I got this call [from Fox] and they were so persistent about getting me on the "O'Reilly" show because they found out I was on the advisory board and signed a statement that was against the war—and that I was directly impacted by 9/11 [...] The reason I was hesitant [was] because I knew that he was this right-wing hack that I didn't take seriously... [and] I wasn't really trying to parade this personal hurt.

After several of Glick's friends and colleagues persuaded him to take on the "Factor" host, he decided to use his well-trained mind to prepare for his killer exam with the former high school teacher:

> The success that I had on the O'Reilly show had to do with success in my life and political work in my life, but it also [had to] do with just practice and preparation. What I did was I taped the shows—I had somebody tape the shows for a couple of weeks. I had a stopwatch that I used for running sprints in high school and I would see when he has a hostile guest where he knows that he's going to anticipate profound disagreement and I would time how long it takes for him to cut them off and then try to figure out what did I want to say and how am I going to say it in a way where he's not going to flip it and manipulate it, and how can I anticipate the objections that he's going to say.

When Glick arrived at the "Factor" studio, he did not receive the chilly reception he may have expected. In fact, Glick recalled, O'Reilly "was very pleasant to me," and that they were "chatting it up." Glick noted that "before we started, we were talking about Rutgers and he was convinced that I was doing a really good job because it was a very fine school and [he] started telling me about how he used to be a teacher."

However, there were signs that the lulling was only for show—Glick was asked not to bring his notes because they made O'Reilly "nervous." Glick also felt ill at ease for another reason: because of O'Reilly's height, Glick felt as if the host "lorded over" him. Glick may have felt uneasy, but he did not lose his cool.

One important point should be made clear: Bill O'Reilly wouldn't have achieved the level of success in his chosen career unless he was an excellent judge of other people's strengths and weaknesses. Nightly verbal sparring takes strategy, risk and the ability to know where, when and how to strike at your opponent. People have every reason to feel intimidated by O'Reilly. This gladiator is the best at what he does because he can read his marks efficiently and accurately.

But Jeremy Glick may have proven an enigma for O'Reilly: the young man was endearing and had an infectious smile. His youth and student status may have also contributed to the impression that Glick was something of a greenhorn pushover. He was an unabashedly progressive activist, which many people erroneously equate with flaky weakness. Finally, Glick was decidedly antiwar despite having an easy reason to support bloodlust. Or maybe O'Reilly was just so used to winning every fight that he became a little careless. In any case, O'Reilly seems to have sized this contender up as an easy mark.

Yet Glick was nobody's fool. He wasn't merely a student—he was a PhD candidate at a prestigious university; his intellectual prowess and critical thinking skills would have to be in top form. And Glick used those same skills before coming on to the show: he quietly researched O'Reilly's methods before agreeing to take a dangerous ride in the No Spin Zone. Glick also made sure to keep his goals simple and attainable: he had one point to make—that George Bush the elder, through his actions as director of the CIA, enabled the al Qaeda network to flourish, hence why would Glick give the benefit of the doubt to Bush Junior—and in that he would succeed. His work with inner city youths who served in juvenile detention would require him to be capable of holding his own with the disenfranchised. He was no ordinary man. It also meant Glick was capable of connecting to vastly different audiences very quickly. Though Glick maintained that he was "not overly charismatic or even that bright" (an overly modest remark given his credentials), his unique combination of skills and experiences would work in his favor.

Jeremy Glick would prove to be every bit as intelligent, brave, resourceful and shrewd as Bill O'Reilly. He may have been young, but he wasn't a helpless little pantywaist. He was a grown man who had a brilliant mind that could assess, negotiate and solve puzzles that lesser minds could not. Unlike others who recklessly went through O'Reilly's glass funhouse, Glick studied the layout and the sequence of events and formed a plan to hold his own without running into the distorting mirror.

Glick also had two other powerful qualities going for him: for one, beneath that million dollar smile was a young man who had lost his father through horrendous national tragedy. That one event would transform his entire life: to have good news, bad news, any news that he could no longer share with a loved one is a hard reality to have to face for the rest of one's life. It is a pain that doesn't go away. Closure is a poor fool's paradise: one familiar phrase or anniversary and the wounds open up again.

However, this young man didn't choose to ignore the tragedy or blindly follow someone else's ideas for vengeance; he chose to address the problem in his own way, not by stooping to his father's murderers' negative and primal level, but by attacking the problem in a different and intellectual way. He used his suffering to guide his mind. Glick didn't just have brains on his side, he had the conviction of an innocent who was horribly wronged. Glick would fight, but not in the same way other victims' families would choose. He would opt for something different. It was his unpredictability and righteous energy that would make him a worthy opponent to the "Factor" host. The assessment of Glick was elementary, but for whatever reason, O'Reilly never saw it coming.

The much anticipated gladiatorial bout between reigning champ Bill O'Reilly and the new contender Jeremy Glick started off this way on the February 4, 2003 edition of the "O'Reilly Factor":

> **O'REILLY:** In the "Personal Stories" segment tonight, we were surprised to find out that an American who lost his father in the World Trade Center attack had signed an antiwar advertisement that accused the USA itself of terrorism.

As a set up to the upcoming brawl, it couldn't have been more suspenseful. As usual, showman O'Reilly was careful to frame the debate in a way that would make it clear to his audience not only who the "offending" bad guy was in this match, but that Glick was an isolated character:

O'REILLY: The offending passage read, "We too watched with shock the horrific events of September 11... we too mourned the thousands of innocent dead and shook our heads at the terrible scenes of carnage—even as we recalled similar scenes in Baghdad, Panama City, and a generation ago, Vietnam." With us now is Jeremy Glick, whose father, Barry, was a Port Authority worker at the Trade Center. Mr. Glick is a co-author of the book *Another World is Possible*. I'm surprised you signed this. You were the only one of all of the families who signed...

Glick would quickly intercede O'Reilly with a quick counter punch:

JEREMY GLICK: Well, actually, that's not true.

O'REILLY: Who signed the advertisement?

GLICK: Peaceful Tomorrow, which represents 9/11 families, were also involved.

If nothing else, O'Reilly does his homework and must have felt confident when he could duck and deliver an easy jab to his guest:

O'REILLY: Hold it, hold it, hold it, Jeremy. You're the only one who signed this advertisement.

GLICK: As an individual.

Glick conceded on this point and it looked like smooth sailing for the "Factor" powerhouse. It didn't matter if other 9/11 survivors held Glick's views, what mattered was that O'Reilly's audience heard that Glick—and only Glick—put his name on an "offending" petition. Glick did not offer any resistance at this early stage. If the debate ended right there, O'Reilly would have had yet another cakewalk.

But an overly self-assured O'Reilly would make a tactical blunder by pursuing his point just a little too long with the following statement:

O'REILLY: Yes, as—with your name. You were the only one. I was surprised, and the reason I was surprised is that this ad equates the United States with the terrorists. And I was offended by that.

This repetition and expected posturing may have bought Glick enough time to quickly counter O'Reilly in an unexpected way. In a breathtaking rebuttal, Glick sucker-punched the usually primed O'Reilly with the one point the young man came on the show to make:

GLICK: Well, you say—I remember earlier you said it was a moral equivalency, and it's actually a material equivalency.

And just to back up for a second about your surprise, I'm actually shocked that you're surprised.

If you think about it, our current President, who I feel and many feel is in this position illegitimately by neglecting the voices of Afro-Americans in the Florida coup, which, actually, somebody got impeached for during the Reconstruction period—our current President now inherited a legacy from his father and inherited a political legacy that's responsible for training militarily, economically and situating geopolitically the parties involved in the alleged assassination and the

murder of my father and countless of thousands of others.

So I don't see why it's surprising...

Ouch.

Glick's mission was officially accomplished. He almost immediately managed to take control away from the normally alert O'Reilly: the ability to set the agenda is critical in any debate and Glick managed to grab control away from his unsuspecting opponent. It's easy to win a game in which you make up the rules, but when someone else figures out those rules and plays the game better than you—particularly a person who doesn't seem to have either the gall or the smarts to outfox you—the nature of the contest suddenly changes. It was here where the once untouchable "Factor" host was blindsided and soundly knocked to the ground by a simple, but effective sucker punch. The rope-a-dope did its trick and Glick slipped in his message without losing his composure or being tricked into wasting his time trying to defend his actions and honor.

O'Reilly's defeats are few and far between, but this time was different. For him to easily lose control of the debate as early and quickly as it did must have been a shock to his system. The regular O'Reilly outbursts are merely ruses to make it seem as if an irate host will physically strike his prey. His outbursts are meant to strike fear and suppress thought in his hostile guests. At all times, O'Reilly maintains full control of his emotions. His raised voice and insults throw his hostile guests for a loop; ergo, giving him the upper hand. What happens is that his guests run for cover while he continues to manipulate them and their messages. O'Reilly creates chaos in his opponent's mind so that he can win the match.

But this fight was different. At this point the wounded host must have seen how badly he misjudged his pigeon. In a moment of fury, O'Reilly's wits left him alone with his real rage. Glick would quickly find himself in O'Reilly's crosshairs.

Perhaps he was more angry at himself than at Glick for allowing himself to be so easily outmaneuvered, or maybe there was some real anger projected at the serene young turk, but by now O'Reilly was out for revenge. In an attack that can only be described as wicked, O'Reilly laid into the young man—and this time the tirade was genuine. Suddenly, Glick could not complete a thought without getting smacked by O'Reilly's relentless fury:

> **O'REILLY:** All right. Now let me stop you here. So...
>
> **GLICK:** ...for you to think that I would come back and want to support...
>
> **O'REILLY:** It is surprising, and I'll tell you why. I'll tell you why it's surprising.
>
> **GLICK:** ...escalating...
>
> **O'REILLY:** You are mouthing a far left position that is a marginal position in this society, which you're entitled to.
>
> **GLICK:** It's marginal—right.

It wasn't just O'Reilly's words and voice that encircled the guest; according to Glick, he "started pointing [his] finger and arching over like he was going to kill me." O'Reilly's anger did not ebb for a second:

O'REILLY: You're entitled to it, all right, but you're—you see, even—I'm sure your beliefs are sincere, but what upsets me is I don't think your father would be approving of this.

GLICK: Well, actually, my father thought that Bush's presidency was illegitimate.

O'REILLY: Maybe he did, but...

GLICK: I also didn't think that Bush...

O'REILLY: ...I don't think he'd be equating this country as a terrorist nation as you are.

GLICK: Well, I wasn't saying that it was necessarily like that.

O'REILLY: Yes, you are. You signed...

GLICK: What I'm saying is...

O'REILLY: ...this, and that absolutely said that.

It was now O'Reilly's turn in the No Spin Zone with a cool Glick playing the puppet master. The young man didn't exactly play it O'Reilly's way—far from it. What Glick did was simply point out an irrational O'Reilly's logical flaws without losing his logic or stooping to name calling in the process:

O'REILLY: I don't want to debate world politics with you.

GLICK: Well, why not? This is about world politics.

O'REILLY: Because, number one, I don't really care what you think.

GLICK: Well, OK.

O'REILLY: You're—I want to...

GLICK: But you do care because you...

O'REILLY: No, no. Look...

GLICK: The reason why you care is because you evoke 9/11...

O'REILLY: Here's why I care.

GLICK: ...to rationalize...

O'REILLY: Here's why I care...

Glick wasn't falling for any sophomoric tricks. O'Reilly was desperately trying to regain control of the situation, but his guest was having none of it. Glick was used to working with angry, energetic youth who challenge authority; his current opponent's tricks must have seemed familiar to him. O'Reilly's groping for an exit led his interrogation from being rude to crude:

GLICK: Let me finish. You evoke 9/11 to rationalize everything from domestic plunder to imperialistic aggression worldwide.

O'REILLY: OK. That's a bunch...

GLICK: You evoke sympathy with the 9/11 families.

O'REILLY: That's a bunch of crap. I've done more for the 9/11 families by their own admission—I've done more for them than you will ever hope to do.

GLICK: OK.

Rude wasn't doing it and neither was crude. While a roaring O'Reilly began talking down and threatening the placid Glick, the guest merely pointed out a certain truth:

O'REILLY: So you keep your mouth shut when you sit here exploiting those people.

GLICK: Well, you're not representing me. You're not representing me.

Threatening wasn't getting O'Reilly any more control than his other desperate gambits did. His back was up against the distorting mirror and his guest still didn't break. O'Reilly couldn't risk turning around, but he did keep a stash of mud handy in case of such emergencies:

O'REILLY: And I'd never represent you. You know why?

GLICK: Why?

O'REILLY: Because you have a warped view of this world and a warped view of this country.

O'Reilly's aim missed its mark and the young man was still standing tall and proud. This was galling and unacceptable. O'Reilly's moves were uncharacteristically unplanned and ineffective. His plucky guest was taunting him by remaining calm. Well, if the young man was close to his family and lost his father, then perhaps an emotionally manipulative low blow would throw the kid off balance:

O'REILLY: Man, I hope your mom isn't watching this.

GLICK: Well, I hope she is.

Now what? It was too late: Glick was victorious by being straightforward, cool and remembering what the point of a debate was. Not once did the young man falter or try to justify his actions. O'Reilly would still hit below the belt, but even as he did, it was obvious he was trying to cut his losses as quickly as he could:

O'REILLY: I hope your mother is not watching this because you—that's it. I'm not going to say any more.

GLICK: OK.

O'REILLY: In respect for your father...

GLICK: On September 14, do you want to know what I'm doing?

There is nothing worse than when the person who just defeated you keeps replying to your outbursts with an even-tempered "OK." Winners are supposed to gloat over their conquests, not be agreeable to their requests. O'Reilly lost the bout and he just wanted to push it all away:

O'REILLY: Shut up. Shut up.

GLICK: Oh, please don't tell me to shut up.

O'Reilly shouldn't have told Glick to shut up for tactical reasons. Because the "Factor" host was yelling at a young man who lost his father through terrorism, O'Reilly was simply making Glick seem increasingly sympathetic. What kind of man viciously attacks someone whose loved one died in a national tragedy? No matter what else would transpire from that moment on, O'Reilly handed his critics tangible proof of his nefariousness. It doesn't matter that Glick could take care of himself;

it doesn't even matter that O'Reilly hurt himself in the process. It doesn't matter what else he does in his life, O'Reilly's detractors will never let him live the Glick debacle down. Nor should they. His on-air sore loser behavior was despicable.

His immediate off-air behavior was even worse. As the May 2003 edition of *Harper's* magazine reported, O'Reilly told Glick: "Get out! Get out of my studio before I tear you to fucking pieces!" O'Reilly may claim his studio is a No Spin Zone; he never claimed it wasn't a no assault zone. No doubt: Bill O'Reilly was having a really bad day.

Glick remained cool off air, too. As he later recalled:

> I went in the green room to eat a bagel... and O'Reilly's executive producer called me to ask what my intention was and why I was still staying in the building. I was like, "I'm relaxing before I take the car service back to New Brunswick. The executive producer and the assistant encouraged me to leave the building because they were concerned that "if O'Reilly ran into me in the hallway that he would end up in jail."

The victory bagel may have been a pointed statement on Glick's part, but O'Reilly's wits weren't coming to rejoin the rest of him. Strangely enough, for a man who has the distinct ability to unnerve his targets, he couldn't calm his nerves down enough to conduct a much-needed self-evaluation and honest post-mortem of his mistakes. The Glick incident could have been a learning experience for O'Reilly; instead, it proved that his darker side can control and inhibit much of his thinking when things don't go according to plan.

Jeremy Glick held his own on O'Reilly's show.

If O'Reilly truly was morally outraged by Glick at all, then why give a platform to Glick in the first place? Wouldn't silence be more potent than publicity? Perhaps. But to discredit his prey, O'Reilly lured the young man to appear on his show just so he could have a quirky opponent to defeat. The episode may have been abusive, twisted, gratuitous and pseudo-moralizing, but it was also very calculated and strategic: Bill O'Reilly didn't gain prominence in his career holding the hands of his guests—he made it by becoming a more palatable Morton Downey Jr. or Wally George. The problem is that his methods aren't 100% effective.

So how did O'Reilly succumb to a bad case of brain cramps? In his drive to find a new opponent to beat up, he forgot to assess his own morals on the issue. If O'Reilly truly was moved by his ethics in this case, he would have had enough empathy to know that a young man who lost his father through extreme violence (not to mention seeing his students die senseless, violent deaths on the streets) might not want to see any more violence or death, especially not in the name of his father. Watching countless media replays of the collapsing towers and knowing that a relative was forced to spend his final moments in fear, pain and without his loved ones is a heavy burden for someone to live with. There are some people who do not wish to see others suffer the same fate. O'Reilly's quick assumption that being antiwar meant being anti-moral worked against him.

Instead of yelling at Glick, a cynical but collected O'Reilly could have surprised the young man by being human and showing compassion. If O'Reilly truly believed Glick was outrageously misguided, wouldn't the "Factor" host try to reason with this young man? Why demonize a victim? Why assume he's up to no good? Could this not be his own way of dealing with grief?

A savvier and more compassionate O'Reilly could have said any number of things to Glick: "I know you mean well, but..." or, "I know you probably had your fill of violence, but..."—he could have said anything along those lines to get through to someone who he believed was misguided. He could have tried to reach out to the young man or even offered a rebuttal that a father's actions can't serve as any prediction to the success of his son's actions. There were countless ways O'Reilly could have saved face and sparred with dignity.

But that's not what his regular viewers want—they want their host to pulverize and destroy all opposition to their stifling worldviews; they want him to attack ruthlessly and prove that their hatred is right. O'Reilly had no room to maneuver; he was trapped.

Fortunately for O'Reilly, his viewers have virtually no comprehension of the finer points of psychological warfare. For the most part, they are a simple folk who have no clue how brilliant O'Reilly really is or what a fantastic thrashing he received from Glick. Many of them who wrote letters to the show praising their hero for that night's performance had absolutely no clue that O'Reilly lost control, face and the battle with Glick; they just heard their heartthrob O'Reilly's regular yelling and assumed the host was merely smacking the kid around as usual. Bless their heads. It may have been a hollow victory, but there was still opportunity for damage control.

Glick was an easy target; too-good-to-be-true cannon fodder for O'Reilly's show. O'Reilly baited the young man to come on his program; Glick proved more resourceful than many other seasoned guests and managed to hold his own against O'Reilly's tricks. When it became obvious that Glick was a man who wasn't going to waver, back down or cower in the corner, an unhinged O'Reilly quickly shut off the mike. Not that O'Reilly couldn't later salvage the incident, nor was he helpless in striking back, but in a real way, it was O'Reilly and not Glick who was ill-prepared for battle.

All right, O'Reilly was still smarting over his miscalculation with Glick, but it didn't mean he was going to let the Glick episode drop and be forgotten, OK? It must have bothered O'Reilly more than he let on, or he figured he could spin or milk that confrontation to his liking, which is what he precisely did on his February 5 program:

> **O'REILLY:** Thousands of letters about Jeremy Glick, the war protester who lost his father on 9/11. Mr. Glick thinks America is an evil place.

Glick neither said nor implied this sentiment; this "fact" was entirely an invention concocted by sore loser O'Reilly. As for some viewers, they misinterpreted what they saw:

> **O'REILLY:** Sharon Leary, New Fairfield, Connecticut, "O'Reilly, I know you were embarrassed by your guest, Mr. Glick, but no need to apologize. His interview proved to me that some antiwar people are really ridiculous." I'm glad you got something out of the interview, Ms. Leary, but I'm sorry I gave the guy a forum to spout anti-American hatred.

Glick never spouted any anti-American hatred, but why let facts get in the way of a good story? However, not every O'Reilly viewer is naïve, and a few actually comprehended what went down. Those sharper, dissenting viewers also got a crude verbal slapping for defending Glick:

> **O'REILLY:** Diane Alt, West Virginia, "Mr. O'Reilly, I watched in disgust as you berated that young man. How dare you treat a guest like that? Most intelligent people know how biased Fox News is." Well, Ms. Alt, from your letter, I assume you are an ideologue with a political axe to grind, just as Glick was, so I understand your sympathy for him.

If Glick won the battle, there was no way he could win the war: in ancient Roman days, the defeated gladiator would be put out of his misery and the victor didn't have to ever worry about having to deal with a sore or vindictive loser spinning and sassing off later on. For better or for worse, these days televised verbal sparring leaves both parties still breathing, with the loser free to exact his revenge any way he wants to. What that meant for Glick was that even though he managed to get out of the glass fun house unscathed, O'Reilly still owned the attraction and could control what his audience would see and hear long after Glick was gone. Glick did not have a nightly show where he could rebut the vengeful O'Reilly.

When other journalists and commentators chastised O'Reilly for being a boor, he used his show to defend his actions while attacking Glick. On September 19, 2003, O'Reilly retorted to one of his critics on his program, "Wow, that sounds bad. Doesn't it? Sounds like I'm just the worst guy ever. Well, here's the truth. And [Joel] Connelly [a columnist for the *Seattle Post Intelligencer*] knows the truth. He's so blatantly dishonest, he would never write it." O'Reilly may not have been "the worst guy ever" but his treatment of Glick was one of the worst moments in television journalism. O'Reilly's Glick-bashing continued:

> **O'REILLY:** We invited him [Glick] on the "Factor" last February because he signed an advertisement accusing the USA of being a terrorist country.
>
> Here's what Glick said to us. "Our current President now inherited a legacy from his father that's responsible for training militarily, economically and situating geopolitically the parties involved in the alleged assassination and murder of my father and countless thousands of others." Alleged assassination? Glick was saying without a shred of evidence that President Bush and Bush the elder were directly responsible for 9/11.

O'Reilly's foul temper tantrum continued unimpeded on the program:

> **O'REILLY:** Now that kind of stuff is not only loony, it's defamation. So I terminated the interview, after which Glick had to be escorted out of the building by Fox security because of his demeanor.

Loony? Pretty harsh and defaming words from the "Factor" emcee, indeed. O'Reilly also made it sound as if Glick was acting like a raving madman on the set; in fact, Glick was the opposite—that's what seemed to have unnerved O'Reilly in the first place. He was asked to leave because flunkies said they feared what O'Reilly would do to Glick, not the other way around. O'Reilly couldn't let go; he continued with his sporadic Jeremy-Glick-is-un-American-and-evil monologues.

During this time O'Reilly rival Al Franken had decided to try to help the young man sort out the mess. After unsuccessfully trying to get someone who worked for O'Reilly to point out to the anonymous employee's boss that he was slandering Glick and playing loose with his facts, Franken decided to illuminate O'Reilly himself. As Franken recalled:

> I just went on C-SPAN... and I did a speech [at] the University of Missouri at Columbia, Missouri, and I just told the story. And I told it so that it would be on record somewhere... I said it partially to defend Jeremy, and partially just so that it's out there so that O'Reilly couldn't continue to do it.

The drubbing didn't cease for long, as O'Reilly spun furiously over a year later on one of his July 2004 programs:

> **O'REILLY:** [Glick] said America itself was responsible for the 9/11 attack because it is an imperialistic, aggressive nation. Glick was dismissed from the "Factor" because he was completely off the wall. Security actually had to take the guy out of the building, he was that out of control.

No, the only one "out of control" that night was a defeated and humiliated O'Reilly. Though the never-ending soap opera called O'Reillygate continues to unspool, Glick's place in O'Reilly lore remains assured, even if he had to pay a higher than expected price for it.

Blame Canada, They Seem Easier to Push Around Than China

Canadians, for the most part, pride themselves on their modesty, politeness, helpfulness and even-temperedness. The calm demeanor has helped the country and its people go about their lives without getting themselves into too many conflicts in its history. Canadians may not always be the grandest of tippers or the most flamboyant of personalities, but they can be counted on to be reasonable and keep a collective level head in a crisis.

Yet even the most peace-loving nation can be the target of Fox fury. At times, according to a certain perpetually-sourball Fox News host, Canada seems to be a more sinister threat to the United States than the usual suspects with deep ties to terrorist networks that openly vow to destroy the Land of the Free. Who knew the Axis of Evil secretly included the neighbors to the North?

So what was the unforgivable sin that Canadians committed to warrant a Fox attack?

All the Canadian government ever did was not agree with the United States government on every single issue (just like Larry Johnson) and request to see concrete proof of evidence before committing lives on the front line. But to at least one of those talking heads at Fox, those actions were enough to call for crippling and punitive economic sanctions against a country whose national symbol is a beaver. So much for international democracy and diplomacy.

Leading the charge of gutting Canada was none other than Fox's official excitable loud mouth Bill O'Reilly. O'Reilly asked this loaded and leading question during his interview with Canadian-born

ABC news anchor Peter Jennings on October 17, 2002:

O'REILLY: Canada is a socialistic country, and America is a capitalistic country. So I'm going to ask you, since you know both systems, which one is better?

But unbeknownst to both Canadians and Americans alike, O'Reilly's seemingly recalcitrant grudge against Canada would continue to fester and boil, culminating in a somewhat coherent if paranoid ideation about what those slippery Canadians were really up to: mass brainwashing of that country's youth, OK? Programming teens from Vancouver to Halifax was the evil plot afoot and, who knows, maybe even the Canadian tradition of its citizens wearing those little red paper flowers on their coat lapels in November could be all part of the same sinister scheme, too, all right?

> The Canadian government did not agree with the United States government on every single issue, which made them a suspect to Fox.

In any case, O'Reilly's vast clandestine Canadian conspiracy theory was revealed to his viewers on his August 4, 2004 show:

O'REILLY: But my point was that the Canadian media and the Canadian education system is now skewing their reportage about America so that all of these children, millions of Canadian children, feel that we are an evil force in the world. They're not providing perspective to the children up there, and I believe I'm absolutely correct, sir.

O'Reilly was anything but "absolutely correct"—he failed to mention the small fact that these are the same children who watch U.S. films, shows, sports events and listen to American music. He made it sound as if mass indoctrination of young Canadians was taking place with resounding success—and as if Canucks weren't already so inundated with U.S. news outlets that Canada's tourism slogan to Americans might as well be, "Canada: the official getaway for Americans who get homesick easily! Come visit us: you won't know the difference watching television."

The facts didn't stop O'Reilly from making this loaded cat-and-dog remark on January 29, 2003:

O'REILLY: A poll taken in Canada said that 84% of Canadians believe America was partially responsible for the attack on us on 9/11. Canada has also a very lenient immigration policy and a wide open border.

But even before O'Reilly decided that a peaceful and non-threatening nation had to be punished for being peaceful and non-threatening, he had already hurled his meaningless threats to New Democratic Party (a small left-leaning Canadian political party) leader Jack Layton on March 27, 2003:

O'REILLY: But the perception of the American people toward your leader, Chretien, is that he is a guy who just doesn't have any use for us, and the problem here is that he has a right to his opinion as the elected leader of your country, and he has a right to express it.

But we have a right to take economic reprisals against Canada, if we see or we

think that you're not looking out for our best interests and, if we do, you guys
are in big, big trouble, Mr. Layton.

Threatening a party leader who has a snowball's chance of ever becoming his nation's leader was truly a futile effort on O'Reilly's part: even if the progressive Layton wanted to play fairy godmother to O'Reilly's wishes, he had no power to do so, anyway.

In the months that followed, it never occurred to O'Reilly that a country with a relatively small population wanted to see evidence of Hussein's alleged weapons of mass destruction before committing and condemning young soldiers to possible death—a real possibility considering how many U.S. soldiers had lost their lives in the conflict. Nor did it occur to O'Reilly that then-Canadian Prime Minister Jean Chretien (who served three terms in office) was the elder statesman who had international seniority over the then-rookie President Bush: Bush's imperious attitude was most likely off-putting to the scruffy, street fighter Prime Minister.

Historically, upstarts who intentionally or otherwise slight those with more experience find themselves suddenly getting the cold shoulder. Blazing and brash young turks who always get their way only work in teen escapist movies; in real life adults who try those same tricks at home find themselves receiving a chilly reception from those senior peers to whom they've shown little respect or regard. In the real world, experience and seniority still count for something. Bush's colossal diplomatic blunder may have played well with his fan boy constituents at home who saw it as their aggressive leader taking charge, but abroad, it resulted in strained international relations. Your dad always seemed to be cooler to you than he did to your friends.

The lack of international support stemmed from the simple fact that the Bush administration did not make a convincing enough case to world leaders who had far more intelligence and knowledge about the situation than did the less initiated public citizens. The President's home turf advantage did not translate as well to other countries and, for once, Canada did not behave like a sycophantic and obedient little yes man. The lack of WMD proved that prudence was the way to go. But to Bill O'Reilly, details are unimportant.

Some may think O'Reilly's Canadaphobic tirades stemmed from nationalistic patriotism, but there is also another, more self-serving reason for O'Reilly's perplexing and tedious Canada-bashing that has little to do with politics or ideological bent: at the time, the Fox News Channel was not welcome in Canada.

Though other American news channels are free to air in Canada, the FNC is not one of them. News Corp applied for a license to the Canadian equivalent to the FCC (in this case the CRTC) to air in that country, but unlike other cases, this time Murdoch and company had to wait in line like everybody else. Yes, Fox News was available to Canadian politicians, but it had to follow the rules before it could air in the rest of the country. A potential audience of thirty million was at stake (though if O'Reilly's idea of a boycott took place, there really was no point in courting penniless and starving Canucks, eh?)

While the country occasionally debated whether to grant a license to a network that wished the country irreparable harm, John Doyle, a television critic and columnist with the *Globe and Mail*, a Canadian national daily newspaper based in Toronto, wrote about Fox's attempts to gain a foothold in Canada. As Doyle mused to readers in his April 19, 2004 column:

> [...S]ome honchos in the cable-TV racket are applying for permission to offer the Fox News Channel in Canada.

> Beauty. Bring it on, I say. We're all in need of a good laugh. The barking-mad Fox News Channel is something that most Canadians have only heard about. It's time we saw it for ourselves, and made up our own minds about the phenomenon. We'll find out if this Bill O'Reilly fella is as stupendously pompous and preening as he appears to be in the rare clips we see of Fox News.

Doyle went on to describe Fox News style and format to his uninitiated readers:

> Me, I've seen the Fox News Channel on visits to the United States. It is a splendid thing entirely. You have no idea how funny it is. The Fox News Channel is a kind of live theatre of the airwaves, with right-wing pundits playing journalists in an ongoing soap opera. In this soap opera there are good guys and bad guys. The bad guys are the Democratic Party and a dark force that is sometimes known as The Liberal Media Elite and sometimes known as The Loony Left.

Doyle was merely expressing his opinion, and for better or worse, his readers could decide for themselves whether they would agree with him or not.

Not that an American audience would have known that from watching the "O'Reilly Factor." Bill O'Reilly called the *Globe and Mail* the "far left Toronto *Globe and Mail*"—a very strong exaggeration for a newspaper whose business reportage is considered to be second to none in the country. For a man who has no qualms calling others boobs and idiots, he certainly couldn't take a far gentler ribbing in return.

But a "stupendously pompous and preening" Bill O'Reilly would have none of it on his April 19, 2004 program. The poor man's feelings must have been hurt by that tough Canadian bully—why else did the "Factor" host rant, "So they see rare clips, but think we're laughable. The *Globe and Mail* sounds like a real responsible enterprise, doesn't it? Hey, you pinheads up there, I may be pompous but at least I'm honest"? And don't forget thin-skinned and uncivilized (though Jeremy Glick may disagree with O'Reilly on that "honest" part).

The tantrum-throwing over a single newspaper column continued without any sign that O'Reilly was going to get a "time out" or a "hot-saucing" for his misbehavior. Response to Doyle's column (which was reprinted in the *New York Times*) was fast and furious: he was deluged with obnoxious and semiliterate letters from Fox News supporters in the U.S. Doyle's response? "Before the channel has even appeared, I can tell you I was in stitches reading the voluminous response from Fox News supporters in the U.S. By Monday evening, I was so paralytic with laughter I had to call off the writing of yesterday's column. I was incapacitated with the hilarity," he wrote in an easy-to-fill follow up column that featured some of the goonier jeers.

But then the governmental body responsible for regulating Canadian airwaves came down with its dose of Tabasco: the FNC was denied a license to broadcast to Canada (at the time regulations stipulated Fox News had to have Canadian content on their channel, though the rule was recently dropped, making it possible for Fox News to reapply successfully, which it did as a digital channel that made its debut on Canadian television in January 2005) while the Aljazeera network was granted a conditional license. It seemed as if the Canadian government really was taking sides against the U.S. on its "War on Terror."

Or so it seemed. In fact, the CRTC's restrictions on Aljazeera were so prohibitive and restrictive (namely, any cable provider would have to continuously monitor and censor the network for hateful content) that the decision was a de facto shut out. In other words, don't expect to see Aljazeera on the Canadian airwaves anytime soon. The vigorous baby-sitting and screening required to please the CRTC isn't worth it.

Yet the FNC played it up as if were in bed with the terrorists. Apparently not having any better issue or current event to discuss on his show, O'Reilly continued to grouse about the snub, even though the country of thirty-odd million people was already being served by numerous national and local all-news channels from Canada, the United States and other nations. O'Reilly again took it upon himself on April 29, 2004 to scold his Northern neighbors on April 29, 2004 (who, unfortunately for O'Reilly, could not watch his accuracy-deprived rant on their televisions since they did not have access to the FNC):

> **O'REILLY:** It's simply hard to believe what's going on up there. Some Toronto news-papers, the CBC [a Canadian public television and radio network], some liberal politicians are brutal toward the USA. As we reported last week, a new poll says 40% of Canadian teenagers think the USA is an evil country.
>
> Fox News Channel has petitioned the Canadian government for access. So far, we have been denied. You can't get FNC on Canadian cable. But you can get Aljazeera, of all things. The Canadian government recently approved that operation for viewing.

The approval had so many strings attached that Canadians couldn't see the network from all that rope—but that factoid didn't work for O'Reilly. The "Factor" kahuna wanted to vent and he found a couple of well-respected Canadian journalists to take it out on:

> **O'REILLY:** Joining us now from Toronto is Rick Salutin, who writes for the Globe and Mail, a paper that's been overly hostile to me, and Peter Worthington, a colum-nist for the *Toronto Sun*.
>
> All right, Mr. Worthington, let me begin with you. A lot of Americans just simply don't understand the vast changes that have taken place in Canada in the past twenty years. We're not talking about the Canada that our grandfathers knew, are we?

O'Reilly had a couple of months to settle down and get over the snub, but it didn't work out that way; so he continued to gripe about the Northern Rejection on his program. The real motive behind the host's Hate-Canada kick was again hinted at on July 6, though O'Reilly started with the usual blustering quasi-Presidential-sounding threats to Rondi Adamson, a freelance reporter he found who apparently was capable of only uttering one single word...

O'REILLY: Do people understand that if Americans get angry, as we are with France...

RONDI ADAMSON: Right.

O'REILLY: ...with Canada, you know, these deserters aren't sent back, I'm going to call for a boycott of Canada. And that means that I'm going to ask Americans not to visit there.

ADAMSON: Right.

O'REILLY: And not to buy Canadian products if they can help it.

ADAMSON: Right.

O'REILLY: Does Canada understand the Armageddon that that would cause?

...but then O'Reilly uncharacteristically regressed to a bafflingly whiny *"It's not fair!"* tangent to the arid freelancer who expanded his writer's vocabulary:

O'REILLY: We can't do anything to you politically, but we can choose to spend our money in other places, as we are now with France. So I'm sorry. I love Canada. I think it's a great country, but I've been reading the *Toronto Globe and Mail* and it's awful. The CBC is awful.

ADAMSON: Oh, the CBC's appalling, I agree.

O'REILLY: And they won't let Fox News in to balance it.

The CBC is hardly the only network available to Canadians, who prefer to watch other networks, from CTV to the American NBC (as for Adamson's comforting jab that the CBC is appalling, it could hardly be considered indicting: most Canadian reporters do not like the CBC until they get a job there). There isn't anything that the FNC has that Canadians need or can't find elsewhere—in-house or abroad.

Though he has been passionate and relentless with his neighbor-bashing, O'Reilly's various swipes at Canada seem to have been met with indifference from most of his viewers, who most likely could not care less about Canada. However, Fox News' anti-Canada pieces are so insidious that more paranoid people with way too much free time on their hands may be wondering whether the FNC has been engaging in subliminal swipes at Canucks (after all, Fox News' motto "fair and balanced" is an anagram for "brain fled Canada," quite an uncalled for slight against a nation of percolated coffee drinkers). While those who draw their salary from Fox News may see Canada as the bastion of left-leaning American-bashing refuseniks, the truth is that the country is politically and regionally diverse (it can still function with conservatives, progressives, moderates and even separatists duking it out in the government).

But O'Reilly and company should be careful what they wish for: Canadian audiences can be a snarky and fickle bunch who can make an amateur night at the Apollo look like a love-fest if the main act in question has an attitude problem. Northern audiences do enjoy watching arrogant pontificators,

and they like someone they can relentlessly bash and humble. If O'Reilly took offense to Doyle's comments, he would not fare well against a chorus of much harsher voices. Regardless, as of this writing, President O'Reilly's decree for economic sanctions against Canada is still waiting to be enacted.

FNC Memo to Larry Johnson: Don't Hit Yourself on the Way Out

It may be natural that the FNC is xenophobic; after all, they are one of the most inexperienced of all the television news outfits, they are owned by someone who is not American by birth and they market themselves as outsiders. Both their real and self-imagined differences with other media outlets seem to make the Fox News kids suspicious of those outside their network. But how are the insiders treated?

If security consultant Larry Johnson's experience is any indication, network patriotism is crucial for insiders to stay insiders. As Peter Hart observed, "The rules are pretty clear to everyone who is participating in this game, even the people who are supposedly liberal in those panel discussions: they know that to challenge the guests and the other hosts too forcefully, [Fox News] will certainly find someone else to stand in [his] place if that's the case."

Sometimes it isn't even a "liberal" who finds himself exiled for not toeing the party line; it's a conservative who doesn't agree with everything in the FNC bible. Larry Johnson is a security consultant and worked in the U.S. State Department's counterterrorism office as well as the Central Intelligence Agency. His credentials in assessing the United States' abilities on its various antiterrorism campaigns were sound.

From January 2002 to January 2003, Johnson was also a paid contributor for the Fox News Channel, giving his on-air assessment on different aspects on the White House's "War on Terror." As Johnson recalled:

> I came in and was always [going] to call it as I saw it and give people my unvarnished viewpoint. I think they initially liked it because they thought I was a conservative, but then they saw over time that I wouldn't always toe the party line.

It was one of his rebellious moods that would prove to be fateful. Johnson was asked to appear on "Hannity and Colmes" to discuss the U.S. campaigns in Iraq and Afghanistan:

> I went on the show and the question came up about the ability of the United States to fight two wars simultaneously, and Sean Hannity, being the right-wing cheerleader that he is, was just incensed that I had the temerity to suggest that we couldn't. Facts don't seem to have any effect upon him. But as I said at that time, the United States did not have the airlift and the logistics resources in place to sustain a two-front war. So, if we're going to commit forces to something like Iraq, we were going to be tied up there for quite awhile.

Johnson's reply to Hannity's assertion went this way on the November 13, 2002 edition of "Hannity and Colmes":

LARRY JOHNSON: [...] The concern I have is at least over the short-term that going into Iraq is going to divert resources and attention that should be focused on al Qaeda. Right now, the one that—you know, we look back over the past twelve years, the folks with blood on their hands for killing Americans are al Qaeda, not Iraq.

Larry Johnson: Cold-shouldered by Fox.

Hannity did not seem too pleased with Johnson's reply and made his feelings known to his guest:

HANNITY: Thanks for being with us. Well, I couldn't disagree with both of you more in terms of—we do have the ability and the resources to—we're able to walk and chew gum. We can handle the situation in Iraq, which I think needs to be dealt with and in fairly short order, and we can still finish the job of protecting against al Qaeda and another attack. I don't see why you think we're incapable really of doing both and doing both well.

However, Johnson would not back down from his un-Foxified position:

JOHNSON: Well, let me tell you why I take that position. I have been involved in scripting the counterterrorism exercises for the U.S. military forces that have that specific mission. And I know how these things go.

While in theory the United States can fight two-front wars, in fact, what happens is when the resources end up getting diverted, and particularly the air-lift assets required to support special operations forces on the hunt for bin Laden are going to be diverted and used in the campaign in Iraq. So it really is going to end up—at least it's going to be a temporary diversion.

The host took the typical FNC route when dealing with a hostile guest—and did most of the talking:

HANNITY: See, I take the position, I think they're connected, because it's all part of an ongoing war on terror. Al Qaeda is a threat or a part of a threat. But yet so is—so is Iraq and Saddam Hussein.

But look, that's neither here nor there. We now know U.S. officials are telling Fox News tonight that there is little doubt that the voice on the tape is, in fact, his...

JOHNSON: Right.

HANNITY: ...which means he is alive and that there is no doubt. And some real concern in the intelligence community is that this tape could signal another wave of al Qaeda attacks, and that they say the chatter about al Qaeda action has been as much or more than what they heard prior to 9/11. No matter what we do, we

are vulnerable still. And they're planning on killing us. So...

JOHNSON: No, that is true. We're vulnerable but they've also suffered some significant losses.

Soon afterwards, Johnson would feel the consequence of his actions: even though there would be more on-air chit chats about his area of expertise, he himself would become a virtual persona non grata on the network as Johnson recalled:

> It almost seemed that there was a deliberate effort not to use me, but I could never put my finger on it. I could never get a clear answer. It was later in talking with one of my friends who was still with Fox, who described [how] they laid out very clearly how every morning there was a detailed list of subjects to talk about and not talk about... After my appearance on "Hannity and Colmes" the only other program I was called to appear on was the "O'Reilly Factor" and I attributed that to the fact that O'Reilly still tends to call his own shots... but ultimately even the great Bill O'Reilly apparently succumbed to the pressure and they stopped using me.

If Johnson thought that the sub was all in his head, he soon discovered on multiple occasions that he truly was no longer welcome on Fox News:

> I've had at least eight experiences since going out from under contract where I received a phone call from one of the bookers, the lower-level bookers at Fox and they said, "Hey, we'd like to have you on the air today." I said, "Really? Have you checked this to make sure it's not a problem?" They said, "What do you mean?" I said, "My understanding was that there was a problem." They said, "Oh, that can't be; we'll get right back to you." I have yet to have a phone call back in any of those eight cases.

> [...] What I find funny is that you have an organization that doesn't even have the guts to stand up and say, "Hey, we don't like your views," or "we don't think you're articulate," or "you're so ugly, you're scaring the viewer."

Though Johnson was not a full-fledged Fox News personality, he is not the only one to feel that all employees must conform to the FNC's unwritten manifesto, as one former Fox employee recalled:

> It seems pretty unique because I've talked to many people and several have signed confidentiality agreements, and then other people hang up the phone on me with their voice quivering. I've not encountered this level of fear in anything else that I've done.

> [...]It's a sense of brutality that I think was unheard of before Fox News. Now, it wasn't unheard of in politics, [where] Roger Ailes and his style of brass knuckles politics has been around for awhile... I had one person at Fox News, a manager, describe it to me as a civil war. And Roger Ailes was Robert E. Lee and you either stay on the battlefield fighting for him, or when you try to get off, he shoots you in the back.

Another former employee witnessed what happens when even the most patriotic of employees don't follow the FNC rules to the letter:

After 9/11, there was a sudden move among management at Fox News to have all their on-air talent wear little [American] flag pins. I witnessed a reporter whose suits say "Made in the USA," who has the Unite, Union of Needlepoint and Industrial Textile Employees because that reporter had witnessed factories [and textile mills] being closed, and yet when that reporter said to management "I'm not going to wear a flag pin because viewers don't need to know on the surface of my jacket that I care about America. I know because of what's inside the jacket that I care about America because the suit is made in America." Management still went crazy and said, "You got to wear that flag pin; you're either one of them or you're one of us, and this is going to prove it."

One former Fox employee described the mentality of some fellow coworkers at the strident cable newser:

I think most of the reporters that I worked with were very hard workers, very good reporters, writers and editors. And they struggled with the fact that despite their own personal preference in politics, they were having a certain agenda shoved down their throats and they were conscious of the fact that they were acting as the foot soldiers for the Murdoch army and they really had no other place else to go.

Even when a Fox News employee does find a place to go, they will be punished for their disobedient and perceived disloyalty—just ask Paula Zahn.

Paula Zahn: A Little Too Sexy for Fox?

Sometimes you don't need to be a comedian, left-wing activist or independent-minded world leader to be the target of scorn and derision at Fox; at times, even being a sought-after employee will be enough to trigger Fox's fury. Just ask Paula Zahn, who saw herself being described by her Fox colleagues as a low-class journalist wannabe after previously being scored as a competent, if underrated journalist—all because she was in demand.

The relationship between Fox brass and Zahn seemed to be one of a smitten, if brash young man wooing the pretty young thing he fancies. Prior to her stint at the vixen network, Zahn co-anchored a morning news show at CBS, but the program never caught on with viewers, as did rivals "Good Morning America" or "Today." Yet despite her lack of journalistic draw, Fox News brass seemed genuinely enamored with their choice when they first recruited Zahn for their young network back in 1999. In fact, the blonde anchor was good enough to host her own program called "The Edge," and she was good enough to boost ratings for her designated time slot. Ailes seemed to have nothing but praise for Zahn when he said of her, "She's a good interviewer who was underused. This will give her a chance to really show her stuff."

But two years later, when CNN finally noticed Zahn's stuff on Fox and then suddenly began courting the comely journalist, the love affair abruptly ended. Fox brass not only fired Zahn six months before her Fox contract expired, but they also filed an unsuccessful lawsuit against her for her move to CNN. Though Richard Leibner, Zahn's high-profile agent (whose clientele included Diane Sawyer

and Dan Rather) maintained that the negotiations were above board, Ailes still reportedly called him a "liar."

However, that insult would prove to be less offensive than those hurled at Zahn. A Fox publicist compared her to an outdoor toilet and not-so-discreetly accused her of being a pseudo-journalist. Even Ailes was sounding more like a jilted boyfriend than a former employer when he told the *New York Times*, "I could have put a dead raccoon on the air this year and got a better rating than last year." Ailes could very well have had a point: if anyone continued to watch the Fox News Network after he openly stated his disdain and disrespect for an audience he thought was so stupid and obedient that they would watch vermin carcasses decay on-air, then Fox viewers are getting the network they so richly deserve.

Fox has never stopped trashing Paula Zahn— because she stopped working for them and went to work for CNN.

Though one would think a failed lawsuit and public trashy barbs would be cathartic enough, Zahn's Fox detractors would continue to taunt her for another couple of years. Like Ailes, Bill O'Reilly also sounded like the proverbial bitter and sarcastic ex-boyfriend with his occasional jabs at Zahn. Among the low-lights:

◆ On January, 2002, when CNN's now-infamous Zahn television ads were broadcast (marked with a zipper sound with an announcer declaring that Zahn was "a little bit sexy"), O'Reilly couldn't resist making fun of his colleague, though she had nothing to do with the ad. O'Reilly asked viewers on his program, "My question is, if Paula Zahn is getting that kind of copy, why can't your humble correspondent? Well, wait a minute. Don't answer that question. It could be ridiculous." He later dedicated an entire segment of the "Factor" on the "sexy flap." His column on the matter also made reference to the episode. Why he felt the incident needed any more play than some more important issues of the day was never explained by him.

◆ On September 25 of that same year, O'Reilly publicly took Zahn to task for her allegedly sympathetic interview with Madelyne Toogood, the Indiana mother who was caught on a Wal-Mart security camera hitting her child in her vehicle. As O'Reilly opined to the faithful on his program, "And perhaps the worst example of this whitewash, Paula Zahn asked Madelyne Toogood, quote, 'What is it you're trying to teach Americans about what went wrong that day?' With all due respect to Miss Zahn, a former colleague, come on! It is simply irresponsible to allow that woman to teach America anything on national television. She is a disgrace. And some of the media gave her a phony platform that is also disgraceful."

◆ Almost two years after Zahn left Fox, O'Reilly still had the little bit sexy Paula on his mind, as witnessed by his steady references to the fair-haired journo. Whether O'Reilly felt it necessary to taunt or there was another emotion at play, during his "Most Ridiculous Item of the Day" segment, O'Reilly may have bored his viewers when he remarked, "Our pal, Paula Zahn, is supposed to be competing against us over at CNN, but she hasn't shown up for work in nearly a month. Where's Paula? Has anybody seen her? Should we put out a Paula alert? If you have seen her, please let us know. We're worried. We hope nothing ridiculous has happened." OK, we get the picture, Bill, all right?

The method of attack is almost always the same: isolate the target, vilify him or ridicule him, and repeat this process enough times for regular viewers to remember who it is they are being asked to hate (though in the case of Larry Johnson, his punishment was to be shut out of Fox and never to be used as a talking head again). Fox is not only partisan, it is also personal: personal vendettas are settled when cameras are rolling. It is not only opinion that has replaced news at Fox, but grudges have also replaced editorial content. Talk about a young man who signed a petition, talk about a former colleague who left to accept a more lucrative offer, talk about a country who doesn't want to watch your program but whatever you do, don't talk about real issues.

Even though there have been an increasing number of people, groups and even countries who have been attacked by the Fox News Channel, it doesn't mean that everyone who has been abused has been taking those relentless strikes lying down.

Part Five:

Fox HUNTING

Chapter 17

After the Fox

"We have no alternative—we must see the job through."

Rupert Murdoch on why the
"Coalition of the Willing" should not pull out of Iraq

There is no doubt that the Fox News Channel is in top form: its caché of convulsing opinionists disguised as newsmen can mesmerize the frustrated and then transform their nightly fits into instant bestsellers. The FNC's ratings have steadily improved over the years, until it became a cable news powerhouse. During the 2004 Republican National Convention, it even surpassed network news in the ratings war. Fox News' ascension is an ominous sign for the Big Three Establishment networks: new generations are now growing up without the sense that ABC, NBC or CBS are any different than HBO or CNN. When it comes to newsgathering, CNN was always there for them, then MSNBC and Fox News. When more Gen Y-ers are getting their news from comedians and talk show hosts, their standards for their news sources are a lot lower than those of the older viewers advertisers shun. If it really is all the same to younger audiences, and a comedian, talk show host and pundit are equally viable sources for news, then what has journalism been reduced to? Snappy opinions and sound bites devoid of context, facts and analysis?

This is hardly elitist snobbery: doctors, accountants, lawyers and even hair stylists are licensed and trained to do their jobs properly. Journalists are not licensed and many aren't trained, and news gathering skills take time and experience to develop; however, they are being replaced with people who have no qualms with infecting the information stream with uninformed opinion just so they get to mug for the camera for another five seconds. Worse, those who give a forum to the opinion-spewers are actively encouraging unqualified people to disseminate information—and leading the charge to make journalists obsolete is the Fox News Network.

Murdoch-O-Vision: The world's reality tunnel.

Even if Fox News is a Bush Republican faction opinion channel—why care about it at all? Isn't everyone entitled to their own opinion? True, but being entitled to an opinion is one thing: misrepresenting yourself and your facts is despicable and dangerous. If Fox News brass insist on peddling opinion instead of getting off their rear ends to dig for information, then as long as they refer to themselves as an opinion station and drop their "real journalism—fair and balanced" motto, there would be no underlying dishonesty or false pretense. But Fox News reports on events while it skews, omits and distorts critical information that can change an event's meaning and interpretation. The FNC serves up palatable propaganda: it was thanks to the network that the Iraq War looked like a justified event.

Instead of providing information, Fox News would rather make viewers feel good about themselves and their world-views. The vixen network is a reliable escort service for the nation's frustrated Republicans. Fox News yappers may wear suits, but they are no different than the cheesecakes that pose topless in Murdoch's British newspapers. Both are there to satisfy baser desires.

But that shameless pandering leads to a dilemma: when a manipulator tries to get what he wants by playing up on pigeons' false beliefs, the seducer loses respect for the audience. It's hard to respect the pigeon who is buying your lies. In the long run, Roger Ailes did not insult Paula Zahn when he retorted that a dead raccoon would do just as well in the ratings as her—you cannot have one shred of respect for your audience if that is your true belief. Fox News is dependent on the very audience that they are pandering to: without them, Murdoch and his crew are powerless. An entire empire is dependent on catering to people who have no clue as to the power they yield or the put downs they are being subjected to by the very people they are watching, but they will continue watching Ailes' parade of dead raccoons in order to prove group affiliation and brand loyalty.

However, not everyone is mesmerized by the FNC's roadkill: some people see the insults to viewers and decide to do what they can to slow down the Fox News juggernaut—by watching or doing something else. Others have done the opposite: they've taken a closer look at the newser and analyzed what they see a little more carefully.

Dumbing Down America—Fox Style

In 2003, PIPA (the Program on International Policy Attitudes) conducted a study on Americans' views and knowledge about the Iraq war. Their results were surprising: how much people knew and the accuracy of their beliefs were highly dependent on which news source they primarily relied on for their information.

The study found that viewers who relied on Fox News flunked the test: people who watched Fox held the most mistaken beliefs about the Iraq war, while those who tuned in to PBS and NPR held the fewest. The average rate for misperceptions was 45% for Fox viewers, 31% for CNN viewers, 25% for print readers and 11% for NPR/PBS listeners/viewers. Among the misconceptions:

- 67% of Fox viewers thought that the U.S. found "clear evidence in Iraq that Saddam Hussein was working closely with the al Qaeda terrorist organization." Only 16% of PBS/NPR audiences believed the same erroneous factoid. Even more illuminating, 78% of Bush supporters who watched Fox News thought that there was evidence of ties between Iraq and al Qaeda, while 50% of Bush supporters who tuned in to NPR/PBS held the same mistaken belief (on the other hand 48% of Democratic supporters who watched Fox thought so, while 0% of Democratic supporters who tuned in to NPR/PBS did).

- 33% of Fox viewers thought U.S. soldiers found WMD in Iraq, while 20% of CNN and 11% of NPR/PBS viewers/listeners did.

- 35% of Fox News viewers mistakenly believed that the U.S. war against Iraq had international support, while 5% of NPR/PBS consumers thought that.

- Republican Fox News viewers had more mistaken beliefs than those Republicans who tuned in to NPR/PBS.

Political affiliation had very little to do with swallowing misinformation. Those who watch the Fox News Channel got their facts all wrong. That's hardly why someone invests time watching a newscast—they expect to not have their minds stuffed with garbage. But at the FNC, that's exactly what happened in this case—and they couldn't pin their factual bungling on those pesky elite liberal media people.

Making the News Fit the Demographic

In one 2004 Pew study, respondents were asked about the media outlets they read and watch, as well as their political affiliations and background. Among the findings:

- In 2000, 18% of Republican respondents watched Fox News, by 2002, the number had grown to 25% and by 2004 it had increased to 35%.

- The typical cable news viewer is male and conservative: 43% of respondents who said they were regular cable news viewers described themselves as conservative; only 14% of regular cable news respondents called themselves liberal. Of regular cable news viewers, 41% were male and 35% were female. 49% of male respondents who were over fifty said they watched cable news regularly; 35% of female respondents who were between the ages of thirty to forty-nine responded similarly.

◆ 46% of respondents who were over 65 regularly watched cable news, compared to 29% of respondents who were eighteen to twenty-nine.

◆ Of the Republican respondents, 45% said they liked their news to share their personal point of view, while 36% of Democrats and 29% of Independents felt the same way.

Some interesting patterns emerged for Bill O'Reilly fanboys:

◆ Despite his insistence that he is politically independent, 72% of respondents who watched the "O'Reilly Factor" described themselves as conservative; the only personality to have a higher score was Rush Limbaugh at 77%. Interestingly, in 2002, only 56% of regular "Factor" viewers saw themselves as conservative.

◆ Ironically, despite O'Reilly using his show as a soapbox to air his own gripes and opinions, 49% of respondents who sought hard news stories watched the "Factor."

◆ 34% of respondents who watch the "Factor" were college graduates; 52% were over the age of fifty.

◆ The typical "Factor" viewer is male, over fifty, white and a Republican.

A FAIR and Balanced Study

Fairness and Accuracy in Reporting has also conducted several studies on the content of the FNC. When FAIR first analyzed the content of Fox News broadcasts in 2001, 71% of one-on-one guests on "Special Report With Brit Hume" were conservatives. Though the ratio has improved somewhat, the FNC is still by and large a GOP love-fest.

The latest study consisted of twenty-five weeks of monitoring one-on-one interviews on "Special Report." There were 101 guests in total, and FAIR found the following:

◆ 57% of "Special Report" guests were conservatives, 20% were non-ideological, 12% were centrists, while only 11% were progressives.

◆ Of forty-two partisan guests that were interviewed, seven were Democrats, but thirty-five were Republican. Of the seven Democrats that made the Fox cut, most were centrist or conservative.

◆ "Special Report" guests were predominantly white males; in 2003, the only woman of color to be interviewed was National Security Advisor Condoleezza Rice. In terms of percentages, in 2002, FAIR found that only 7% of guests were women and 11% were nonwhite. Of the seven women who did snag a seat, four were conservative and two were centrists. No woman interviewed was a progressive.

PIPA Knowledge/Networks Poll — October 2003

Has the U.S. Found WMD in Iraq?

Fox viewers who say yes	33%
PBS-NPR viewers/listeners who say yes	11%

Does World Opinion Favor the U.S. Invasion of Iraq?

Fox viewers who say yes	35%
PBS-NPR viewers/listeners who say yes	5%

Has the U.S. Found Links Between Iraq and al Qaeda?

Fox viewers who say yes	67%
PBS-NPR viewers/listeners who say yes	16%

◆ Of the seven guests of color, five were conservative and one was progressive.

Steve Rendall of FAIR noted, "We found that Republicans appeared five times as often as Democrats on "Special Report," one on one, newsmaker interviews. That means that made up 83% of the partisan guests on the show. In addition, the few Democrats that were interviewed for the show tended to be centrist and conservative Democrats often brought on to affirm Bush administration policies." As Rendall noted, "For instance, Jim Marshall, a Democratic representative from Georgia who is a centrist, or Senator Zell Miller, a conservative Democrat who is actively campaigning for George W. Bush."

Peter Hart made an interesting observation about the awkward role Brit Hume plays on the Fox News Channel:

> On Sunday when Brit Hume is saying there is no reason to believe Richard Clarke; he's partisan; he has an ax to grind. Well, on Monday through Friday, does the fact that he thinks Richard Clarke has zero credibility enter into Brit Hume's mind? Of course it does. And that's where you see the main bias at Fox in the "news" is the story selection; what's important, what's elevated to a certain position. What stories are not considered very key to understanding the world that week. So stories that undermine someone like Richard Clarke, those are the stories that you'll see...

Hart also observed that "when you watch the newscasts, you watch Peter Jennings and 'Special Report With Brit Hume' on Fox, it's very different news [...] Fox is motivated by a political agenda and that, I think, skews the stories they select and the stories they tend to diminish." He adds, "When Fox does panel discussions and roundtables, they are overwhelmingly biased in favor of conservative voices...

Fox takes a tendency in the media to emphasize conservative voices and just runs away with it to an extreme that's unlike almost anything else you'll see in mainstream journalism." Rendall noted that, "if Fox were the bastion of fairness and balance that it claims to be, we'd see a lot more balance in this prominent interview segment on the network's most prestigious show. Instead, the numbers indicate that Brit Hume and 'Special Report' choose their guests based on political consideration, rather than news judgment."

Another study conducted by the Center for Media and Public Affairs at George Mason University with Media Tenor also came to a similar conclusion. The 2004 Presidential Election proved Fox's red stripes based on a sampling of the network's political coverage:

◆ 17% of Fox News stories on Democratic candidate John Kerry were positive, while 45% of their stories on George Bush were positive, meaning that "Kerry's evaluations were negative by a five-to-one margin."

◆ In comparison, on average, 41% of network news stories on Kerry were positive, while 43% of their stories on Bush were positive.

Connecting the Dots

What do all those studies mean? Separately, each one points to a different survival tactic at Fox News, but take them together, and they say something specific about the Fox News mindset and its methods for winning more viewers.

The vixen network takes no chances; it knows exactly who's watching television and which of the largest audiences will likely fall under its spell. A smattering of lefties won't bring in decent ratings or impress advertisers who need a steady stream of loyal pro-consumerists. The above studies reveal a lot about the network's audience-building strategy:

1. Fox's ideological bent conveniently coincides with a typical cable news watcher. Television is a business and it stands to reason that if a network wants to be profitable, the programs it broadcasts should be created based on who is most likely going to be talked into watching. Rupert Murdoch's detractors have accused him of pandering and only doing what is economically pragmatic, and they may have a point. More conservatives watch cable news channels than progressives (43% versus 14%), meaning that close to half of the pool of potential viewers is conservative, while only slightly more than a tenth are progressive. Of those who are conservative, 45% like news to reflect their point of view, while 35% of progressives feel the same way.

Unlike network news where audiences are measured in the millions of viewers, cable contents itself with hundreds of thousands—or merely thousands—of viewers. The tighter margins mean that a

ratings win can be achieved by attracting one or two thousand more viewers than the next guy. Why fight to gain the less common progressive viewer who isn't as picky about the ideological bent of the news as the more plentiful conservative viewer? Cable news is a white man's distraction; the FNC is merely hunting the prey that is the most readily available.

2. Fox News guests and hosts reflect the typical demographic of cable news viewers.
People like to watch themselves and hear that their points of view are the correct ones. A network that admonishes its viewers for being immoral is not going to be as popular as one who does the opposite. Fox News caters to the grumpy old man set since they are the ones who watch cable news; women are less enthralled with rerun newsers. Older viewers still care about current events; younger audiences are generally too consumed with other media (film, music, video games) to care about who holds power over their lives. There are front and center hard news stories that affect youth (a possible looming military draft, rising tuition costs, slowing economy), but those stories aren't in demand; therefore Fox News doesn't carry them. Why bother trying to entertain an apathetic crowd when it's easier to amuse an already aroused one?

3. Fox News produces content based on ideological, not factual considerations.
Since conservative viewers tend to gravitate toward channels that cater to their own worldview, the FNC has taken out the welcome mat and set up shop as a network that caters to the ideologically rigid. This faction of Republicans turns to Fox News. Viewers may hold more misconceptions about the Iraqi war and its consequences, but that's the way they want it: they'd rather have an outlet that is willing to indulge their erroneous beliefs than have one that will challenge them with the truth. When Bill O'Reilly went mano a mano with director Michael Moore on July 27, 2004, it would be only natural for regular Fox News viewers to make the Iraq-al Qaeda link:

O'REILLY: Yes. There are terrorists in Iraq.

MOORE: Oh really? So Iraq now is responsible for the terrorism here?

O'REILLY: Iraq aided terrorists. Don't you know anything about any of that?

MOORE: So, you're saying Iraq is responsible for what?

O'REILLY: I'm saying that Saddam Hussein aided all day long.

MOORE: You're not going to get me to defend Saddam Hussein.

O'REILLY: I'm not? You're his biggest defender in the media.

MOORE: Now come on.

O'Reilly's exaggeration and misrepresentation was off the money, but his loyal viewers will believe every word he says—after all, many already think it, and their pal O'Reilly has just enabled their illusions.

Getting Away From the Fox

The Fox News Channel has begun a dangerous news trend: opinion has replaced news, yelling has replaced rational debate and manipulation has replaced information. But are television news viewers destined to watch more hateful propagandized advertorials instead of detached newscasts? Will news be a thing of the past or is there a way for news consumers to reclaim their news?

Some see the Internet as some sort of savior for news, but that assessment is a little too optimistic, according to Mark Cooper, Director of Research at the Consumer Federation of America, who noted that in a "survey in which we asked people that question very carefully, what they use, what influences their opinions about local news issues, and the Internet was almost never mentioned, which is exactly right because studies on the content of the Internet [show] that there's very little local content available on the Internet." He added that "the fascinating thing is that when you ask them where they go... [on] the Internet for their news, it turns out they go to the websites of the major TV stations and newspapers. So that the Internet is a distribution medium or mechanism, but it's not a real independent source."

> The Fox News Channel has begun a dangerous news trend. Opinion has replaced news. Yelling has replaced rational debate. Manipulation has replaced information.

Television has to compete with cyberspace for audiences—with the Internet giving access to a larger array of news sites and perspectives. But with more news outlets beginning to charge for their stories—and with the fact that the sites people turn to are ones owned by the same media conglomerates—television news is still the most cost effective way (aside from radio) to get informed. But why simply walk away from one news outlet when there are ways to make them more accountable and responsive? Besides, as John Dunbar noted:

[...T]he media itself may or may not have your best interest at heart. Chances are it doesn't have your best interest at heart. The media corporations in this country, they're beholden of their shareholders; they're not beholden of the public. So whatever sells, whatever makes them the most money, that's going to be chief on their list of priorities. What people don't realize... is that the means by which these media corporations are making their money is a public asset. They're using airwaves that are owned by the public.

The networks don't own the airwaves: all citizens do and there is no reason why those who own those airwaves can't make demands for more—not less—news (or as Dunbar referred to it, a "public interest obligation"). As *Air America* founder David Goodfriend quipped, "Here's what I'd love to have happen—a family from Nebraska goes to Washington for their family vacation. We're going to visit the Air and Space museum, we're going to visit the mall, we're going to visit the Viet Nam memorial and we're going to visit the FCC to see a commissioner or two to tell them about what we care about. When that happens, we might start to see a little more attention. It ain't going to happen if you don't try it." Yet change can't happen if citizens remain comatose and apathetic, nor will others with vested interests motivate or encourage citizens into exercising their rights, as Mountaineering

Information Network executive director Wally Brown noted:

> One thing I have come to recognize is that our current undemocratic media system treats citizens as consumers and spectators; it doesn't draw people into public life; it doesn't help people of like minds meet and organize. In fact, our media system is set up to keep people isolated and distracted and somewhat depressed about their ability to do anything. So it's a disempowering media system.

The FNC has learned a very simple, but effective parlor trick: as long as its newscasts cater to esteem-building, rather than beefing up the editorial content, they will attract a loyal following. So how does someone inoculate themselves from the agitating effects of Foxaganda? It's easy if you can not only spot lies from fact, but also learn how to think just like a real Fox News kid.

Chapter 18

Thinking Outside the Fox

*"I figured [Mort Zuckerman] would assume
that I would assume that he was misleading me,
and would never print what would have been a
great scoop. So I did."*

Rupert Murdoch on why he had ordered the *New York Post*
to run the erroneous and infamous front page story that
Democratic Presidential nominee John Kerry picked
Dick Gephardt as his running mate

Frank Zappa may have described rock journalism as "people who can't write interviewing people who can't talk for people who can't read," but Fox News journalism could be described as people who can't report fairly reporting about people who can't take criticism for people who can't cope. What Fox promises is a simple world with simple heroes and even simpler villains. Everything about life is conveniently packaged and served in digestible and edible bites.

Except, of course, that life is a messy complicated affair with messy and complicated people. Political or ideological allegiance to the right gives no one immunity from making mistakes or being colossally in the wrong. Fox News brass may try to pretend that they give an accurate and truthful account of unfolding events because they claim to be "fair and balanced." Unfortunately, neither the word fair nor the word balanced remotely implies truthfulness or accuracy. Anyone watching the FNC and expecting a straightforward newscast is naïve. A viewer has to ignore the shivering American flags, the come-ons, the flash, the façade and the attitude in order not to be taken in.

When it comes to truth in advertising, the FNC's motto is troubling, but at least it can be construed as being honest—so long as you are good at parsing phrases. Fox News is fair, but only to certain people. The FNC is balanced, but it balances opinion with entertainment. Fox News is a lot of things, but it almost always skirts around the issue of what it isn't. Though it continues to insist that its product is "real journalism," its content and delivery only seem like reenactments of the real thing. If

we were to take "real journalism" to be whatever the FNC presents, then real journalism must mean adhering to these following principles:

◆ Holding prolonged and recalcitrant grudges against critics and reporting on such personal vendettas as if they were newsworthy events;

◆ Spending hours engaged in petty quibbling and bickering over past events that are of no usefulness to the average viewer;

◆ Speculating on future events without data, expertise or research;

◆ Speculating on someone's motives without sufficient information;

◆ Hosts offering uninformed opinions about non-newsworthy events;

◆ Interviewing poorly mannered and uninformed people with no real life credentials or logical relevance for their advice and opinions;

◆ Interviewing other journalists on topics they do not cover;

◆ Resorting to name calling and bullying of critics or guests;

◆ Becoming a disgruntled former employer because one employee left to work somewhere else;

◆ Inviting guests on a news show to explain their positions, then preventing them from explaining their positions by cutting off their microphones or repeatedly interrupting them while they speak;

◆ Obsessing over the fortunes of rivals instead of concentrating on improving the editorial content;

◆ Underreporting and ignoring bad domestic news;

◆ Overreporting or exaggerating good domestic news;

◆ Hosts, journalists and anchors disseminating information in an angry or jeering demeanor;

◆ Wasting airtime promoting and endorsing products of guests who are expected to offer analysis to viewers;

◆ Openly praising certain guests on air;

◆ Getting angry or critical towards others for living their lives on their own terms;

◆ Equating someone who has a different nonviolent political ideology with being a terrorist;

◆ Reporting on foreign news without having a sufficient number of foreign bureaus;

◆ Disseminating information without proper investigation;

- Engaging in personal attacks and using logical flaws (e.g., artificial forced choice, appeal to authority) as a legitimate reporting style;

- Scraping information from other television networks, then not giving proper attribution;

- Not removing reporters who have a conflict of interest from their assignments;

- Asking guests loaded questions.

If spoiled and unruly children ran the news, they too would most likely adhere to the above Fox News principles. The Fox News formula decrees that partisan and sensational stories are interwoven with uninformed opinion and eye candy. The obsession with toys, coolness, sarcasm, laziness, personal wants, threats, attention and temper tantrums dominates the FNC airwaves, while civility, hard work, patience and respect for others are nowhere to be found. What can be found is a rotating roster of predictable stories told in predictable ways. The news value of the stories themselves will be low, but they will be presented in a way that suggests viewers are being actively informed. However, looking at typical FNC stories makes you wonder what audiences are really getting informed about:

1. Nice dead women.

Laci Peterson, Dru Sjodin, Tamara Dunstan and Lori Hacking were all, by all accounts, very nice and attractive women who led private lives with their families. Though each lived in different parts of the country and held different jobs, these all-American beauties shared one disturbing trait in common: they were gruesomely murdered and their bodies were callously dumped in demeaning resting places.

Despite the traumatic implication for the victims' families, these are local stories that shake individual communities and, for the most part, squarely belong in the pages and airwaves of the town's local media. But if there is a murder of a pretty young thing, Fox News will be there to play up on the sensational details, though some of those details may be lacking. During one April 19, 2004 teaser for "On the Record," Greta Van Susteren simply referred to Dunstan as that "pregnant twenty-nine-year-old woman in Georgia."

Fox News must love dead lovelies an awful lot, since they air so many stories about them. Sometimes the cadaverous cutie in question was accused of naughty antics, such as Chandra Levy, who had an affair with a married politician, but for the most part these women are the saintly everyday victims who did nothing to deserve their cruel fate. The soccer mom set can clearly identify with these women. What woman couldn't identify with Laci Peterson; the pretty and genial-looking Californian mother-to-be with the megawatt smile whose body was thrown into a watery grave? And for what reason?

It was an important local story that took national headlines, but the FNC treatment of the case was less than respectful. The network shamelessly played up on the gory details as Geraldo Rivera's soliloquy did on May 15, 2003:

RIVERA: Let me just give people a caution before I start this [...]It can take some graphic details as to the state of what was done to twenty-seven-year-old Laci Peterson and by extension to her unborn son, Connor.

As Fox News reported exclusively yesterday and despite repeated denials by the coroner and other officials involved, the parties in the Peterson murder case, that is the prosecutor and the defense, have received copies of the victims' autopsies. That according to John Gould, the deputy chief district chief attorney of Stanislaus County.

The delay up until now has been [a] long three months, [and] was apparently caused by the difficulty in pinpointing the cause of Laci's, quote, "horrendous death." That from a defense source.

How horrendous? Quote, "awful, awful, awful." That's what I was told last night by a highly placed, very reliable source within the defense camp.

[...] The source then went on to recount some injuries allegedly suffered by Laci. Quote, "She was carved up," the source told me. "And the head is not the only part that is missing," end quote.

When Peterson's husband Scott was arrested and put on trial for her murder, the FNC, particularly "On the Record" and the "O'Reilly Factor," had discussed the micro-details of Scott's affair with one Amber Frey whose taped telephone conversations with Peterson were salacious nightly fodder for their programs. Melodrama and superlatives are used to describe the grisly details of each new sensational trial. In one August 2004 broadcast, Stan Goldman told Bill O'Reilly with a straight face that he had "tried 300 cases as a criminal lawyer. This was, this morning, one of the most dramatic, perhaps the most dramatic, and I'm talking about some major things, that I sat in on the McVeigh trial, for example, one of the most dramatic mornings ever spent in a courtroom." That a simple homicide was more dramatic than the mass slaughter of innocent men, women and children is a chilling idea—was it more chilling because the victim was more photogenic than those in Oklahoma?

2. Naughty naked women.

Though Fox News stories and guests tend to skew male, it doesn't mean that women can't get an invite to the newser. While some of those women who are considered newsworthy enough to warrant coverage aren't actually breathing, sometimes a real live woman is deemed newsworthy, too. The problem is, sometimes you have to get naked in order to get the FNC treatment.

If you're too shy about reading *Adult Video News* to find out what's happening with your favorite porn star, the vixen network will gladly give you an update. Of course the anchors will harshly chastise and insult these surgically enhanced nymphets, but don't forget that the spanking and domineering of easy women is a fine, long standing tradition for the sexually debauched.

This is not to say that all female guests are required to be in an X-rated film to get to be a guest on one of FNC's programs; in fact some female guests are employed elsewhere (heck, even Janeane Garofalo was allowed on "Hannity and Colmes" without being escorted out by bouncers). It's just that in a world full of female newsmakers, women who make their living in the sex trade are over-represented on the FNC. Those career nymphets are brought in or discussed in less-than-respectful terms; they are to be slapped about and insulted to help the folks back home feel more moral than the guests.

But even if a woman isn't a porn star, if she shows her breasts in public, she is going to be treated just as roughly. For example, a grampaw-esque Bill O'Reilly gave Janet Jackson a what-for for exposing her breast on CBS' Super Bowl half-time program on his February 5, 2004 show:

> **O'REILLY:** Bad behavior must be confronted. And for far too long, it has not been in our popular culture. Time after time, people excuse bad behavior by pointing to worse behavior. That is intellectually dishonest and leads to no standards at all.
>
> As "Talking Points" mentioned, the Janet Jackson situation is a huge loss for the secular movement in America because now everybody knows that anything goes in our culture. And people are starting to get angry.

O'Reilly made Jackson sound like a hardened criminal who was capable of torturing small children:

> Those of you who are older than thirty-five can remember a country where Janet Jackson, if she did what she did, that couldn't have happened. If she flashed, say, back in the sixties, her career would have been ruined, and she might have even been arrested.
>
> Now we are more progressive, but all the secularism is redefining the country. And I think it's dangerous. The society of 300 million Americans without discipline or standards will fall apart, period.

Fox News also dedicated resources covering a porn actress' murder by a photographer and the porn industry's tizzy over the slate of HIV infections. When New York's Learning Annex was offering porn director Joe Gallant's course on making DIY adult films, Fox News jumped for the chance to interview him. If you make a career out of displaying the silicon bags that were implanted in your chest, it wouldn't hurt to send a press release to Fox News, though you may want to bring the paddle of your choice to be used against you during the interview.

3. People demanding some rights.

Whether you call it hypocrisy, poor memory, lack of ideological continuity, lousy logic or just plain psychotic thinking, according to the Fox News Channel, the United States is either in need of a complete overhaul, or is just fine the way it is. Either children and women are in constant danger because of perverts, Democrats or foreigners, and therefore drastic overhauling of the system is needed, or everything is just perfect with the U.S. and anyone making any demands is just plain sick. Antiwar activists don't know how good they got it, and gays who want to marry and be a family with their lovers are just trying to destroy the American family and ruin the social fabric of the country with their unpatriotic demands. So is everything just fine or falling apart according to FNC logic? So long as people do not ask for rights or freedoms in America, everything in the country is just wonderful for the Fox News Channel. Anyone pressing for the opposite is a heretic and faceless being

who is just trying to make trouble for Gertrude Whipple of Sandusky, Ohio and all of her kind.

But if those making demands look like everyone else, the FNC is likely going to quietly drop the issue without conceding that it may have been wrong in its slanted coverage. James Wolcott observed that Fox News "did stir it up on gay marriage, but I think that they got sort of blindsided, when the marriages started taking place in San Francisco; they all of a sudden couldn't show the usual footage they used to show because they [were used to showing] footage of the parades and the black leather and the drag queens. Then they had very normal-looking, dumpy, middle-aged couples getting married and smooching on the steps of City Hall; so I've noticed a certain kind of zest going out of the gay marriage thing."

4. Various bogeymen that don't look American.

Foreigners don't fare particularly well on the FNC. The "them" are usually viewed with suspicion: while foreigners who resemble Americans such as Canadians and French have gotten a verbal thrashing on the FNC, countries that are visually different from the U.S. are portrayed as even worse. Just as cults separate members from their family and friends, the FNC seems to work overtime in isolating the United States from its global brothers and sisters.

If the foreign country in question is also at odds with the U.S., coverage will be especially unfavorable. As John Gibson opined on the August 18, 2004 edition of his program the "Big Story With John Gibson":

> **GIBSON:** Yes, but, [in] general, the South Koreans are undergoing rampant anti-Amer-
> icanism at any given moment. They are trying to kiss and make up with North
> Korea and the sunshine policy. Surely there is a point at which we don't need
> 37,000 Americans in South Korea and certainly not up there in the DMZ. Where
> the crazy men in the North could incinerate them in a moment's notice.

Maligning the rest of the planet may be a cynically enterprising way of making alternate information and analysis seem less credible in viewers' eyes, but sooner or later, picking on an expanding list of nations also means maligning a viewer's heritage. It's a risky gambit, but the FNC still knocks foreign countries and their mindsets, anyway.

5. Snappy, happy wars.

The FNC's presentation of easy, fun and bloodless wars doesn't seem the least bit realistic or possible, but Americans still tune in to the vixen network to get their information about the Iraq war. The Iraq war looked like an easy victory for both American troops and President Bush, but when the U.S. soldier death toll after the so-called conclusion overtook the toll during the battle, the FNC's coverage looked suspect. As Dave Korb noted:

> The [Iraq] war had begun taking a turn for the worse, and it was becoming clear that
> maybe President Bush had jumped the gun in announcing "Mission Accomplished."
> The senior producer told the two or three writers for her news hour for which she was

responsible, "now just keep in mind, it's all good. This is such a fair and balanced issue. Don't write about the number of dead or troops being under fire or under attack. Not that somebody might have died, keep it positive. We've got to emphasize all the good that we're doing." I think she, at that point, made a reference to rebuilding schools, bringing democracy into Iraq, and then she said, "see? Big progress. Hoo hoo for us." Things were actually, at that point, going quite badly.

Korb recalled the orders he received about his producer's sins of omission:

> The same senior producer told us when it was clear that there were no weapons of mass destruction to be found in Iraq, she said, "Leads, copy teasers. We make no mention of WMD. It's just making the problem worse."

Korb also recalled that another senior producer did not want to make mention of WMD because Fox News couldn't "bring attention to it."

But writers could bring attention to the actions of antiwar protesters. According to Korb, higher-ups encouraged that the protesters were to be made to look stupid, and writers were instructed to only use video that showed small crowds of protesters that seemed to embody the drugged out liberal— and that the opposition to the war was confined to a smattering minority.

The FNC's version of the Iraq War seemed like a fun exercise that benefited everyone. Iraqis who saw their homes destroyed or their family members killed by the bloodshed were grateful for the invasion without a hint of resentment or grief. As James Wolcott observed, "[Fox] showed an [American] soldier handing out flyers to Iraqi kids and the Iraqi kids laughing and waving at the camera... you almost expected the soldier to give them candy bars, but one of the things you noticed was barbed wire around the place, and... the kids weren't even looking at the fliers; so it wasn't like they were taking in the message." He adds, "There was a sense that things are not as bad as you're being told in the other media."

The fairy tale images of war may have made for good television, but to get them took a little creative editing, as John Nichols noted: "When the statue of Saddam Hussein was torn down in that square in Baghdad, Americans saw, especially on Fox... repeated images day after day of the statue coming down. In fact Fox made it into a promo advertisement that they ran all the time on the network[...] The Brits—remember, our partners in this war—saw the BBC and Reuters photographs and images of it which were of the whole square which of course showed that the square was essentially empty. There was a small wrecking crew that came in to take the statue down and it was all a matter of how you framed the photo. The Fox network especially framed the photo so close that it looked like there was a teeming mass of happy Iraqis... taking down the statue."

Clean war coverage is propaganda, plain and simple. As Bruce Page noted, "I regard Fox as simply a government propaganda system. Its coverage of the war in Iraq is a major disgrace. You would have to look at a Soviet system or indeed a Chinese one to find a bias towards the government as insane, as unprofessional as this." Page added that, "the kind of stuff that Fox... puts out... simply has no relation to serious news coverage of any kind at all... To pretend that the First Amendment

gives you the right to pump out government propaganda in wartime is nonsense [...N]obody in the war business in America should imagine that Rupert is a stalwart battler who will see it through to the end because if it starts going pear shaped, Murdoch will be out of there so fast you won't see him." But Peter Hart summed it up best when he said, "Any time you're sending Geraldo Rivera into war zones as your correspondent, it does demonstrate that you're not serious about journalism."

6. Protecting the Bush Republican enclave at all costs.

A true democracy allows for different people to hold different political beliefs and not automatically assume that either side is wrong. People have differing life requirements: an inner city teacher battling breast cancer has different needs than a wealthy man who is getting pistol whipped by a disgruntled former employee. A young person who opposes war is not an idealist since he knows that if his country chooses to force him to enlist, he would likely lose his health, sanity or life in the bargain. To savage someone for believing in the importance of health care, peace or policing is revealing a profound lack of empathy, logic and emotion. A true news network presents multiple sides of an issue from multiple perspectives. People have competing interests and conflicts; it is those conflicts that make news. As Nichols noted, "I think it's fair to say that what Fox does is they start with the end of the story. They start with the conclusion and then they work back to create a story that tells it." Fox News simply frowns upon complexity and personal choice: when a news outlet decides to take sides in those disputes, it turns the news outfit into a propaganda mill.

Same to You, Pal!

Fox News has no remorse; it does not believe in self-analysis or anything that resembles a mea culpa. Being a Fox News kid means never having to say you're sorry. Bill O'Reilly can continue to destroy the reputation of Jeremy Glick and Al Franken. Sean Hannity can continue to demonize people who do not agree with his childish worldview. O'Reilly can call people idiots and Sean Hannity can accuse progressives of having nefarious motives on national television, and neither ever has to worry about issuing a retraction or an apology.

On and off camera, there is a deep and disturbing sickness somewhere in the dark and malodorous bowels of the Fox News Channel that compels employees to not only attack, but to destroy their critics' reputations. When a critic does voice a complaint against the FNC, they usually respond in one of these predictable and clichéd ways:

- The critic is mentally unstable or, as Fox spokesman Rob Zimmerman once so eloquently stated, "nuts." Whether anyone at Fox has the appropriate degree or state license to make these sensitive diagnoses is questionable, but it has been employed;

- The critic is jealous of Fox's success;

- The critic is a poor sport with no sense of humor;

- The critic is petty and/or pathetic;

- The critic is a "media whore" who is looking for attention at the expense of Fox;

- The critic is a "nobody." This form of critic-emasculation should be the most troublesome for Fox viewers: most of them are "nobodies" in the sense that they aren't famous or powerful, which means that if any one of them disagreed with an FNC stand, they too would be dismissed as a "nobody." Isn't it nice that the network you watch has such a low opinion of you? Does that mean that only the rich, famous or powerful are entitled to criticize? Are regular citizens to be relegated to the "put up and shut up" dumpyard?

Of course, the seething attack dogs at Fox can think of other, more decrepit put-downs when the situation warrants. Just remember that, according to FNC logic, the critic is never in the right or even entitled to a difference in opinion: he is just a bad, vindictive and unbalanced person trying to make trouble.

Even dissatisfied viewers aren't immune from a Fox bite. Bill O'Reilly must have the most fun, insulting viewers who disagree with him while endlessly justifying his callow behavior:

- November 13, 2002: "'Bill, you're rapidly losing me as a viewer. Your debates are supposed to be meaningful, not feature emotional outbursts.' Well, Mr. Heaney, this isn't NPR. Sometimes emotion is appropriate."

- July 8, 2002: "About my interview with the President of the American Atheist Group, Renee Gossen, Charlotte, NC. 'O'Reilly, they say bias is like a backpack. You can't see your own. You were very rude and arrogant to atheist Ellen Johnson. You use your media power to promote your beliefs and exclude others.' Hey Ms. Gossen, that's a bunch of baloney and you know it. "

- December 6, 2001: "'O'Reilly, I've been watching Chris Matthews on MSNBC, but thought he was too harsh with his guests. So I switched to you. But after watching you cut off those parents in New Hampshire, I became very upset. I'm a parent who would not let my child watch that horrific terror attack. You are arrogant and rude, and I will not watch you again.' Well, you seem to be a very sensitive person, Ms. Wilkinson, so perhaps the No Spin Zone is a bit too much for you."

Buy My Book!

The trendy way to gain fame in modern-day America takes one of two forms: win first prize on a soap opera game show or get a bratty shtick down pat, come up with a few sassy lines for the nice audience and then try to stretch those few catch phrases to a lucrative book that can be plugged by the hosts of various Fox News shows. No Oprah book club needed for these pundits—they have the Fox News book club shill it for them.

Hawking the books of various hosts and guests is a common feature on the fair and balanced network. Perhaps it is a form of sly product placement, but whatever the reason, Republicans can expect endorsement of their various works:

◆ On the April 12, 2004 edition of "Hannity and Colmes":

COLMES: [...W]e're joined by Fox News military analyst Lieutenant General Tom Mc-Inerney and Major General Paul Vallely who have written a new book called *Endgame: The Blueprint for Victory in the War on Terror*, a fascinating book whether we agree or disagree. A well-written book.

HANNITY: (later on): Let me first applaud both of you. *Endgame: The Blueprint for Victory in the War on Terror*, this is a great book, folks. This is what it is.

◆ On the January 6, 2003 "Hannity and Colmes":

HANNITY: We're continuing with nationally syndicated radio talk show host superstar Dr. Laura Schlessinger. Her new book is called *The Proper Care and Feeding of Husbands*. By the way, I read almost all of it tonight. It's an easy read and I loved it. It's a great book.

◆ Another shameless plug for Dr. Laura on the August 4, 2004 "Hannity and Colmes":

HANNITY: [...J]oining us first is the author of *Woman Power*. Well, it's—and by the way, this is destined to be a best seller. *Transform Your Man, Your Marriage, Your Life*. This was a great idea. First of all, I love the first...

SCHLESSINGER: It wasn't mine.

HANNITY: Who was it? It's your book.

SCHLESSINGER: The readers of *The Proper Care and Feeding of Husbands* kept writing to me and saying, "We need more information. We want questions to ask ourselves, things to do, things to think about. We get in women's groups; we're in church groups. We need more information." It really came from the readers.

HANNITY: You know—you know what's really cool about this book? I mean this sincerely, and you should be proud of yourself.

◆ Clinton living nightmare Ken Starr got his plug on October 15, 2002:

HANNITY: All right, joining us finally now is Ken Starr, author of the great new book, *First Among Equals: The Supreme Court in American Life*. All right, we're going to have to bring you back, Ken, because we don't have a lot of time here. Congratulations on a great book.

◆ On the November 22, 2002 edition of his show, Hannity lavished praise on Senator Orrin Hatch's literary efforts:

HANNITY: Joining us now, our good friend, the next chairman of the Senate Judiciary Committee, Utah Senator Orrin Hatch. And by the way, terrific, terrific read. I read this book, *Square Peg: Confessions of a Citizen Senator*. I enjoyed it, Senator. Congratulations on a great book.

HATCH: Well, thank you. I've had people all over the country say they're really enjoying it because they're getting some of the really behind the scenes information. But I loved your book, too. I got to tell you, it's selling well all over the country.

HANNITY: Thank you. Well, thank you, Senator. I'm proud of it. You did a good job with it.

◆ Michael Savage got this Hannity endorsement on January 17, 2003, "It's a great book. Get it."

◆ J.C. Watts was praised by Hannity on October 22, 2002: "*What Color is a Conservative: My Life, My Politics.* I've been reading it. It's a great book. This is destined to be a bestseller, ladies and gentlemen. Congratulations."

The "great book" plug was also used to describe Oliver North, Bill Bennett, G. Gordon Liddy, Jeannie Pirro and Dick Armey books, too. That doesn't mean that there have been other less-than-creative ways that the Fox News kids have peddled wares to the people they are supposed to be informing:

◆ Tony Snow plugged regular contributor Juan Williams' book on February 2, 2003: "...Juan Williams, national correspondent for National Public Radio and author of, among other books, his latest, *This Far by Faith*, fresh off the presses. Go buy it— that's an order."

It seems like a lot of work to insult guests, hustle guests' books and also plug their own work on their shows, but somehow FNC personalities have the energy, as Hannity did on January 28, 2004: "It's a great book, and it's in bookstores everywhere. I put it on my website, hannity.com. If people want to get it there."

Alan Colmes "interviewed" Hannity on his second effort on February 16, 2003:

COLMES: His first book, *Let Freedom Ring*, was a *New York Times* best seller. His new book is sure to be a success, already doing well on Amazon.com.

Joining us for a "Hannity & Colmes" exclusive—how did we get him—the author of *Deliver Us From Evil: Defeating Terrorism, Despotism and Liberalism*, my co-host and friend, Sean Hannity.

HANNITY: We can be friends.

COLMES: That's right.

HANNITY: Even though—thank you.

COLMES: You want to start already. I'll ask the questions. I telegraphed the question last week, the first question.

HANNITY: You did.

COLMES: The title, *Defeating Terrorism, Despotism and Liberalism*. Are you then equating liberalism with terrorism and despotism?

HANNITY: Now that you've read the book—you did read it?

COLMES: I did read a good part of it.

The FNC has perfected the art of the twenty-four hour commercial; getting the twenty-four hour news thing's been just a little harder.

Trained Parakeets

Repetitive phrases are easy to spot on Fox News, and the FNC uses the same phrases liberally. Left-wingers will be described as "weak"; right-wingers will be described as "strong" and "brave." It is never just the "media"; competitors are the "elite liberal media." Bill O'Reilly can be counted on to say any number of phrases over and over again.

Even Fox spokespeople are frighteningly uniform in their responses to their various critics, as the following excerpts show:

- ◆ In the September 11, 2001 edition of the *Atlanta Journal and Constitution*: "'The numbers speak for themselves,' Fox News spokesman Robert Zimmerman said of the report."

- ◆ In the October 29, 2002 edition: "'The numbers speak for themselves,' Fox News spokeswoman Tracey Spector said of the "Hannity and Colmes" victory."

- ◆ In the April 10, 2003 edition of *USA Today*: "'The numbers speak for themselves,' says Fox News spokeswoman Irena Steffen."

The phrase is meaningless: it does not address the quality or accuracy of the information presented, nor does it address the criticism directly. The statement is a dodge used to dismiss criticism while evading the real issue. The numbers may "speak for themselves," but since millions of Americans do not watch Fox News, what do these publicists have to say about *those* numbers?

The FNC may shy away from digging for real and credible sources, but they do have their own version of Deep Throat, called "Some People Say." As Hart noted:

> Other journalists use phrases like "some people say" or "officials say" when they're trying to insert anonymous information in a story that sort of advances the storyline. Fox does it a different way. "Some people say" is Fox's cue that there is a political opinion that we're trying to push here, and we don't have a guest on to say this. I'm pretending to be an anchor; so I can't say this is my opinion, or this is Roger Ailes' opinion, but "some people say." Journalistically, it's a very peculiar technique because the idea behind journalism is that you're sourcing who you're referring to. You're talking to people on the record and you're using their names. This is just sort of a clever way of inserting political opinion when you know it probably shouldn't be there."

Some people also say that the earth is flat and that goat's eggs exist, but none of those people are credible. What people? How credible are they? Who are they? You may ask, but don't expect a Fox News kid to get off his keester and find out for you.

Outfoxing the Fox

A serious-looking guy standing in front of the White House holding a microphone and wearing a suit and tie is just a serious-looking guy standing in front of the White House holding a microphone and wearing a suit and tie. The fact that a television camera is recording his every word and that those images are dancing on your television screen means nothing. What is this man telling you? Why is he telling you this? What are his qualifications and intentions? What is his proof? What research did he do? Where did he get his information and how reliable are his sources? How free is he to speak the truth? Who is this man's employer and what values and motives does he hold?

The serious-looking guy standing in front of the White House holding a microphone and wearing a suit and tie can only be a journalist if he's digging, pushing, researching, probing, analyzing, consulting, fighting, taking abuse from evasive sources and standing up to those bullies; otherwise, he's an impostor.

The Fox News Channel has perfected the real journalism look and lingo to the point of looking *better* than your average TV news outfit. Their reality is better than the one we've been given. They can stand up to criticism better in their studios than they can outside them. Their arguments seem sacrosanct against the critics they choose to challenge them on their programs, but hardly so to the ones that they don't. The Fox News world seems more certain and simple than the one in which it's housed. Even the women who prance on their programs look hotter than the ones walking the streets. Good and evil are separate and distinct entities that are easily identifiable. Solutions to problems can be found falling from the lips of the all-knowing hosts.

The fairy tale world of the Murdochian kingdom is an epic one of heroes and villains; valiant knights and deadly dragons. King Murdoch's ever-expanding empire grows at the expense of the reputations of his critics and rivals; the FNC has become his most powerful weapon in inoculating and protecting his kingdom from the assaults of criticism and competition. With the FNC, Murdoch has created a safe haven for disenfranchised viewers seeking shelter from a seemingly brutal reality; the price they may have to pay in the long run for the hospitality isn't considered. They may feel comfort in watching the knights throwing mud at people the warriors assure the public are their enemies, but the unevenly matched opponents don't seem to clue in the audience that perhaps the beaten enemies may not be a threat at all. Few of the refugees question the filthy weapon of choice.

A news channel like the FNC wouldn't have been possible without promiscuous media consolidation: in the drive to become the biggest, the richest and the most powerful media company, many companies never considered also trying to be the best, most informative or the most useful information provider. The Fox News Channel was created in order to dominate rivals in the race for ratings, not quality. News was gathered on the cheap, but the FNC reached its goal, breaking the backs of rivals and critics one person at a time. Murdoch, with the help of Roger Ailes, John Moody, Brit Hume and Bill O'Reilly, created a news powerhouse that is run on opinion, vitriol, flash and attitude, but not on actual news.

Viewers looking for truth in their news should look to multiple sources from multiple outlets. Getting divergent voices and sources becomes increasingly difficult in today's media's shrinking landscape— but citizens have an obligation to themselves and their country to look for the raw, unfiltered and sometimes homely truth, wherever it may lie.

But wherever the truth resides, it isn't on the Fox News Channel.

References

Interview Transcripts

Alterman, Eric.
Anonymous ex-FNC employee 1.
Anonymous ex-FNC employee 2.
Anonymous ex-FNC employee 3.
Barkin, Joel.
Brock, David.
Brown, Wally.
Burnett, David.
Cafasso, Joseph.
Chester. Jeff.
Cohen, Jeff.
Cooper, Mark.
Cronkite, Walter.
Cyril, Malkia.
Dunbar, John.
Dupree, Jon.
Franken, Al.
Frenk, Clara.
Glick, Jeremy.
Goodfriend, David.
Green, Mark.
Hart, Peter.
Hill, Len.
Johnson, Larry.
Kimmelman, Gene.
Kippen, Alexander.
Korb, Dave.
McChesney, Bob.
Miller, Mark.
Mirsky, Jonathan.
Morantz, Paul.
Nichols, John.
O'Donnell, Frank.
Page, Bruce.
Pingree, Chellie.
Rendall, Steve.
Sanders, Bernie.
Westin, Av.
Winthrop, Diana.
Woolcott, James.

Memos

Burke, J. (2003). May 3.
Gaffney, B. (2003). May 2, May 9.
Lacorte, K. (2004). April 9.
Moody, J. (2003). May 9, May 22, May 29, June 2, June 3.
Moody, J. (2004). March 12, March 16, March 19, March 23, March 25, March 26, March 31, April 1, April 4, April 6, April 8, April 18, April 20, April 21, April 22, April 23, April 26, April 27, April 28, April 30, May 3, May 4, May 5.

Broadcast Transcripts
Fox News Channel

"The Beltway Boys" (2004). "Trail Dust: Gay Marriage Hot Potato." February 14.
"The Beltway Boys" (2004). "Trail Dust: Pulling Ahead?" October 1.

"The Big Story With John Gibson" (2004). "What's the Best Way to Stabilize Iraq?" May 21.
"The Big Story With John Gibson" (2004). "How Do We Stop the Terrorists?" June 18.
"The Big Story With John Gibson" (2004). "Did Kerry Flip Flop on Redeployment?" August 18.
"The Big Story With John Gibson" (2004). "Can Kerry Make Up Lost Ground?" September 7.
"The Big Story With John Gibson" (2004). "Campaign Messages: Which Side Is Winning?" October 4.
"The Big Story With John Gibson" (2004). "How Will Edwards' Trial Skills Help Him in the Debate?" October 5.
"The Big Story With Rita Cosby" (2003). "Interview With Tabitha Stevens." November 8.
"The Big Story With Rita Cosby" (2004). "FOX Exclusive: Defense Secretary Donald Rumsfeld." October 2.
"Cavuto Business Report" (1999). "Boeing – CFO – Interview." October 14.
"Cavuto Business Report" (1999). "AT&T Business Services – President – Interview." December 7.
"Cost of Freedom" (2004). "Bulls and Bears." May 8.
"Cost of Freedom" (2004). "Cavuto on Business." July 17.
"Cost of Freedom" (2004). "Bulls and bears." July 31.
"Fox Files" (1999). "A New Exotic Dancer." March 11.
"Fox Files" (1999). "Pornography Industry." March 25.
"Fox Files" (1999). "Russian Sex Industry." May 27.
"Fox Files" (1999). "Prostitution Parties." June 3.
"Fox News Sunday" (2003). "Below the Fold." April 20.
"Fox News Sunday" (2003). "Secretary Rumsfeld with Tony Snow." May 4.
"Fox News Sunday" (2003). "Iraqi Administrator L. Paul Bremer on 'Fox News Sunday.'" August 24.
"Fox News Sunday" (2004). "Condoleezza Rice on 'Fox News Sunday.'" June 6.
"Fox News Sunday" (2004). "Condoleezza Rice on 'Fox News Sunday.'" June 27.
"Fox News Sunday" (2004). "Dowd, Gingrich on 'Fox News Sunday.'" August 1.
"Hannity and Colmes" (1999). "Interview with Michael Moore." May 24.
"Hannity and Colmes" (1999). "John F. Kennedy, Jr." July 26.
"Hannity and Colmes" (1999). "Gennifer Flowers Highlights." August 20.
"Hannity and Colmes" (2002). "Interview With Betsy Mccaughey and Laura Ingraham." January 23.
"Hannity and Colmes" (2002). "Interview With Brent Wilkes and Michelle Malkin." February 19.
"Hannity and Colmes" (2002). "Interview With Michael Moore." February 20.
"Hannity and Colmes" (2002). "Interview With Laura Ingraham and Ellen Rattner." February 28.
"Hannity and Colmes" (2002). "Interview With Ted Hayes, Maria Foscarinis." April 26.
"Hannity and Colmes" (2002). "Interview With Michelle Malkin and Chris Byrne." May 1.
"Hannity and Colmes" (2002). "Interview With Ann Coulter." June 25.
"Hannity and Colmes" (2002). "Interview With Ann Coulter." July 15.
"Hannity and Colmes" (2002). "Interview With Ann Coulter; Lynn Gold Bikin." August 2.
"Hannity and Colmes" (2002). "Interview With Oliver North." August 21.

"Hannity and Colmes" (2002). "Interview With Bill Bennett." September 10.

"Hannity and Colmes" (2002). "Interview With Michelle Malkin." September 12.

"Hannity and Colmes" (2002). "Interview With Laura Ingraham, David Corn." September 27.

"Hannity and Colmes" (2002). "Interview With Michelle Malkin." September 27.

"Hannity and Colmes" (2002). "Interview With Ken Starr." October 15.

"Hannity and Colmes" (2002). "Interview With J.C. Watts." October 22.

"Hannity and Colmes" (2002). "Did Sniper Strike In Alabama First?" October 24.

"Hannity and Colmes" (2002). "Interview With Michelle Malkin." October 24.

"Hannity and Colmes" (2002). "Interview With Larry Johnson." November 13.

"Hannity and Colmes" (2002). "Interview With G. Gordon Liddy." November 20.

"Hannity and Colmes" (2002). "Interview With Orrin Hatch." November 22.

"Hannity and Colmes" (2002). "Interview With Ellen Rattner." December 9.

"Hannity and Colmes" (2002). "Interview With Ann Coulter, Al Sharpton." December 13.

"Hannity and Colmes" (2002). "Interview With Terry O'Neill, Laura Ingraham." December 13.

"Hannity and Colmes" (2003). "Interview With Michael Savage." January 17.

"Hannity and Colmes" (2003). "Hollywood Coming Out Against War." January 22.

"Hannity and Colmes" (2003). "Did Bush administration Already Make Determination About Iraq Before Seeing Today's Report by Weapons Inspectors?" January 27.

"Hannity and Colmes" (2003). "Interview With Gloria Allred, Mike Gallagher." February 17.

"Hannity and Colmes" (2003). "Do France and Germany Have a Secret Agenda for Their War Opposition?" February 21.

"Hannity and Colmes" (2003). "Analysis With Mansoor Ijaz." March 6.

"Hannity and Colmes" (2003). "Backlash Against Dixie Chicks for Comments on Bush." March 17.

"Hannity and Colmes" (2003). "Interview With Newt Gingrich." March 25.

"Hannity and Colmes" (2003). "Interview With Newt Gingrich." April 1.

"Hannity and Colmes" (2003). "Interview With Henry Kissinger." April 3.

"Hannity and Colmes" (2003). "Analysis with Ann Coulter, Ellis Henican." May 14.

"Hannity and Colmes" (2003). "Autopsy Report Says Laci Peterson Was Cut Up." May 15.

"Hannity and Colmes" (2003). "Was Blix Objective on Iraq?" May 26.

"Hannity and Colmes" (2003). "Was Hillary Lying in Her New Book?" June 5.

"Hannity and Colmes" (2003). "Analysis with Laura Ingraham, Peter Fenn, Michael Emanuel." June 9.

"Hannity and Colmes" (2003). "Interview With Ann Coulter." June 25.

"Hannity and Colmes" (2003). "Interview With Xavier Becerra, Mike Reagan." August 1.

"Hannity and Colmes" (2003). "Interview With Michelle Malkin." August 8.

"Hannity and Colmes" (2003). "Author Says Hollywood Elite too Outspoken on Social Issues." September 15.

"Hannity and Colmes" (2003). "Interview With Alan Keyes." September 19.

"Hannity and Colmes" (2003). "Laura Ingraham and Richard on the 2004 Race." October 1.

"Hannity and Colmes" (2003). "And Justice for... Criminals?" October 6.

"Hannity and Colmes" (2003). "Is the Economy Turning Around?" October 15.

"Hannity and Colmes" (2003). "Dick Armey Publishes Book of Axioms." October 17.

"Hannity and Colmes" (2003). "Will Hillary Run for President?" October 20.

"Hannity and Colmes" (2003). "Discussion: Rumsfeld's Memo, Boykin's Religious Statements." October 22.

"Hannity and Colmes" (2003). "Are Senate Democrats Blocking a Judicial Nominee Because She's a Black Conservative?" October 23.

"Hannity and Colmes" (2003). "Analysis with Bill Bennett." December 2.

"Hannity and Colmes" (2003). "Dean Attacked for Not Releasing Records." December 5.

"Hannity and Colmes" (2004). "Interview With Former Forbes Campaign Manager Bill Dal Col." January 22.

"Hannity and Colmes" (2004). "John Kerry: Fighter or Flip-flopper?" January 27.

"Hannity and Colmes" (2004). "Interview with Pat Robertson." January 28.

"Hannity and Colmes" (2004). "Next Round of Elections to be Swan Song for Some Presidential Hopefuls?" January 28.

"Hannity and Colmes" (2004). "Will CBS Face Fines for Super Bowl Show?" February 2.

"Hannity and Colmes" (2004). "Kerry Under Fire for Changing Stance on Death Penalty for Terrorists." February 11.

"Hannity and Colmes" (2004). "Alan Interviews Sean About New Book." February 16.

"Hannity and Colmes" (2004). "Is Bush Ready for the Fight?" February 18.

"Hannity and Colmes" (2004). "Is George W. One of the Greatest Presidents?" February 19.

"Hannity and Colmes" (2004). "Interview With Michelle Malkin, Darrell Issa." February 23.

"Hannity and Colmes" (2004). "Analysis with Tony Snow." March 1.

"Hannity and Colmes" (2004). "Could Hillary Be the V.P. Choice?" March 2.

"Hannity and Colmes" (2004). "Kerry's 'Crooked Liar' Remarks Stirs Controversy." March 11.

"Hannity and Colmes" (2004). "Is Kerry Flip-Flopping on Iraq?" March 22.

"Hannity and Colmes" (2004). "Was Richard Clarke a Disgruntled Employee?" March 22.

"Hannity and Colmes" (2004). "What Do Anti-War Protesters Want?" March 22.

"Hannity and Colmes" (2004). "Bush, Kerry Battle Over Gas Prices." March 30.

"Hannity and Colmes" (2004). "Strategy to Thwart Terror At the Root." April 12.

"Hannity and Colmes" (2004). "Bush's Critics Unfair in Terrorism Critiques?" April 14.

"Hannity and Colmes" (2004). "Hannity Appears on Today Show." April 16.

"Hannity and Colmes" (2004). "U.S. Soldier Kidnapped in Iraq." April 16.

"Hannity and Colmes" (2004). "Analysis with Dick Morris." April 19.

"Hannity and Colmes" (2004). "Should Gay Couples Have a Right to Wed?" April 22.

"Hannity and Colmes" (2004). "Do Kerry's Medals Matter to the Election?" April 26.

"Hannity and Colmes" (2004). "Did Kerry Throw Away his War Medals?" April 27.

"Hannity and Colmes" (2004). "Jesse Jackson Makes Controvercial War Comments." April 27.

"Hannity and Colmes" (2004). "What Will Bush, Cheney Testify?" April 28.

"Hannity and Colmes" (2004). "Has Kerry Flip-Flopped on Abortion?" May 21.

"Hannity and Colmes" (2004). "Neil Cavuto Shares Stories of Triumphs Over Tragedy." June 1.

"Hannity and Colmes" (2004). "Dean Scream, Part Two." June 4.

"Hannity and Colmes" (2004). "Liberals Criticize Conservative Talk Radio." June 4.

"Hannity and Colmes" (2004). "Has Gore Gone Too Far?" June 14.

"Hannity and Colmes" (2004). "Teresa Kerry Draws Fire." June 15.

"Hannity and Colmes" (2004). "Did Dean Scream Speech Happen?" June 16.

"Hannity and Colmes" (2004). "Is Scott Peterson Headed for a Mistrial?" June 17.

"Hannity and Colmes" (2004). "Was Clinton Victim of Conspiracy?" June 17.

"Hannity and Colmes" (2004). "Does Clinton Book Tell the Truth?" June 21.

"Hannity and Colmes" (2004). "Does Clinton's Book Revise History?" June 22.

"Hannity and Colmes" (2004). "Gore Criticizes Bush for Linking al Qaeda and Saddam." June 24.

"Hannity and Colmes" (2004). "Should We Reinstate the Draft?" July 1.

"Hannity and Colmes" (2004). "Nader Says He'll Stay in Race." July 6.

"Hannity and Colmes" (2004). "Interview With Alan Keyes." July 12.

"Hannity and Colmes" (2004). "Newt Gingrich on Elections, WMD." July 14.

"Hannity and Colmes" (2004). "Is Republican Party Getting Too Moderate?" July 15.

"Hannity and Colmes" (2004). "Linda Ronstadt Fired for Praising Michael Moore." July 20.

"Hannity and Colmes" (2004). "Republicans to Do Damage Control in Boston." July 22.

"Hannity and Colmes" (2004). "Interview With Ann Coulter." July 26.

"Hannity and Colmes" (2004). "Interview With Janeane Garofalo." July 30.

"Hannity and Colmes" (2004). "Interview with Pat Robertson." July 30.

"Hannity and Colmes" (2004). "Interview With Robert F. Kennedy, Jr." August 3.

"Hannity and Colmes" (2004). "Dr. Laura Gives Advice to Women on Marriage." August 4.

"Hannity and Colmes" (2004). "Is Mrs. Kerry Bad for His Campaign?" August 4.

"Hannity and Colmes" (2004). "Has Kerry Changed Views on Iraq?" August 11.

"Hannity and Colmes" (2004). "Analysis With James McGreevey." August 12.

"Hannity and Colmes" (2004). "Congressman Tells Why He Jumped the Democratic Ship." August 12.

"Hannity and Colmes" (2004). "Is John Kerry Winning the Security Debate?" August 17.

"Hannity and Colmes" (2004). "Rudy Giuliani Under the GOP's Big Tent." August 25.

"Hannity and Colmes" (2004). "Interview with Mary Carey." August 27.

"Hannity and Colmes" (2004). "Is National Guard Story Evidence of Bias?" September 14.

"Hannity and Colmes" (2004). "What's the Fallout from Thursday's Debate?" October 1.

"Hannity and Colmes" (2004). "Ann Coulter Explains How to Talk to A Liberal..." October 4.

"On the Record With Greta Van Susteren" (2003). "Interview With Playboy Founder Hugh Hefner." December 5.

"On the Record With Greta Van Susteren" (2004). "Interview With Girls Gone Wild Attorney Aaron Dyer." March 10.

"On the Record With Greta Van Susteren" (2004). "Major Terror Attack on U.S. Soil for Summer?" May 25.

"On the Record With Greta Van Susteren" (2004). "Scott Says Laci Knew of Affair With Frey." August 11.

"On the Record With Greta Van Susteren" (2004). "RNC Straight Talk With John McCain." August 25.

"On the Record With Greta Van Susteren" (2004). "Giuliani: 'RNC Exceeded All Expectations.'" September 1.

"O'Reilly Factor" (1999). "Back of the Book: Al Franken." February 12.

"O'Reilly Factor" (1999). "Impact: Project No-Spank." February 23.

"O'Reilly Factor" (1999). "Impact: Avoiding Foreign Conflicts." April 7.

"O'Reilly Factor" (1999). "Impact: Business as Usual for President Clinton." May 17.

"O'Reilly Factor" (1999). "Unresolved Problems: Censoring Television." May 26.

"O'Reilly Factor" (1999). "Unresolved Problems: JonBenet Ramsey Case." July 1.

"O'Reilly Factor" (1999). "Personal Story: Choice of Sexuality." July 8.

"O'Reilly Factor" (1999). "Unresolved Problems: Russia's Biological Weapons Program." July 14.

"O'Reilly Factor" (2001). "Interview With Bill Mirro." November 2.

"O'Reilly Factor" (2001). "Mail: Fox News Conservative?" December 6.

"O'Reilly Factor" (2001). "Unresolved Problem: Interview With Michelle Malkin." December 17.

"O'Reilly Factor" (2001). "Unresolved Problem: Interview With Terry McAuliffe." December 20.

"O'Reilly Factor" (2002). "Mail: O'Reilly on O'Reilly." January 7.

"O'Reilly Factor" (2002). "Follow Up: Interview With Tammy Bruce and Laura Ingraham." January 9.

"O'Reilly Factor" (2002). "Follow Up: Interview With Gavin De Becker." February 11.

"O'Reilly Factor" (2002). "Unresolved Problem: William Baldwin." February 18.

"O'Reilly Factor" (2002). "Unresolved Problem: Interview With Vincent Cianci." March 12.

"O'Reilly Factor" (2002). "O'Reilly vs. Harvard." May 6.

"O'Reilly Factor" (2002). "Follow Up: Interview With Michelle Malkin." May 7.

"O'Reilly Factor" (2002). "Impact: Interview With Laurence Leamer." May 9.

"O'Reilly Factor" (2002). "Top Story." May 31.

"O'Reilly Factor" (2002). "Unresolved Problem." June 5.

"O'Reilly Factor" (2002). "Most Ridiculous Item of the Day." June 19.

"O'Reilly Factor" (2002). "Most Ridiculous Item of the Day." July 8.

"O'Reilly Factor" (2002). "Factor Follow-Up: Interview Nedra Ruiz." July 15.

"O'Reilly Factor" (2002). "Top Story." July 16

"O'Reilly Factor" (2002). "Top Story." August 5.

"O'Reilly Factor" (2002). "Top Story: Interview With James Payne."

September 25.

"O'Reilly Factor" (2002). "Unresolved Problem." October 11.

"O'Reilly Factor" (2002). "Interview with Peter Jennings." October 17.

"O'Reilly Factor" (2002). "Impact: Interview with Michelle Malkin." October 29.

"O'Reilly Factor" (2002). "Impact." November 4.

"O'Reilly Factor" (2002). "Talking Points: Interview With David Dukcevich." November 7.

"O'Reilly Factor" (2002). "Villain of the Week: Analysis of Eminem." November 8.

"O'Reilly Factor" (2002). "Most Ridiculous Item: James Bond Drinks Bottled Water." November 13.

"O'Reilly Factor" (2002). "Follow Up: Derek and Alex King Are Sentenced." November 14.

"O'Reilly Factor" (2002). "Talking Points; Interview With Steve Rendell." November 21.

"O'Reilly Factor" (2002). "Follow Up: Interview With Curt Smith." November 22.

"O'Reilly Factor" (2002). "Talking Points: Moyers Versus O'Reilly." December 4.

"O'Reilly Factor" (2002). "Back of the Book: Interview with Ira Kramer; Most Ridiculous Item of the Day." December 5.

"O'Reilly Factor" (2002). "Talking Points: The Factor Versus CNN." December 5.

"O'Reilly Factor" (2002). "Back of the Book: Interview With Mark Lubet, Most Ridiculous Item of the Day." December 12.

"O'Reilly Factor" (2002). "Follow Up: Interview With Robert McKee." December 12.

"O'Reilly Factor" (2003). "Talking Points: ACLU Attack on the USA." January 2.

"O'Reilly Factor" (2003). "Talking Points: When Politicians Don't Enforce the Law." January 7.

"O'Reilly Factor" (2003). "Unresolved Problem: Interview With Peter Nunez, Isabel Garcia." January 9.

"O'Reilly Factor" (2003). "Talking Points: The Collapse of Public Education in the USA." January 10.

"O'Reilly Factor" (2003). "Talking Points: Jesse Jackson's Bad Advice." January 16.

"O'Reilly Factor" (2003). "Unresolved Problem: Interview With Susan McDougal." January 17.

"O'Reilly Factor" (2003). "Talking Points: George Clooney, Bill Moyers Misbhaving?" January 20.

"O'Reilly Factor" (2003). "Daimler Chrysler VP Says Conservatives 'Myopic.'" January 24.

"O'Reilly Factor" (2003) "Is it un-American for Protest Group to Challenge Stance in Iraq?" January 27.

"O'Reilly Factor" (2003). "Personal Story: Interview With Canadian Consul General Pamela Wallin." January 29.

"O'Reilly Factor" (2003). "Man Whose Father Died in Trade Center Signs Anti-War Ad." February 4.

"O'Reilly Factor" (2003). "Back of the Book: Interview With University of Maryland's Luke Jensen, Most Ridiculous Item of the Day, Viewer Mail." February 5.

"O'Reilly Factor" (2003). "Personal Story: Interview With Former Prosecutor Cynthia Alksne." February 6.

"O'Reilly Factor" (2003). "Ludacris, Russell Simmons and O'Reilly." February 13.

"O'Reilly Factor" (2003) "A Hip-Hop Magazine Attacks O'Reilly For Criticizing Thug Rappers." February 18.

"O'Reilly Factor" (2003). "Villain of the Week." February 21.

"O'Reilly Factor" (2003). "Back of the Book: Interview With Porn Star Jenna Jameson, 'Most of the Ridiculous Item of the Day,' Viewer Mail." February 25.

"O'Reilly Factor" (2003). "Back of the Book: Interview With Journalist Robert Peecher, 'Most Ridiculous Item of the Day,' Viewer Mail." February 26.

"O'Reilly Factor" (2003). "Are Protesters Bad Americans if They Continue to Protest After War Breaks Out?" February 27.

"O'Reilly Factor" (2003). "Analysis With Newt Gingrich." March 6.

"O'Reilly Factor" (2003) "Is God on America's Side in Iraq Situation?" March 11.

"O'Reilly Factor" (2003). "Personal Story: Interview With Dr. Robert Lichter, FAIR's Steve Rendall, Time Paris Bureau Chief James Graff." March 25.

"O'Reilly Factor" (2003). "Talking Points: Slanting The War Coverage." March 25.

"O'Reilly Factor" (2003). "Personal Story: Interview With Jack Layton." March 27.

"O'Reilly Factor" (2003). "Back of the Book: Interview With Travis Tritt." April 3.

"O'Reilly Factor" (2003). "Follow Up: Is Arnett Guilty of Treason?" April 3.

"O'Reilly Factor" (2003). "Most Ridiculous item of the Day." April 3.

"O'Reilly Factor" (2003). "Personal Story: Analysis With Michelle Malkin, Dick Morris." April 3.

"O'Reilly Factor" (2003). "Canada: Would Not Turn Over Captured Hussein Regime Leaders to U.S." April 16.

"O'Reilly Factor" (2003). "Talking Points: Using Economic Clout to Form Policy." April 17.

"O'Reilly Factor" (2003). "Most Ridiculous item of the Day." April 21.

"O'Reilly Factor" (2003). "Personal Story: Interview With C.O.R.E.'s Niger Innis, New York Daily News Editor Richard Schwartz." April 24.

"O'Reilly Factor" (2003). "Talking Points: Interview with Wade Jessen, Rebecca Hagelin." April 25.

"O'Reilly Factor" (2003). "Personal Story: Far Left's Position in Laci Peterson Case." May 5.

"O'Reilly Factor" (2003). "Personal Story: Interview with 'Progressive' Magazine's Matthew Rothschild." May 19.

"O'Reilly Factor" (2003). "Talking Points: Corruption at U.N." May 21.

"O'Reilly Factor" (2003). "Follow-Up: Interview With Kansas State Senator Mary Wagle, Interview With KTVX Reporter Heidi hatch." May 28.

"O'Reilly Factor" (2003). "Personal Story: Allegations the Pentagon Staged Lynch Rescue." May 29.

"O'Reilly Factor" (2003). "Talking Points: Profiting From Malice." June 2.

"O'Reilly Factor" (2003). "Back of the Book: Interview With Sharon Osbourne, 'Most Ridiculous Item of the Day,' Viewer Mail." June 3.

"O'Reilly Factor" (2003). "Talking Points: The Truth, the Whole Truth, and Senator Hillary Clinton." June 5.

"O'Reilly Factor" (2003). "Rev. Jesse Jackson and Liberia's Charles Taylor." July 9.

"O'Reilly Factor" (2003). "Unresolved Problem." July 11.

"O'Reilly Factor" (2003). "Headlines and Main Story." July 17.

"O'Reilly Factor" (2003). "Unresolved Problem: Interview With Author Ann Coulter." July 22.

"O'Reilly Factor" (2003) "APA Defines Conservatives." August 7.

"O'Reilly Factor" (2003). "Most Ridiculous Item of the Day." August 12.

"O'Reilly Factor" (2003). "Run DMC's Joseph Simmons Defends Gangsta Rap." September 15.

"O'Reilly Factor" (2003). "Most Ridiculous Item of the Day." September 18.

"O'Reilly Factor" (2003). "Dishonesty in Media." September 19.

"O'Reilly Factor" (2003). "Smear Merchants." October 8.

"O'Reilly Factor" (2003). "George Soros Supports MoveOn.org." November 11.

"O'Reilly Factor" (2003). "Personal Story." November 12.

"O'Reilly Factor" (2003). "Massachusetts to Rule on Gay Marriage." November 14.

"O'Reilly Factor" (2003). "Personal Story: Interview With Publicist Lizzie Grubman, Psychologist Linda Miles." November 14.

"O'Reilly Factor" (2004). "Interview With Attorney in Dog Mauling case." January 2.

"O'Reilly Factor" (2004). "Personal Story: Interview With Seattle Post-Intelligencer Columnist Joel Connelly." January 8.

"O'Reilly Factor" (2004). "Interview With Alan Keyes." January 21.

"O'Reilly Factor" (2004). "Janet Jackson Punishment Unfair." February 5.

"O'Reilly Factor" (2004). "Impact: Hillary to Run on Kerry Ticket?" February 12.

"O'Reilly Factor" (2004). "Kerry Wins Wisconsin." February 18.

"O'Reilly Factor" (2004). "Personal Story: The Media Is Losing Its Clout." March 1.

"O'Reilly Factor" (2004). "Gay Marriage Anarchy Continues." March 3.

"O'Reilly Factor" (2004). "Factor Follow-Up: Interview With Jayson Blair." March 10.

"O'Reilly Factor" (2004). "Legislation Could Lead to Crackdown on hock Jocks." March 12.

"O'Reilly Factor" (2004). "Impact: Judge Rules in Favor of Gay Sex in Park." March 16.

"O'Reilly Factor" (2004). "Personal Story: Media meets with Democratic Candidate." March 22.

"O'Reilly Factor" (2004). "Personal Story: Laci Peterson's Parents Work to Pass Law." March 24.

"O'Reilly Factor" (2004). "Talking Points: Dishonest Liberal Media." April 2.

"O'Reilly Factor" (2004). "Popular Shows Conceal Anti-Bush Messages." April 8.

"O'Reilly Factor" (2004). "Talking Points: Some 9/11 Families Use Tragedy to Promote Ideology." April 15.

"O'Reilly Factor" (2004). "Most Ridiculous Item of the Day." April 19.

"O'Reilly Factor" (2004). "Personal Story: Photographer Sued Over Wet T-Shirt Contest; Ohio Anchor Loses Her Job from Key West Striptease Caught on Internet." April 22.

"O'Reilly Factor" (2004). "Talking Points: Using Iraq to Advance Left Wing Ideology." April 22.

"O'Reilly Factor" (2004). "Unresolved Problem: Enforcing Immigration Law." April 22.

"O'Reilly Factor" (2004). "Impact: Election Rhetoric Getting More Vicious." April 26.

"O'Reilly Factor" (2004). "Unresolved Problems: Jesse Jackson Using Power in Dubious Ways." April 26.

"O'Reilly Factor" (2004). "Impact." April 27.

"O'Reilly Factor" (2004). "Personal Story: Dick Morris Discusses His New Book and Hillary." May 6.

"O'Reilly Factor" (2004). "Vice President Dick Cheney Talks with Tony Snow." May 11.

"O'Reilly Factor" (2004). "Factor Flashback: Factor Flashback: Does Gangsta Rap Harm Kids?" May 14.

"O'Reilly Factor" (2004). "Al Gore Lashes Out at the Bush Administration." May 26.

"O'Reilly Factor" (2004). "Personal Story." May 27.

"O'Reilly Factor" (2004). "Back of the Book." May 31.

"O'Reilly Factor" (2004). "Back of the Book: Interview with Donna Brazile." June 1.

"O'Reilly Factor" (2004). "Personal Story: Interview with Laura Ingraham." June 14.

"O'Reilly Factor" (2004). "Most Ridiculous item of the Day and Mail." June 28.

"O'Reilly Factor" (2004). "D.C. Reacts To Michael Moore's New Film." June 30.

"O'Reilly Factor" (2004). "Unresolved Problem: Kerry's Vice Presidential Pick?" July 1.

"O'Reilly Factor" (2004). "Personal Story: School Systems Push Rapper Book." July 2.

"O'Reilly Factor" (2004). "Follow-up: Status of Two Army Deserters." July 6.

"O'Reilly Factor" (2004). "Factor Original: O'Reilly Discusses Media Politics." July 9.

"O'Reilly Factor" (2004). "Personal Story: Are Anti-Bush Comments Fair?" July 12.

"O'Reilly Factor" (2004). "Talking Points: Dissent or Dishonor?; Analysis of Growing Bitterness in Politics." July 12.

"O'Reilly Factor" (2004). "Talking Points: Smearing Continues." July 13.

"O'Reilly Factor" (2004). "Washington Insider: Hillary Clinton Upset at Snub." July 14.

"O'Reilly Factor" (2004). "Talking Points: Truth about Gay Marriage." July 15.

"O'Reilly Factor" (2004). "Most Ridiculous Item of the Day." July 19.

"O'Reilly Factor" (2004). "Personal Story." July 19.

"O'Reilly Factor" (2004). "Talking Points Memo and Top Story." July 19.

"O'Reilly Factor" (2004). "Canada Gets Aljazeera But No FNC!" July 20.

"O'Reilly Factor" (2004). "Most Ridiculous Item of the Day: O'Reilly Discusses Michael Moore." July 26.

"O'Reilly Factor" (2004). "Moore: Bush 'Didn't Tell the Truth.'" July 27.

"O'Reilly Factor" (2004). "Follow-up: Analysis of Convention." July 29.

"O'Reilly Factor" (2004). "Personal Story: O'Reilly Discusses John Kerry." July 29.

"O'Reilly Factor" (2004). "Back of the Book." August 2.

"O'Reilly Factor" (2004). "Personal Story." August 2.

"O'Reilly Factor" (2004). "Back of the Book: O'Reilly Discusses Canadian Media." August 4.

"O'Reilly Factor" (2004). "Personal Story." August 5.

"O'Reilly Factor" (2004). "Factor Flashback: O'Reilly Discusses Medical Marijuana." August 6.

"O'Reilly Factor" (2004). "Frey Testifies Against Scott Peterson." August 12.

"O'Reilly Factor" (2004). "Most Ridiculous Item of the Day: O'Reilly Discusses the Olympics." August 12.

"O'Reilly Factor" (2004). "What on Earth Is Happening in New Jersey?" August 12.

"O'Reilly Factor" (2004). "Flashback: NY Times Attacks Fox News." August 18

"O'Reilly Factor" (2004). "Flashback: Interview With Paul Krugman." August 19.

"O'Reilly Factor" (2004). "Talking Points: Republican Convention Begins." August 30.

"O'Reilly Factor" (2004). "Bono: Not Facing AIDS Crisis 'Foolhardy.'" September 1.

"O'Reilly Factor" (2004). "Personal Story: O'Reilly Interviews Bill Maher." September 2.

"O'Reilly Factor" (2004). "CBS Imitates Fox News Slogan." September 8.

"O'Reilly Factor" (2004). "Talking Points: Mud and the Media." September 14.

"O'Reilly Factor" (2004). "Talking Points: CBS Faces Scrutiny." September 15.

"O'Reilly Factor" (2004). "Personal Story: O'Reilly Discusses 'The Daily Show.'" September 17.

"O'Reilly Factor" (2004). "Terry Gross and Bill O'Reilly: Round

OUTFOXED

Two." September 21.

"O'Reilly Factor" (2004). "Bush Talks to O'Reilly." September 27.

"O'Reilly Factor" (2004). "Bush Talks to O'Reilly, Part 2." September 28.

"O'Reilly Factor" (2004). "A Look At Tomorrow's Presidential Debate." September 29.

"O'Reilly Factor" (2004). "Bush Talks to O'Reilly, Part 3." September 29.

"O'Reilly Factor" (2004). "How Do Europeans Feel About Kerry, Bush?" September 29.

"Special Report With Brit Hume" (1999). "Special Report Roundtable." March 8.

"Special Report With Brit Hume" (1999). "Interview with Trent Lott." June 24.

"Special Report With Brit Hume" (2001). "Special Report Roundtable." December 7.

"Special Report With Brit Hume" (2002). "Grapevine: BBC Editor Calls Fox Coverage 'Embarrassing.'" October 21.

"Special Report With Brit Hume" (2003). "Below the Fold." January 12.

"Special Report With Brit Hume" (2003). "More Allegations, Discoveries in Iraq." January 20.

"Special Report With Brit Hume" (2003). "Roundtable." February 2.

"Special Report With Brit Hume" (2003). "All-Stars Debate fate of Arnett; Rivera; Propaganda War." March 31.

"Special Report With Brit Hume" (2003). "Roundtable." April 1.

"Special Report With Brit Hume" (2003). "Operation Iraqi Freedom." April 7.

"Special Report With Brit Hume" (2003). "All-Star Panel Discusses Criticism of Bush's Motivations for War on Iraq, Controversial Reporters of The New York Times." May 21.

"Special Report With Brit Hume" (2003). "Chief Weapons Inspector Says He's Found No Weapons Of Mass Destruction In Iraq; Car Buying Frenzy In Iraq." October 2.

"Special Report With Brit Hume" (2004). "All-Star Panel Discusses Howard Dean's Unusual Concession Speech in Iowa." January 20.

"Special Report With Brit Hume" (2004). "All-Star Panel Discusses Democratic Presidential Candidates." February 18.

"Special Report With Brit Hume" (2004). "Presidential Candidate Howard Dean Bows Out of Race." February 18.

"Special Report With Brit Hume" (2004). "Four Marines Die During Intense Fighting in Ramadi." April 6.

"Special Report With Brit Hume" (2004). "An Independent Inquiry Will Investigate Illegal Revenues In Oil For Food Program." April 21.

"Special Report With Brit Hume" (2004). "Senator Kerry Says The U.S. Mission In Iraq Is In Danger Of Failing; Ralph Nader Says Democrats Should Get Over His Race For the Presidency." April 30.

"Special Report With Brit Hume" (2004). "Senator Kerry's Proposals on Nuclear Arms Control Mirror." June 1.

"Special Report With Brit Hume" (2004). "Senator Kerry Postpones Campaigning This Week In Respect To Reagan's Death, As Republicans Favorably Compare The Presidencies Of Reagan And Bush." June 8.

"Special Report With Brit Hume" (2004). "Exclusive Interview With Bush 41." June 14.

"Special Report With Brit Hume" (2004). "Grapevine: Guantanamo Bay Detainees Help Foil Summer Olympic Attack." July 13.

"Special Report With Brit Hume" (2004). "Political Headlines." August 30.

"Special Report With Brit Hume" (2004). "All-Star Panel Discusses Senator Miller's Fiery Convention Speech." September 2.

"Special Report With Brit Hume" (2004). "Political Grapevine; Many News Outlets Including a CBS Anchor Believes CBS Was Duped by National Guard Memos." September 15.

"Special Report With Brit Hume" (2004). "All-Star Panel Discusses Whether Those at CBS Involved with Documents Fiasco Should Step Down." September 22.

"Special Report With Brit Hume" (2004). "Down in the Polls, Can Kerry Afford to be Aggressive?" September 30.

"Your World With Neil Cavuto" (2003). "Michael Powell, Chairman of the FCC." June 2.

"Your World With Neil Cavuto" (2003). "Sir Richard Branson, CEO and Chairman of Virgin." October 15.

"Your World With Neil Cavuto" (2004). "Interview With Don Evans." January 5.

"Your World With Neil Cavuto" (2004). "Billionaire Tycoon Richard Branson on a Quest for the Best." May 20.

"Your World With Neil Cavuto" (2004). "Neil's Heroes: Richard Branson." May 31.

"Your World With Neil Cavuto" (2004). "Neil's Heroes: John Duffy." June 1.

"Your World With Neil Cavuto" (2004). "Neil's Heroes: Paul Orfalea." June 2.

"Your World With Neil Cavuto" (2004). "Neil's Heroes: Jon Huntsman." June 7.

"Your World With Neil Cavuto" (2004). "Interview With Dick Cheney." June 25.

"Your World With Neil Cavuto" (2004). "Profit Percolates?" July 22.

"Your World With Neil Cavuto" (2004). "Losing Its Grip." July 23.

"Your World With Neil Cavuto" (2004). "Business for Bush?" August 4.

"Your World With Neil Cavuto" (2004). "Uninsured Americans." August 26.

Other

Transcript. (2004). CBS Television. "60 Minutes." "Bill O'Reilly: 'No Spin.'" September 26.

Transcript. (2004). *Outfoxed: Rupert Murdoch's War on Journalism.* Greenwald, R. (director).

Articles and Books

Ailes, R. (2004). "'Elite, Arrogant, Condescending...'" *Wall Street Journal*, June 2, page A14.

Angwin, J. (2004). "Liberals Step Up Political Assault Against Fox News." *Wall Street Journal*, July 20, page B1.

Anonymous. (1997). "Murdoch's falling star." *The Economist*, August 30, volume 344.

Anonymous. (2001). "Editorial: The Fox-ification of cable news." *University Wire*, August 6.

Anonymous. (2003). "Kellner out at Turner Broadcasting." cnn.com, February 19.

Anonymous. (2003). "We decide, you shut up." *Harper's*, May, Vol. 306, 1836, page 17.

Anonymous. (2003). "FOX drops Franken suit." *Montreal Gazette*, August 26, page D6.

Anonymous. (2003). "Roger's Balancing Act." *Broadcasting and Cable*, October 27, 133, 43, page 28.

Anonymous. (2003). "Why Ailes." *Broadcasting and Cable*, October 27, 133, 43, page 48.

Anonymous. (2004). "Murdoch backs Bush and wants troops to stay." *Sidney Morning Herald*, April 7, www.smh.au.

Anonymous. (2004). "Fox News gets foothold in House of Commons." *Globe and Mail*, June 1, page B2.

Anonymous. (2004). "Dialogue: Rupert Murdoch; the News Corp. chairman discusses how DirecTV is the 'missing link' in his global media empire." *Hollywood Reporter*, June 22, www.hollywoodreporter.com.

Anonymous. (2004). "FOX News Channel Garners More Than Half of Cable News Audience During Second Quarter; FNC Captures Nine Out of Top Ten Cable News Shows." *Business Wire*, June 29, home.businesswire.com.

Anonymous. (2004). "Fox and Gophers." *Wall Street Journal*, July 19, page A10.

Anonymous. (2004). "Activists sue FOX News for use of slogan." *The Telegram*, July 20, page A7.

Anonymous. (2004). "Murdoch's media vision." *Media Channel*, August 25, www.mediachannel.org.

Anonymous. (2004). "Keyes Says Christ Would Not Vote For Obama." September 7, NBC5.com.

Anonymous. (2004). "KVI, Fox News Partner For First Fox-Branded Radio Station." October 1, www.radiolink.com.

Anonymous. (2004). "Editorial: Fox's blunder/Brushing aside a staffer's hoax.' *Star Tribune*, October 8, www.startribune.com.

Anonymous. (2004). "Fox News: Hannity still heading to UVSC." *Salt Lake Tribune*, October 8, sltrib.com.

Anonymous. (2004). "O'Reilly: Female Aide In $60M Extort Bid; Fox News star denies sex harassment, claims political motivation." October 13, www.thesmokinggun.com.

Anonymous. (2004). "O'Reilly Hit With Sex Harass Suit; Female Fox coworker details lewd behavior of cable TV star." October 13, www.thesmokinggun.com.

Anonymous. (2004). "O'Reilly Sues Manhattan Attorney, His Law Firm and Employee in Extortion Scheme." *Business Wire*, October 13.

Anonymous. (2004). "Bill O'Reilly." Undated, foxnews.com.

Anonymous. (2004). "O'Reilly: Hand over the tapes." October 20, thesmokinggun.com.

Applebaum, A. (2004). "Old-fashioned beliefs led to his downfall." *Kitchener Waterloo Record*, January 23, page A11.

Arango, T. (2004). "Save Our Butts!" *New York Post*, June 10, www.nypost.com

Associated Press. (1995). "Murdoch backed Gingrich fete." June 23.

Associated Press. (1998). "Rupert Murdoch denies European press monopoly." April 6.

Associated Press. (2002). "Brown raps Van Susteren." March 28.

Associated Press. (2003). "CNN's Tucker Carlson angry over phone flap." September 29.

Associated Press. (2004). "CNN, FOX resume battle of the billboards." July 9.

Associated Press. (2004). "CNN hires new boss." November 22.

Barwick, S. (1998). "My regrets, by Murdoch." *Daily Telegram*, November 9.

Bates, S. (1989). *If No News, Send Rumors: Anecdotes of American Journalism*. New York: St. Martin's Press.

Bauder, D. (1999). "FOX criticizes MSNBC for North hire." *Associated Press*, January 29.

Bauder, D. (2001). "CNN reporter detained in China." *Associated Press*, April 12.

Bauder, D. (2001). "CNN, FOX battle heats up as war correspondent abruptly switches." *Associated Press*, October 2.

Bauder, D. (2002). "FOX still badmouthing Zahn." *Associated Press*, October 7.

Bauder, D. (2004). "O'Reilly Says He's Ready to Fight Charges." *Associated Press*, October 14.

Berkowitz, H. (1996). "Time Warner says Rudy has 'political agenda.'" *New York Newsday*, October 26, page A23.

Bianculli, D. (2003). "CNN exec knocks Fox News; 'We're a Rolex – they're a Timex.'" July11, *New York Daily News*, www.nydailynews.com.

Block, A.B. (2004). "FOX News plays hardball with press." July, 25, www.tvweek.com.

Boyd, D. (2004). "The Descent of an enigma." *BC Business*, February, vol. 32, page 21.

Bruce, H. (2003). "Lord Black's comeuppance: how sweet it is: Many a journalist has been berated by Lord Black through his newspaper years." *Truro Daily News*, November 29, page A6.

Campbell, C. (2003). "It's scary to imagine Atlanta without CNN." *Atlanta Journal and Constitution*, October 12, page E2.

Campbell, C. (2004). "War for ratings over, but FOX's jabs continue." *Atlanta Journal and Constitution*, May 4, page B2.

Canadian Press. (2004). "Not angry at Canadians, O'Reilly says." May 3.

Carroll, J.S. (2004). "The Wolf in Reporter's Clothing: The Rise of Pseudo-Journalism in America." *Los Angeles Times*, May 6, www.latimes.com.

Carter, B. (1997). "Fox's use of Footage Irks ABC." *New York Times*, January 23, page B11.

Carter, B. (2001). "FOX News fires a star host over CNN bid." *New York Times*, September 6, page C1.

Cioli, R. (1996). "A Conservative view?" *New York Newsday*, October 7, page B5.

Colapinto, J. (2004). "Mad Dog." *Rolling Stone*, August 11, www.rollingstone.com.

Colford, P.D. and Ortega, R.R. (2004). "Post gaffe: Rupe keeps his distance." *New York Daily News*, July 8 www.nydailynews.com.

Collins, S. (2004). "Television; Outfoxing CNN; A new book tells how Bill O'Reilly and Roger Ailes changed the future of cable news." *Los Angeles Times*, May 2, page E25.

Collins, S., Jensen, E., James, M., Tyrell, J, and Wilson, S. (2004). "Fox News' Bill O'Reilly Is Accused of Sexual Harassment." *Los Angeles Times*, October 14, www.latimes.com.

Cook, J. (2004). "O'Reilly scolds guest who outed gays, then calls judge a lesbian." *Chicago Tribune*, July 21, www.chicagotribune.com.

De Moraes, L. (2001). "Only CNN gets the picture." *Washington Post*, April 12, page C1.

De Moraes, L. (2004). "In a Tuesday night showdown, FOX News Channel outdraws the Big Three." *Washington Post*, September 9, page C7.

Doyle, J. (2004). "FOX News. Not here yet, but already hilarious." *Globe and Mail*, April 21, page R2.

Doyle, J. (2004). "Who's afraid of the big bad FOX? Certainly not us." *Globe and Mail*, April 19, page R2.

Durbin, J. (2004). "Who's winning the News Wars? FOX squares off against CNN." *Maclean's*, October 4, pages 28-30.

Dvorkin, J.A. (2003). "Gross vs. O'Reilly: Culture Clash on NPR." *Media Matters*, October 15, npr.org.

Edgers, G. (2004). "Taking on mainstream media, Fox's Hume faces political views head-on." *Boston Globe*, September 1, www.boston.com.

Eviatar, D. (2001). "Murdoch's FOX News: They Distort. They Decide." *The Nation*, March 12, 272, 10, page 11.

Eyal, J. (1994). "Look what happened in Asia: The BBC's World Service." *Independent*, March 28.

Fabrikant, G. (1998). "News Corp. to sell shares in new unit." *New York Times*, June 30, page D1.

Fallows, J. (2003). "The Age of Murdoch." *Atlantic Monthly*, September, vol. 292, 2, page 81.

Farhi, P. (2001). "The Afghan War's Media Magnet; Ashleigh Banfield Is Gaining More Notice Than Viewers." *Washington Post*, December 5, page C1.

Fraser, N. (1999). "The Perpetual predator." *George*, February pages 56-61.

Furman, P. (2004). "Fox News has topper for CNN." *New York Daily News*, June 10, www.nydailynews.com.

Gay, V. (1996). "The All-news wars heat up: FOX's new channel arrives, gunning for CNN and MSNBC – led by cagey corporate warrior Rupert Murdoch." *New York Newsday*, October 7, page B4.

Gay, V. (2001). "Roger Ailes is crazy like a FOX." *New York Newsday*, December 11, page B2.

Gillis, C. (2004). "Is Canada ready for Loudmouth TV?" *Maclean's*, October 4, pages 23-27.

Gitlin, T. (2001). "How TV killed democracy." *Los Angeles Times*, February 14, page B11.

Goodway, N. (2004). "Black's six deals to 'milk' Hollinger." *Evening Standard*, May 11, www.thisismoney.com.

Gross, D. (2004). "FOX News threatens lawsuit over flamboyant billboard near CNN." *Associated Press*, May 8.

Grove, L. (2002). "Roger Ailes-Bob Woodward Smackdown?" *Washington Post*, November 19, page C3.

Grove, L. and Morgan, H. (2004). "Heated exchange at 'Fahrenheit'?" *New York Daily News*, June 15, www.nydailynews.com.

Grove, L. and Morgan, H. (2004). "Hardball or 'slimeball'?" *New York Daily News*, August 24, www.nydailynews.com.

Grove, L. and Morgan, H. (2004). "O'Reilly, running man?" *New York Daily News*, September 6, www.nydailynews.com.

Grove, L. and Morgan, H. (2004). "The briefing." *New York Daily News*, October 6, www.nydailynews.com.

Gunther, M. and Brown, E. (1996). "CNN envy together, Microsoft and NBC are gunning for global news power in cable TV and cyberspace. Rupert Murdoch wants to play the game too." *Fortune*, July 8, page 120.

Gunther, M. (1998). "The Rules According to Rupert Flouting tradition and betting billions, Rupert Murdoch built the Fox network and made news Corp. into a global media giant..." *Fortune*, October 26, page 92.

Hagan, J. (2004). "Fox News Embraces ABC Memo Story Over Cameron's Pleas." *New York Observer*, October 18, page 21.

Heilmann, J. (2004). "Rupert Murdoch They Watch His Every Move." *Time*, April 26, 163, 17, page 73.

Henican, E. (1996). "Ink-stained: Tainted coverage in clash of network titans." *New York Newsday*, October 23, page A4.

Hickey, N. (2003). "Cable Wars." *Columbia Journalism Review*, January, volume 41, page 12.

Hilyard, N.B. (2003). "Clash of the Titans: how the unbridled ambition of Ted Turner and Rupert Murdoch has created global empires that control what we read and Watch." *Library Journal*, May 15, 128, 9, page 144.

Hoberman, J. (2003). "Nixon's Shadow: The History of an Image." *The Nation*, December 8, 277, 19, page 40.

Hoffmann, B. and Gilmore, H. (2004). "John a 'Bronze' Star." *New York Post*, September 29, www.nypost.com.

Honigsbaum, M. (1997). "The Napoleon Complex." *Independent on Sunday*, July 27, page 21.

Horsman, M. (1996). "Censorship fears as BBC closes Arabic TV." *Independent*, April 10, page 2.

Houpt, S. (2004). "Fair and balanced – and maybe outfoxed." *Globe and Mail*, July 17, page R3.

Huff, R. (2004). "Bush story has Hume on the air from the air." *New York Daily News*, June 14, www.nydailynews.com.

Johnson, P. (1996). "Fox seems a natural for ANC's Brit Hume." *USA Today*, August 4, page 6B.

Johnson, P., Levin, G., and Bianco, R. (1999). "Zahn trades CBS' reach for face time on Fox News." *USA Today*, January 25, page 2D.

Johnson, P. (2003). "For cable news, Iraq war is clear ratings victory." *Tulsa World*, April 10, page D6.

Kane, E. (2004). "O'Reilly may be in no-spin zone." *Milwaukee Journal Sentinel*, October 18, www.jsonline.com.

Kasindorf, M. (1995). "Newt: I met Rupert; Speaker: no impropriety in pre-deal visit." *New York Newsday*, January 13, page A22.

Kempner, M. (2001). "Trust study: Fox gains on CNN." *Atlanta Journal and Constitution*, September 11, page D1.

Kempner, M. (2002). "Zahn on ratings roll Morning show on CNN still nowhere near 'FOX and Friends.'" *Atlanta Journal and Constitution*, September 25, page D1.

Kempner, M. (2002). "King no longer king of 9pm time slot." *Atlanta Journal and Constitution*, October 29, page D1.

Kirkpatrick, D.D. (2003). "Media Deregulation Foes Make Murdoch Their Lightning Rod." *New York Times*, May 29, page C6.

Kitty, A. (1998). "Objectivity in Journalism: Should we be skeptical?" *Skeptic*, Vol. 6, No. 1, pages 54-61.

Krauss, C. (2004). "When a Canadian insults FOX News, them's [expletive] fighting words." *New York Times*, April 25, page 16.

Kull, S. (2003). "Misperceptions, the Media, and the Iraq War." Program on International Policy Attitudes/Knowledge Network, October 2.

Kurtz, H. (1993). "Weeding Out Liberals At WTTG?: News Chief Backs Off Memo About Staff." *Washington Post*, September 9, page D1.

Kurtz, H. (1998). "Colleagues are uneasy with Brinkley's decision to turn pitchman." *Washington Post*, January 12, page E3.

Kurtz, H. (2002). "Over Wall Strett, a Clash of Ego and Bio." *Washington Post*, May 20, page C1.

Kurtz, H. (2004). "For anchor Tom Brokaw, a race with a finish line." *Washington Post*, January 26, page C1.

Kurtz, H. (2004). "Scrambling for Cover – and Coverage; Spiraling Iraq Violence Keeps Reporters Away from Action." *Washington Post*, May 17, page C1.

Kurtz, H. (2004). "O'Reilly's 'No-Spin' Control Prompts Guest to Cry Foul." *Washington Post*, June 30, page C3.

Kurtz, H. (2004). "Up Next: The News In Red and Blue." *Washington Post*, September 27, page C1.

Landler, M. (1997). "The logic of losing ay all-news TV." *New York Times*, June 22.

Larson, M. (2000). "Fox out of the woods." *Mediaweek*, November 6, 10, 43, page 46.

Larson, M. (2003). "What's ahead for Ted?" *Mediaweek*, February 3, 13, 5, page 6.

Lengel, A. and Priest, D. (2004). "Investigators Concluded Shelby leaked message; Justice Dept. Declined to Prosecute Case." *Washington Post*, August 5, page A17.

Lewis, R. (1996). "When reporters become news." *Maclean's*, September 23, vol. 109, page 2.

Lichtblau, E. (2004). "Fabricated Kerry Posting leads to Apology from Fox News." *New York Times*, October 3, www.nytimes.com.

Lieberman, D. (1994). "Taking to new stump – CNBC's Ailes dares to raise cable stakes." *USA Today*, April 28.

Lieberman, D. (1996). "Ailes tackles toughest assignment; cable channel battles budget, clock, rivals." *USA Today*, September 23, page 9B.

Lieberman, D. (1997). "FOX News sets sights on prey Network looks to outsmart MSNBC." *USA Today*, September 15, page 8B.

Mackenzie, R. (2003). "Action and reaction, particularly in cable news." *Richmond Times-Dispatch*, May 1, page A15.

Malkin, M. (2004). "Ambush journalism...or my evening with caveman Chris Matthews." August 20, michellemalkin.com.

Mathews, J. (2004). "Hide this, Bill O'Reilly." *New York Daily News*, June 28, www.nydailynews.com.

Maull, S. (2004). "Woman files new charges Vs. FOX, O'Reilly?" *Associated Press*, October 19.

Maull, S. (2004). "O'Reilly, producer settle legal dispute." *Associated Press*, October 28.

Mayberry, C. (2004). "DirecTV 10th anniversary." *Hollywood Reporter*, June 22, www.hollywoodreporter.com

McCarroll, T. and Burton, S. (1993). "New star over Asia: New media baron Rupert Murdoch buys Asia's hottest TV service. But will 3 billion Asians buy Homer Simpson?" *Time*, August 9, page 53.

McChesney, R.W. (2004). "The Escalating War Against Corporate Media." *Monthly Review*, March, 55, 10, page 1.

McClintock, P. (2004). "FOX news beats all rivals." *Variety*, September 28, news.yahoo.com.

McFarland, M. (2004). "CNN's Brown sounds off on TV and politics." *Seattle Post-Intelligencer*, September 30, seattlepi.com.

Memmott, M. (2004). "Filmmaker Moore, talker O'Reilly spar in Boston." *USA Today*, July 27, www.usatoday.com.

Mink, E. (2003). "Does 'fair and balanced' really mean 'destroy your opponents'?" Knight-Ridder/Tribune News Service, July 23.

Montgomery, S. (2003). "How the mighty have fallen." *Montreal Gazette*, November 23, page D8.

Moore, M.T. (2000). "Bush cousin helped FOX make call." *USA Today*, November 14, page 15A.

Morano, M. (2004). "Protesters Deounce Fox News for 'Twisted View' of World." CNSNews.com, September 1.

Murray, S. (2001). "Rivera is easy target for critics." *Atlanta Journal and Constitution*, December 20, page F1.

Nelson, L.E. (1994). "Murdoch's blue license to scoff." *New York Newsday*, June 5, page A40.

Nelson, L.E. (1995). "Murdoch's art of book deal." *New York Newsday*, February 2, page A6.

Nichols, A. (2004). "Fox moves to fire accuser; Tells judge it's not retaliation." *New York Daily News,* October 16, www.nydailynews.com.

Nichols, A. (2004). "Her dad mad as hell, out to whup O'Reilly." *New York Daily News*, October 21, www.nydailynews.com.

Noble, C. (2004). "News Corp. board OK's move to U.S." August 10, cbsmarketwatch.com.

O'Brien, G. (2004). "Way is now clear for Fox News." *Cablecaster*, September 17, www.cablecastermagazine.com.

Olive, D. (2004). "Slothful directos the real scandal." *Toronto Star*, September 1, www.thestar.com.

O'Reilly, B. (2003). "Keeping it Simple; Villain of the Week." foxnews.com, February 3.

O'Reilly, B. (2003). "Is O'Reilly a Cry Baby?" www.foxnews.com, October 23.

O'Reilly, B. (2004). "The worst of *Times*: A once-great newspaper has adopted a radical agenda." *New York Daily News*, June 21, www.nydailynews.com.

O'Reilly, B. (2004). "The Most Liberal Ticket, Ever." www.foxnews.com, July 8.

O'Reilly, B. (2004). "It's War Between FNC and the New York Times." foxnews.com, July 21.

O'Reilly, B. (2004). "Turbulent Times." www.foxnews.com, October 14.

Orol. R. (2004). "News Corp. flouts FCC order." www.thedeal.com, October 11.

Paris, G.A., Savage, G.W., and Seitz, R.. G.H. (2004). "Report of investigation by the special committee of the board of directors of Hollinger International Inc." August 30, online.wsj.com.

Pennington, G. (2001). "TV Anchors are restrained, while Americans are fixated by reports of 'orgy of terrorism.'" *St. Louis Post-Dispatch*, September 12, page A19.

Pew Research Center for People and the Press. (2004). "2004 Pew Reseach Center for People and the Press Media Consumption and Believability Study." June 8.

Piazza, J. and Stevenson, M.G. (2004). "FOX bitten by reporter's joke quotes." *New York Daily News*, October 2, www.nydailynews.com.

Porteus, L., Rhiner, C., Cameron, C., and Asher, J. (2004). "Trail Tales: What's That Face?" October 1, www.foxnews.com.

Purnick, J. (2004). "It's the News The Way We'd Like It." *New York Times*, July 19, page B1.

Reuters. (2004). "US court keeps stay on media rules." June 24.

Rivers, W. (1970). *The Adversaries*. Boston: Beacon Press.

Rendall, S. and Hollar, J. (2004). "Still Failing the 'Fair & Balanced' Test: 'Special Report' leans right, white, Republican & male." Fairness and Accuracy in Reporting.

Robertson, A. (2004). "Dual listing denied to News Corp." June 23, www.abc.net.au.

Robison, P. (2004). "Hollinger's Black 'victimized' company, re-

port says." *Bloomberg*, August 31.

Rogers, P. (1998). "NBC exec: Deals reach 'insane level.'" *Atlanta Journal and Constitution*, January 15, page F1.

Roh, J. (2004). "Protesters March on FOX News." www.foxnews.com, September 1.

Rohan, V. (1996). "CNN faces invasion by network challengers." *Bergen County Record*, January 22m page A1.

Rose, D., Rush, G., and Dillon, N. (2004). "What a big Bill! Paying millions in sex-harassment case." *New York Daily News*, October 29, www.nydailynews.com.

Rush, G. and Molloy, J. (2004). "Were porn stars an O'Reilly factor?" *New York Daily News*, October 19, www.nydailynews.com.

Rutenberg, J. (2001). "Cable's Instinct For the Racy And Repetitive." *New York Times*, July 30, page C1.

Rutenberg, J. (2001). "Defining terms." *New York Times*, October 3, page E6.

Rutenberg, J. (2002). "At Fox News, the Colonel Who Wasn't." *New York Times*, April 29, page C1.

Rutenberg, J. (2003). "Is this CNN?: Connie Chung's tabloid-style show is at the centre of a fight at CNN between old-timers and those trying to update the venerable news network and to improve ratings." *National Post*, February 25, page AL5.

Rutten, T. (2003). "FOX biased? Ex-producer says yes." *Los Angeles Times*, November 3, page B2.

Rutten, T. (2004). "The news: A nation divided." *Los Angeles Times*, July 7, www.latimes.com.

Sanders, B. (2004). "Fox News and the Iraq War: Fact vs. Fox-tion." March 31, www.buzzflash.com.

Sanger, E. (1996). "Ailes quits at NBC/Had no role at new NBC Microsoft channel." *New York Newsday*, January 19, page A57.

Sanger, E. (1996). "Ailes to Head News Channel; Murdoch hires conservative to give CNN competition." *New York Newsday*, January 31, page A35.

Saranow, J. (2004). "Fox News Redesigns Site With Advertisers in Mind." *Wall Street Journal*, June 14, online.wsj.com.

Saunders, D. (1998). "Ratings spin sends NBC into 'Reality' check." *Denver Rocky Mountain News*, December 14, page 2D.

Shafer, J. (2004). "How to Beat Bill O'Reilly; Kill him with kindness." *Slate*, September 23, www.slate.com.

Shah, S. and Griffiths, K. (2004). "News Corp begins charm offensive over US move." *Independent*, October 5,.

Shaw, D. (2004). "News as entertainments is sadly becoming the norm." *Los Angeles Times*, July 11, www.latimes.com.

Shister, G. (2003). "Fox News Channel uses Arnett incident in promotions." Knight-Ridder/Tribune News Service, April 3.

Steinberg, J. and Carr, D. (2004). "Murdoch said to be source of Post's Gephardt 'exclusive.'" *New York Times*, July 9, www.nytimes.com.

Steinberg, J. (2004). "Fox News, Media Elite." *New York Times*, November 8, www.nytimes.com.

Stoltzfus, D. (1993). "Roger Ailes to head CNBC." *Bergen County Record*, August 31, page C1.

Streitfeld, R. (2004). "Hannity to follow Moore at Pageant." *Student Life*, October 1, www.studlife.com.

Streitfeld, R. (2004). "Hannity cancels appearance." *Student Life*, October 6, www.studlife.com.

Strupp, J. (2004). "Murdoch Says Fox Would Have Been 'Crucified' for CBS Mistake." *Editor and Publisher*, September 22, www.mediainfo.com.

Szalai, G. (2004). "Murdoch takes on NYC leaders." *Hollywood Reporter*, June 29, page 4.

Thomas, E. (2001). "Life of O'Reilly." *Newsweek*, February 12, page 28.

Tumulty, K. and Rudulph, E. (1995). "Congress: When Rupert met Newt." *Time*, January 23, page 34.

Unknown (2004). "FoxOops." June 30, homepage.mac.com/mj-smitho/FoxNewsPornSlip/FoxOpps.html.

Usborne, D. (1996). "Murdoch plans global TV news operation." *Independent*, January 31, page 17.

Usborne, D. (1996). "Rupert meets his match." *Independent*, November 11, page 15.

Vines, S. (1997). "Murdoch dreams of a Chinese empire." *Independent*, January 10, page 10.

Vitello, P. (1998). "A Huckster In Reporter's Clothing." *New York Newsday*, January 6, page A8.

Waller, J.M. (2002). "FOX outraces the old dogs." *Insight on the News*, October 29, vol. 18, page 18.

Wasserman, B. (2004). "COMMENTARY: You Can Report, but We Will Decide; The conservative media's handling of the Swift boat dispute is a case study in bias." *Los Angeles Times*, August 24, www.latimes.com.

Wayne, W. (2002). "FOX news sweeps to TV marketer of year." *Advertising Age*, November 4, 73, 44, page 1.

Weber, T. (2004). "Hollinger branded 'kleptocarcy.'" *Globe and Mail*, August 31, www.theglobeandmail.com.

Wharton, D. (1993). "FOX News memogate." *Variety*, September 10.

Whitelaw, K. (1996). "Reporting live: FOX takes on CNN." *U.S. News and World Report*, October 7, page 51.

Wilbert, C. (2003). "Franken beats FOX, lands on 'Crossfire." *Atlanta Journal and Constitution*, August 23, page F1.

Wilbert, C. (2003). "FOX News billboard takes jab at CNN." *Atlanta Journal and Constitution*, October 9, page E1.

Wilbert, C. (2003). "Saddam drama helps CNN, but FOX News carries day." *Atlanta Journal and Constitution*, December 17, page C1.

Williams, R. (1994). "Murdoch." *Independent*, December 29, page 10.

Zerbisias, A. (2003). "'The press self-muzzled' its coverage of Iraq war." *Toronto Star*, September 16.

Zimmerman, T. (1996). "All propaganda, all the time." *U.S. News and World Report*, November 11, pages 48-49.

Zoglin, R. (1996). "And in other news...FOX has a fledgling Sunday Show and big plans. But in TV News, Rupert Murdoch still has lots to prove." *Time*, May 20, page 66.

About the Authors

Alexandra Kitty is a freelance journalist who has written for *Elle Canada, Maisonneuve, Presstime, Current, Quill, Critical Review, Skeptic* and *Editor & Publisher*, and is the author of the book *Don't Believe It!: How Lies Become News*. She has an Honors B.A. in Psychology from McMaster University and a master's degree in Journalism from the University of Western Ontario. She was a Professor of Language Studies at Mohawk College, and now teaches writing at the Sheridan Institute. She won the 2004 Arch Award from McMaster University, and lives in Hamilton, Ontario.

Robert Greenwald is the director/producer of *Outfoxed: Rupert Murdoch's War on Journalism* (2004), as well as the executive producer of the trilogy of "Un" documentaries: *Unprecedented: The 2000 Presidential Election* (2002), *Uncovered: The Iraq War* (2003), which Greenwald directed, and *Unconstitutional: The War on Our Civil Liberties* (2004).

In addition to his documentary work, Greenwald has produced and/or directed more than 50 television movies, miniseries and feature films, garnering 25 Emmy nominations. Greenwald was awarded the 2002 Producer of the Year Award by the American Film Institute and was the recipient of awards and honors for his political work by the ACLU Foundation of Southern California, the L.A. chapter of the National Lawyers Guild, Physicians for Social Responsibility and the Office of the Americas. Greenwald is a co-founder (with Danny and Victor Goldberg) of RDV Books, as well as the co-founder (with Mike Farrell) of Artists United, a group of actors and others opposed to the war in Iraq, which continues to work toward publicizing progressive causes. Greenwald has also lectured at Harvard University for the Nieman Fellows Foundation for Journalism. He lives in Los Angeles.

OUTFOXED